Invest in ASEAN

Lorenzo Riccardi · Giorgio Riccardi

Invest in ASEAN

Countries Analysis and Treaties

Springer

Lorenzo Riccardi
Shanghai University
Shanghai, China

Giorgio Riccardi
RsA Asia
Shanghai, China

ISBN 978-981-15-5377-6 ISBN 978-981-15-5378-3 (eBook)
https://doi.org/10.1007/978-981-15-5378-3

This Springer imprint is published by the registered company Springer Nature Singapore Pte Ltd.
The registered company address is: 152 Beach Road, #21-01/04 Gateway East, Singapore 189721, Singapore

Introduction

The ASEAN Declaration (Bangkok Declaration) was signed on 8 August 1967 in Bangkok, Thailand, giving rise to the Association of Southeast Asian Nations, or ASEAN. The Founding Fathers of ASEAN were Indonesia, Malaysia, Philippines, Singapore and Thailand. Brunei Darussalam then joined on 7 January 1984, Vietnam on 28 July 1995, Lao PDR and Myanmar on 23 July 1997, and Cambodia on 30 April 1999, making up the ten Member States of ASEAN.

The ASEAN Member States have adopted the following fundamental principles, as contained in the Treaty of Amity and Cooperation in Southeast Asia (TAC) of 1976:

- mutual respect for the independence, sovereignty, equality, territorial integrity, and national identity of all nations;
- the right of every State to lead its national existence free from external interference, subversion or coercion;
- non-interference in the internal affairs of one another;
- settlement of differences or disputes by peaceful manner;
- renunciation of the threat or use of force; and
- effective cooperation among themselves.

In the Bangkok Declaration are stated the aims and purposes of ASEAN, namely:

- to accelerate the economic growth, social progress and cultural development in the region through joint endeavors in the spirit of equality and partnership in order to strengthen the foundation for a prosperous and peaceful community of Southeast Asian Nations;
- to promote regional peace and stability through abiding respect for justice and the rule of law in the relationship among countries of the region and adherence to the principles of the United Nations Charter;

- to promote active collaboration and mutual assistance on matters of common interest in the economic, social, cultural, technical, scientific and administrative fields;
- to provide assistance to each other in the form of training and research facilities in the educational, professional, technical and administrative spheres;
- to collaborate more effectively for the greater utilization of their agriculture and industries, the expansion of their trade, including the study of the problems of international commodity trade, the improvement of their transportation and communications facilities and the raising of the living standards of their peoples;
- to promote Southeast Asian studies; and
- to maintain close and beneficial cooperation with existing international and regional organizations with similar aims and purposes and explore all avenues for even closer cooperation among themselves.

ASEAN countries have adopted the ASEAN Vision 2020, by which they agreed on a shared vision of ASEAN as a "concert of Southeast Asian nations, outward looking, living in peace, stability and prosperity, bonded together in partnership in dynamic development and in a community of caring societies".

Motto

"One vision, one identity, one community"

Flag

Emblem

Day

8th August

Secretary General

Le Luong Minh

ASEAN countries

Brunei, Cambodia, Indonesia, Laos, Malaysia, Myanmar, Philippines, Singapore, Thailand, Vietnam

ASEAN observers

Papua New Guinea, Timor Leste

Contents

Country Profiles

Country Profiles—Members 3
Brunei 4
  Country Introduction 4
  Economy 6
  Investment Area 11
  Finance and Taxation 15
  Risk Assessment 16
Cambodia 19
  Country Introduction 19
  Economy 23
  Investment Area 28
  Finance and Taxation 31
  Risk Assessment 35
Indonesia 41
  Country Introduction 41
  Economy 43
  Investment Area 49
  Finance and Taxation 54
  Risk Assessment 58
Laos 61
  Country Introduction 61
  Economy 64
  Investment Area 68
  Finance and Taxation 74
  Risk Assessment 78
Malaysia 80
  Country Introduction 80
  Economy 82

Investment Area 88
Finance and Taxation 93
Risk Assessment 98
Myanmar 104
Economy 107
Investment Area 111
Finance and Taxation 114
Risk Assessment 117
Philippines 122
Country Introduction 122
Economy 125
Investment Area 128
Finance and Taxation 133
Risk Assessment 137
Singapore 141
Country Introduction 141
Economy 144
Investment Area 148
Finance and Taxation 153
Risk Assessment 160
Thailand 164
Country Introduction 164
Economy 166
Investment Area 169
Finance and Taxation 173
Risk Assessment 181
Vietnam 183
Country Introduction 183
Economy 186
Investment Area 189
Finance and Taxation 192
Risk Assessment 195

Country Profiles—Observers 199
Papua New Guinea 200
Country Introduction 200
Economy 202
Investment Area 204
Timor Leste 208
Country Introduction 208
Economy 211
Investment Area 213

Relevant Treaties

Treaty of Amity and Cooperation in Southeast Asia 219
Chapter I. Purpose and Principles 219
Chapter II. Amity 220
Chapter III. Cooperation 220
Chapter IV. Pacific Settlement of Disputes 222
Chapter V. General Provision 223

Basic Agreement on ASEAN Industrial Projects 225
Chapter I. Purposes and Principles 225
Chapter II. Equity 226
Chapter III. Board of Directors 227
Chapter IV. Financing 227
Chapter V. Preferential Trading Arrangements 228
Chapter VI. Taxation 228
Chapter VII. Incentives 229
Chapter VIII. Repatriation of Foreign Exchange 229
Chapter IX. Protection of Minority Shareholders 229
Chapter X. Pricing Principles 230
Chapter XI. Project Scope 231
Chapter XII. Institutional Arrangements 231
Chapter XIII. Consultations 232
Chapter XIV. Bankruptcy 232
Chapter XV. Supplementary Agreement 232
Chapter XVI. Amendments 233
Chapter XVII. Entry into Force 233

ASEAN Agreement of Customs 235

ASEAN Agreement on Transboundary Haze Pollution 241
Part I. General Provisions 242
Part II. Monitoring, Assessment, Prevention and Response 244
Part III. Technical Co-operation and Scientific Research 248
Part IV. Institutional Arrangements 249
Part V. Procedures 250
Part VI. Final Clauses 252
Annex: Terms of Reference of the ASEAN Co-ordinating Centre for Transboundary Haze Pollution Control 254

Protocol Governing the Implementation of the ASEAN Harmonised Tariff Nomenclature 257
Interpretative Notes of the Protocol Governing the Implementation of the ASEAN Harmonised Tariff Nomenclature 261

Agreement on the Establishment of the ASEAN Development Fund . . . 265

ASEAN Trade in Goods Agreement . . . 271
Chapter 1. General Provisions . . . 272
Chapter 2. Tariff Liberalisation . . . 279
Chapter 3. Rules of Origin . . . 284
Chapter 4. Non-tariff Measures . . . 293
Chapter 5. Trade Facilitation . . . 295
Chapter 6. Customs . . . 298
Chapter 7. Standards, Technical Regulations and Conformity Assessment Procedures . . . 303
Chapter 8. Sanitary and Phytosanitary Measures . . . 308
Chapter 9. Trade Remedy Measures . . . 311
Chapter 10. Institutional Provisions . . . 311
Chapter 11. Final Provisions . . . 312

ASEAN Petroleum Security Agreement . . . 315

ASEAN Multilateral Agreement on Air Services . . . 323
Annex I: Scheduled Air Services . . . 336
Annex II: Implementing Protocols . . . 337

Framework Agreement on the Facilitation of Inter-State Transport . . . 339
Part I. General Provision . . . 341
Part II. Designation of Inter-State Transport Routes and Frontier Posts . . . 342
Part III. General Conditions for Road Transport . . . 343
Part IV. Customs Control, Sanitary and Phytoanitary Measures . . . 345
Part V. Miscellaneous Provisions . . . 346
Part VI. Institutional Arrangements . . . 347
Part VII. Final Clauses . . . 348

ASEAN Agreement on the Movement of Natural Persons . . . 351

Country Profiles

Country Profiles—Members

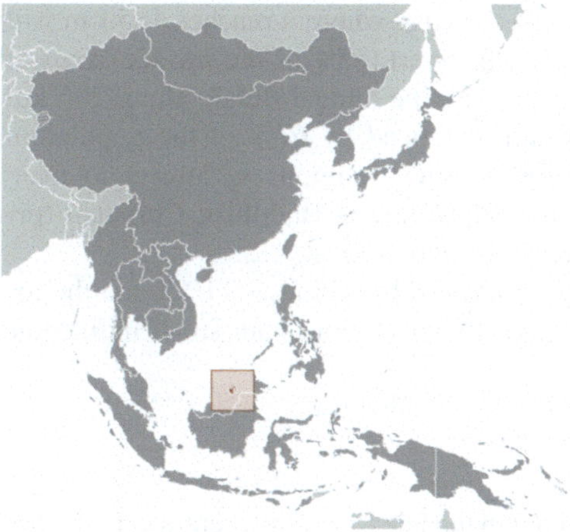

BRUNEI

Official name
Negara Brunei Darussalam
Capital
Bandar Seri Begawan
Area
5,765 sq. km
Population
0.44 mln
Languages
Malay (official), English, Chinese
Main ethnic groups
Malay 66%, Chinese 10%

Main religions
Muslim (official) 79%, Christian 9%, Buddhist 8%
Government type
Absolute Monarchy
Urbanization
77.6%
Life expectancy ratio
78 years
Fertility rate
1.8 children born/woman
Currency
Brunei Dollar BND

L. Riccardi and G. Riccardi, *Invest in ASEAN*,
https://doi.org/10.1007/978-981-15-5378-3_1

Brunei

Country Introduction

Population, Location, Geography, Climate

The Sultanate of Brunei (officially referred to as Negara Brunei Darussalam, i.e. the State of Brunei, Abode of Peace) or simply Brunei, is a state located on the island of Borneo, in Southeast Asia. Brunei is only, and completely, bordered by Malaysia, with the exception of the coast overlooking the South China Sea.

The country counts 440,000 inhabitants, with an average density of 69 inhabitants per km^2 and an urbanization rate of 73%.

The country is constituted of very humid, coastal plateaus (55% of the territory). The rest is rather mountainous; especially in the east, where it reaches 1850 m with Mount Bukit Pagon. The territory is essentially forest (85% of the surface), crossed by two major rivers: the Tembrong and especially the Sungai Belait, along 206 km.

The official state religion is Sunni Islam, practiced by 67% of the population, whose summit is the Sultan. The practice of other religions is subject to many limitations and restrictions. The rest of the population is Buddhist; Christian (primarily Catholic, and Anglican and Protestant); and animist.

The main ethnic group is Malay (66%); followed by Chinese (11%); and the rest is to be shared between white Anglo-Saxon, Indian, Indonesian, small indigenous groups of Borneo and mestizos.

The national language is Malay, but English is also used.

Internal Policy

The Islamic Sultanate of Brunei was founded in the late fourteenth century. In the first three centuries of existence, the Sultanate was a sort of constitutional monarchy. In fact, the Sultan did not exert direct legislative power, which was reserved exclusively for the Council of Princes—It only possessed executive duties. The golden age of this period can be placed during the reign of the fifth sultan, Bolkiah (1485–1521). He managed to develop most of the commercial activities by maturing Brunei as a sorting center in goods between China, India, and European countries. He also was able to extend its domain in the entire northern Borneo, even in the Philippines. In the sixteenth century, it began to make relations with Portugal and Britain, which gradually became the main trading partners of the country. On the contrary, there were bad relations with Spain, with whom the Sultanate fought long for dominion over the Philippines; unfortunately, the Sultanate lost at the end of the sixteenth century.

Meanwhile, in the seventeenth century, the Sultanate of Brunei developed into a more absolutist governance while also increasing the Islamic religious connotation. In fact, the Sultan was able to take a direct legislative power at the expense of the principles of the Council. In the eighteenth century, the Sultans developed important pacts with the British, certainly opting for their protection. This ultimately forged alliance with the Dutch East Indies. Significantly, in the nineteenth century there are the excellent relations with the nearby Maharaja White Sarawak James Brooke and all the British Governors Malaysians. The Sultanate envied their autonomy and in the nineteenth and twentieth centuries was always careful not to be overly inclusive Malays in business, particularly its Muslim outpost in Asia. In 1941, during the Second World War, Brunei was occupied by Japan. The town was used as a Japanese naval base and suffered because of the shortage of food and medicine, until the surrender of the Japanese garrison on September 10, in 1945. The Protectorate was endowed in 1959 with a constitution that proclaimed the internal autonomy was accomplished. In 1962, the Sultan witnessed the unsuccessful attempt to establish the constitutional monarchy through parliamentary elections. The majority of the population opted clearly for the absolute monarchy. Parallel, during the sixties, he refused to join the newly formed Federation of Malaysia and upheld the Protectorate. In 1967, the Sultan abdicated in favor of the eldest son, Hassanal Bolkiah, the 29th Sultan as of today since the founding Sultanate. In 1984, he proclaimed full independence from the British Empire.

Nowadays, the country is ruled as a monarchy based on heredity. It is ruled by a Sultan, who is head of state and prime minister. Therefore, all powers are concentrated in one, supported by 4 Tips: religious and private (both advisory), ministers (assisting the sultan in the exercise of executive power) and inheritance (which decides, in case of need, the succession to the throne). Legislative power is exercised by means of the Legislative Council. Prior to its elimination by the king in 2005, the constitution (1959), amended in 1965 and 2004, brought the number of Legislative Council Members to 45. The judicial system in each country is based on British law and Islam and divided into three levels of courts: courts of magistrates and religious courts (lower level); the Courts of Appeal (second degree); and the High Court (upper level) which has unlimited civil and criminal skills. The death penalty is formally in force. The armed forces are divided into the three conventional branches (army, air force, navy) and military service is carried out on a voluntary basis. The State, engaged for decades in improving the school system, has undertaken several measures to support education in the country; it includes the building of schools in remote areas and the cover of a range of expenses such as, transportation costs and housing for students who live far from the school within a specified range and part of the costs incurred by students living abroad. Thanks to these measures, the illiteracy rate in Brunei is low.

International Relations

The international relations of Brunei are the following:

- Brunei became a member state of the United Kingdom Commonwealth in 1984;
- Brunei joined ASEAN on 7 January 1984, one week after resuming full independence, and gives its ASEAN membership the highest priority in its foreign relations;
- Brunei joined the United Nations in September 1984;
- it also is a member of the Organization of Islamic Cooperation (OIC), the Asia-Pacific Economic Cooperation (APEC) forum and the Commonwealth of Nations;

- founding member of the World Trade Organization (WTO) in 1995;
- Brunei hosted the APEC Economic Leaders' Meeting in November 2000. In 2005 it attended the inaugural East Asia Summit;
- since 2009 Brunei and the Philippines signed a Memorandum of Understanding (MOU) that seeks to strengthen the bilateral cooperation between the two countries in the fields of agriculture and farm-related trade and investments.

Brunei has a number of diplomatic missions abroad and close relations with Singapore, sharing an interchangeable currency regime as well as close military relations with the latter island-state. Aside from relations with other ASEAN states, of which the Philippines, Indonesia, and Malaysia are key partners, Brunei also has extensive relations with the Islamic and Arab world outside its region.

The country has bilateral relations with a number of countries including Australia, Bangladesh, Burma, Cambodia, Canada, China, France, Germany, India, Indonesia, Japan, Laos, Malaysia, New Zealand, North Korea, Oman, Pakistan, Philippines, Qatar, Russia, Singapore, South Korea, Thailand, United Kingdom, United States, and Vietnam.

Economy

Macroeconomic Overview

	Unit	2000A	2018	2020F
GDP, current prices	USD (billions)	6.66	14.08	14.28
GDP per capita, current prices	USD	20,511.08	32,423.92	32,073.37
GDP based on PPP per capita	Current International dollar	66,767.38	79,529.86	90,104.82

Source IMF Outlook (2019)

In 1970, the Government was able to create foreign currency reserves and invest all around the world for the benefit of their posterity. This was possible due to increased revenues from oil exports and the effort to maintain low public spending. The gains arising from oil export revenues were also utilized to finance the annual government deficit. However, in 1986, oil exports decreased and consequently, public spending started to increase. As a result, Brunei's government was constantly running a deficit. The disappearance of a public surplus made Brunei's economy more vulnerable to fluctuations in oil prices. Brunei's gross domestic product (GDP) soared with the increase of the petroleum price in the 1970s, to a peak of $5.7 billion in 1980. It declined slightly in the next five years, then fell by almost 30% in 1986. This drop was the result of a combination of sharply lower petroleum prices in world markets and voluntary production cuts in Brunei.

The GDP recovered somewhat since 1986, growing by 12% in 1987, 1% in 1988, and 9% in 1989. In recent years, GDP growth was 3.5% in 1996, 4.0% in 1997, 1.0% in 1998, and an estimated 2.5% in 1999. However, the 1999 GDP was still only about $4.5 billion, well below 1980's peak. The Asian financial crises in 1997 and 1998, coupled with fluctuations in the price of oil have created uncertainty and instability in Brunei's economy. In addition, the 1998 collapse of Amedeo Development Corporation, Brunei's largest construction firm whose projects helped fuel the domestic economy, caused the country to slip into a mild recession.

Structure of output (% GDP)	2000	2005	2010	2015	2018
Agriculture	1.0	0.9	0.7	1.1	1.0
Industry	63.7	71.6	67.4	60.2	62.2
Services	35.3	27.5	31.9	38.7	36.7

Source Asian Development Bank (ADB, 2019)

Recent trends show an acceleration of Brunei economy and, in general, the following elements characterize the recent period:

- pickup in oil and gas production (conversely, activity in the non-energy sector slowed, dragged down by declining government spending);
- Brunei's government is struggling to diversify the hydrocarbon-dependent economy and improve its business environment;
- the government is also immersed in an austerity drive, seeking to reduce public spending;
- the effects of low oil prices on the economy are still being felt.

Structure of expenditure (% GDP)	2000	2005	2010	2015	2018
Final consumption	50.6	40.9	36.9	44.8	43.6
Gross capital formation	13.1	11.4	23.7	35.2	41.1
Exports of goods and services	67.4	70.2	67.4	55.2	51.9
Imports of goods and services	35.8	27.3	28.0	37.7	42.0
Statistical discrepancy	4.8	4.9	0.0	5.4	5.3

Source Asian Development Bank (ADB, 2019)

Economic Policy

Foreign Trade Policy

Brunei Darussalam's foreign trade policy objectives:

- to promote an external environment conducive to research and for trade and investments in Brunei Darussalam;
- to explore and identify the market opportunities for companies in Brunei;

- to increase the economic activities and contribute significantly to economic diversification (i.e. away from oil and gas);
- to optimize the benefits of international outlook and regional prominence.

Main Pillars of Brunei Darussalam's foreign trade policy:

- The World Trade Organization (WTO) provides the stable framework of multilateral trade rules that ensure the free flow of goods and services.
- Participation in regional economic forums is based on the concept of "open regionalism".
- Free Trade Agreements (FTAs) with key trading partners can help to facilitate trade liberalization and strengthen trade links.

Guiding principles of Brunei Darussalam's foreign trade policy:

- exercise of free trade and open in the context of multilateral trade rules;
- support for a multilateral open trading system based on non-discriminatory rules;
- use of "open regionalism recognition" as a building block towards multilateral trade liberalization.

Brunei Darussalam's FTA Policy

Brunei Darussalam sees Free Trade Agreements (FTA) as an essential part of its foreign trade policy to maximize the potential of free and open trade for its people in an ever more globalized world. With a relatively free and open trading system and a small but highly educated workforce, Brunei Darussalam sees the commitment of Free Trade Agreements as a fundamental step to make sure that people, services, and investments have continued access to open markets worldwide.

Brunei Darussalam, widely viewed in the international community as an important oil and gas producer, is currently engaged in a series of projects attempting to further diversify its economy. The Government of Brunei Darussalam believes strongly that the active commitment to free trade agreements with many partners will open the strategic markets for exports. In addition, it is hopeful that Brunei services will also facilitate the flow of foreign direct investments in Brunei Darussalam.

Industrial Policies

Industrial policies, including labor, property, government's support, and facilities remain open and flexible to all categories of industrial activities. Brunei Darussalam maintains a realistic approach in which a variety of arrangements are feasible. Property policies allow for full, majority, or minority foreign ownership according to the type of industry and location. Only activities related to the national food safety and those based on local resources require a certain degree of local participation. Industries for the local market (not related to national food security) and industries for total exporting can entirely be under foreign property.

Brunei Darussalam, in its vast territory, offers a variety of services in all four districts of the country. Most of 12 currently developed industrial sites are available and ready for occupation. Moreover, large spaces for agroforestry and aquaculture are available. Terms of rental and lease agreements are competitive, and the sites offer a range of services, infrastructures and resources. Brunei Darussalam gives priority to ensuring the Natural Environment Stability.

All sites are free from pollution and are environmentally balanced. The philosophy of the Government is linked to sustainable development. Therefore, all polluting industries are prohibited and the criteria will continue to consider each participant's impact on the environment.

The Ministry of Industry and Primary Resources coordinates the Industrial Development Activities. The Ministry is the one-stop agency coordinates for Investments in Brunei Darussalam. It is very easy to start a sector in Brunei Darussalam. A private development does not require government structures and only needs an approval to begin. Those who require government assistance and facilities can just deal with the Ministry, who will liaise with other agencies and accelerate applications.

The Ministry realizes the importance of time frames and clear decision-making processes to businesses. The entire procedure has four stages:

- approval of the concept;
- approval of firm proposal;
- approval of physical plans;
- approval to operate.

In all four stages, the Ministry of Industry and Primary Resources act as one-stop agency.

Banking System

The evolution of financial institutions in Brunei has marked rapid growth over the last decade. This is demonstrated by the presence of financial institutions' numbers of international standing and reputation (e.g. Bank of China has received permission to open a branch in Brunei in April 2016), the advent of new financial instruments, the development of securities, the extensive nature of the financial transactions that are entered into and the numerous financial services that are now provided. Citibank, which entered Brunei Darussalam's financial system consists of a dual financial system comprising Islamic and conventional financial institutions. The banking system represents the core of the financial system.

The Banking System in Brunei Darussalam comprises of commercial banks, which play an important role in Brunei financial sector. Nine banks presently licensed to conduct businesses within the country, six are foreign owned and represented by branch operations. The only banking institution which provides Islamic banking services is the Islamic Bank of Brunei Berhad. It was officially launched on 13 January 1993, giving opportunities and fair options for the public to choose. This also helps to enhance the financial sector by creating fair competition among the other conventional financial institutions.

All banks are required to submit the following financial returns:

- direction of lending for all banking operations in Brunei Darussalam (quarterly);
- consolidated monthly statement of Assets and Liabilities for all banking operations in Brunei Darussalam (monthly);
- SSS Appendix II. a Schedule (Reserve requirement—monthly);
- SSS Appendix III Schedule (Statement of Assets and Liabilities—monthly);
- capital adequacy computation monthly.

Regulation and supervision are continuously being strengthened to ensure that financial stability prevails in the financial system, in line with international best regulatory practice. Authority Monetary Brunei Darussalam (AMBD) will remain vigilant of risks and external factors that may affect the domestic financial sector and economy. AMBD, through the banking supervision unit, is responsible for licensing, regulating, and supervising the banks and finance companies. The primary objective of AMBD's banking supervision unit is to ensure safety and soundness of banks and finance companies, as well as protecting the interests of consumers and public.

During recent years, the overall key financial soundness indicators in the banking sector continued to be at healthy levels:

- aggregate capital adequacy ratio of 18.4% in 2018;
- the banks are highly liquid, having a "liquid assets to total assets" ratio in 2018 of 51.6%;
- the financing to deposit ratio (excluding government deposits) was 40.9% in 2018;
- the assets and deposits of the banking system have declined by 8.9% from $18.7 billion in 2014 to $17 billion in 2015, and 11% from $16.0 billion in 2014 to $14.2 billion in 2015 respectively (the fall in assets is mainly due to the decrease in placements with banks and financial institutions abroad by 24%).

According to the statistics directly from Brunei Ministry of Energy and Industry, "[The] decline in deposits is mainly due to decrease in institutional deposits. Asset quality continued to improve with a net non-performing loans financing ratio (NPLF) of 4.8% in 2018. Brunei's household debt accounted for 15.9% of the country's Nominal GDP in Dec 2018, compared with the ratio of 17.7% in the previous year. As part of AMBD's aspiration to encourage lending/financing of the banks to the productive sector, credit growth was evident in the corporate sector with a steady growth starting by. Mainly the manufacturing and services sectors contributed to the increase. Total deposits of the finance companies have increased marginally from 2014. Finance companies, whose main activities are hire purchase transactions, faced significant falls in total assets and total financing by 7.7% from $2.3 billion to $2.2 billion and by 10.7% from $2.0 billion to $1.8 billion respectively." (Brunei Ministry of Energy and Industry).

It is worth mentioning the role of the Brunei Currency Board (BCB). BCB was established in 1967 by the Currency Act. Under Section 9(1) in Chapter 32 of the Laws of Brunei, and it has the sole right to manage and issue currency notes and coins in Brunei Darussalam. Its main mission is to ensure the integrity of the currency issue and that the public's interest is safeguarded. At the same time, Brunei Currency Board also seeks to provide the highest standard of service to both the banks and the public. The objectives of Brunei Currency Board are:

- to maintain strict control over the amount of currency in circulation whereby the external and liquid assets must exceed the statutory limits of 70% and 30% respectively;
- to ensure that the demand for currency notes and coins is adequately and sufficiently met by coordinating its activities with the banks;
- to assist other departments within the Ministry of Finance in implementing the nation's monetary policy;
- to ensure the highest degree of protection for the Board's assets and custody items held by it;
- to ensure prudent management of the Currency Fund and the Currency Reserve Fund.

Interest rates (% per annum; period averages)	2000	2005	2010	2015	2018
On deposits					
Savings	N/A	1.01	0.47	0.29	0.34
Time: 6 months	N/A	1.20	0.58	0.45	0.46
12 months	N/A	1.63	0.82	0.75	0.80

Source Asian Development Bank (ADB, 2019)

Investment Area

Despite many advantages promoted by the Sultanate, the Foreign Direct Investments (FDI) is discouraged due to the reduced size of the domestic market. Those advantages include tax incentives and customs duties exemptions on certain sectors, especially non-oil investments and freedom of investment in all sectors, with the exception of certain fields in which local participation is required. Since 2011, foreign invest has been growing. However, a study of the APEC Business Advisory Council (ABAC) provided that there were many weaknesses among many sectors within the business climate. The Company Act was amended in January 2015, with the overall objective to increase transparency and strengthen corporate governance. The new version aims to simplify the business climate. The Government of His Majesty the Sultan of Brunei, through its Wawasan 2035, has set out the directions for its economic goals with a growing emphasis on attracting

FDI as an important driver of growth, focusing mainly on economic activities that bring new knowledge, new industries, new technologies, new markets as well as new business and employment opportunities for its people. The Economic Strategy that has been established calls for, among others, the following policy directions:

- ensuring continued macroeconomic stability;
- ensuring high rates of economic growth;
- promoting national economic competitiveness through policies that encourage productivity, economic openness and competition;
- investing in downstream oil and gas industries and other economic clusters;
- investing in the world class infrastructure that is required to attract foreign and domestic investment in new export industries.

The Brunei Economic Development Board (BEDB) has identified several key industry clusters within the export-oriented manufacturing and services sectors that have the potential to bring value added activities to Brunei and create spin-off opportunities. Furthermore, the readily available industry cluster-specific sites throughout the country make Brunei as an ideal location for the establishment of the following industry clusters: manufacturing (Pharmaceuticals and Food and Food Ingredients; Petrochemicals, Integrated Petrochemical Refinery and Renewable Energy); services (Information and Communications Technology; Supporting Industries); emerging new technologies.

Manufacturing

Within the manufacturing sector, Brunei focuses on many different industries. According to the food and food industry, it is obvious to see a multiplicity of opportunity. From sourcing, to manufacture, to distribution, the size of the market within the region of Brunei is perfect. With the utilization of authentic foods and ingredients, Brunei has the potential to capitalize on the establishment of research and development centers to expand successfully and globally. In addition to its well-established guidelines and standards for the handling and manufacturing of halal food products, Brunei has also launched its very own Brunei Halal Brand with the objective to make Brunei as one of the major players of the global trade in Halal food production and certification. With its strong Islamic background, the global market can be assured that Brunei's Halal Certification is both stringent and credible for businesses to penetrate the Muslim markets. In addition to the food industry, the pharmaceutical industry is growing just as rapidly. Many Pharmaceutical's companies established in Brunei, giving rise to a surge of research and development opportunities that provide a source of innovation. Brunei promotes international investments from well-established companies to utilize its location, strategically for expansion.

Services

Among the service industry, Brunei wishes to expand and capitalize on the growing economy, domestically and globally, through utilizing its highly-skilled workforce and readily available infrastructure. In doing so, Brunei capitalizes on the establishment of ICT-related activities to introduce itself as a regional hub for ICT.

In an effort to make Brunei as a regional hub for ICT, the Sultan has identified ICT as one of the key catalysts for sustainable socio-economic development and thus the development of ICT industry continues to be a top priority. Brunei is safe and perfectly centralized in accessibility to neighboring markets, making it ideal for data centers, disaster recovery centers, software development, wireless communication, and multimedia. Furthermore, Brunei's utility rates are amongst the lowest in the region. Brunei is also very competitive when it comes to the data center industry as it offers one of the most competitively priced utilities in the region. In addition, Brunei has an abundant bandwidth capacity through its web of international submarine cables and state-of-the art telecommunications infrastructure which enables efficient connectivity with the rest of the world. Finally, the BEDB has identified several logistic activities that can be further exploited through the utilization of Brunei's readily available infrastructure in order to sustain the growth of supporting industries. They include aviation support services, air and sea logistics, marine support services as well as oil field support services.

Emerging New Technologies

Brunei is in the position to grow as a new technology developer within the next 20–30 years. The BEDB is currently promoting new frontiers of science and technologies to develop in Brunei, to create economic activities that are driven by accelerated technology developments. Subject to further research and dialogue with experts, the potential new technologies may be found within the identified sectors of healthcare, food security, advanced manufacturing processes, material sciences, electronics.

Domestic Markets

Brunei derives its massive wealth from the abundance of oil and gas resources. As the source of his wealth is its massive hydrocarbon resources, the industrial sector dominates the structure of the economy with 74%. The service sector follows with 25%, while the agricultural sector is negligible with 1%. Other numbers that highlight domination of economy by the oil and gas sector are the following: hydrocarbon production represents about 50% of GDP and 90% of exports and government revenues. The government plans to diversify into Islamic banking and IT-sector. Furthermore, its investment in the development of the two sectors will greatly improve the prospects of the country, since the labor force is very small. Currently, the public sector employs the majority of the population. The government is also seeking to privatize many public-sector enterprises. However, progress is slow in terms of economic diversification and privatization as the government has a slow approach. If there are no new oil and gas fields locations, the country will run out of oil in 20–30 years. It is quite advisable that they accelerate diversification to prevent an economic collapse.

The current account surplus has always been significant in Brunei, entirely due to the trade balance. In 2019, the trade surplus was BND 281.4 million, lower than the BND 283.1 million recorded in 2018. The value of exports is BND 687 million, it fell by 9.9% in 2019. The value of imports is BND 405 million, it shrinks to 15.4%. Brunei imports come mostly from ASEAN. The smaller import partners are the United States and the EU. The country's major export partners are Japan and South Korea, with which Brunei has long-term supply agreements.

The large current account surpluses mean that any external funding is required. However, the sustainability of these surpluses is based on the availability of hydrocarbon resources.

External trade (USD millions)	2000	2005	2010	2015	2018
Exports, fob	3906.0	6247.3	8887.4	6338	6575
Imports, cif	1106.7	1448.0	2535.4	3235	4167
Trade balance	2799.3	4799.3	6352.0	3104	2408

Source Asian Development Bank (ADB, 2019)

Main commercial partners (USD millions)	2000	2005	2010	2015	2018
Exports					
1. Japan	998	2039	3863	2309	2281
2. Korea, Rep. of	307	1103	1483	992	617
3. India	0	547	495	578	493
4. Thailand	411	82	78	545	687
5. Malaysia	4	33	132	295	500
6. Australia	205	685	918	223	580
7. Singapore	311	114	251	223	555
8. Taipei, China	0	2	4	437	397
9. China, People's Rep. of	101	184	585	95	234
10. Indonesia	49	1241	631	103	44
Imports					
1. China, People's Rep. of	19	120	199	377	1636
2. Singapore	203	221	484	688	573
3. Malaysia	175	290	599	457	552
4. United States	88	134	246	341	359
5. Japan	47	141	252	341	161
6. United Kingdom	38	34	109	303	123
7. Thailand	26	65	136	246	109
8. Korea, Republic of	9	50	56	113	98
9. Germany	21	39	78	125	76
10. Indonesia	16	42	65	86	72

Source Asian Development Bank (ADB, 2019)

Finance and Taxation

Tax

In Brunei there are no Personal Income tax, Sales Tax, Payroll Tax, Export Tax, Manufacturing Tax, and no Capital Gains Tax. An individual person is categorized as a resident if he/she resides in Brunei and is physically present or exercises an employment (other than as a director of a company) in Brunei for 183 days or more in the preceding year of assessment.

Corporate Income Tax

The corporate income tax standard rate is 18.5%. In the long-term, the Brunei Corporate Tax Rate is projected to trend around 19% in 2020.

Any company that resides in Brunei is considered a resident of Brunei and is subject to tax. A company is resident in Brunei if it is managed and controlled in Brunei. Any income accrued within Brunei, domestic or foreign, is subject to income tax. Trade, business, investment, interest, and royalty income are all forms of taxable income with few exceptions, such as nonprofit organizations and some governmental positions. Companies with revenue that does not exceed BND 1 million are exempt from corporate tax. Furthermore, capital gain is not taxed. There is also a limited tax credit available to foreign-source income; it is assessed at half rate. Tax credits are also available to specific salaries and training. Instead of a corporate tax, approved export companies can pay a fixed rate of 1%.

Withholding Taxes

- Dividends—Brunei does not levy withholding tax on dividends that have been assessed to tax, regardless of whether paid to a resident or a non-resident;
- Interest—Interest paid to a non-resident is subject to a 2.5% withholding tax;
- Royalties—Royalties paid to a non-resident are subject to a 10% withholding tax;
- Technical service fees—Technical service fees are subject to a 10% withholding tax. Fees paid for the use of scientific, technical, industrial, or commercial knowledge or information are subject to a 10% withholding tax.

Tax rate	%
Corporate tax	18.5
Personal income	0
Sales tax	0

Source Trading Economics (2019)

Audit and Accounting

Brunei Darussalam Accounting is under the Brunei Darussalam Accounting Standards Council (BDASC). Under the International Accounting Standards Board, BDASC has applied the International Financial Reporting Standards (IFRS) to public accountable companies within Brunei. The full adoption of the IFRS took place on 1st of January 2014, applying to all public accountable companies. Following the adoption is a push for the full adoption of IFRS. Several large multinational corporations have started using IFRS for their foreign subsidiaries/ branches. All public accountable companies such as banks, financial institutions, and insurance companies are required to adopt full IFRS. Until BDASC changes the principles, companies that do not have public accountability will apply generally accounting principles. Furthermore, companies that have no public accountability are although encouraged to adopt IFRS.

Risk Assessment

The largest risk to sustainable growth is the oil dependency of the country. Yet despite the potential short-term impact on oil exporters' margins and tax revenues, what really worries the government is the long-term picture: namely, how the economy will support itself when the sultanate's hydrocarbon reserves run out. The government has developed its long-term national development plan, Wawasan Brunei 2035 (Vision Brunei 2035). Wawasan directly addresses the concern of Brunei's dependency on gas, as Brunei's oil reserves are projected to be depleted within twenty years and thirty years, the country will run out of natural-gas. If the country does not turn to success within non-energy-based industries and services, it may fall into an economic collapse. Wawasan Brunei 2035 focuses on the development of a non-energy-industry based economy. Furthermore, Wawasan Brunei 2035 also encourages the production of administration whom plan to aid in the sustainability of the sultanate, in a long-term. With the encouragement of small businesses and investment in other industries other than oil production, there is a hope for sustainability. Currently, the major focus is the development of tourism. The government is targeting to increase tourism by 50%. In its development of the non-energy sector, Alcoa, a large United States based aluminum producer, has extended studies to open an aluminum-smelting plant within the sultanate.

This is ultimately an extremely difficult challenge for the sultanate. Cultural values may clash with the controversial behavior that comes along with worldwide tourism. Although Brunei has a great potential for ecotourism, it is a predominantly conservative Muslim country. There are strict laws on alcohol, which may inhibit its potential for growth in the ecotourism sector. Success of the plan is not completely secured. With the development of the Sungai Industrial Park, there has been much investment in construction of a methanol plant, in addition to many other investments. To create many jobs and the development of transshipment hubs, the government has embedded large investment in the Pulau Muara Besar port. This development with hopefully allow the financial sector to grow, although it will not be enough to keep the economy afloat. It is also projected that there will be differences in the current tax system as the development within a non-energy-based economy incurs. Successfully implementing this will pose a larger challenge to the Sultanate, than attracting investors. In addition to transferring the economy off energy-based industries, the country is a large promoter of sustainability in energy and energy conservation. There is governmental cap of oil production at 200,000 barrels a day. As retail fuel prices are subsidized by the government, it is quite difficult to shift all of these challenges among the citizens of Brunei.

Political Risks

The economics of Brunei has also played a major role in the politics surrounding its dependency. Currently, political activity is negligible. Brunei does not have a democratic elected legislature and to reiterate, power is held by the Sultan. He is not under pressure from the body of his citizens to speed up political reform among the tensions of potential economic collapse. With the living standard being quite high and the government's dependency on the political quiescence of the population is probably further explained by the fact that Brunei's neighbors are mainly less prosperous South-East Asian economies. However, in the long-term, depletion of oil and gas reserves will make it more difficult for the government to provide the large range of benefits that Bruneians have come to expect. This may increase popular demand for a more accountable government, and thus for democratization. It is rare that political advocacy breaks out among the populous, yet when they do it is quite peaceful. Furthermore, there have recently been many anti-western demonstrations that have been triggered by international influence.

External Risks

Brunei Darussalam's banks and financial institutions do not have any significant cross border exposures, so external risks such as the Greek debt crisis or possible slowdown of the global economy are not significant risks to the bank's loan/ financing books.

Terrorism and Crime

Generally, the threat of terrorism in Brunei is relatively low. But foreigners are still anxious due to the more world-wide fear of terrorism aimed specifically at the western community. Crime is relatively low in Brunei; other than petty crimes such as pick pocketing. There have been few reports of drug smuggling across Asia and Brunei being used as a transit. Anyone caught bringing drugs into the country are faced with the death penalty. Alcohol sales are prohibited; while non-Muslims over seventeen years old may import duty free, two bottles of wine/spirits and twelve cans of beer upon entry (must declare at customs). Furthermore, any alcohol brought within the country must also be consumed in private. There also must be a 48-h delay between imports.

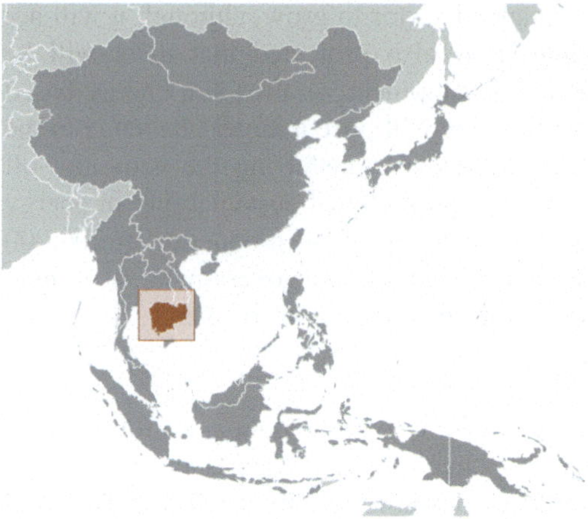

CAMBODIA

Official name
Kingdom of Cambodia

Capital
Phnom Penh

Area
181,035 sq. km

Population
16.5 mln

Languages
Khmer (official)

Main ethnic groups
Khmer 98%

Main religions
Buddhist (official) 97%, Muslim 2%

Government type
Parliamentary Constitutional Monarchy

Urbanization
23.4%

Life expectancy ratio
70 years

Fertility rate
2.5 children born/woman

Currency
Cambodian Riel KHR

Cambodia

Country Introduction

Population, Location, Geography, Climate

The Kingdom of Cambodia was a former French territory, gaining its independence in 1953. Located at the Southern Region of the Indochina Peninsula in South East Asia, Cambodia ranks as the 69th most populous country in the world, consisting of a population of 16.5 million. Cambodia contains 0.21% of the world's entire population, making one in every 487 people in the world, a citizen of Cambodia. The majority of the country's population age from 15 to 64 years. However, the country also has a large and rising younger population—under the age of 15 years. The smallest percentage of the population are those who are 65+ years.

Cambodia's ethnic demographic is made up of Khmer's, Cham's, Khmer Loeu's, Chinese and Vietnamese. 90% of the population is of Khmer origin, the other 5% Vietnamese, 1% Chinese and the other demographics make up the other 4%. The main languages spoken in Cambodia are Khmer with 96% of the population speaking the language. French and English are also spoken throughout the country. Religion in Cambodia plays an important part in the local way of life; 95% of Cambodians practice the official religion, Theravada Buddhism. The two Islamic communities in Cambodia consist of the Chams and Chveas. There are also a number of indigenous hill tribes who live in the remote north-east of Cambodia.

The capital of Cambodia is Phnom Penh, which has over 1 million people in residence. Phnom Penh is also the political center of Cambodia, which is considered a Constitutional Monarchy. It is also home to its Ceremonial head of state. Cambodia is well known for its rich heritage and ancient traditions. The capital city embraces cultural influences from a number of different Asian countries, including China in which merchants usually play the middleman in many economic cycles. Cultural influence in the capital is also taken from France and the United States. Unfortunately, the disastrous cultural impact of the Vietnam War (1975–77) and the Khmer Rouge genocide (1975–79), in which approximately two million people died, is still lingering over the country.

As a largely rural country, Cambodia covers 176,515 km^2 of land and 4520 km^2 of water, making it the 90th largest nation in the world with a total area of 181,035 km^2. This is about half the size of Germany and slightly smaller than the US state of Oklahoma. 20% of Cambodia is agricultural land and about 61% is covered by flat forested land. Cambodia is considered a part of the tropics as its most southern extension is 10° above the equator. Cambodia consists of 24 provinces, with Phnom Penh having both the highest population and the highest population density. It is, however, the second smallest province in terms of land area. In contrast, Mondulkiri, which is the largest province by area also has the lowest population density. The smallest province is Kep, which is also the least populated.

Cambodia shares its borders with three other South East Asian economies. This includes Thailand to the North and West, Laos to the North, Vietnam to the East and Siam Gulf to the South-West. Its main landscape features include the Tonle Sap Great Lake, which is one of the most productive freshwater ecosystems in the world. Nevertheless, the surroundings of the Lake are among the poorest in Asia. The Lake connects to the Mekong River, that is the 9th largest river in the world running throughout South East Asia, which is an important river trade route linking China to India and the rest of South East Asia. Remarkably the current of the mighty Mekong River expands until it pushes the Tonle Sap to reverse its direction, pushing upstream from the ancient capital. This reversal of the river is celebrated throughout the country with a Water Festival in November every year.

Cambodia has two main seasons. The wet season ranges from May to October and the dry season ranges from November to April. The wet and dry seasons are similar in length and the average temperature is around 27 °C. The climate is usually humid throughout the year as well as monsoonal, which is typical of the rest of the South East Asian countries.

A majority of Cambodian citizens makeup the rural areas and engage in agricultural production. Most villages are settled along major bodies of water within Tonle Sap Basin-Mekong Lowlands region. Cham origin is usually what makes up most the Cham villages. But there are large Chinese communities, known as Khmer villages, among the central and southeast. Vietnamese usually work with agricultural production, while Chinese usually work with commerce.

Cambodia is well known for its Tonle Sap Lake, which exceeds 12,000 km^2 during the monsoon floods, and shrinks to 2500 km^2 by the end of the dry season. The area also flourishes in rich culture as the ancient city of Angkor with its famous Angkor Wat temple is located close to Siem Reap at the lake's northwestern corner. Angkor Wat is the most renowned of the temples, as it is the largest. In addition to the Bayon, it makes up some of historical carvings of all the Angkorian temples. Quite interestingly, that Angkor Wat is the only temple that was designed facing the west rather than how the others were designed, towards the East. For more than 500 years, Angkor was the capital of the Khmer Empire, which controlled mainland Southeast Asia from the 9th to the thirteenth century and was South East Asia's largest empire. The Khmer Empire began to gradually decline through the thirteenth century, and Angkor was completely abandoned in 1432, following an attack by the Ayutthaya Kingdom. Siem Reap is one of the most popular cities in Cambodia, with thousands of tourists flooding to the city every year, mainly with the intention to see "one of the wonders of the world"—Angkor Wat temple. Other popular cities in Cambodia include Sihanoukville, which is well known for its beautiful beaches, Battambang, which is well known for being the rice basket of Cambodia and Takeo, which is often referred to as being the "cradle of Cambodian civilization".

Cambodia has a number of abundant natural resources including biodiversity, oil, gas, timber, gemstones, some iron ore, manganese and phosphate. The country as a whole is rather peaceful and friendly, being one of the up and coming Asian economies. The prospects for the country are huge due to its young labor population and strategic location.

Internal Policy

After years of destruction and conflict, the signing of the Paris Peace Agreements in October 1991 was the beginning of a political restructuring. The first national elections occurred in 1993, in which a constitution was adopted, that outlines the rights and obligations of Cambodian citizens, defines the policymaking process, and includes numerous other subject matters. Cambodia is a "multi-party democracy under a Constitutional Monarchy". This means that the King who is head of State appoints the prime minister from the representatives of the ruling party in the National Assembly. The Prime Minister is head of Government, elected every five years, and appoints cabinet members but is accountable to the National Assembly.

The National Assembly consists of 10 deputy prime ministers, 17 senior ministers, 172 secretaries of state and 28 ministers. Cambodia has a two-tier parliament structure, consisting of a lower house and an upper house. The lower house consists of the National Assembly, which is made up of 123-members, which all sit for a term of five years. The upper house consists of a 61-member Senate, which sits for a term of six years. The National government as of 2013 includes the Cambodian People's Party (CPP) who secured 68 seats at the July 2013 general election, while the opposition Cambodia National Rescue Party (CNRP) won 55 seats. The lower house and upper house election both took place in 2018.

The National Assembly constitution, which was amended in 1999 to establish a Senate states that its political system stands for liberal democracy and a multiparty system. The constitution states that the Cambodian citizens are masters of their own country and therefore hold all power, which they exercise through the National Assembly, Senate, Royal Government and the Judiciary. It also states that all Khmer citizens, which are the majority ethnicity in Cambodia have the right to establish associations and political parties.

Cambodia's liberal democracy and pluralism policy approach includes power being separated between Legislative, Executive, and Judicial branches. The Judiciary Branch consists of the Supreme Council of the Magistracy, Supreme Court (and lower courts), which have judicial authority. Judges and magistrates are appointed, promoted and dismissed by the Supreme Council of the Magistracy, which is chaired by the King. The Supreme Council of the Magistracy consists of the Minister of Justice, the President of the Supreme Court, the Prosecutor General of the Supreme Court, the President of the Appeals Court, the Appeals Court Prosecutor and three elected judges, each with a five-year mandate.

The local Governments are separated by provinces and municipalities, and each has its own courts and is run by The Ministry of Interior. There are 24 provinces and four municipalities. (Phnom Penh, Sihanoukville, Kep, and Pailin). Each municipality is divided into sections (khan) and each section is divided into quarters (sangkat). Each province is divided into districts (srok) and each district into communes (khum). In addition, there are groups of villages (phum), although they are not considered as the formal administrative units.

It must be noted however that even though Cambodia's courts are independent, meaning the Government should not get involved in private disputes. Foreign investors prefer to not go to the courts as they are perceived to be unreliable and highly corrupt. As a result, the Cambodian government enacted the Law on Court Structure in July 2014, creating the Commercial Court.

International Relations

Since the 1980s the two main Cambodian regimes continued to seek a foreign policy based on peaceful coexistence. During this time, Cambodia's main trading partners were limited to Vietnam, the Soviet Union, and a small number of countries in Europe including East Germany and Poland.

The geographical location of Cambodia positioned between both Thailand and Vietnam; two large economies have had a strong influence on Cambodia's foreign relations. After the dispute between Vietnam and Cambodia in February 1979, Cambodia signed a Treaty of Peace, Friendship, and Cooperation with Vietnam that formally strengthened "solidarity and cooperation" between the two countries. As a result, trade relations between the two countries have strengthened and Vietnam is now Cambodia's third largest import source after China and Thailand. This relationship can also be attributable to the large ethnic Vietnamese community in Cambodia. However, bilateral relations with Thailand is under pressure following the coup in Thailand in recent years. The ongoing Cambodia-Thailand border dispute has also damaged the relationship. Interestingly Cambodia's perception of the ineffective response by the ASEAN group in response to the Cambodia-Thailand border dispute has led to its confidence in ASEAN fading. Nevertheless, it is noted that ASEAN has been the foundation of Cambodia's foreign policy.

As China's rising economy has an impact on many world countries, Cambodia is not exempt. The bilateral relationship, which was once rooted in suspicion, mistrust, and uncertainty, due to the involvement of China in Cambodia's civil war, and its support for the Khmer Rouge regime has now improved since 1997. A remarkable transformation has taken place over the last decade. In December 2010, both, China and Cambodia, improved bilateral ties to a 'Comprehensive Strategic Partnership of Cooperation.' This has led to China playing an increasingly important role in the development of the Cambodian economy. China is Cambodia's main trading partner and its largest FDI contributor. The large pool of a Chinese community in Cambodia is also a contributing factor to the strong China-Cambodia links.

Outside of Asia, Cambodia has successfully attempted to become increasingly integrated into the world economy. This has happened by Cambodia becoming a member of The United Nations in 1955, a member of The Asian Development

Bank (ADB) in 1966, a member of ASEAN in 1999, and a member of the World Trade Organization in 2004. As of June 30, 2016, Cambodia has received $2.38 billion in Asian Development Bank (ADB) lending, grants, and technical assistance. ADB who is Cambodia's largest multilateral development partner has supported a number of projects such as helping to provide 96,000 rural households with access to improved water supply and connecting 40,000 rural households to lower-priced electricity. These examples show how Cambodia's increasing relationships within organizations are having a positive impact on its economy.

It must also be noted that Cambodia relies heavily on foreign assistance because between 30 and 40% of the central government's budget depends on donor assistance. Considering the fact that there has been a constant tension between the US and Cambodia due to Cambodia's human rights policies, the bilateral relationship between the US and Cambodia has improved drastically. US assistance currently makes significant contributions to the country's development. In 2014, Cambodia received $77.6 million in assistance from the US for programs in health, education, governance, and economic growth. US President Barack Obama also became the first incumbent US president to visit the country during the November 2012 East Asia Summit. The US-Cambodia relationship is also strengthening due to US interests in cooperating with Cambodia on counterterrorism efforts and responding to China's growing economic influence in the region.

Economy

Macroeconomic Overview

Cambodia has adopted a market-based economy in 1989. This economic structural change has been achieved by implementing various economic reforms. This includes the structural adjustment reforms, required by the World Trade Organization since becoming a member in 2004. Cambodia has effectively improved its integration with regional and global activities and has established trading relationships with various partners such as the EU, Japan, and many other East Asian countries.

As a result of a shifting market structure and the development of strategic relationships, Cambodia has received more than $25 billion in Foreign Direct Investment (FDI). This upsurge in investment can also be attributed to Cambodia's large pool of low-cost labor and attractive investment incentives. The majority of this investment occurs within Cambodia's garments footwear and construction sectors. Nonetheless compared to its neighboring South East Asian countries, Cambodia is still trailing behind in its development of infrastructure.

	Unit	2000A	2018	2020F
GDP, current prices	USD (billions)	3.67	24.52	29.30
GDP per capita, current prices	USD	299.98	1508.82	1750.40
GDP based on PPP per capita	Current International dollar	1084.34	4334.75	4985.05

Source IMF Outlook (2019)

The country attained the lower-middle-income status with gross national income (GNI) per capita reaching US$1070 in 2015 and has experienced an economic boom over the past 15 years with an average annual real Gross Domestic Product (GDP) growth rate of 8%. GDP peaked at 10.8% in 2006 before growth contracted to its lowest point of 0.1% in 2009 due to the global financial crisis. Since then, Cambodia has had an average GDP growth rate of 8%. In 2015, the economic growth rate was 7%, which is the second largest growth rate in South East Asia behind Myanmar. In 2015, the GDP rate was worth $18.05 billion, which represents 0.03% of the world economy. In 2018, the GDP rate was worth $24.52 billion, and according to forecasts it will reach 29.30 billion in 2020. This economic growth has been driven largely by an increase in Government spending as well as an increase in trade within the garment, footwear, construction, and manufacturing sector. There are approximately 280,000 skilled and unskilled workers within the garment industry, which has been a major factor in stabilizing the economy. Nevertheless, the textiles garments industry is under threat due to increased international competition.

Agriculture is also a major sector within the economy, which accounts for over half of the labor force. The main products being produced include rice, rubber, corn, and vegetables. However, agricultural growth is highly dependent on rainy season's rice production. As a result, the growth of the agricultural sector has been slowing recently. For example, rice production in 2015 was estimated by the authorities, being lower than in 2014, due to factors such as drought. Interestingly, industry contributes the majority of the country's GDP at 42.3% but employs only 29.6% of the workforce. In contrast, agriculture employs over 50% of the population but the sector contributes the lowest amount of GDP at 28.2%. Considering that the agricultural sector employs over half of the Cambodian labor force, contributing a significant amount to the country's GDP as most of the country's poor live in rural areas and depend on agriculture for their livelihoods, the development of the sector will be vital in enhancing the economy. Furthermore, enhancing infrastructure such as roads will help to circulate improved agriculture technology and provide microfinance to farmers to increase and diversify agriculture production. It is interesting to note that Cambodia's continued growth in industry and services and diversification in garments and light manufacturing sectors means that strong growth of the export sector should help to offset a slowdown in agriculture. As a result, Cambodia is expected to continue to have strong economic growth over the next two years.

The Tourism sector, which relies primarily on its gambling and betting services is also recovering slowly. It saw a rise in tourists into the country by 3.4% in January–July 2016, which contrasts to a contraction of tourist arrivals in 2015 by 4.9%. This decline was partly due to political unrest in Thailand. The main source of tourists is coming from Asia, contributing almost 85% of the total increase in arrivals over the past five years. Thailand is Cambodia's second largest import source and has been a key investor in Cambodia, including in the tourism sector. The initial recovery of regional tourism activity within Thailand is expected to have a continued positive impact on Cambodia tourism sector.

Cambodia's import growth is driven largely by domestic demand. Import increased from 59.5% in 2010 to 63.3% in 2018. Domestic demand pressures are also increasing imports of consumer goods, particularly for items such as food and beverages.

Structure of output (% GDP)	2000	2005	2010	2015	2018
Agriculture	37.9	32.4	36.1	28.2	23.5
Industry	23.0	26.4	23.2	29.4	34.4
Services	39.1	41.2	40.8	42.3	42.1

Source Asian Development Bank (ADB, 2019)

Structure of expenditure (% GDP)	2000	2005	2010	2015	2018
Final consumption	91.9	90.1	87.6	82.2	75.6
Gross capital formation	16.9	18.5	17.4	22.5	23.4
Exports of goods and services	49.9	64.1	54.1	61.7	61.6
Imports of goods and services	61.7	72.7	59.5	68.1	63.3
Statistical discrepancy	3.0	0.1	0.4	−0.2	2.7

Source Asian Development Bank (ADB, 2019)

Cambodia's Current Account recorded a deficit of 1.5 USD bn in Jun 2019, compared with a deficit of 947.0 USD millions in the previous quarter. A reduced deficit has also been financed by FDI inflows. In 2016, the budget reflected expansionary fiscal policy, with spending increasing by 3.6% of GDP, of which 1.4% is due to rising wages and the rest to capital expenditure and non-wage spending. Transport received the largest portion of the Government's capital budget, which was 35% of GDP. In contrast, most investors still face operational challenges due to the countries underdeveloped transport and infrastructure utilities, meaning that many businesses fix broken roads, causing substantial risk to supply chains. The agriculture, energy, and health sectors follow next, receiving 20, 10, and 5% of the total capital budget, respectively.

There has been strong revenue performance with tax revenue increased from 10% of GDP in 2010 to 15.1% in 2015. This increase in revenue can be attributed to improved revenue administration such as auditing methods. Cambodia now compares revenue collection levels, which are similar to other ASEAN economies.

Cambodia also has a stable credit rating score of 30, which is encouraging for foreign investors.

Cambodia's main trading export partners in 2016 were United States, United Kingdom, and Germany who contributed $2.1 billion, $953.23 million, $903.84 million respectively in exports. Its main import partners include China, Thailand, and Vietnam, who contributed $4.55 billion, $1.91 billion, and $1.42 billion respectively. The country's long-term economic growth prospects remain positive, with currently 5299.40 billion KHR exports.

Furthermore, as growth has increased, the poverty rate has fallen drastically; in 2011, the percentage of poor people decreased by half within seven years to around 20%. However, inequality between the rich and the poor is growing with Cambodia's upper and middle class—mainly located in the capital and other urban areas. Furthermore, despite the large poverty reduction, nearly 20.5% of the population still live under its national poverty line. For example, the increase in growth in the capital has been associated with an expansion of slum settlements, which is creating additional pressures on the informal sector.

Due to these challenges, Cambodia's economic climate can be described as bleak and weak compared to other South East Asian economies. The success of Cambodia's economy is further hindered by weak infrastructure, inadequate healthcare and educational system, poor environmental sustainability, poor governance, and ineffective management of land and natural resources.

Economic Policy

Economic Policy within Cambodia is based on the foundation of rules and regulations adhering to a free market economy. The Government has largely used fiscal policy, which has been the main policy instrument to maintain macroeconomic stability and to mitigate shocks; this is because Cambodia's monetary policy is constrained due to the high level of dollarization.

The benefit to Cambodia is that the country hosted the 2017 World Economic Forum on East Asia. Commerce Ministry spokeswomen Ms. Sophari stated, that "The key reason for choosing Cambodia is that the economic growth is remarkable, especially for the region. Cambodia can be chosen as the role model among the less developed countries."

According to the Supreme National Economic Council (SNEC), the next stage of Cambodia's industrial development strategy focuses on transforming the economic structure of Cambodia, by providing more value-added from a wider economic base that can ensure sustained growth with equity. The objective is to upgrade the economy through promoting the development of the industrial sector, which would lead Cambodia towards a 'new phase of economic base diversification', through the use of its endowments and relying on Cambodia's comparative advantages.

As a developing economy, Cambodia faces economic policy challenges such as the demographic problem of having a young workforce, as 50% of the population is under 22 years old, the majority of which are low skilled labor. Low skilled labor in the informal sector accounts for around 80% of Cambodia's GDP. Although many firms state that Cambodia's low-cost labor is beneficial for their firms and therefore choose to conduct operations in the country, Cambodia faces competition with neighboring countries such as such as Myanmar in maintaining multinational companies in the economy due to rising labor costs resulting from tight labor markets.

Cambodia can adopt policies in order to keep its exports industries competitive by developing the productivity of human capital. This can be achieved through both educational reform and increasing training and retooling programs. Additionally, by Cambodia prioritizing factors such as its high energy costs, the regulatory environment in conducting business, and infrastructure bottlenecks, this could improve growth.

Banking System

Three types of banks in Cambodia are Specialized, Commercial and Microfinance Institutions (MFIs). All banks operate under the National Bank of Cambodia (NBC), which offers registrations, licenses, and regulation to them. Cambodia's financial sector includes 36 Commercial banks, 8 Representative offices, 13 specialized banks, 54 Micro-finance institutions and 23 insurance companies. The National Bank of Cambodia (NBC) raised the minimum capital requirement for commercial banks to \$37.5 million, which all banks conformed to by the end of 2010.

Overall Cambodia's banking system has been strengthened due to numerous factors. This includes an increase in private sector growth credit at 27% year on year. The total credit provided by banks is rising. Credit growth is providing the necessary financing to facilitate an increase in investment and domestic consumption. Additionally, borrowing costs have reduced as the weighted average of short-term lending rates dropped to 11.6% per year in 2015, down from 22.04% per year in 2010. There has also been increased confidence within the banking system, which has led to increased private sector deposits. This grew at an average rate of 23% per year over the same period. Furthermore, the introduction of the liquidity coverage ratio and the directive on the minimum registered capital of banking and financial institutions issued by the central banks has strengthened the banking system. Furthermore, due to Cambodia's limited capital markets, the country is likely to be protected from global financial volatility.

Currently, Cambodia's banking system does not have any restrictions on transferring funds in or out of Cambodia through banks. This includes the repatriation of profits or capital from Cambodia. The Foreign Exchange Law of 1997 states that there should be no restrictions on foreign exchange operations, however, these operations can only be performed through an authorized financial institution.

Interest Rates (% per annum; period averages)	2000	2005	2010	2015	2018
On deposits					
Savings	6.13	2.08	1.18	1.43	1.14
Time: 6 months	7.40	5.83	5.49	5.65	4.69
12 months	7.20	6.83	6.58	6.64	6.11

Source Asian Development Bank (ADB, 2019)

Direct Investment

"Direct investment provides capital funding in exchange for an equity interest without the purchase of regular shares of a company's stock". All investment must be registered at the Ministry of Commerce. Investors are required to obtain operating permits from the relevant line ministries. Foreign investors must register and obtain approval by the Council for the Development of Cambodia or Provincial-Municipal Investment sub-committee before seeking investment incentives for a Qualified Investment Project.

Indirect Investment

Moving money into and out of Cambodia is relatively simple. Transfers from overseas accounts or transit through a correspondent bank in the USA may allow the correspondent bank to charge a processing fee—as may the originating bank for incoming transfers or the destination bank in the case of outgoing payments.

Corporate accounts require more documents and will depend on the bank's specific requirements.

The Riel, which is Cambodia's national currency, may be chosen as a means of payment and settlement. However, Cambodia still operates on a predominantly cash-based system and the use of the US dollar is very widespread in Cambodia. Large transactions are generally conducted in dollars with riel in the equivalent of cents since Cambodia does not use coin exchange.

Investment Area

Cambodia's investment climate has been relatively positive since it shifted to a free market economy and started receiving FDI in 1989. Since then Cambodia has adopted a competitive investment strategy with political stability, a low-cost labor pool, and its abundant natural resources, all have an impact on the increase in FDI entering the country.

The Cambodian 1994 Law on Investment allowed for an open investment regime, allowing more foreign investment. This includes allowing all sectors of the economy to become open to foreign investment. The government also allows 100% foreign ownership of companies in most sectors. Local equity participation or prior authorization from authorities is needed in sectors such as cigarette manufacturing and radio and television. Free remittance of foreign currencies abroad is also permitted. Significantly in 2010, a law was passed, which enables non-Cambodian citizens access to property.

The launching of Cambodia's stock exchange in 2011 has also resulted in opening for foreign investors to invest in the Cambodian market. Companies are encouraged to list on the stock exchange due to various incentives such as tax reductions for the first three years. The majority of FDI (90%) Cambodia receives is derived from its Asian neighbors with China acting as its leading investor. South

Korea, Vietnam, Malaysia and Taiwan are also major investors in Cambodia. The majority of this investment occurs in the construction industry (primarily textiles), agriculture, and tourism sectors. The construction sector attracts the largest share of foreign investors, which is expected to increase as urbanization increases. One of the main construction projects was initiating a hydroelectric dam in 2015, which was financed by a Chinese company for USD 500 million. The hydroelectric dam began producing electricity by 2018.

As a result of trade policy review recommendations from the WTO, Cambodia has implemented reforms, which include but are not limited to execution of online business registration; adoption of a competitive hiring process for Ministry of Commerce staff, and Implementation of risk evaluation measures for the Cambodia Import-Export Inspection and Fraud Repression.

Encouraged Investment Sectors

The Cambodian Government are encouraging investment and have explored the potential to expand growth into a number of sectors. These include:

- food processing;
- economic land concessions for agro-industry;
- electronics;
- car assembly;
- oil and gas.

Although the Government attempt to expand investment into broader and more diverse areas, all sectors above require human resources development, which requires long-term investment and commitment.

It must also be stated that although Cambodia is ranked 127th out of 189 countries in 2016 according to its business climate, it does have a dynamic and low-cost labor force compared to other Asian economies, which is beneficial for the economy. Furthermore, Cambodia provides investment incentives in order to stimulate investment and increase growth and has focused on its special economic zones to attract FDI, which are located in Phnom Penh, Koh Kong, Kandal, Kampot, Sihanoukville, and near the borders of Thailand and Vietnam. The main investment sectors in these zones include "garments, shoes, bicycles, food processing, car and motorcycle assembly, and electrical equipment manufacturing. The Phnom Penh Special Economic Zone has attracted more than USD 100 million in investments from several large American companies, including Coca-Cola and Tiffany & Co." (IBP Inc., 24).

Investment Incentives for Foreign Companies

- 100% foreign ownership of companies;
- 20% Corporate Tax rate after the incentive period ends (8 years);
- Duty-free import of capital goods;
- No restrictions on capital repatriation.

It must be noted that whilst these incentives are attractive to foreign investors and even whilst Cambodia is actively seeking and encouraging investment, due to the political instability during its 2013 national elections, its limited supply of skilled labor, bureaucracy within its legal system and inadequate infrastructure (including high energy costs), still it remain significant obstacles to overcome for international investment.

Domestic Markets

Cambodia has benefited from becoming a member of the WTO in 2004 as the country has committed to binding all of its tariffs. Cambodia's tariff structure is bound at four levels: 0, 7, 15, and 35%. This offers certainty to importers, who know in advance, what the maximum tariff rates are for any product that seek to import into the country. This is in contrast to other countries in Asia such as India, who have committed to binding less than 75% of tariffs. The economy is robust, underpinned by solid export performance and strong domestic demand, according to the latest edition of the World Bank's Cambodia Economic Update report released. However, real growth is decelerating to 7.0% in 2019, down from 7.5% in 2018.

Even though Cambodia has a favorable tariff structure, its domestic market continues to be influenced negatively by a number of factors. This includes the appreciation of riel (CR) against the US dollar, which makes Cambodian exports less competitive on the world market. Furthermore, the impact of the Trans-Pacific Partnership (TPP) and the free trade agreement (FTA) between Vietnam and the EU has caused a significant risk to investment and export diversion away from Cambodia. As a result, Cambodia's export market, which contributes to the majority of Cambodia's GDP, is under threat. It must be stated that even though Cambodia's has a flourishing textile sector, the exports industry is extremely limited, and Cambodia should seek to develop its trade diversification. Infrastructure also requires heavy investment to be made into the Cambodia economy in order to build a solid base for industrialization.

Adopting a Public-Private Partnership (PPP) structure will also prove vital in enhancing and improving Cambodia's domestic economy. PPP is defined as partnerships between the public and private sectors to design, plan, finance, construct and/or operate projects traditionally provided by the Government. The use of PPPs in Cambodia will reduce the fiscal and revenue burden on the Government and focus on corporate social responsibility of private companies.

External trade (USD millions)	2000	2005	2010	2015	2018
Exports, fob	1397.1	2908.0	3905.9	9336.3	12,962.7
Imports, cif	1935.7	3918.3	5755.6	13,285.1	18,806.5
Trade balance	−538.6	−1010.3	−1849.7	−3948.8	−5843.8

Source Asian Development Bank (ADB, 2019)

Main commercial partners (USD millions)	2000	2005	2010	2015	2018
Exports					
1. United States	738.9	1597.4	1903.3	2136.8	2821.9
2. United Kingdom	81.6	124.2	235.1	869.0	897.0
3. Germany	66.0	225.3	112.3	748.4	983.8
4. Japan	10.7	62.9	89.4	571.6	880.4
5. Canada	4.8	107.1	274.1	551.0	805.9
6. China, People's Rep. of	23.7	14.2	64.9	405.5	983.0
7. Belgium	3.0	10.1	63.8	282.5	606.3
8. Spain	6.4	33.9	101.2	273.6	599.4
9. France	27.7	52.2	57.3	298.3	448.0
10. Thailand	22.8	15.2	149.9	346.2	365.2
Imports					
1. China, People's Rep. of	112.8	423.5	1184.8	3926.2	6761.4
2. Thailand	221.7	290.5	689.9	1561.5	2665.8
3. Singapore	106.0	136.1	155.5	503.3	2929.8
4. Viet Nam	91.5	181.6	486.7	927.0	1301.8
5. Hong Kong, China	254.3	449.7	552.6	714.3	671.0
6. Taipei, China	174.8	291.1	476.5	546.2	647.7
7. Japan	58.3	100.2	156.4	423.0	623.0
8. Korea, Rep. of	76.8	150.6	247.8	459.6	463.8
9. Indonesia	68.4	82.6	175.0	335.5	381.5
10. Malaysia	64.1	92.5	165.3	187.5	216.6

Source Asian Development Bank (ADB, 2019)

Finance and Taxation

Tax

The principal taxation law of Cambodia is the Law on Taxation (LoT). The main categories of tax imposed in Cambodia are Personal Income Tax, Corporate Income Tax (CIT)/Tax on Profit (ToP), Value Added Tax (VAT), Patent Tax, Specific Tax and certain Merchandise and Services (STCMS) and Import and Export Duties.

There is only one tax regime, which is the Real Regime Tax System (RRTS). This is further divided into three classes of taxpayers. This includes small taxpayers (250–700 million KHR) medium taxpayers (700–2000 million) and large taxpayers (more than 2000 million). The small taxpayers are required to adhere to the simplified accounting procedures, which includes submitting a monthly tax return in one single form, whereas the medium and large taxpayers are required to adhere to the international accounting standard of Cambodia, which includes submitting and paying taxes to the General Department of Taxation (GDT) on an annual and monthly basis. The classification is also dependent upon the form of the enterprise as well as the business activity.

Taxable income is defined as the net profit obtained from all types of business operations including capital gains realized during the business operation.

Corporate taxpayers are classified as either resident or non-resident taxpayers. Resident taxpayers are enterprises that manage and carries out businesses within Cambodia. Resident taxpayers are subject to ToP (Tax on Profit) or CIT (Corporate Income Tax) for income from both domestic and foreign incomes. Non-resident taxpayers are enterprises that do not have management within Cambodia, yet, and has a Cambodian source of income. Non-residents are subjected to ToP and CIT by only Cambodian source income. Cambodia doesn't impose additional capital gain taxes. Gains from property/asset disposal are subjected to ToP rate as an ordinary source of income.

The Cambodian Corporate income tax/annual ToP rates are as follows:

- 20% for the profit obtained by a legal person.
- a tax on profit prepayment equal to 1% of turnover must be paid each month.
- 30% for the profit from an oil or natural gas production sharing contract and the exploitation of natural resources including timber, ore, gold, and precious stones.
- 0% for the profit of QIP during the tax exemption period as determined by CDC.
- 5% on gross premiums received in Cambodia for Insurance Companies engaged in the insurance or reinsurance of life, property or other risks and 20% on non-insurance income.

Cambodia currently operates its own system of filing CIT/ToP, which are completed on an annual basis and due on 31st March on the year following the income tax year.

Personal Income Tax or a tax on Cambodian and foreign sourced income is only applicable for residents in Cambodia, who are Cambodian nationals or those who have been residing in Cambodia for more than 182 days.

Tax rate on salary	%
KHR 0–500,000	0
KHR 500,001–1,250,000	5
KHR 1,250,001–8,500,000	10
KHR 8,500,001–12,500,000	15
KHR 12,500,001 and above	20
Non-residents	20 flat rate
Fringe benefit	20

Source SantanderTrade.com

The personal income tax operates as a progressive system ranging from 0% tax for those earning up to 500,0000 (KHR) per month to 20% to those earning over 12,500,000 KHR. For non-tax residents, a flat rate of 20% is applied on the income derived from Cambodia.

A patent tax is a yearly business registration tax, which all enterprises carrying on business activities in Cambodia are required to pay by the 31st of March. A "patent tax certificate" will be issued by the GDT upon registration. The standard patent tax payment is KHR 1140,000 (approximately $285).

In Cambodia VAT is chargeable on a wide range of goods and services as well as on the importation of goods. VAT is either taxable at 10%, which is the standard rate, or the 0% rate, which is applicable to the export of goods and services and certain charges in relation to international transport of people and goods. Exempt supplies are not subject to VAT and include but are not limited to, public services including post, healthcare, dental services, transportation systems. Insurance services and the primary financial services are also exempt from paying VAT tax. The taxpayer must self-assess to check which incentives are applicable according to the current tax regulations.

VAT registration must be made at the commencement of business operations or within 30 days in which the taxpayer becomes a taxable person. VAT returns and payment are due to be filed and paid to the GDT by the 20th day of the following month.

Import duty rates vary depending on the nature of goods involved and origin of the goods. Currently, the duty rates are 0, 7, 15, and 35%. Exemptions can also be obtained as part of the tax incentives offered in Cambodia. These incentives are promoted by the Council for the Development of Cambodia (CDC), which has the ultimate aim to stimulate investment in Cambodia. These incentives include:

- ToP exemption for up to 9 years (specific conditions apply)
- accelerated depreciation on manufacturing assets
- import duty exemption on production equipment, raw materials, and inputs to manufacturing
- rights to employ foreign labor.

In order to receive these investment incentives, investors are required to submit an Investment Proposal to either the CDC or the PMIS to obtain a Qualified Investment Project (QIP) status depending on capital level and location of the investment project in question. In 2003, a "negative list" was created into Government legislation, which means that the investment incentives apply to all sectors not included in the "negative list". Cambodia also implements the Common Effective Preferential Tariff Scheme (CEPT) for the ASEAN Free Trade Area (AFTA).

Cambodia has not entered any Double Tax Agreements (DTA) with other countries. There is also no "general anti-avoidance" provision in the Cambodian tax law.

Tax rate	%
Corporate tax	20
Personal income tax	20
Sales tax	10

Source Trading Economics (2019)

Audit and Accounting

All enterprises are required to submit their annual financial statements to be audited by an independent auditor. The audit shall be carried out by an auditor registered with the Kampuchea Institute of Certified Public Accountants and Auditors (KICPAA): enterprises must meet two of the following criteria below to have their financial statements audited by an independent external auditor.

The requirements include:

- annual turnover above 3,000,000,000 Riels (approximately USD 750,000)
- total assets above 2,000,000,000 Riels (approximately USD 500,000)
- more than 100 employees
- for QIPs registered with the Council for the Development of Cambodia in accordance with the law on Investment, annual Financial Statements have to be submitted and audited by an independent auditor registered with the KICPAA.

According to the US Department of State, the National Accounting Council of Cambodia has adopted the Cambodian International Financial Reporting Standards for Small and Medium-sized Entities (CIFRS for SMEs) and Cambodian International Financial Reporting Standards (CIFRS) issued by the International Accounting Standard Board (IASB) effective for Financial Statements with the period beginning on or after January 1, 2010 and January 1, 2012, respectively.

On April 11, 2016, the Law on Accounting and Auditing became effective. The accounting requirements needed to be adhered to include but are not limited to:

- enterprises and not-for-profit organizations are required to prepare financial statements within 3 months following the year-end.
- financial statements form the basis for fulfilling tax obligations.
- accounting records must be maintained, and the underlying transaction shall be supported by proper vouchers.
- accounting records and financial statements should be in Khmer language and Khmer Riel, and a secondary set of accounting records and foreign-related financial statements may be prepared in a foreign currency and in the English language.
- enterprises and not-for-profit organizations have to maintain accounting records for ten years.

Generally, the tax and accounting year is the calendar year. The tax audit period in Cambodia can be for a maximum of 3 years after filing the tax return. There are three main types of tax audits, desk audit, limited audit, and comprehensive/final audit. A tax year is considered "closed" when it has been audited by the comprehensive/final tax audit.

Risk Assessment

Cambodia is considered to be a less developed country (LDC) but is continuing to take measures to disconnect from its developing status by 2030. The measures, that Cambodia has taken to become increasingly integrated into regional and international activities, have had a strong impact on the economy with Cambodia's economic climate pursuing a steady growth rate of 7%. Economic activity remains strong driven by exports, real estate, and construction. However, GDP growth is projected to decline to around 6.3–7.0% until 2021, with the assumption that there will be a small amount of product diversification and supportive policies to support this growth.

Economic growth will be supported by the Government's main macroeconomic tool of fiscal policy with Government spending expected to rise. Inflation is also set to rise in line with an expected rise in global oil prices. In 2019, the country's exports reached KHR 5299.40 billion. Imports, on the other hand, reached 7084.10. In the preliminary 2017 budget, the government plans to target a budget deficit of 2.6% of GDP. Cambodia recorded a Current Account deficit of KHR 6210 billion in the second quarter of 2019.

In the long term, the ease of doing business in Cambodia is expected to worsen to 133 by 2020 due to tighter regulations. Furthermore, Cambodia's medium-term growth is projected to decline to around 6.3% by 2021, due to a moderation in the credit cycle and challenges in economic diversification.

The main sectors contributing to the Cambodian economy are agriculture, industry, and services. The agriculture industry, which correlates to over one-third of Cambodia's GDP, is expected to continue to have a negative impact on the growth of the sector due to falling commodity prices. As a result, it is expected that the poverty rate will continue to fall, but at a slower pace due to the slow growth in the agricultural sector.

The Cambodian Government has explored other areas to increase investment and stimulate the economy. Current opportunities to stimulate the economy exists in mining, hydrocarbons and natural gas. Offshore hydrocarbon reserves have recently been discovered. As a result, this is a significant advantage for the Cambodian economy as many Asian economies in power supply want to invest in Cambodia. There are many projects with regional backing underway.

Looking ahead, the main risks facing Cambodia include a significant slowdown in China which will spill over through less FDI, financial sector vulnerabilities, fiscal pressures, and the loss of competitiveness from higher wage pressure. It must also be stated, that the country is and will continue to remain heavily dependent on foreign aid including loans and FDI. It is interesting to note that the Government has approved the 2017 budget of $5 billion, which was funded using loans of nearly $1 billion. Therefore, the budget remains unbalanced. Cheang Von, chairman of the National Assembly's Foreign Affairs Commission, said, "I firmly believe, that the 2017 national budget is important to support economic growth, create more jobs for people, eliminate poverty by one percent a year, build human resources, particularly youth, and build physical infrastructure which facilitates transporting agriculture products." It is also interesting to note that Agriculture, which is one of Cambodia's main economic drivers, was not in the top seven priority sectors of the budget.

Overall, Cambodia's economic and political development can be hindered by social unrest in the country, difficult relationships with neighboring Thailand, a weak economic structure and business environment, rapid credit growth, which threatens price stability and banking sector stability, high current account deficits, and an extremely vulnerable export base, that is highly concentrated within the garment sector.

Economic Risks

According to Mr. Tukuafu, ADB continues to support Cambodia through investing in agriculture, transport, logistics, tech, and vocational education.

It must be noted that although economic growth within the country is rising, this growth is not considered to be sustainable due to the heavy reliance on its garment and tourism industry, which are easily affected by external markets and demand. For example, the slow growth of the export sector can be attributed to factors such as: increases in the minimum wage and competition from other low-cost countries like Myanmar. Additionally, the country's national currency is pegged to the US dollar, which is continuing to appreciate effects the price competitiveness against Cambodian exports.

Policymakers seem to recognize Cambodia's reliance on its exports as an issue. Even the prime minister stressed the importance of Cambodia's need to modernize its economy through promoting the development of the industrial sector in order to achieve sustainable growth during the opening of the Fourth Cambodia Economic Forum in 2013. The World Bank also addressed this issue. World Bank country economist Sodeth Ly stated, that "The garment sector is characterized as a footloose industry, and footloose industries can move quickly from one country to another." As a result, Cambodia's diversification is extremely important.

"Most of the country's labor force is young, but often not equipped with skills that match business needs, so the challenge for policymakers is to address this gap and mismatch," said ADB Chief Economist Shang-Jin Wei. "Developing a more educated, employable, and productive workforce is essential for Cambodia to broaden its economy beyond the current four mainstays of garment manufacturing, tourism, construction and agriculture and to sustain high growth."

According to the IMF's annual Article IV mission to Cambodia report, "The main downside risk arises from rapid credit growth, increasingly concentrated in real estate, which threatens to undermine economic and financial stability. External risks include a significant slowdown in China, an appreciating US dollar, weaker growth in Europe and increased uncertainty from the Brexit referendum result, and a sharper-than-anticipated tightening in global financial conditions."

The IMF argue that the policies the Cambodian Government should "focus on include securing sustained growth and mitigating financial sector vulnerabilities, including by enhancing resilience and building buffers". This is in line with ADB's view, Hiroyuki Aoki, Senior Financial Sector Specialist at ADB's Southeast Asia Department states that "Cambodia's economy has been performing well but achieving inclusive growth has been a challenge, particularly among people who don't have access to formal financial services." As a result, ADB is committed to helping Cambodia "develop its financial sector to reduce financial exclusion and promote inclusive growth."

Political Risks

The political stability in Cambodia has recovered since its last election in 2013, in which a political dispute occurred due to the Cambodian National Rescue Party (CNRP) rejecting the result of the ruling Cambodian People's Party (CPP). This rejection by the CNRP led to chaos as the CNRP boycotted the National Assembly, seeking electoral reform. This occurred for approximately 12 months, meaning no economic or political progress was achievable. The dispute was resolved in 2015 when the National Assembly passed new election laws, which were approved by both parties. Without consulting the opposition, the prime minister decided to postpone the 2018 elections by five months. This tension has now been reignited earlier this year due to the killing of Kem Ley in the capital of the country, who was a critic of the Cambodian Government. As a result, political tension is lingering in the air. BMI state, "We see a growing threat that the recent crackdown by the government on the opposition and civil society will spark a return of potentially-violent street protests."

Political tensions are also running high due to the Cambodia-Thailand border and illegal migration dispute, which began in 2008. The Cambodian government considers the Thai military presence along the border as a direct national security threat. This has led to Cambodia reaching out for worldwide support in order to defend its sovereignty from what it considers deliberate acts of aggression by Thailand. This has affected Cambodia's bilateral relationship with Thailand and has led to disunity within the ASEAN group. In 2015, the controversy led to violent conflict between Cambodian border activists and Vietnamese residents along the border. This dispute has reignited bad flames between Cambodia and Vietnam as Cambodian policymakers are still aware, that its stronger neighbors remain a security threat to the kingdom's territorial integrity. From July 2014 and June 2015, Cambodian authorities deported 2058 illegal Vietnamese immigrants.

It must be noted, that even though the relationship between Cambodia and Vietnam remain uncertain, it is clear that Cambodia will grow closer to China. This explains Phnom Penh's inconsistency on the dispute of the South China Sea, between China, Vietnam, and a number between other South East Asian economies.

The Lower Mekong Sub-region could also see a rise in conflict over the coming years due to the growing need for power, as well as the desire for economic growth. This has driven most of the South East Asian countries to drastically increase their hydropower capacity in the Lower Mekong River. Cambodia and Laos are both building dams along the river at the irritation of its Asian neighbors. As a result, Vietnam's economy and its river delta will be affected negatively.

It must be noted, that political stability in Cambodia has and is continuing to improve. However, compared to other South East Asian countries, Cambodia still has a long way to go. Political stability is especially important to Cambodia in order to continue to attract FDI in order to stimulate the economy.

Corruption Risks

According to the Transparency International (T.I) index, Cambodia ranks 152 out of 163 in the corruption index. Preap Kol, executive director of T.I Cambodia, said Cambodia's score landed it in the "highly corrupt" category. Cambodia is now perceived to be the most corrupt country out of all of the other ASEAN countries, with Singapore being the best performing ASEAN country members.

A study by Sophal Ear from the Department of Diplomacy and World Affairs found that Corruption in Cambodia is widespread and anti-corruption efforts are limited because of the lack of political will. This view is reinforced by TI who ranked the key Cambodian institutions from 0 to 100 (0 being very weak to 100 being very strong).

The Cambodian judiciary had the lowest rating, with a score of 16, followed by law enforcement agencies, with a score of 22. The civil society scored the highest rating with a score of 48. Considering civil society received the highest rating, but the score is still below the half-way mark: these are signals, that Cambodian institutions are highly corrupted. This has a massive impact on Cambodia's trading environment and limits its impact of receiving FDI, especially due to the large amount of bureaucracy that exits within the business environment for obtaining a limited number of licenses and permits.

As Cambodia is a relatively poor country in comparison to other Asian countries and even more so on an international scale, corrupt officials diverting revenue away from public services (e.g. health and education into their own pockets) has a detrimental effect on the economy, more than it would do in other high-income countries. Furthermore, considering the fact, that Cambodia relies heavily on donor assistance, corruption undermines and wastes the money of the countries providing assistance including the ADB, World Bank, and other multilateral institutions.

A number of countries and organizations have addressed the issue of corruption in Cambodia. For example, in January 2016 US Secretary of State, John Kerry, met with Cambodian policymakers about concerns regarding the Government's record on human rights and corruption. Furthermore, ADB states that many of the country's laws on public finances are not being implemented and that public procurement of goods and services needs to be improved at all levels of government. Additionally, ADB argues that Cambodia's police, judges, courts, and other public service institutions are the most corrupt.

It must, however, be stated, that the Cambodian Government is aware of the corrupt practices within the country and therefore, have taken steps in order to prevent corruption occurring within the regional, and international activities that Cambodia has actively integrated into. These steps have included implementing the Anti-Corruption Law in 2010, in order to combat corruption through education, prevention, and more effective enforcement. The implementation of the Public Financial Management Reform Program has had a slight impact on reduced negative perceptions of corruption. Furthermore, the setting up of the Rectangular Strategy, which has the aim to improve governance and other reforms such as judicial and civil administration reform has been implemented. The Government has also set up the Government–Private Sector Forum, which allows the private sector to express their criticisms and complaints to the Government, which the Government than attempt to address. These steps show an attempt by the Cambodian Government to make a commitment to improving governance, the rule of law and the establishment of an appropriate regulatory environment. Further steps to combat corruption need to include an amendment of existing anti-corruption measures, which are designed with loopholes. However, implementation of these amendments remains a struggle.

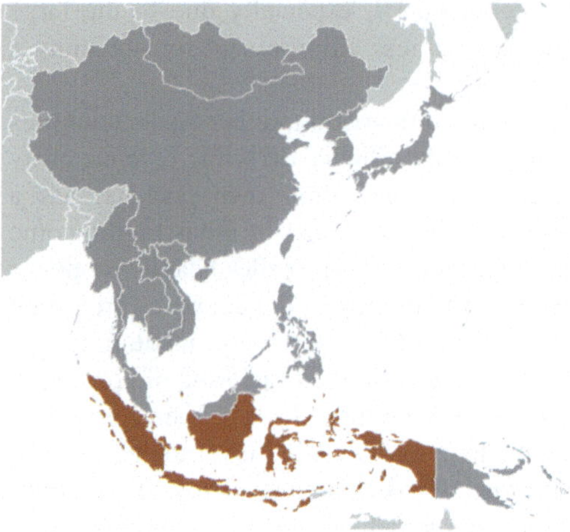

INDONESIA

Official name

Republic of Indonesia

Capital

Jakarta

Area

1,904,569 sq. km

Population

266 mln

Languages

Bahasa Indonesia (official)

Main ethnic groups

Main religions

Muslim 88%, Christian 7%

Government type

Presidential Republic

Urbanization

55.3%

Life expectancy ratio

70 years

Fertility rate

2.3 children born/woman

Currency

Indonesia

Country Introduction

Population, Location, Geography, Climate

Indonesia has a population of about 266 million and it is the fourth most populated country in the world after China, India, and the United States. Over two-thirds of the population live in Java, the island where capital city Jakarta is located, the center of the country's economic and political power. The majority of Indonesians are of Malay extraction. Major ethnic groups are Javanese (45%), Sundanese (14%), Madurese (7.5%), Coastal Malays (7.5%), and others. There are also ethnic Chinese, Indians and Arabs concentrated mostly in urban areas throughout the archipelago. Furthermore, six religions are formally recognized in Indonesia and about 87% of the population is Muslim, 10% is Christian (Protestant and Roman Catholic) and approximately 3% is Hindu, Buddhist or Confucian.

The official language of Indonesia is Bahasa Indonesia which is a strong unifying factor in a country where more than 300 distinct regional languages are still spoken. English is spoken in international and high-level business contexts in large cities. However, in rural areas, it may be difficult to find someone who speaks English unless it is a tourist destination. Some older Indonesians may understand Dutch, as they may have attended Dutch schools.

Indonesia is composed of seventeen thousand islands that stretch over five thousand miles along the equator and it borders with Malaysia, Timor-Leste, and Papua New Guinea by land, and Christmas Island, India, the Philippines, Singapore, Thailand, Vietnam, Australia, and Palau by sea.

The area of Indonesia is 1,904,569 km^2 and it is the world's largest archipelago. Indonesia is an ideal destination for adventure and eco-travel since it offers a stunning variety of topography and ecologies Mist-shrouded volcanoes and mountains, unexplored rainforests, thousands of miles of beaches, and endless offshore reefs support a dazzling abundance of wildlife.

The great majority of Indonesia's islands are negligible size, but it holds several islands that are enormous in size. These include Sumatra, Kalimantan (formerly Borneo, and shared with Malaysia), Sulawesi, and Java. The Indonesian state of Irian Jaya occupies the western half of New Guinea, which is the world's second largest island (behind Greenland). The most populated Indonesian islands by far is Java, where the country's capital city, Jakarta, is located. Other notable islands include the exotic, popular resort island of Bali, Lombok, Catholic Flores, and Komodo which is home of dragons.

The two seasons of Indonesia are divided among a dry season from June to October and the rainy season, from November to March. Both seasons are hot yet, the coastal regions and mountains tend to stay cool.

Internal Policy

Indonesia is a republic with a presidential system, and predominantly adopts the civil law system, intermixed with customary law and the Roman-Dutch law. The President acts as the Head of State, Head of Government, and the commander-in-chief of the Indonesian National Armed Forces, and has the power to appoint his/her cabinet members. Furthermore, the President responsible for domestic governance, policy-making, and foreign affairs. The president is elected every 5 years by an absolute majority vote.

The highest level of the judicial branch is the Mahkamah Agung (supreme court). The constitutional court rules on constitutional and political matters, and the judges are controlled by the judicial commission. A judicial commission nominates the supreme court judges and the president with the concurrence of parliament appoints them. The president, supreme court, and parliament are recommended by the constitutional court, and the president appoints judges.

The two legislative bodies for Indonesia are the Majelis Permusyawaratan Rakyat and the Dewan Perwakilan Rakyat. Dewan Perwakilan Daerah are elected by single non-transferable vote, and the Dewan Perwakilan Rakya are elected by open-list proportional representation in multi-member constituencies. Both bodies are elected every 5 years.

International Relations

Indonesia's foreign policy priorities include strategically balancing in its relationships with China and the US and raising its international profile by working through ASEAN. In other words, Indonesia is focusing on maintaining and building economic and political collaboration with the Western countries, and it also maintains close relationships with its neighbors in Asia and is also a founding member of ASEAN and the East Asia Summit as well as a member of the United Nations, the World Trade Organization, and APEC.

Furthermore, Indonesia maintains a close relationship with the Netherlands. Due to their shared history and past, the two countries maintain close cultural relations and have a special bilateral relationship. Dutch firms are making considerable investments in Indonesia's fast-growing economy and Indonesia is a Dutch partner country for development cooperation, with an emphasis on water management, food security, and the justice sector.

Indonesia is a member of the Association of Southeast Asian Nations (ASEAN), Asian-Pacific Economic Cooperation (APEC), the World Trade Organization (WTO), the World Health Organization (WHO), UNESCO, G-20 and many others. The country maintains bilateral relations with the most members of these organization. In other words, Indonesia maintains bilateral relations with the ASEAN countries, EU countries, Australia, New Zealand, Japan, China, India, USA,

Canada, Mexico, Argentina, Brazil, South Africa, Morocco, and Egypt. Furthermore, Indonesia has signed bilateral agreements for the protection of investment with 57 countries.

Japan (1st), China (2nd), United States of America (3rd), Singapore (4th) and India (5th) are the largest exporter of Indonesia. Furthermore, the top importers of Indonesia are China (1st), Singapore (2nd), Japan (3rd), South Korea (4th) and Malaysia (5th).

Economy

Macroeconomic Overview

	Unit	2000A	2018	2020F
GDP, current prices	USD (billions)	179.48	1022.45	1208.86
GDP per capita, current prices	USD	870.15	3870.56	4479.50
GDP based on PPP per capita	Current International dollar	4646.85	13,229.54	14,892.57

Source IMF Outlook 2019

Indonesia's economy has expanded strongly during the last 10 years, despite the sharp economic contraction that occurred during 1997–1998. At this pace, Indonesia has become globally important to the worldwide economy. Its growth has made it the fourth largest economy in East Asia, following China, Japan, and South Korea. It has the 15th largest economy in the world based on Purchasing Power Parity (PPP). The Indonesian economy has changed drastically, specifically on the focus of its agricultural sector. Within the 1950s and 1960s, the government promoted self-sufficiency in the agricultural sector, boosting its economy significantly.

Urbanization and industrialization began in the late 1960s. It sped up in the 1980s when the government of Indonesia diversified the economy from oil exports and focused more on manufacturing exports. By the mid-1980s, the Indonesian economy became globalized as trade barriers were reduced. From 2008 to 2009, the economy slowed in moderation in relation to the worldwide crisis concurrently happening.

Since overcoming Asian financial crisis of the late 1990s, Indonesia's gross national income per capita has constantly risen. Today, Indonesia is ranked as the fourth most populated countries in the world.

Indonesia's economic planning follows a 20-year development plan, spanning from 2005 to 2025. It is divided into 5-year medium-term plans, each one with different development priorities. The current medium-term development plan (2015–2020), focusing on infrastructure development and social assistance programs.

A continued fall in demand for commodities has led to moderate GDP growth. Trade has slowed, as well as the expansion of fixed investment, and domestic consumption. These developments have led to a slower pace of poverty reduction.

While the poverty rate declined by 1% annually from 2007 to 2011, since 2012 poverty has declined by an average of only 0.3% points per year. Hence out of a population of 252 million, more than 28 million Indonesians still live below the poverty line. Approximately 40% of the entire population remains vulnerable to falling into poverty, as their income hover marginally above the national poverty line, set at 330,776 rupiahs per person per month.

Another challenge to try reducing poverty and to help 1.7 million youth who enter the workforce each year, in order to create jobs. Employment growth less than population growth.

There have been many efforts to improve the standard of living by increasing the standard of basic public services. Yet, the quality of hospitals and schools is divided by middle-income standards—contributing to health concerns.

The government continues to announce policy reforms intended to bureaucracy, in order to promote investment and economic growth. Investors welcome the policy reforms, which include opening up sectors for investment and reducing high logistics costs. A long-anticipated cabinet reshuffle also reflects the government's commitment to further reforms, as well as the consolidation of the political coalition supporting the administration.

Indonesia has a large domestic consumption base and the country's middle class with increasing levels of disposable income. The purchasing power has grown from 38% of the population or 81 million in 2003 to 56.6% or 131 million in 2010.

The World Bank report indicated that the middle class grew by 61.73% over this 7 years' period, with over 7 million people being elevated to the middle class. The middle class live on 4.50 USD to 22.50 USD a day and have consumption patterns starting to resemble those of a typical "middle class". Controlled wage growth provided accompanied by a sustained improving employment outlook.

Due to the vast population, many people believe in the foreign investment in countries in South-east Asia due to the available consumption base. Comparisons of Indonesia having the same economic growth and investment potential as the "BRIC" countries are now not so relevant given the major economic downturns in Brazil and Russia and slowdown in China. India is the only remaining BRIC country worthy of direct comparison.

Indonesia is now being grouped with Mexico, Nigeria, and Turkey as one of the MINT countries. From 2000 to 2010, Indonesia's population grew at a rate of

15.8%. It is forecasted to have 263 million people by 2020. The Central Statistics Agency (BPS) has estimated that between 2010 and 2035 the country's population will grow to over 305 million at 3 million per year. Another report refers to estimates of Indonesia's population exceeding the USA by 2043. The country is the most populous nation and is also the largest market in Southeast Asia.

Indonesia's 250 million people make up 40% of the 625 million of combined ASEAN countries. Indonesia was ranked the world's 16th largest economy with a GDP of 862 million USD. It is predicted that Indonesia with be the seventh largest economy, worldwide, by 2030. By taking advantage of the large consumer class, the economy can be continually boosted, maximizing the country's attractiveness for foreign investment. In April 2014, the World Bank report rated Indonesia as already having the 10th largest economy in the world, contributing 2.3% of global economic output.

The report assessed economies based on purchasing power parity (PPP) with Indonesia moving up 6 places and passing more developed countries such as Canada, South Korea, and Spain. The report found that middle-income economies of Indonesia, China, India, Russia, Brazil, and Mexico accounted for 32.3% of world GDP compared to 32.9% contribution of the six largest high-income economies: USA, Japan, Germany, France, the UK, and Italy.

However, based on Real GDP, the country ranks 16th with an output of 795 billion USD in 2014. Other observations referred to an uneven growth rate and a widening gap between rich and poor, with real consumption rates in a selected 7-year period for the poorest 40% of households being just over 1% compared to nearly 6% for the richest 20%. In terms of the financial sector, bank loans were the equivalent of 26% of Indonesia's GDP.

As at 2015, Indonesia's national debt was 27% of GDP, which was comparably low to the nearby China, Singapore, South Korea, Malaysia, and Thailand, whom of which had relatively high debts to GDP. In 2018, the national debt of Indonesia amounted to around US 316.25 billion.

Following the 1997 Asian Economic Crisis, Indonesia went through a period of economic and political instability that ended with the collapse of the banking system. However, ten years later, Indonesia was less affected by the GFC compared to many neighboring economies.

An important further factor is that the Indonesian banking industry had become one of the most open and tightly regulated in the world, having dramatic transformation and consolidation. Following the Asian economic crisis, Indonesia liberated its banking system through structural adjustment reform, where 39 billion USD was spent.

Indonesia is in a lower economic growth period since 2017. It is relevant however that many of the world's other emerging economies are also growing slower.

Structure of output (% GDP)	2000	2005	2010	2015	2018
Agriculture	15.6	13.1	14.3	13.9	13.3
Industry	45.9	46.5	43.9	41.3	41.4
Services	38.5	40.3	41.8	44.7	45.2

Source Asian Development Bank (ADB, 2019)

Structure of expenditure (% GDP)	2000	2005	2010	2015	2018
Final consumption	68.2	72.5	65.2	67.2	65.9
Gross capital formation	22.2	25.1	32.9	34.1	34.6
Exports of goods and services	41.0	34.1	24.3	21.2	21.0
Imports of goods and services	30.5	29.9	22.4	20.8	22.1
Statistical discrepancy	−0.9	−1.7	0.0	−1.6	0.6

Source Asian Development Bank (ADB, 2019)

Economic Policy

Throughout the decade following the Asian Crisis, Indonesia's economy performed exceptionally well. However, growth has moderated in recent years, reflecting weaker international demand and slow investment growth.

Indonesia is still trying to catch up to growth and has recently slowed in growth as protectionist measures have been adopted. Internal and external factors continue to challenge the implementation of monetary policy. Indonesia is adopting standards maintaining macroeconomic stability, adopting a broad range of structural reforms, and creating fiscal space to expand government expenditures in priority areas such as education, health, poverty alleviation, and infrastructure.

Recently, Indonesia has removed many fuel subsidies. Yet, low commodity export prices and slower growth means that tax revenue needs to be carefully designed to improve the current low levels. There is also room to improve the efficiency and targeting of public spending at both central and sub-national levels. Indonesia has pushed against poverty, relative to the increase in per capita income growth and the multiplicity of programs aimed to reduce poverty. However, income inequality is high. The current mix of social programs, including cash transfers conditioned on school attendance and a subsidized rice program, although encouraging headway is being made in developing a single registry of vulnerable households.

There are some programs that harm economic and social development—hindering investment in new or existing businesses. Failing to have conformity between both, national and sub-national, laws and regulations will pose an issue.

The Administration has been trying to interfere against corruption by establishing the Corruption Eradication Commission. The capacity of the civil service is quite inconsistent—which discourages investment in both, domestic and foreign businesses. Budget execution at all levels of government also remains a problem; measures have recently been taken to address this issue.

Since 2012, the Indonesian economy has both varied and grown. In 2013 GDP growth fell below 6% for the first time since the financial crisis, and growth continued to mitigate through 2014. Although it faced an economic downturn, Indonesia's economic growth has outperformed many others ASEAN countries. This performance can be attributed to macroeconomic policies, such as inflation targeting and fiscal prudence.

Until mid-2014, consumption had been supported by firming increasing, cash transfers to poor families, strong wage gains and improving labor market outcomes. Despite a surge in exports in late 2013, as exports of mineral ores were brought forward before the enforcement of the export ban, the contribution of external demand to growth has been disappointing, exacerbating current account worries starting in mid-2011 and again in mid-2014. Investment also weakened in 2013–14, led by slowing investment in machinery and transportation equipment. This should be focused on due to the effect it causes in productivity and its growing share in GDP: one quarter in 2013, up from one fifth in 2000.

The economy grew at 5% in 2014 and then it accelerates somewhat during recent years, as exports accelerate thanks to the lower exchange rate, and a pickup in government investment. A rapidly expanding middle class, combined with improving confidence, can help to sustain consumption and lift private investment.

If the core inflation remains low and begins to stabilize, the depreciated currency could help to contain imports. Bank Indonesia (BI) needs to remain cautious about official interest rates, especially in light of the continuing reliance on external sources of funding in the context of global financial uncertainty. Indonesia recorded a Government Budget deficit equal to 1.76% of the country's Gross Domestic Product in 2018. Government Budget in Indonesia averaged −1.14% of GDP from 1988 until 2018, reaching an all the time high of 3.02% of GDP in 1995 and a record low of −2.58% of GDP in 2015.

With such a large population, Indonesia has a large domestic consumption base. The country's middle-class, with increasing levels of disposable income and purchasing power, has grown steadily till now.

A World Bank report indicated that the middle class grew by 61.73% over this 7-year period, with over 7 million people being elevated to the middle-class segment. The definition of "middle class" is now being re-evaluated and debated.

According to the World Bank, 44 million (18%) middle class live on 4.50 USD to 22.50 USD a day and consumption patterns which look like a typical middle-class model.

Economic growth, joined with a political stability of the country, helps to strengthen the confidence of international markets in the continuation of a harmonious development in the medium to long-term, thanks to the maintenance of prudent fiscal and monetary policies. Indonesia has long since embarked on a virtuous circle of solid macroeconomic fundamentals, a progressive decline in the cost of capital and reforms.

The Government aims to raise the infrastructure for a total of $420 billion through the scheme of the "Public-Private Partnership", to contribute to growth. The infrastructure plan is based on the development of six "economic corridors":

- Sumatra: mining and agriculture (in particular palm oil);
- Java: manufacturing and services; Kalimantan: mining; Sulawesi: agriculture, plantation, fishery;
- Bali-Nusa Tenggara tourism and food production;
- Papua-Maluku: natural resources.

Following the corridors and their development, it should be added pro-growth policies to support consumption and domestic investment, in order to maintain the growth of the GDP.

During 2015, the Indonesian government has allocated 3.18 billion of dollars in infrastructure (+19.3% over the previous year), especially in the maritime sector.

Banking System

Indonesian banking sector after the economic collapse of 1998, has experienced a long-term consolidation and restructuring process and now looks solid and capitalized. The supervision of the banking system is the Bank of Indonesia.

The banking system of the country includes four state banks: Bank Mandiri, Bank Negara Indonesia (BNI), Bank Rakyat Indonesia (BRI), Bank Tabungan Negara (BTN), which controls 37.5% of total assets; there is also a group of commercial banks in private ownership, active mainly in households and SME market (Bank Central Asia, Bank Danamon, Bank Panin, Bank International Indonesia—Maybank, CIMB Niaga). Most of them have created joint ventures with foreign groups.

There exists a network of 1635 rural banks with 4678 branches. The new and capitalization criteria adopted by the Central Bank would like to push local entities to aggregate to reach the minimum capitalization threshold.

Regarding the operational point of view, some challenges persist, including a weak legal system, high levels of corruption, deficiencies in terms of governance and transparency—that may increase the potential loss of credit banks and the related operating costs.

Since 2014 it exists OJK (Indonesian Financial Service Authority), an independent institution, which has the tasks to overview, to supervise, to manage and to investigate on Indonesian financial services.

Interest Rates (% per annum; period averages)	2000	2005	2010	2015	2018
On deposits					
Savings	8.86	4.32	3.92	1.7	1.3
Time: 6 months	13.31	10.17	7.20	8.5	7.1
12 months	12.17	10.95	7.88	8.5	6.5

Source Asian Development Bank (ADB, 2019)

Indonesian Central Bank is conducting an anti-crisis expansionary monetary policy since 2008, and in 2015, it has cut the benchmark rate by 25 basis points, bringing it to 7.50%, with deposit rates reduced to 5.50% and the loan kept all 8.00%.

The banks tend to support the investment plans of the national companies. Access to credit from retail customers is still limited to—albeit growing—middle class, with about 20% of the adult population that benefits, according to OECD data, the formal financial services.

Nowadays, banking system is focusing more and more on the expansion of access to credit by the population and SMEs, key elements for the sustainable development of national economy, after years whom the attention has been focused on the safety against potential critical phenomena.

Economic growth is picking up slightly, and there are no signs of large-scale stress on corporate balance sheets. Indonesia's rated banks also show strong buffers, in terms of a high level of pre-provision income, loan loss coverage and capital, against a deterioration in asset quality.

On Indonesia's recently passed financial safety net law, legislation has both positive and negative implications for the level of systemic support that the banks will receive in times of stress.

Investment Area

Foreign direct investment in Indonesia rose 7.8% year-on-year to 99.7 trillion IDR in the third quarter of 2016. It is the highest value on record as investment grew the most in metal and electronic, mining, and property sector with Singapore being the biggest investor. In dollar terms, FDI is equivalent to 7.4 billion USD. Foreign Direct Investment in Indonesia averaged 66,033.33 IDR billion from 2010 until 2018, reaching an all-time high of 99,700.00 IDR billion in the third quarter of 2016 and a record low of 35,400.00 IDR billion in the first quarter of 2010.

Oil Plants

Palm oil is one of the most widely produced and consumed oil in the world. It is a competitive product and always shows price stability and it is used in a wide variety of food, cosmetic and health products, and can be used as a biodiesel source. Most palm oil is produced in Asia, Africa, and South America since palm trees require the abundant warm temperatures, sunshine, and rain to maximize production.

Indonesia and Malaysia dominate the world's palm oil production. Production from these two countries accounted for about 90% of the total global production of palm oil. Over the past 20 years, the palm oil industry in Indonesia has shown tremendous growth as seen from the figures of production, export, and the expansion of oil palm plantations.

Driven by the increase of global demand and a higher yield, oil palm cultivation has expanded significantly by the farmers and the Indonesian conglomerate.

Foreign Direct Investment in the Agribusiness sector (crude palm oil and palm oil for cooking) has reached 675.2 million USD and an increase of 150.1% in 2014. Similarly, Domestic Direct Investment has reached 376.9 million USD in 2014 and increase of 18.7%.

Potential for the Investment

- The area of palm oil plantations in Indonesia has doubled over the last 20 years, to 8 million ha today. It is estimated that the number will rise to 13 million ha in 2020.
- In 2020, it is estimated that palm oil production will reach 40 million tons; while world consumption per year is expected to reach 60 million tons. At this rate, Indonesia will be able to fulfill the 80% of world demand.
- Vegetable oil demand was able to reach 6 million tons annually; 2 million tons for the Indonesian market and 1.5 million tons for the Malaysian market. This means that there are 3.5 million tons of market opportunities to meet the needs of the palm oil industry.
- More than 21 million of skilled laborers work in plantations in Indonesia. This makes Indonesia the country who has no match in the agricultural labor force in ASEAN regional.

Rubber

In line with its economic growth, Indonesia has become one of the investment destinations for rubber industry. Indonesia, the second largest rubber producer in the world, is supplying many of rubber products to the international market. The rubber industry is also significantly contributing to state revenue from non-oil and gas international trade and plays an important role to trigger the growth of new economic centers in the rubber development region.

Approximately 70% of the world's natural rubber is being produced in Thailand, Indonesia, and Malaysia. As many as 15% of rubber production in Indonesia is used for domestic materials industry, meanwhile, the remaining 85% is exported. Nearly half of Indonesia's rubber production is exported and sent to other Asian countries, as well as North America and Europe. The main importers of Indonesian rubber are United States, China, Japan, Singapore, and Brazil. Meanwhile, the domestic rubber consumption is contributing to the supply to Indonesia's manufacturing industry through the automotive sector and technical rubber products.

The rubber industry in Indonesia is currently more focused on the production of semi-finished goods than to finished goods. However, for domestic consumption, most Indonesia's natural rubber is consumed by the industry which accounted for 61%, while consumption to produce gloves, shoes, and other products respectively 14, 12, and 13%.

Potential for the Investment

- International Rubber Study Group (IRSG) estimates world's rubber consumption in 2020 will increase at an average growth rate of 6.7%.

- Since the 2000s, Indonesian rubber industry has shown a steady increase in production. Indonesia's dry rubber production has increased by 54%.
- There are 385 companies in the downstream rubber industry which employs 107,927 people.
- Average labor cost per head in Indonesia is more efficient than the four other major ASEAN countries.

Textile

The textile industry is one of the oldest and most strategic industries in Indonesia. Despite the needs of diverse fashion which is growing continuously, the large number of Indonesia citizen population becomes several factors for the growth and development of this industry. In 2010, the textile industry was capable to employ up to approximately 11% of the total industrial workforce, or 1.34 million people in 2853 companies and contributed 8.9% of the total exports of the country.

The textile industry in Indonesia has the ability to develop in both upstream and downstream sector. From raw material to the finishing stage, create a highly efficient supply chain, and capable to provide 'one door solution' for local and international markets. Some great local garment manufacturers even seek to raise capital to acquire assets that will help them to streamline the supply chain.

Indonesia has succeeded in positioning themselves as an alternative of production market for world's fashion brands and including become the top 10 textiles and garments exporter. Indonesian Textile Association (API) claimed that 80% of their global apparel produced in Indonesia. Textile factories which are mainly located in Bandung, Bekasi, and Bogor are being the supplier of the expensive brands such as Hugo Boss, Giorgio Armani, Guess, Marks and Spencer, Mango, and many other famous brands. The export products of these factories have reached developed markets such as Japan, UK, USA, and other high-end markets.

Up to 2014, the investment realization in Indonesia's textile industry has reached 9.53 trillion IDR or increase 9.4% from the previous year. Accumulation from the period of 2009 to the third quarter of 2014 showed that the Domestic Direct Investment (DDI) increased by 33.6% or 11.8 trillion IDR, while Foreign Direct Investment (FDI) increased by 36.4% or 23.2 trillion IDR.

Potential for the Investment

- The labor cost is low, political stability, availability of raw materials and lower price of industrial land. Compared to China, the average wage of a textile worker there has risen to 247 USD per month, higher than Indonesia that was 140 USD.
- Indonesia becomes the industrial base for foreign companies that specialized in manufacturing textile products such as geotextile; military uniforms, which have been exported to around 30 countries. One of those was for the army of North Atlantic Treaty Organization (NATO); Anti-Nuclear and uniforms which have been exported to Saudi Arabia and Malaysia.

- Industry of garments and other textiles is one of the largest employers in Indonesia. In 2013, the number of workers who work in this field reached nearly 850,000 people, increase from 2009 to about 690,000 people.

Energy

Indonesia has a high potential for renewable energy such as solar, wind, hydro and geothermal energy due to its geographical location and agriculture. In addition, renewable generation sources supplied 5–6% of Indonesia's electricity in 2018, and Indonesia has targeted to generate 26% of electricity from renewable sources by 2025. The Indonesian government also has planned US$6.47 billion worth of energy projects by 2020, 70% of the budget is needed from foreign direct investment.

Others

There is also a potential for the investment in the mining sector, telecommunication, transport, construction, medical and pharmaceutical, and the chemical industry. Potential foreign investors can consider also these industries as the investment option since these sectors also provide a good opportunity for the investors and industries need investment to expand and become even better.

Domestic Markets

A continued slump in demand for commodities (mainly fuel) has led to moderating GDP growth, and Indonesia's economic boom in the past decade. Trade, fixed investment, and domestic consumption has slowed. Furthermore, the country has a very high level of unemployment and employment growth is now slower than population growth.

Agriculture is a key sector which contributed to 14% of the nation's GDP in 2015. Currently, 30% of Indonesian land is used for agricultural production and employs around 39% of total Indonesian workforce. Indonesia's important agricultural commodities are rubber, palm oil, poultry, beef, forest products, shrimp, cocoa, coffee, medicinal herbs, essential oil, fish, and tropical spices.

Industries contributed 41% of Indonesian GDP and it employed only 13% of the country's population in 2015. The most important industries to Indonesia are goods in petroleum and natural gas, textiles, automotive, electrical appliances, apparel, footwear, mining, cement, medical instruments and appliances, handicrafts, chemical fertilizers, plywood, rubber, processed food, jewelry, and tourism.

Services contributed 45% of the country's GDP and it is the highest contributing sector, and it also employed 48% of the Indonesian labor force in 2015. Unemployment Rate dropped to 5.28% in Aug 2019, from the previously reported number of 5.34% in Aug 2018.

Exports from Indonesia dropped 6.13% from a year earlier to USD 14.93 billion in October 2019, better than market consensus of an 8.38% decline and after a marginally revised 5.73% fall in the prior month. Oil and gas exports slumped by 40.07% to USD 0.93 billion on the back of mining products (−45.85%), including crude oil (−71.46%) and natural gas (−34.39%), and sales of non-oil and gas products decreased by 2.48% to USD 14.01 billion. Exports in Indonesia averaged 4490.66 USD Million from 1960 until 2019, reaching an all the time high of 18,647.83 USD Million in August of 2011 and a record low of 30 USD Million in January of 1961.

External trade (USD millions)	2000	2005	2010	2015	2018
Exports, fob	62,124.0	85,660.0	157,779.1	150,366	180.215
Imports, cif	33,514.8	57,700.9	135,663.3	142,695	188.711
Trade balance	28,609.2	27,959.1	22,115.8	7671	−8496

Source Asian Development Bank (ADB, 2019)

Main commercial partners (USD millions)	2000	2005	2010	2015	2018
Exports					
1. China, People's Rep. of	2768	6662	15,693	15,045	27,127
2. Japan	14,415	18,049	25,782	18,014	19,480
3. United States	8489	9889	14,302	16,267	18,472
4. Korea, Rep. of	4318	7086	12,575	19,542	8,996
5. Singapore	6562	7836	13,723	12,650	12,992
5. India	1151	2878	9915	11,713	13,726
7. Malaysia	1972	3431	9362	7662	9437
8. Thailand	1026	2246	4566	5530	6819
9. Philippines	820	1419	3181	3921	6825
10. Taipei, China	2378	2475	4838	5037	4649
Imports					
1. China, People's Rep. of	2022	5843	20,424	2411	45,538
2. Singapore	3789	9471	20,241	18,022	21,440
3. Japan	5397	6906	16,966	13,264	17,977
4. Thailand	1109	3447	7471	8083	10,953
5. Korea, Rep. of	2083	2869	7703	8427	9089
6. Malaysia	1131	2148	8649	8531	8603
7. United States	3393	3885	9416	7617	10,212
8. Australia	1694	2567	4099	4816	5826
9. Saudi Arabia	1598	2712	4361	3422	4911
10. India	525	1052	3295	2741	5017

Source Asian Development Bank (ADB, 2019)

Finance and Taxation

Tax

Corporate Income Tax

In Indonesia, the Corporate Income tax rate is a tax collected from companies. Its amount is based on the net income companies obtain while exercising their business activity, normally during one business year. Corporate Income Tax is set at a flat rate of 30%. In addition, after-tax profits of a branch are also subject to withholding tax at 20%, regardless of whether such profits are remitted to the home country. However, small and medium-sized domestic companies are entitled to a 50% reduction of the tax rate. The reduced rate applies to taxable income corresponding to a gross turnover of up to 4.8 billion IDR. Individual and corporate taxpayers that generate an annual gross turnover of no more than 4.8 billion IDR and meet the criteria set out by the government are subject to a final income tax of one percent of monthly gross turnover. Moreover, special tax rates are also granted to petroleum, mining, construction, foreign drilling, non-resident international shipping companies and airlines. In addition, Indonesia has enacted several international treaties for the avoidance of double taxation.

Indonesian accounting standards have adopted IFRS principles which are mainly based on the use of 'fair value', and this new accounting system will oblige corporations to do fiscal adjustments before they can assess and settle their tax obligations and file the corresponding tax returns.

Withholding Taxes

Payments to a non-tax resident of Indonesia are, by default, subject to 20% final withholding income tax and may apply based on the enforceability of a tax treaty.

If Non-residents can provide a certificate from the Indonesian and their home country (DGT-1 form) tax authority, they have the opportunity to benefit from the reduced rate provided for in the applicable tax treaty.

Payments of a passive income nature such as interests, royalties, or dividends, to any special purpose vehicles that are beneficially owned by Indonesian tax residents, must not receive any such benefit.

Income tax withholding is also applied towards certain types of transactions, such as:

- Importation of goods.
- Sale of goods to the government.
- Sale or purchase of certain products.
- Sale or purchase of luxurious goods.
- Payment of certain services.

Personal Income Tax

In Indonesia, the Personal Income Tax Rate is a tax collected from individuals and is imposed on different sources of income like labor, pensions, interest and dividends. Revenues from the Personal Income Tax Rate are an important source of income for the government of Indonesia. Indonesian residents are subject to personal income tax on their worldwide income, and non-residents are subject to tax on their Indonesian-source income only. Unless otherwise specified by an applicable tax treaty, an individual is considered to reside in Indonesia when:

- present in Indonesia for more than 183 days within any 12-month period;
- present in Indonesia for less than 183 days but intends to reside in Indonesia.

Income tax is payable on all employment income, business income, director's fees, and investment income.

For tax calculation purposes:

- The following items can be deducted from gross revenue:
  - occupational support amounting to five percent of gross income, up to a maximum of 500,000 IDR per month;
  - contribution paid by the employee to a pension fund that has been approved by the Minister of Finance;
  - contribution paid by the employee to BPJS 'Ketenagakerjaan' (the old-age benefit of the obligatory social security program).
- Insurance premiums paid by the employer should constitute part of the revenue.
- The following annual allowances can be deducted from taxable income:
  - for the concerned taxpayer 36,000,000 IDR;
  - for spouse (if married) 3,000,000 IDR;
  - for dependents (maximum 3) 3,000,000 IDR (each).

Tax rate on salary	%
1–50,000,000 IDR	5
50,000,000–250,000,000 IDR	15
250,000,001–500,000,000 IDR	25
500,000,001 + IDR	30

Source HSBC (2019)

Tax rate	%
Corporate tax	25
Personal income tax	30
Sales tax	10

Source Trading Economics (2019)

Income earned by a non-tax resident individual is subject to the default 30% final income tax rate or a lower rate if provisions of the relevant tax treaty apply, and income that is already subject to final tax, such as dividend income, shall not be subject to the above progressive rates, and shall be excluded from the annual tax calculation.

Other Taxes

VAT is a transaction tax where the cost of which ultimately falls on the end customer. Most VAT transactions involve the supply of goods, services, and imports. VAT is indirectly collected at each level of production, with the application of an offsetting mechanism.

All businesses engaged in the supply of goods and services liable to VAT must register for VAT as 'taxable entrepreneurs', unless they qualify as small entrepreneurs which is any business with an annual turnover of less than 4.8 billion IDR. This requirement also extends to permanent establishments of non-resident businesses.

Under the VAT Law, the Indonesian government may set VAT rates from five to 15%. Nevertheless, the government has not changed such rates since the pronouncement of the VAT Law back in 1984.

VAT is applied to:

- sale/delivery of any goods and services within Indonesia, at the rate of 10%;
- exportation of any goods and limited types of services as set out by the Regulation of the Minister of Finance, at the rate of 0%;
- importation of any goods and services, at the rate of 10%.

LGST is similar to the VAT. LGST is a tax which falls on the end-users of goods/services that are considered as luxurious products. LGST is only applicable upon the importation of luxury good or, upon subsequent manufacture, upon the delivery from the manufacturer. Unlike VAT, LGST does not use a single rate but may be imposed at different rates, depending on the category of goods. Under the VAT and LGST Law, the rates may range from 10 to 200%.

Import and export duties are applied on various goods upon importation at various rates, as set out by the Indonesian government on a regular basis. The exportation of goods is generally free from any export duty. Certain commodities are subject to export duty at various rates, depending on the type, grade of products, and other criteria.

Land and building tax (PBB), is chargeable each year at a rate of up to 0.3% of the government determined value. The tax is payable within six months upon issuance of the PBB assessment.

Transfer of land and building rights are subjected to a five percent "Acquisition of Land and Building Right Levy" (BPHTB). It is to be calculated based on the transaction value or the government determined value or whichever is higher.

Stamp duty is applied towards legal receipts and documents, at the nominal amount of either 3000 IDR or 6000 IDR. Payment of stamp duty is made by way of fixing a stamp duty on the signing section of the relevant document, whereby the signing officer or one of the concerned parties should sign across it. Subsequent payment through the Post Office is permitted.

Audit and Accounting

Every business in Indonesia is required to have a bookkeeping system that is maintained in the Indonesian language and using Indonesian Rupiah as its reporting currency. However, on behalf of the Minister of Finance and the Indonesia Tax Authority, the usage of the English language and US Dollars currency may be allowed upon application but no other currency and language is allowed.

Typically, the accounting period is the calendar year, from the first of January to the end of December each year. However, companies may determine their own financial years from their respective dates of establishment. Any change of the fiscal year would be subject to notification to the Minister of Law and Human Rights, and approval from the Indonesian Tax Authority, on behalf of the Minister of Finance for tax reporting purposes.

By law, every business must maintain their books, records, and other supporting documentation in Indonesia at their place of domicile for at least 10 years following the end of the applicable fiscal year.

Bookkeeping must be maintained on an accrual basis, and financial statements must be prepared at least once a year by the management board of each respective business. Under the Limited Liability Company Law, the management board must present their annual report, which includes the financial statements, before and for the ratification by the General Meeting of Shareholders each year, within six months upon closing of the reported financial year. The management board of a corporation shall be individually and jointly liable for any losses incurred due to any misleading or incorrect financial statements.

A complete set of financial statements of one financial year is presented on a corresponding basis with the previous year, and should consist of the following:

- statement of financial position;
- statement of comprehensive income;
- statement of cash flows;
- statement of changes in equity;
- notes to the financial statements.

Even though there is no statutory audit requirement for companies, businesses in certain sectors and those that meet the following criteria, are required to have their books audited, and subsequently report the audited financial statements to the Minister of Trade, the Ministry of Law and Human Rights, Indonesian Stock Exchange authority, and other relevant departments:

- companies that accumulate and manage public funds;
- companies that issue debt instruments to public;
- public listed companies;
- certain types of state-owned enterprises;
- companies having assets at least 25 billion IDR;
- companies having assets and annual turnover at least 50 billion IDR;
- foreign companies conducting business in Indonesia with authority to enter contracts;
- other criteria as may be set by specific laws and regulations.

Furthermore, being a counterparty in a private business transaction, such as a bank creditor as mentioned above, may also invoke the need for a company to have its books audited.

Risk Assessment

Indonesia is one of the largest economies in Southeast Asia. It is a diverse nation, with more than 300 ethnic groups. Since the financial crisis in the late 1990s, Indonesia has had a massive amount of economic growth. Since 2000, the gross national income per capita has risen from $857 to $3603 by 2016. Being the fourth most populated countries in the world, having the tenth largest economy (PPP), and as a member of G-20, Indonesia is rapidly growing in its development. It is soon to be classified as middle-income earning country as it rises out of poverty. It has cut its poverty in half throughout the 1990s, leaving it at 11.2% in 2015. Yet, as much success Indonesia has seen, there is the difficulty with finding investors that are willing to face the environment, the Chinese demand, and the high levels of corruption.

The main difficulty to investment lies in the high cost of illegal deductions, which can be as much as 60%. There are many limitations on investing in Indonesia. There are several challenging procedures, formalities, regulations, for the threshold of initial capital. The World Bank did a study showing that Indonesia is quite less efficient than other Asian Countries. Legality in Indonesia is often denounced and there is quite a lot of corruption within the justice system, providing for inefficiency in business regulation. Taxes and customs are usually found to be corrupted by the officials and difficult for businesses—especially foreign investors.

Indonesia has low-interest rates and it is decreasing every year. For the potential foreign investors, low-interest rates mean small return, therefore, investment in Indonesia becomes less attractive to investors. Also, return for certain industries depend on the demand of the Indonesian goods and services, so there is a high risk associated with the investment in Indonesia, however, due to low-interest rates the return does not pay back the risk it is associated with. The potential investors might decide that it does not worth to invest in Indonesia due to low-interest rates and high risk.

China is the largest exporter of raw materials of Indonesia. Therefore, raw materials' demand depends on China which means that investing in the raw material industries can be risky for the foreign investors due to the turbulence of the raw materials demand. This means that when Chinese demand is high the return from the investment will be high as well, however, if the Chinese demand is lawing the return from the investment will be low or the investors may end up not having any returns.

As mentioned above, Indonesia has a high level of corruption which can be a problem for the potential investors. Furthermore, the level of corruption is very high in the big cities where most of the investment opportunities are which makes even harder for the potential investors to operate in the corrupted environment. Indonesian government tries to resolve this issue; however, it is still unsuccessful. The risk for investors is that it will be hard to manage and operate in an environment where corruption can be creating problems or barriers in any activities they conduct.

LAOS

Official name
Lao People's Democratic Republic
Capital
Vientiane
Area
236,800 sq. km
Population
6.8 mln
Languages
Lao (official), French, English
Main ethnic groups
Lao 55%, Khmou 11%, Hmong 8%, Thai 4%
Main religions
Buddhist 67%, Christian 2%
Government type
Communist State
Urbanization
35.0%
Life expectancy ratio
68 years
Fertility rate
2.5 children born/woman
Currency
Lao Kip LAK

Laos

Country Introduction

Population, Location, Geography, Climate

Laos is a landlocked country in the center of Indochina. It shares its borders with Cambodia to the south, Vietnam to the east, Thailand to the west and China and Myanmar (Burma) in the north and north-west respectively.

Seventy percent of its total land area (236,800 km^2) comprises of mountain and plateau areas. The Annamite mountains goes along part of the east border with Vietnam and on average is 1200 m in height. The Mekong river is one of the longest rivers in the world and it flows along the border with Thailand. The river flows through nearly 1900 km of Lao territory and has always been a lifeline for the country in terms of fish supplies, transportation routes and agriculture. Several hydro-electric facilities, situated on the tributaries of the Mekong, generate electricity for export to Thailand.

Laos enjoys a warm, tropical climate with two distinct seasons: the rainy season from the beginning of May to the end of September and the dry season from October through to April. Temperatures and rainfall very considerably throughout the year and according to latitude and altitude from November to February the temperatures are lower and cool breezes bring a pleasant and refreshing change from the humidity of the rainy season.

Laos is a Socialist, one party government. The Lao people's Democratic Republic was established in 1975 and since the instigation of new forward-thinking economic policies and their imminent entry into ASEAN, Lao PDR has seen rapid growth and development in the last 10 years. New infrastructures and services have transformed the capital, Vientiane into a thriving and prosperous city with a great deal to offer visitors. The provincial areas of the country are also seeing flourishing change and development.

The estimated population of Lao PDR is around 6.5 million (2015) of which about 790,000 people live in the capital, Vientiane. The rest of the country is very sparsely populated, comparative to other Asian countries, with 85% of people living in rural areas. New comprehensive research shows classification of 47 ethnic groups. So far, no one gives a complete list of 68 ethnic groups. These are divided into three main ethnic categories—Lao Loum (Lao landers), Lao Theung (lower mountain dwellers) and Lao Soung (highlanders). The Lao Loum, the largest group, have traditionally been subsistence rice growers along the Mekong river while the Lao Theung live on the mountain slopes, bartering with their produce of coffee, tobacco, mountain rice and cotton. The Lao Soung comprise hill tribes originally from Burma, Tibet and southern China who live high up in the mountains raising animals and producing opium crops. The latter two groups are animist (believing in earth spirits) but about 60% of the population are Theravada (Hinayaan) Buddhists.

Although Hinayaan Buddhism was introduced into the country in the fourteenth century, Mahayaan is known by Laotians as the beginning of the Silk Roads, long before they came into the land forming the Lang Xang Kingdom. But Buddhism was very slow to spread in Lao and there was quite a reluctance by those holding animist beliefs to adopt its doctrines. Nonetheless, today Buddhism is an inherent feature of daily life and costs a strong influence on Lao society. Most Lao Buddhism try to gain 'merit' for a better next life by giving donations to the temple and through regular worship. The temples are important places of private worship and also provide many opportunities for social gatherings.

Internal Policy

Laos is divided into 17 provinces (khouang) and one prefecture (kamphaeng akhon) which includes the capital city Vientiane (Nakhon Luang Viangchan). Provinces are further divided into districts (muang) and then villages (ban). An "urban" village is essentially a town.

The Lao People's Democratic Republic, along with China, Cuba and Vietnam, is one of the world's four or five remaining socialist states that openly oppose Communism. The only legal political party is the Lao People's Revolutionary Party (LPRP). The head of state is President Bounnhang Vorachith, and he is the General Secretary of the Lao People's Revolutionary Party. The head of government is Prime Minister Thongloun Sisoulith, who is also a member of the Lao Communist Party's Politburo. Government policies are determined by the party through the all-powerful eleven-member Politburo of the Lao People's Revolutionary Party and the 61-member Central Committee of the Lao People's Revolutionary Party. Important government decisions are vetted by the Council of Ministers. The Socialist Republic of Vietnam maintains significant influence over the Politburo of Laos and the one-party communist state apparatus and military. In 1992 elections were held for a new 85-seat National Assembly with members, nominated by the one-party communist government, elected by secret ballot to five-year terms. The elections were widely disputed and questioned by Lao and Hmong opposition and dissident groups abroad and in Laos and Thailand. This National Assembly, which essentially acts as a rubber stamp for the LPRP, approves all new laws, although the executive branch retains authority to issue binding decrees. The most recent elections took place in April 2011. The Lao People's Armed Forces (LPAF) are small, poorly funded, and ineffectively resourced; its mission focus is border and internal security, primarily in countering ethnic Hmong insurgent and opposition groups; with the Lao People's Revolutionary Party and the government, the Lao People's Army (LPA) is the third pillar of state machinery and, as such, is expected to suppress political and civil unrest and similar national emergencies. The LPA has upgraded skills to respond to avian influenza outbreaks; there is no perceived external threat to the state and the LPA maintains strong ties with the neighboring Vietnamese military.

Human rights violations remain a significant concern in Laos. Prominent civil society advocates, human rights defenders, political and religious dissidents, and Hmong refugees have disappeared at the hands of Lao military and security forces. Ostensibly, the Constitution of Laos that was promulgated in 1991, and amended in

2003, contains most key safeguards for human rights. For example, Article 8 makes it clear that Laos is a multiethnic state and is committed to equality between ethnic groups. The Constitution also contains provisions for gender equality, freedom of religion, freedom of speech, and freedom of press and assembly. On 25 September 2009, Laos ratified the International Covenant on Civil and Political Rights, nine years after signing the treaty. The stated policy objectives of both the Lao government and international donors remain focused upon achieving sustainable economic growth and poverty reduction. However, the government of Laos frequently breaches its own constitution and the rule of law, since the judiciary and judges are appointed by the ruling communist party—an independent judicial branch does not exist. According to Amnesty International, Human Rights Watch, The Centre for Public Policy Analysis, and other independent human rights organizations and non-governmental organizations (NGOs), serious human rights violations are ongoing.

Amnesty International raised concerns about the ratification record of the Laos Government on human rights standards, and its lack of cooperation with the UN human rights mechanisms and legislative measures both impacts negatively on human rights. The organization also raised concerns in relation to freedom of expression, poor prison conditions, restrictions on freedom of religions, protection of refugees and asylum-seekers, and the death penalty.

The Centre for Public Policy Analysis, Amnesty International, Human Rights Watch, US Commission on International Religious Freedom, the Lao Veterans of America, Inc. and other non-governmental organizations (NGO) have reported egregious human rights violations, religious persecution, the arrest and imprisonment of political and religious dissidents as well as extrajudicial killings, in Laos by government military and security forces.

International Relations

It is a member of the Asia-Pacific Trade Agreement (APTA), Association of Southeast Asian Nations (ASEAN), East Asia Summit and La Francophonie. Laos applied for membership of the World Trade Organization (WTO) in 1997; on 2 February 2013, it was granted full membership.

In 1989, the PDR Lao government reached an agreement with the World Bank and the International Monetary Fund on additional reforms. The government agreed to introduce fiscal and monetary reform, promote private enterprise and foreign investment, privatize or close state firms, and strengthen banking. In addition, it also agreed to maintain a market exchange rate, reduce tariffs, and eliminate unneeded trade regulations. A liberal foreign investment code was enacted and appears to be slowly making a positive impact in the market. Enforcement of intellectual property rights is governed by two Prime Minister's Decrees dating from 1995 and 2002. In an attempt to stimulate further international commerce, the PDR Lao Government accepted Australian aid to build a bridge across the Mekong River to Thailand. The "Thai-Lao Friendship Bridge," between Vientiane Prefecture and Nong Khai Province, Thailand, was inaugurated in April 1994. Although the bridge has created additional commerce, the Lao government does not yet permit a completely free flow of traffic across the span.

Besides, for the most recent projects to be mentioned, the country operations business plan (COBP), 2020–2022 of the Asian Development Bank (ADB) for the Lao People's Democratic Republic (Lao PDR) is consistent with ADB's country partnership strategy (CPS) 2017–2020 for the Lao PD. The indicative resources available for commitment for 2020–2022 total $322.6 million, including $45.0 million from the disaster risk reduction resources, comprising $30.0 million in concessional ordinary capital resources lending (COL), and $15.0 million in Asian Development Fund grant resources.

Economy

Macroeconomic Overview

	Unit	2000°	2018	2020F
GDP, current prices	USD (billions)	1.57	18.43	22.01
GDP per capita, current prices	USD	291.74	2720.32	3156.90
GDP based on PPP per capita	Current International dollar	1792.92	7924.64	9122.07

Source IMF Outlook (2019)

The government of Laos, one of the few remaining one-party communist states, began decentralizing control and encouraging private enterprise in 1986. The results, starting from an extremely low base, were striking—growth averaged 6% per year from 1988 to 2008 except during the short-lived drop caused by the Asian financial crisis that began in 1997. Laos' growth exceeded 7% per year during 2008–13. Despite this high growth rate, Laos remains a country with an underdeveloped infrastructure, particularly in rural areas. It has a basic, but improving, road system, and limited external and internal land-line telecommunications. Electricity is available in 83% of the country. Laos' economy is heavily dependent on capital-intensive natural resource exports. The labor force, however, still relies on agriculture, dominated by rice cultivation in lowland areas, which accounts for about 25% of GDP and 73% of total employment. Economic growth has reduced official poverty rates from 46% in 1992 to 26% in 2010. Lao PDR posted an impressive economic growth rate of 8% in 2012 and 7% for the whole of the past decade—among the highest in the region. Per capita GDP growth is expected to reach to 6.5% by 2020 to the highest proportion in the last 5 years. Inflation rate has been relatively low, even being under 1% in 2017 and around 2% predictions for the next 3 years. According to ADB estimates, Current Account deficit will be decreasing by half, accounting for 8.4% of GDP by 2020. The government has put considerable effort into reducing poverty in the economy. As a result, poverty incidence has declined remarkably on the back of solid economic growth, successive five-year plans focused on poverty reduction, and aid support for remote communities. The economy also has benefited from high-profile foreign direct investment in hydropower, copper and gold mining, logging, and construction though some projects in these industries have drawn criticism for their environmental impacts. Laos gained Normal Trade Relations status with the US in 2004 and applied for Generalized System of Preferences trade benefits in 2013 after being admitted to the World Trade Organization earlier in the year. Laos is in the process of implementing a value-added tax system. Simplified investment procedures and expanded bank credits for small farmers and small entrepreneurs will improve Laos' economic prospects. The government appears to be committed to raising the country's profile among investors, but suffered through a fiscal crisis in 2013 brought about by public sector wage increases, fiscal mismanagement, and revenue shortfalls. The World Bank has declared that Laos' goal of graduating from the UN Development Program's list of least-developed countries by 2020 is achievable.

The economy of the Lao People's Democratic Republic is on track to meet forecasts of slightly higher economic growth in 2019 and 2020. Electricity generation from the growing number of hydropower plants and the Hongsa lignite-power plant is trending up. Construction on new hydropower projects, residential and commercial buildings, and facilities in special economic zones is contributing to the growth in gross domestic product. Better weather in 2018 has improved prospects for agriculture, though the risk remains that monsoon rains could cause floods. Gold output from two major mines are continuing their rise since 2016, but copper production is declining. Tourist arrivals also falling.

Structure of output (% GDP)	2000	2005	2010	2015	2018
Agriculture	48.5	36.7	30.6	19.7	17.7
Industry	19.1	23.5	29.8	31.0	35.5
Services	32.4	39.8	39.6	49.4	46.8

Source Asian Development Bank (ADB, 2019)

Economic Policy

From 1976 to 1986, Laos' communist rulers progressively switched from Marxist economic policies to free market principles. This remarkable policy restyling, effected in the context of one of the poorest and most assisted economies in the world, reflected a shift in influence from communist to Western aid donors. In terms of influence, the former Soviet Union and the International Monetary Fund (IMF) were leaders of two camps. While combining advice from the IMF and the Soviet Union could be deemed a success from a diplomatic point of view, it has allowed the country to maintain a modest degree of political independence, from an economic viewpoint it was a costly strategy.

The government has put considerable effort into reducing poverty in the economy. As a result, poverty incidence has declined remarkably on the back of solid economic growth, successive five-year plans focused on poverty reduction, and aid for remote communities. The country has also made significant progress towards achieving the Millennium Development Goals (MDGs). The poverty headcount dropped from 46% in 1992–93 to 28% in 2007–08 and is expected to achieve the related MDG target of 25% by 2020. A reflection of the strong commitment to tackling poverty issues, the authorities have adopted poverty eradication as one of their main strategic orientations. They have also placed strong emphasis on macroeconomic stability and on fostering inclusive, sustainable, private-sector-led growth and regional integration. The World Bank Group (WBG) continues to work with the Government of Lao PDR to reduce extreme poverty and boost shared prosperity, supporting the Government's 8th National Socio-Economic Development Plan 2016–2020. The World Bank Group's current Country Partnership Framework (CPF) 2017–2021 was approved at the end of April 2017. The goal is to attain a gross domestic product (GDP) growth rate of at least 8% annually to reach GDP per capita level of at least USD 1700 by 2015. The eighth National Socio-Economic Development Plan (NSEDP) 2016–2020 is geared to achieve the MDGs and the government is pursuing its commitment to addressing social welfare issues. It has made considerable progress towards poverty reduction—the first of the MDGs. In 2010, Laos completed a framework and financing plan for accelerating achievement of the MDGs by setting six specific targets: access to enabling infrastructure; sustainable practices for improved food security and environmental sustainability; universal access to basic education and gender equity; women's equal participation and empowerment; improved maternal and child health; safe water supplies and improved sanitation for all rural areas and remote communities.

Lao PDR's long-term development agenda is based on its gradual transformation from a closed and centrally planned economy to an open, private sector-led economy. The current development strategy aims to support sustainable economic growth and reduce poverty and inequality. However, there are obstacles to inclusive growth that the government needs to bear in mind.

- An increasing lack of educated and skilled human resources that hinder private sector growth and economic diversification.
- An inefficient, underdeveloped financial sector that slows domestic private sector growth.
- Inadequate connectivity between rural and urban areas that restricts the access of families and firms in outlying areas to opportunities in hubs of business, economic, social and cultural activity.
- Poor nutrition and food insecurity that lead to low worker productivity.
- Weak governance arising from weak institutions that slows economic growth.
- Declining competitiveness in the non-resource sector that could affect the economy's potential for achieving inclusive growth.

The current development strategies under the Seventh NSEDP are designed to support sustainable economic growth and reduce poverty and inequality. The strategies involve diversifying and deepening economic activities, significantly scaling up human capital, improving labor productivity, and promoting the inclusion of women, ethnic groups and those living in remote areas. The most important of all is to ensure the quality of growth by achieving the MDGs, protecting the environment, ensuring political stability and peace, working towards regional integration and strengthening linkages with the global economy. The Seventh NSEDP contains five major thrusts:

- national economic development
- rural development and poverty eradication
- the promotion of livelihoods
- improved public administration
- competitiveness.

Towards those five goals, efforts to ensure inclusive growth will focus on rural areas where the majority of the poor live. There will be policy efforts to develop road and energy infrastructure, enhance value chains, improve access to markets and social services, and forge stronger rural urban linkages. Active participation from stakeholders (e.g. businesses, trade unions, nongovernmental organizations, indigenous peoples) should be an inherent part of the development and implementation of national strategies for sustainable development.

Banking System

The Lao banking system is characterized by a marked geographical concentration in banking services in Vientiane and large cities. This concentration is likely to increase. The Lao banking sector can be described as small in absolute terms. It is also relatively small when compared to the size of Laos's economy; the ratio of total assets of the banking system to GDP is about one-fourth. This is particularly low for an economy with a non-diversified financial system (i.e., with no alternative but banks for the supply of loans) and is evidence of a system in its early stage of development. Three quarters of loans were in foreign currencies and the share of loans to the private sector stood at 50%. State-owned commercial banks dominate the market with more than two-thirds of the total assets.

There are only few non-bank financial institutions (NBFI) in Lao PDR, evidence of a narrow, i.e., undiversified financial system where there is still limited alternative to banks for access to financial services. The microfinance system is starting to emerge; there is only one insurance company; and the Social Security system is still in its infancy with little or no accumulated financial surpluses. Institutions such as leasing companies which base their lending on future cash-flow of a rented asset, rather than on past performance and collateral, are missing. Life insurance institutions providing long term capital are also lacking. There is no capital market or arrangements providing equity or debt or standardized debt contracts. Thus, this banking and financial system, dominated by public banks, is unable to perform most expected functions which are to mobilize savings; research and allocate capital; exert corporate control; facilitate trading of goods, services and financial contracts; and facilitate trading, hedging and pooling of risks. However, in order to sustain the stability of the Lao Banking system and thus, to devise plans for handling financial, economic or other relevant crises, considerable updates have been brought into force over the past years. These include the updates on minimum Registered Capital (which has been raised from LAK 100 billion (approx. USD 11.5 million) to LAK 500 billion (approx. USD 58 million), while the minimum registered capital for Lao branches of foreign commercial banks has been raised from LAK 50 billion (approx. USD 5.8 million) to LAK 300 billion (approx. USD 34.5 million), Appointment of Executives, Governance, Reporting and other measures.

Investment Area

The government's policy has emphasized both revenue raising and expenditure containing measures. The result was an open—door policy to create an atmosphere for investment, privatization, liberalization, decentralization, and the initiation of an appropriate regulatory framework to meet the immediate needs of the emerging private sector. Following that, in 1988 the Lao Government adopted a code for foreign direct investment (FDI), hoping to have revenue generated and job opportunities created in the country. Since then the FDI in various fields has increasingly flowed into the country. In parallel to the FDI, the government has begun to transform the centrally planned economy into the market one by fostering the private sector and reforming the public administrative machinery. The primary purpose of public sector reform in the Lao context is to facilitate a market-oriented economy by initiating more private investment, mainly for export-oriented production, and improving public sector performance. The country is also well endowed with all kinds of abundant and untapped natural resources, particularly fertile land suitable for cropping, forestry development and animal husbandry, hydro-power and mining, with the occurrence of numerous types of minerals. These natural resources need proper technology and capital to develop and convert to commodities for export into the world markets.

Agriculture and Tourism

Plains and plateaus offer possibilities for development of agriculture and livestock. Coffee, cotton, sugar, fruits and vegetables can be grown under good soil and climatic conditions. The Lao Government gives special privileges to develop the agricultural sector and investors are invited to bring into the country their capital, know-how and techniques to develop agro-based production for export. The economic growth of the Lao PDR depends to a large extent upon the performance of the agricultural sector, which contributed 51% of the GDP in 1997. Coffee is by far the most promising product for export. The Lao PDR has the most land potential in the Greater Mekong sub-region. There lies large and unexploded fertile land, favorable climatic conditions located in the Bolaven basaltic plateau. This could offer promising opportunities for low-intensive investment in the agro-processing industry for export based on annual and perennial crops. The improvement of main national roads linking major provinces, and the high rate of urbanization has created favorable conditions for investment in the import-substitution agro-processing industries. Forestry is also a valuable sector to Laos's economy. Wood products like lumber are main export earners of the Lao PDR. In view of its long-term sustainable development objectives and the preservation of the environment, the government is implementing a policy of striking a balance between exploitation and conservation and shifting from export of logs and lumber towards the promotion of wood finished-product processing. Due to a shortage of capital and the technical know-how in the country, the development of the wood-processing sub-sector also needs investment and the introduction of new technology from foreign countries.

Mining

In fact, Laos has substantial potential in mineral ores where occurrences of gold, tin, iron lead, zinc, precious stones, coal, lignite, limestone, gypsum, etc., have been identified in many parts of the country. The Lao Government so far has given some concession areas such as oil, gas, gold, lignite and gemstones to foreign investors to explore and develop different minerals. Financial and technological inputs are required to develop these minerals. Foreign direct investment is particularly sought in the mining sector because of its capital-intensive investment combined with scarce domestic financial resources and its high potential for export. From 1988 up to the 19th August 1997 the foreign investment in this sector was ranked third in terms of aggregate value (about US$125,535,764). Fiscal regulations such as royalty rate, corporate income tax and other financial incentives in the mining sector are widely recognized as competitive by international standards. This indicates a firm commitment and strong support of the government to pave the way for foreign direct investment in the sector. The market for fossil fuel in neighboring countries is tremendous. In the short-term, other minerals having high prospect for export would be gemstones, which require simple extraction equipment and could be easily transported.

Energy

Laos has also substantial potential from its water resources for hydropower generation. Many tributaries of the Mekong River offer possibilities for the construction of dams and reservoirs to produce low-cost electric energy for export to neighboring countries, in which the demand for power has increased abruptly year after year. It is estimated that the country possesses over 18,000 MW of hydropower installed capacity, of which only 2% has been so far developed. The government promotes the development of hydropower projects in many locations throughout the country. The hydropower sector will continue to be one of the main foreign exchange earners for Laos with the huge resources located close to the biggest power demand country in the region. Without financial sources, other than public investment funds and external soft loans, hydropower development would probably continue at the same slow rate as experienced in the eighties. This would lead to a loss of opportunity for foreign exchange earners badly needed for the development of other sectors. On this basis, and in line with the new economic policy, the government has begun since the beginning of the 90s to seek the participation of foreign investors in projects beyond the financial capacity of the public and soft loan investments. Since 1988, when the Lao government launched public sector reform resulting from FDI by accepting private participation in hydropower generation for export and the development in the power exporting industry has been very impressive. The government signed MOUs for 18 projects and another 10 of over 100 MW capacity have been initially contacted and site investigations have been undertaken. The development period will depend on the mobilization of funding in which the private investors will be encouraged to participate actively. Assuming the construction is carried out as scheduled, the total installed capacity was 1845 MW with annual generation of 11,837 GWH in the year 2000 and 7279 MW with annual generation of 36,700 GWH in 2010. In addition, the upcoming completion of several large power projects, including the Sayaboury Hydropower Project, is expected to add an extra 2200 MW capacity. This is projected to boost generation capacity to almost 10,000 MW by 2020, of which the majority is exported.

Transport

In Laos, transportation infrastructure is inadequate and considered a major impediment to trade, co-operation and the exploitation of rich mineral resources, particularly those located in the hinterland. Further major commitments are required before minimum standards can be satisfied and most of the shortcomings could be addressed by cooperation efforts such as: priority on the improvement and rehabilitation of existing facilities and sub-regional projects on which there are already agreements among the countries directly concerned; the formulation of projects should consider trade generation impacts, especially economic transportation taking place in the sub-region; transport projects should be implemented in sections and stretches in order to facilitate project implementation and provide immediate benefits. Recent projects on the way to turn the outlook to the positive side are comprised of ongoing construction of the Lao-China railway, the Vientiane-Vangvieng highway, and reconstruction and repair of infrastructure damaged by floods in 2018.

Service

In the field of services like investment in banking, insurance, transportation, communications, hostelry and trade are encouraged. To respond to requirements of the emerging primary and secondary industries in the country, a tertiary industry, such as service development needs to expand.

The Foreign Investment Management Committee (FIMC)

The FIMC is a “one-stop” for the potential investor in Laos. Ultimately the FIMC staff will coordinate the course of and application for investment in the country through the various levels and spheres of approval, informing the investor regularly about the status of the application. Initially, however, the FIMC can and will provide a comprehensive look at Laos and its potential for the investor since it has the latest statistics, such as demographic data, past accomplishments and careful analysis of what can be done. FIMC personnel will listen carefully to the projects that the potential investor has in mind, offer recommendations for alterations based on the needs of the country, government requirements and other feasibility factors. For a very modest fee, the FIMC will provide facsimile materials for the investment application and guide the applicant through the process of completing them, including a feasibility review upon re-submission to the FIMC. Finally, the staff will coordinate movement of the application with various departments concerned.

Investment Projects

These areas of investment are covered here for illustration purposes: hydroelectricity, tourism and textiles. The selection made was based on Laos's enormous capability in these three fields.

Hydroelectricity Investment

Information on electricity and energy in Laos appears in a report of the Foreign Division, the Office of the investment Promotion Committee, revealing that the Lao Government gives first priority to energy production which includes the development of energy from water and the increase of local supplies through the extension of the power grid as well as the distribution of electricity throughout every province with the surplus being exported to earn income for the country, and The Electricity du Laos and its regional units hold responsibility for this. The former oversees generating, supplying and distributing electricity in the Vientiane area and the latter is responsible for generating and distributing electricity in 6 provinces. The Electricity du Lao is also responsible for the approval of the construction of additional station in remote areas. By the end of 1996, The Lao Government had signed contracts with approximately 20 foreign companies for investments in establishing power producing plants in Laos. 2 of these total projects have already begun operating: Nam Theun-Hinboun, and Huey Ho. Moreover, Laos has about 10 more projects of this kind waiting for the foreign companies to invest in. Most of these projects are in the area between Luangnamtha and Luangprabang.

Tourism Investment

Today, tourism receives much more promotion from the Lao Government. After the establishment of the National Tourism Authority of Lao PDR. Currently, 14 tourism companies exist, all of which have been licensed by the government. New regulations on tourism have been set up as well. There are 38 foreign companies counter trading with the company representing the tourism industry of Laos and 17 of those companies belong to Thai's. Revenue from the tourism business of Laos in 1992 amounted to US$9 million, a substantial amount for a country newly opening its door to tourism. Statistics on tourists in 1996 showed an approximately 17% increase, compared with that for 1995. In 1995 Luangprabang, a former capital, was voted to be on the UNESCO world heritage list. Furthermore, 1999 was a Visit

Laos Year and it was expected that the number of foreign tourists will increase considerably. The government cooperated with an economic alliance of Thailand, China and Vietnam in planning its international tourism promotion campaign to prepare efficiently for such situation. Joint visas are applicable at airports and at two international border pass areas. Those areas are Bokeo to Bo Ten, between China and Laos, and Savannakhet to Quang Tri, between Laos and Vietnam. Infrastructure has been improved through the support of foreign investors joining the country's hotel industry. This has enabled Laos to become a sub-regional tourism central and plans have been laid to develop five major provinces—Vientiane, Luangprabang, Huoixai, Champasack and Savannakhet—as points of sale for tourist are set up. Tourist destination in Vientiane include historical sites, ancient ruins, and a shopping centre for foreigners. Luangprabang is to be promoted as the north tourism centre. Tourist attractions in Luangprabang are its natural beauty and the interesting history of the province. Huoixai in Bokeo Province is the focal point of tourism linking the sub-region, or economic quadrangle, as well as Myanmar, China and the north of Thailand. Champasack will be developed for its natural tourist attractions. Major sites here are Khone Phapheng Waterfall and Si Phan Done (4000 islands) with Done Khong as the biggest island. Savannakhet will become a tourism and trade center for Thailand, Laos and Vietnam, with Route 9 linking all three. New zoning of the town is aimed at conserving its beauty. In the conserved area, construction of buildings more than 12 m high—or higher than those that already exist—is not allowed. There is also a provision that any construction must be at least 8 m from the road. The North of the Mekong is considered a development area, as is anywhere there is an important temple with accompanying village without an industry. It should be noted that guides and tour companies are both restricted occupations for those with Lao nationality only.

Textile Investment

Textile investment in Laos draws substantial attention from foreigners, especially Thais, due to a certain extent to the country's capability in this regard. Because of this, Laos has become a major exporter of garments. Key support to textile investment is in raw materials, factory land rents and wage rates. Most importantly, Laos has been granted trade privileges by the European Community, Canada and Japan. Since the promotion of textile factories in Laos in 1988, the sub-regional manufacturing base began to switch from Thailand, by way of the Mekong River, Laos. The transfer contented to 1994. Textile investment in Laos had by then recorded as 63 projects amounting to US$55,130,878.

Domestic Markets

The economy continues to be dominated by an unproductive agricultural sector operating largely outside the money economy and in which the public sector continues to play a dominant role. Still, a number of private enterprises have been founded and some are quite successful in industries such as handicrafts, beer, coffee and tourism. With United Nations, Japanese, and German support the formerly state-controlled chamber of commerce aims to promote private business: the Lao National Chamber of Commerce and Industry, and its provincial subdivisions.

Agriculture, mostly subsistence rice farming, dominates the economy, employing an estimated 85% of the population and producing 51% of GDP. Domestic savings are low, forcing Laos to rely heavily on foreign assistance and concessional loans as investment sources for economic development. Agricultural products include sweet potatoes, vegetables, corn, coffee, sugarcane, tobacco, cotton, tea, peanuts, rice; water buffalo, pigs, cattle, poultry. In mid-2012, the Laos government issued a four-year moratorium for new mining projects. The reasons cited were environmental and social concerns relating to the use of agricultural land.

Tourism is the fastest growing industry in the economy and plays a vital role in the Lao economy. The government opened Laos to the world in the 1990s and continues to be a popular destination amongst tourists. The tourism sector has grown rapidly, from 80,000 international visitors in 1990, to 1.876 million in 2010. Tourism is expected to contribute US$679.1 million to the gross national product in 2010, rising to US$1.5857 billion by 2020. In 2010, one in every 10.9 jobs was in the tourism sector. Export earnings from international visitors and tourism goods are expected to generate 15.5% of total exports or US$270.3 million in 2010, growing in nominal terms to US$484.2 million (12.5% of the total) in 2020. The European Council on Trade and Tourism awarded the country the "World Best Tourist Destination" designation for 2013 for the combination of architecture and history. Luang Prabang and Wat Phu are both UNESCO World Heritage sites, with the Plain of Jars expected to join them once more work to clear UXO has been completed. Major festivals include Lao New Year which is celebrated around 13–15 April and involves a water festival similar, but more subdued than that of Thailand and other Southeast Asian countries. The Lao National Tourism Administration, related government agencies and the private sector are working together to realize the vision put forth in the country's National Ecotourism Strategy and Action Plan. This includes decreasing the environmental and cultural impact of tourism; increasing awareness in the importance of ethnic groups and biological diversity; providing a source of income to conserve, sustain and manage the Lao protected area network and cultural heritage sites; and emphasizing the need for tourism zoning and management plans for sites that will be developed as ecotourism destinations.

Laos is known for its silk and local handicraft product, both of which are on display in Luang Prabang's night market, among other places. Another specialty is mulberry tea.

External trade (USD millions)	2000	2005	2010	2015	2018
Exports, fob	330.3	553.1	1746.4	3653	5295
Imports, cif	535.3	882.0	2060.4	5675	6164
Trade balance	−205.0	−328.9	−314.0	−2022	-869

Source Asian Development Bank (ADB, 2019)

Main commercial partners (USD millions)	2000	2005	2010	2015	2018
Exports					
1. Thailand	69	204	690	1381.8	2299.5
2. China, People's Rep. of	6	23	511	1224.6	1917.6
3. Viet Nam	96	89	265	553.3	399.8
4. India	0	0	18	135.0	16.3
5. Japan	11	7	34	91.9	151.3
6. Germany	21	28	53	75.7	99.4
7. United States	8.82	4.09	56	42.6	133.9
8. United Kingdom	7	38	70	48.0	23.1
8. Netherlands	10	13	14	23.0	52.8
10. Canada	1.5	5.7	7.9	18.5	50.2
Imports					
1. Thailand	419	846	2348	4419.5	4338.2
2. China, People's Rep. of	38	116	524	1352.1	1552.8
3. Viet Nam	78	76	218	554.7	617.4
4. Korea, Rep. of	5	15	123	180.6	88.8
5. Japan	24	21	68	111.0	140.3
6. Singapore	33	44	25	260.4	46.2
7. Germany	4	11	24	48.2	37
8. Russian Federation	2	12	7	16.6	158
9. India	5	5	9	54.7	40
10. Belgium	1	20	20	24.7	31

Source Asian Development Bank (ADB, 2019)

Finance and Taxation

Tax

Corporate Income Tax

Small and medium enterprises that are not registered under the Value Added Tax (VAT) system are subject to lump-sum tax instead of profit tax. This applies to enterprises which have annual revenue of less than LAK 12 million. The CIT rate is 24%, which applies to both domestic and foreign businesses, except for companies registered in the Lao Stock Exchange, which benefit from a five percent reduction of the normal rate for a period of four years from the date of registration in the Stock Exchange. After this period, the normal profit tax rate applies. A 26% profit tax rate applies to companies whose business is to produce, import, and supply tobacco products. Two percent of the tax paid by tobacco companies shall contribute to the Cigarette Control Fund (Article 46 of the Law on Tobacco Control). Small and medium enterprises that are not registered under the VAT system pay lump-sum tax at progressive rates between 3 and 7%, depending on the nature of the business and its revenue. There is no definition of residence for tax purposes in Laos. All companies (i.e. all forms of legal entity) that are registered under Lao law, or that are incorporated under foreign law and are carrying on business in Laos, are subject to Lao profit tax.

Profit tax payments shall be made on a quarterly basis. The quarterly liability for profit tax is calculated based on one of the following:

- the profit tax paid during the previous year;
- the actual profit during the current year;
- the profit of a project as stated in the tax payment plan.

If the profit tax paid within the year is not calculated based on the actual current year profit, and exceeds the actual annual profit tax payable, the excess profit tax shall be offset against profit tax payable in the following year. If the amount paid during the year is less than the actual amount due, the extra will be added to the year-end assessment.

Withholding Taxes

Dividends paid to individuals or legal entities that are registered abroad are subject to withholding tax at the rate of 10%. Royalties paid to individuals or legal entities that are registered abroad are subject to withholding tax at the rate of five percent. Interest paid to individuals or legal entities that are registered abroad is subject to withholding tax at the rate of 10%. These withholding tax rates may be reduced under an applicable tax treaty. As there is limited outward investment from Laos, the tax treaty provisions for relief tend to follow the approach taken by the other country that is a party to the tax treaty. Holding rules Dividends for residents and individuals or legal entities that are registered aboard are subject to income tax at the rate of 10% of the gross dividend received. There is no separate capital gains tax in Laos.

Personal Income Tax

The top rate of income tax is 24%. Employees whose employer has a contract signed with the Government of Laos (e.g. investors with concession agreements) before Presidential Decree No. 001/PS of 1 March 2011, will be subject to personal income tax at a flat rate of 10% until the contract expires or is renewed/extended. The Law on Social Security No 34/NA and the Instruction on Social Security Law (which has been enforced from 1 January 2015) are applicable. There are requirements for compulsory and voluntary registration for the Social Security Fund. Those compulsorily required to register are as follows: Lao Front for National Construction, mass organizations and civil society; Government officers, civic servants, soldiers, police, retired employees, disabled people and their family members; state-owned enterprises, private enterprises, banks, financial institutions, educational institutions, private hospitals, factories, those working with machinery, hotels, department stores, restaurants, farms, and other investment projects; employees who receive salary and wages; local employees working in embassies, consular, Intentional organizations, and NGOs based in Lao P.D.R; and expatriates receiving salary or wages. Those voluntarily able to register are individuals who are working as farmers, merchants, service providers, free lancers and others who wish to be involved in SSO. The Law requires a deduction from gross salary as follows: 6% to be paid by the employer; 5.5% to be paid by the employee. Any salary monies over LAK 2,000,000 per month are not considered when calculating Social Security payments. As a result, the maximum monthly social security payment will be LAK 120,000 per month for employers and LAK 110,000 per month for employees.

Other Rules

Losses (which are agreed to by the National Audit Authority or an independent audit company, with acknowledgment of the tax authorities) may be carried forward for three years. Losses cannot be carried back. There are no grouping provisions in Laos. Share sale and purchase agreements are subject to stamp duty at a rate ranging from LAK 15,000 to LAK 100,000 depending on the purchase value. Income from profit from the sale of shares is subject to income tax at the rate of 10%. However, profits from sale of shares in a stock market are exempt from income tax. In Laos, there are no CFC rules, no transfer pricing rules, no thin capitalization regime. All interest payments must be supported by relevant documentation showing that the payments are made for business purposes. Otherwise, the tax authorities may disallow an element of the interest expense. There are no general anti-avoidance provisions under Lao tax law.

Other Taxes

The standard rate of VAT is 10%. Exclusively, for the exporting of goods to other countries, 0% rate of VAT is applied. VAT applies to a wide range of products, including electricity, water, fuel, and all imported products, unless they receive an exemption from the Government of Laos.

Duties are levied on all types of imported and exported commodities at varying rates from 5 to 40%. Administrative fees are levied at 5% ad valorem on equipment and materials. Excise tax is collected on certain types of goods, including fuel (5–25%), alcohol (50–70%), carbonated drinks and invigorating drinks (5–10%), tobacco products (60%) and cosmetics (20%). Imports of equipment, means of production, spare parts, and other materials used in the operation of foreign investors' projects or in their productive enterprises are taxed at a uniform flat rate of one percent of the imported value. Raw materials and intermediate components, imported for the purpose of processing and then exported, are exempt from such import duties with approval from relevant ministries. Stamp duty rates vary depending on the type of instrument. Land taxes vary on the location and the type of the land. The calculation of land tax is based on both the location and the size of the land and is levied at annual rates per square meter. Land tax is payable in the first quarter of the relevant calendar year. There is no inheritance tax in Laos.

Natural resources tax applies to the oil and gas industry and businesses involved in the exploitation of rare and precious resources, including oil shale/petroleum and natural gas, metallic/non-metallic minerals, construction materials, peat, anthracite, hydro-electric power and land concessions. Tobacco, coffee, tea, and flower seeds are also subject to natural resources tax. The applicable rates vary from 5 to 25% of the sale or export price or are based on a tax per cubic meter. For wood, the taxes vary depending upon the type of wood. Environment Tax Applies to individuals, legal entities, and organizations licensed to conduct activities deemed to be damaging to the environment, ecology, or people's health.

Tax rate on salary	%
Corporate tax	24
Personal income tax	24
Sales tax	10

Source Trading Economics (2019)

Audit and Accounting

All companies, including state-owned companies (SOEs) are required to produce financial statements, including the balance sheets, profit and loss statements, sources and uses of funds, tax returns, and depreciation schedules for fixed assets. Three different levels of accounting methods and reporting requirements (basic, extended, and advanced) are applied to companies depending on their size. The implementing decree generally conforms to the International Accounting Standards (IAS). However, the chart of accounts is standardized for all industries and for example, a hotel business is to follow the same chart as a manufacturing company even though requirements are different. The chart of accounts has been published in Lao, English and French and detailed guidelines on following the chart of accounts have been published in Lao. The structure of the chart of accounts is quite detailed and guidelines are rigid on presentation leading to the concern that form may take precedence over substance. Accounting is used essentially for computation of tax returns, but not yet to measure performance, monitor risks, and business planning.

All public and private enterprises with a capital in excess of 100 million Kip are legally required to have their accounts audited. However, this cannot be enforced in practice because of an acute shortage of qualified certified public accountants (CPAs) in Lao PDR. Formal education for accountancy in local schools is limited to basic bookkeeping and theoretical concepts of accounting, with little or no practical application. The Accountancy Board conducts a 6-month training program as a requirement for registration of government and private auditors. Lao staff of international accounting and auditing firms are sent to overseas branches for further training. Commercial banks are required to conduct a yearly external audit. However, SOCBs have not complied strictly with Article 64 of the Decree Law on Commercial Banks dated March 22, 2000.

Article 46 of the Decree Law on Commercial banks specifies that commercial banks and financial institutions are required to publish their accounts at the end of each financial year. Some foreign branches provide financial figures on the Lao branch operations extracted from the audited accounts or annual reports. There is no such requirement for the SOCBs which are treated differently under the Decree Law although they have occasionally published their financial statements albeit with significant delays. Few private local business enterprises make their annual reports publicly available. Generally, the value of disclosure is not understood and appreciated by the Lao private sector. The exceptions are the subsidiaries of foreign companies, which follow the practices of the parent company and apply the standards of the country of the parent company. By law, all companies are required to submit their financial statements along with the tax returns to the Tax Department of MOF. This requirement applies to banks. In addition, banks are also required to submit financial statements to BOL.

Risk Assessment

Laos has a very dynamic economy which is continuing to grow the country's high growth in the hydroelectric sector. Moreover, Laos is becoming more famous for tourism among Thailand, China and Vietnam, and 80% of tourists are from these three countries. The agricultural sector represents 25% of Laos' GDP and provides work to 70% of the country's population. However, there are several risks that can potential investors face while investing in Laos. The main risk for foreign investors is driven from information accessibility, Laos' sovereign risk and current accounts being in deficit.

It is hard to get access to the information in Laos, and accuracy of the available information is not at international standards. Freedom of the press is rated out of 100 (0 = best, 100 = worst) and indicates the level of freedom in the publication of the information, and Laos' freedom of press index is equal to 84 demonstrating that a lot of information is not published due to governments intervention. Sovereign risk associated with Laos is due to country has a high level of debt. This indicates that the probability of default of the country exists. Furthermore, Laos' current account of the balance of payments is in deficit and country imports twice as much of what it exports. More imports can lead to depreciation of exchange rate of the country's currency and foreign investors can face the risk in terms of Laos' currency depreciation against investors' domestic currency. The return from investment will decrease and investors will receive less due to currency depreciation.

Overall, the risk that foreign investors will face in Laos are associated with not being able to access required information regards important data about the country; the probability of Laos' default and investors being unable to take their money out of the country; and high level of imports which can lead to depreciation of the Laos' currency against investors' domestic currency that will decrease the investment return of the investment return of the investor.

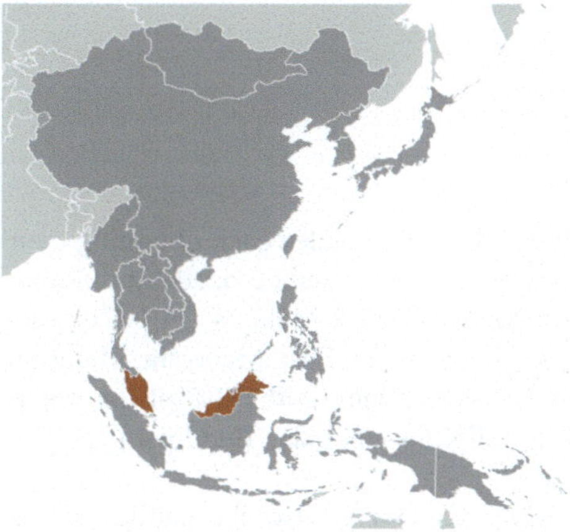

MALAYSIA

Official name
Malaysia
Capital
Kuala Lumpur, Putrajaya (administrative)
Area
329,847 sq. km
Population
32.5 mln
Languages
Bahasa Malaysia (official), English, Chinese
Main ethnic groups
Malay 50%, Chinese 23%, Indigenous 12%

Main religions
Muslim (official) 61%, Buddhist 20%, Christian 10%
Government type
Federal Constitutional Monarchy
Urbanization
76.0%
Life expectancy ratio
76 years
Fertility rate
2.0 children born/woman
Currency
Ringgit MYR

Malaysia

Country Introduction

Population, Location, Geography, Climate

Malaysia is a country in Southeast Asia. It consists of 13 states each obtaining their own structures. Malaysia is a moderate Islamic country characterized by different ethnic groups. The ethnic demographic is made up of 60% Malay's, 24% Chinese, 8% Indian and several indigenous groups which are in East Malaysia. Religion plays a large role in Malaysia. The state religion is Islam, with 53% of the population practicing the religion. The other religions include Buddhism (17%), Hinduism (7%) and Christianity (6.4%).

Kuala Lumpur is the largest city of Malaysia and is also the capital of the Federation. The Malaysian currency is the ringgit, which was formerly the Malaysian dollar, divided into 100 Sen. Malaysia is made up of two regions. These are divided by the South China Sea. The southern tip of the Malacca peninsula is known as West Malaysia whilst the territories of Sarawak and Sabah on the northern coast of Borneo known as Eastern Malaysia. West Malaysia is bounded on the west by the Strait of Malacca and the waters east of the South China Sea and is bordered to the north by Thailand and the south of Singapore. East Malaysia occupies the northern sector of Borneo and is bordered to the south of Indonesia. This is marked by the high peaks of the mountain ranges of Kapuas Hulu of Iran and of Penambo.

The highest peak is in the north. This is where Gunong Tahan reaches 2190 m. There are numerous rivers. The most important are Kelantan, Pahang on the Belum and Muar. The coasts are generally low, mostly sandy or marshy and are faced by several islands, islets and reefs. Furthermore, due to the geographical aspect of the country, a network of ground transportation is unevenly developed. The road and rail communications of Peninsular Malaysia have good destinations. While in Sabah and Sarawak there are many steep hills in the interior regions, impede development and transport particularly through the river network. The road network covers 71,814 km and the rail network, which is operated by the state, stretches for 1667 km. There are four airports, all of which are international, among which the most important is the KLIA to Kuala Lumpur. The ports of the country are very active, the most important is Klang which was privatized in the early nineties. This is followed by George Town, Johor Baharu, Kuantan on the peninsula, Kota Kinabalu in Sabah and Kuching in Sarawak.

The Malaysian climate has high temperatures and abundant rainfall. The monsoon season causes an increase in rainfall from April to August in Malacca

Peninsula and from January to February in Borneo. The average temperature is 27 ° C and precipitation do not fall below 2000 mm annually. The relative humidity exceeds 90%.

Internal Policy

Following independence, in 1957, Malaysia has experienced a political history without disturbances, ruled by a single party, the United Malays National Organisation (UMNO) is the largest in the country and a member of the Barisan National coalition (BN). 56 years of a one-party government have had their basis in UMNO national political force and the sustained economic success of the country. Political stability, however, began to weaken in 2006, due to a series of protests. This was due to corruption and ethical issues. Since the last two elections (2008 and 2013) the ruling coalition have seen their popularity decline. In May 2013 Prime Minister Najib Razak (UMNO) was re-elected for five years but for the second the BN coalition has proved incapable of winning a 2/3 majority in Parliament since they were more victorious against the bloc Pakatan Rakyat (PR) who were the opposition.

The BN coalition government has still achieved the majority of seats and this at first glance should favor political continuity especially given the heightened tensions in the opposition. The obstacles, however, have done nothing but multiply by Prime Minister Najib Razak, who is now trying to counter the growing resistance of hardliners in his own party and other potential leaders and critics, in particular, to its policy of national reconciliation. Therefore, despite having won the primary UMNO last October, Najib saw his position weakened in the party. This explained the measures to assist the Malay ethnicity launched in recent months.

Since independence, the country's political history has been marked by successive coalition governments, which has been dominated by the United Malays National Organization (UMNO) founded in 1946. In the elections of 2008, the coalition government recorded the worst performance in its history while maintaining an absolute majority of seats in Parliament (140 of 222; 62%). The UMNO has lost only one of the 2/3 which allowed the majority to amend the Constitution without the consent of the opposition, which has increased from 19 to 82 seats. The opposition parties (PKR, DAP and PAS), in the wake of electoral success, have formed an alliance called "Pakatan Rakyat" (PR, People's Alliance) under the leadership of Anwar Ibrahim.

After about a year before the elections, following the resignation of Prime Minister Badawi, Najib Tun Razak came to power on 3rd April 2009, becoming the sixth Prime Minister of Malaysia. The last elections took place 5th May 2013, registering a narrow victory of the ruling coalition.

International Relations

Internationally, Malaysia presents itself as a moderate Islamic country, which is open to progress. As evidence of this Prime Minister Najib, spoke to the General

Assembly in September 2010 and proposed the establishment of a “global movement of moderates”, bringing together forces, which are open to dialogue with all religions and marginalizing extremists, referring to the experience of Malaysia as an example of wise restraint in dealing with issues related to the coexistence of different ethnic groups and faiths. The first conference of the “Global Movement of the Moderates” (GMM) was organized by the International Islamic University of Malaysia with the support of the Malaysian Ministry of Foreign Affairs was held in Kuala Lumpur in January 2012.

Malaysia maintains a regional foreign policy, which has a more visible role relating to the situation in Mindanao and in the southern Muslim provinces of Thailand. Kuala Lumpur however is committed to foreign policy on a global level. This is evidenced by the active participation in UN peacekeeping missions (Lebanon, East Timor, Sudan) and its membership in regional and multilateral bodies (ASEAN, OIC, etc.). In 2015 the country has taken the turn of ASEAN chairmanship.

Economy

Macroeconomic Overview

	Unit	2000°	2018	2020F
GDP, current prices	USD (billions)	100.72	354.35	401.99
GDP per capita, current prices	USD	4286.83	10,941.75	12,100.44
GDP based on PPP per capita	Current International dollar	12,788.76	30,859.87	34,284.74

Source IMF Outlook (2019)

Malaysia’s economy has experienced expansionary growth. Although this growth started to slow in 2015. Due to the country’s strong degree of openness to foreign countries it is subject to the dynamics of international markets and the performance of the main macroeconomic indicators. Exogenous and endogenous factors have led to a decline in GDP growth which has fallen from 6% in 2014 to 5% in 2015. The fall in growth can also be attributed to decrease demand from its main trading partner, China; dramatic declines in commodity prices such as oil and palm oil and the volatility of financial markets. An austerity fiscal policy, which led to the contraction of private consumption growth (in part due to the introduction in April 2015 of the GST on consumption) a sharp cut in investment and government subsidies (fuel, sugar and supplies of electric energy) and the sharp depreciation of the Ringgit, which fell 20% against the USD in 2015 has also contributed to the decline in GDP. By 2018, GDP growth had averaged around 5%, seeing 4.7% in the last respective year. While industry and agriculture components dropped to almost their lowest since 2013, service sector achieved its peak with 6.9% alone.

The country's sustained growth has helped to build the foundation of the economy, which has been characterized by macroeconomic stability, modest foreign debt, increasing investment and reduced poverty. It must however be noted that inequalities within ethnic groups have increased. Low unemployment and surplus chronic current have also led to a sustained growth rate. Malaysia is a net foreign creditor with a sustainable debt ratio, with external debt accounting for almost 70% of Gross National Income.

One of the main challenges the country faces is increasing its exports in electrical and electronic goods, which currently stands as almost 50% of industrial output. Small and medium sized enterprises (SMEs) play a large role in the growth of the country. 95.5% of the companies that are registered are SMEs, which contribute around 35% of GDP. The registered unemployment rate in 2015 was 3.2% which was an increase from 2.8% in 2014. Nevertheless, the unemployment rate is still amongst the lowest in ASEAN. The inflation rate, however, fell to 2.1% in 2015 from 2.2% in 2014. The Inflation rate (change in CPI) was stable in 2018, with the proof of only 1% delta since the previous year.

Malaysia has a goal of reaching a balanced budget by 2020. As a result, the government has pursued an austerity policy approach, which has included fiscal deficit reduction. The fiscal deficit reduced from 3.5% in 2014 to 3.2% in 2015 and just under 1% in 2017. The projected forecast deficit is 3.1% in 2016. Public debt was equal to 53.9% of GDP and the private sector was 87.9% of GDP. This ranks amongst the highest in the ASEAN region.

The surplus account matches the current balance of payments surplus to 2.1% of GDP, it is expected to further improve to 2.3% in 2016. The strong performance of the economy can also be shown by the positive trade balance, which was 14.7% in 2015. This was mainly due to the large growth in exports, which increased by 6.8%, which was less than imports, which rose 4.9% in 2015. For the past two years (2017 and 2018), both exports and imports have increased by around 25%. China and Singapore still share the top as being the largest trade partners of Malaysia. Furthermore, the growth of the economy has been impacted by the sharp devaluation of the Ringgit. However, increase in financial account, meaning growth in foreign direct investment flow has helped to increase international reserves, thus strengthening the position of national currency against USD in 2018.

Structure of output (% GDP)	2000	2005	2010	2015	2018
Agriculture	8.3	8.4	10.2	8.4	7.6
Industry	46.8	46.9	40.9	38.9	38.8
Services	44.9	44.7	48.9	52.7	53.6

Source Asian Development Bank (ADB, 2019)

Structure of expenditure (% GDP)	2000	2005	2010	2015	2018
Final consumption	53.9	55.7	60.7	67.0	69.4
Gross capital formation	26.9	22.4	23.4	25.4	23.6
Exports of goods and services	119.8	112.9	86.9	69.4	68.8
Imports of goods and services	100.6	91.0	71.0	61.9	61.7
Statistical discrepancy	0.0	0.0	0.0	0.0	0.0

Source Asian Development Bank (ADB, 2019)

Economic Policy

Malaysia is one of the most open economies, which is continuing to expand in South-East Asia. This is due to the profits of exports and the flow of Foreign Direct Investment (FDI) capital. Whilst 70.1% of this comes from Japan, Singapore, China and Korea 24.5% comes from the EU and the USA.

The local Central Bank ranked Malaysia with the 3rd highest GDP growth rate after China and the Philippines. The financial sector has become increasingly developed with the goal to become a high-income economy by 2020. The country also aims to be among the top 10 most competitive economies in the world in 2016. The country has climbed from the 24th to the 20th position in the "World Competitiveness Yearbook 2014–15 report" and ranks 2nd place, after Singapore. Malaysia ranks 11th out of 144 countries regarding the quality of infrastructure and transport. In 2014, one of the major world markets of Islamic finance, recorded a growth rate of 12% of banks and 65.6% of Islamic bonds (Sukuk), which was issued by Malaysia. The liberalization, which has been initiated in the country allows foreigners to own 100% of the property services company. Joint ventures are permitted within the legal services with foreign participation up to 40%.

Since April 1, 2015, a "Goods and Services Tax—GST" was introduced at 6% and this has led to progressive reductions in subsidies on some food and fuels. From the end of 2014 a trade deal between Malaysia, Russia and New Zealand was introduced using their local currencies, which has had an impact on the US dollar. Furthermore, in 2015, tax breaks have been introduced. The maximum taxation of 26% has been reduced although this is dependable on income of 1–3%. Income tax has also been reduced for enterprises of capital from 20 to 19%. This is for foreign entrepreneurs and start-up owners, whose capital formation must be of 75,000 RM, which entitles them to a work permit for a period of 1 year. In some areas of the country companies can receive tax exemptions of up to 100% for 5 years as this will encourage business development and programs that attract foreign companies operate in the sector of innovative technologies. There is also ongoing liberalization of foreign exchange transactions for citizens and Malaysian companies. Through authorized banks you can make transactions from one foreign currency or you can keep deposits or credit positions on the currency. In the national budget for 2020, the government will make available up to RM1 billion worth of customized packaged investment incentives annually over five years, as part of the strategic push to attract targeted Fortune 500 companies and global unicorns in high technology, manufacturing, creative and new economic sectors. One should also note that the World Bank's Doing Business 2020 report, which ranked Malaysia higher by three spots to 12th place, should continue to place the country on the FDI radar screen.

Banking System

The banking system comprises of commercial banks, investment banks and Islamic banks. These institutions are the primary mobiliser of funds and the main source of financing to support economic activities in Malaysia. The non-banking financial intermediaries include developmental financial institutions, pension funds, insurance companies, and operators. These intermediaries complement the banking institutions in mobilizing savings and meeting the financial needs of the economy. The banking sector in Malaysia accounted for 4.7% of GDP in 2016, boasting assets worth 198.8% of GDP and a workforce equivalent to 3% of the total employed workers in the country in 2016. Various reports point the banking system is stable and has been getting ready for the adoption of IFRS 9 in 2018, and the full Basel III framework in 2019. Supported by its banks, Malaysia aims to be a high-value added, high-income, and cashless economy by 2020.

The Central Bank

The Bank of Negara Malaysia is the Central Bank. This is the top of the monetary and banking structure of the country. Its main objectives as defined in the Central Bank of Malaysia Act 1958 are to:

- issue currency and keep the reserves safeguarding the value of the currency;
- act as a banker and financial adviser to the Government;
- promote monetary stability and a sound financial structure;
- promote the reliable, efficient and smooth operation of national payment and settlement systems and to ensure that the national payment and settlement systems policy is directed to the advantage of Malaysia;
- influence the credit situation to the advantage of Malaysia.

To meet its objectives, the Bank has legal powers under various laws to regulate and supervise the banking institutions and other non-banking financial intermediaries. The Bank also administers the country's foreign exchange control regulations.

Financial Institutions

Banks, including Islamic banks, operate through a network of more than 2200 branches across the country. Six Malaysian banking groups have a presence in 18 countries through branches, representative offices, subsidiaries and joint ventures. There are also 21 foreign banks maintaining representative offices in Malaysia. They do not conduct normal banking business, but provide liaison services and facilitate information exchange between business interests in Malaysia and their counterparts.

The introduction of the framework for investment banks in 2005 provided for the development of full-fledged investment banks through consolidation and rationalization between merchant banks, stockbroking companies and discount houses. Investment banking activities mainly include capital raising activities such as: underwriting, corporate financing, management advisory services, arranging for the issue and listing of shares and investment portfolio management. The development of investment banks will enhance the capacity of financial institutions in Malaysia to improve service to its corporate customers through a wider range of financial and advisory activities on the same level with the services provided by international investment banks.

Malaysia also has a comprehensive Islamic banking system. Currently, Malaysia has fifteen full-fledged Islamic banks, three of which are from the Middle East. These provide a broad spectrum of financial products and services based on Shariah principles. At the same time, there are five conventional banks, three of which are major foreign banks. These offer Islamic banking products and services via the Islamic banking window set up.

The entry of three foreign Islamic banks enhances the competition and stimulates innovation among the Islamic banking players. At the same time this complements the Malaysian players in tapping into strategic growth areas such as investment banking and wealth management. In addition, these institutions also have plans to make Malaysia their financial hub.

Malaysia has several development financial institutions (DFIs) that were set up with specific objectives to develop and promote strategic economic sectors, including the manufacturing and export sectors, small and medium enterprises (SMEs), agriculture, infrastructure and maritime sectors. These DFIs complement the banking institutions by providing a range of financial and non-financial services to support the development of the strategic sectors. These include the provision of medium to long-term loans, equity capital, guarantees for loans and a range of supplementary financial and business advisory services. Bank Perusahaan Kecil & Sederhana Malaysia Berhad or the SME Bank, which was established in October 2005, offer financial products such as term loans and working capital including start-ups and SMEs in new growth areas, particularly to those in professional services, export-oriented activities and franchise businesses. Bank Pertanian Malaysia has recently merged with the Bank Pertanian Malaysia Berhad (Agrobank) to strengthen its role to be more effective in meeting the needs of the entire value chain of agricultural activities including the agro-based industries.

Malaysia as an International Islamic Financial Centre

Malaysia's continuous efforts in strengthening the Islamic financial system domestically and internationally have gained acceptance and recognition by the international financial community. An important initiative that has been introduced to enhance the position of Malaysia as a leading international Islamic financial hub.

In August 2006, the Malaysian Government launched the Malaysia International Financial Centre (MIFC) initiatives. The MIFC initiative is a collaborative effort formed by Malaysia's financial and market regulators together with top officials from relevant Government agencies and participants from the banking and capital market sectors. The establishment of the MIFC as one of the key intermediation linkages in the global marketplace, has an important role in accelerating the process bridging and strengthening the relationship between international Islamic financial markets and thereby expanding the investment and trade relations between the Middle East, West Asia North Africa and East Asia. Situated centrally in the Asian time zone Malaysia presents itself as a meeting place for those with surplus funds and those who seek to raise funds from any part of the world.

As of June 2017, there are eighteen Islamic local and foreign banks operating in Malaysia. Foreign banks with operations in Malaysia are allowed 100% equity participation. Islamic banking is based on Sharia law that disallows the payment of interest in favor of profit-sharing.

Under the MIFC initiatives, Malaysia offers strong value propositions as a key provider of Islamic financial services, with five focus areas:

- Sukuk Origination—a platform for Sukuk origination, distribution and trading.
- Islamic Fund and Wealth Management—a destination for financial investment with a wide range of world class capital market and treasury instruments.
- International Islamic Banking—a center for the establishment of Islamic banks providing international currency financial services.
- International Takaful—center for international takaful and retakaful businesses.
- Human Capital Development—a center of excellence and thought leadership in education, training, consultancy and research in Islamic finance to create a supply of talent for the Islamic finance industry.

Major Incentives Introduced to Attract more Participants to MIFC Include:

- Issuance of new International Islamic Banking (IIB) licenses under the Islamic Banking Act 1983 to qualified foreign and Malaysian financial institutions to conduct the full range of Islamic banking business with residents and non-residents in international currencies either as a subsidiary or a branch. The entity will enjoy full income tax exemption for up to ten years.
- Issuance of a new International Takaful Operator (ITO) licenses to qualified foreign and Malaysian financial institution to conduct a full range of takaful business with non-residents and residents in international currencies, either as a subsidiary or a branch. The entity will enjoy similar income tax exemptions as the IIB entity.
- Islamic fund management companies (IFMC) can invest all their Shariah funds abroad. The entity will enjoy tax exemption on all fees for managing Islamic funds for foreign and Malaysian investors up to year of assessment 2016 under the Income Tax Act 1967.
- Provision of start-up funds by Employees Provident Fund (EPF) for the establishment of foreign IFMC.

Interest Rates (% per annum; period averages)	2000	2005	2010	2015	2018
On deposits					
Savings	2.72	1.41	0.94	1.06	1.04
Time: 6 months	3.50	3.04	2.55	3.19	3.21
12 months	4.24	3.70	2.81	3.31	3.31

Source Asian Development Bank (ADB, 2019)

Investment Area

Basic Pharmaceutical Products and Pharmaceutical Preparations

The healthcare sector in Malaysia is strongly growing and it is expected to reach 971 billion USD, with an annual growth of 24% in 2016. In 2014, Malaysia has approved 15 projects with a total investment of over 500 million Ringgit (60% of this investment came from abroad). There is also a growing demand for the hemodialysis sector which recently had a 230-million-ringgit investment from a foreign operator. The government's main priorities are to encourage the biopharmaceutical industry to create high added value and facilitate growth which can be transferred to the local industry.

Malaysia has planned to invest 9 billion Euros in healthcare over the next years with 17 new private hospitals with about 4500 beds and a total investment of over a billion Euros is expected. Three other private hospitals will expand their facilities for 770 beds. The healthcare sector is also expected to increase the service it provides to foreign patients and about 1900 new beds are expected to be reserved.

In 2014, Malaysia had a large number of tourists who benefited from medical and hospital treatments in over 40 specialized centers and private clinics. There have been over 500,000 people, which have collectively brought in 125 million Euros. It is believed the pharmaceutical industry will grow considerably within the next year. The positive performance has been achieved due to massive foreign and local investment. This investment has permitted the creation of new research laboratories and production facilities.

The medical industry in Malaysia has strong growth and has so far attracted RM 23.6 billion (Euro 5.6 billion) of foreign direct investment, while exports increased to 10 billion RM (Euro 2.4 billion) a year, mostly due to the G3 markets, United States, Europe and Japanese economies. It is also expected that the medical sector will create more than 40,000 jobs within the next five years.

Malaysia currently supplies 80% of the world catheters and over 60% of rubber gloves (including medical ones). In Malaysia there are about 180 manufacturers of latex gloves (these gloves are used for surgical and patient treatment) and there are also some producers with foreign partnerships in catheters, cannulas, intravenous needles and contact lenses. Most medical equipment is imported.

As mentioned, Malaysia has an ambitious plan to become a benchmark for the Asian continent with regards to medical treatment as practiced by a growing number of foreigners. This can be attributed to excellent healthcare facilities and the presence of a multi-linguistic and multi-ethnic communities (Chinese, Malay, and Indian). This greatly facilitates the development of medical tourism. The import of medical equipment consists largely of surgical instruments, sterilizers, instruments for medical and veterinary, orthopedic articles, pacemakers and diagnostic equipment. The weight of exports in this sector is still marginal.

Construction

Malaysia has many investment incentives for foreign investors. The country is ranked second in Asia, for the most attractive for investment in infrastructure with Singapore coming first. This was reported by the "Arcadis Global Infrastructure Investment Index" report. According to this study, the infrastructure is the backbone of the country, which acts as a catalyst for its long-term economic development.

On average, the country has a population growth rate of 1.4%. Therefore, investment in infrastructure will need to increase to strengthen the growth of the Malaysian economy. Malaysia has a goal of becoming a high-income country by 2020. There is also a commitment from Malaysian authorities to invest resources into creating functional infrastructures and productive and livable urban centers which can then be comparable to other world class cities.

Malaysia's high level of infrastructure, efficient network of services, a stable macroeconomic environment and a growing domestic market make Malaysia one of the favorite destinations for foreign investors. Furthermore, Malaysia's efficient banking system and availability of skilled labor at competitive prices contribute to the large number of foreign investors in the country.

The Asia Business Outlook Survey report showed 44% of multinationals that are already in the country have expressed their intention to make further investments. In the ranking of major countries Malaysia rose to 4th place for receiving the largest amount of foreign investment, coming behind China, India and Indonesia. The report also showed investors prefer to use the two hubs of Hong Kong and Singapore because of the high cost of the real estate, personnel, services and the cost of living for expatriates in Malaysia. It is important to note that investors wish to reduce investment in Taiwan, Philippines, Vietnam and Thailand.

The Malaysian Investment Development Authority (MIDA), announced that the total investments in Malaysia had rose to 216.5 billion Ringgit (51.8 billion Euros). This was 30% higher compared to previous years. This amount relates to 5669 projects, including 14 mega-projects which are above 250 million Euros. They are targeted at high-growth sectors and high operating margins. It is expected that the new approved projects will provide approximately 192,000 jobs.

Most of foreign direct investment (FDI) has been invested into the services sector. 24.1% (12.5 billion Euros) has been invested into the manufacturing sector specifically within the electronics, electrical components, fuel, vehicles, and chemicals. The areas receiving most of the investment include: petrochemical, chemical and electronic goods. 40% of FDI is received in the State of Johor (which borders Singapore) 20% is received in Sarawak and 10% in Penang. The main countries investing in the manufacturing sector are: The United States, South Korea, Singapore, Japan and China.

Information Technology and Communications

The Multimedia Super Corridor (MSC) is a status that allows companies operating in the sector of multimedia technologies to obtain numerous tax incentives. Currently 2356 companies have been granted MSC status, of which more than 500 are foreign-owned. The MSC Malaysia is an initiative aimed at developing the Information Communication Technology industry to transform Malaysia into a society of "knowledge", driven by the new economy. The Government is working with Telekom Malaysia to develop high-speed broadband in densely populated areas, such as the area of Port Klang and the capital Kuala Lumpur. The project will require a decade for its realization (2008–2018) and provides connections for over 34,000 industries.

Machinery and Equipment

The manufacturing of machinery and equipment industry has experienced good technological progress. The Malaysian government has launched a development policy to produce machines with high value-added technology, to allow for the continued advancement of the level of industrialization of the country and to tackle the competitiveness of neighboring Asian countries. In addition, the third "Industrial Master Plan" has set the goal of making Malaysia a "regional hub" for the production and distribution of high-tech machinery and equipment as well as a regional center for maintenance, reconditioning and technological improvement special machines. The Government encourages foreign investment to promote innovation, the creation of talent, research and development and marketing to maximize the growth of the industrial sector. Companies of the Italian Federation for Aerospace, Defence and Security, under the support of the Malaysian Ministry of Defence and Security Technology Park (MDSTP) is worth one billion euros. This will undoubtedly help strengthen and develop technological research and industrial cooperation between Italian and Malaysian industries.

Domestic Markets

Malaysia restricts open trade in protected industries such as: the automotive and agricultural sectors. Malaysia protects domestic industries by imposing higher duty rates and excessive taxes. Malaysia also uses a system of import permits or licenses to reduce imports in protected and strategic sectors.

Government restrictions hamper foreign investment in several areas. This includes government procurement contracts, finance, business, professional services and telecommunications. In many cases it is imperative to have a local partner, usually a Bumiputra (ethnic Malay-owned) company, to effectively compete in the market.

Malaysian officials continue to make progress in establishing fair and adequate protection of Intellectual Property Rights (IPR). Although challenges remain Malaysian officials have increased their resources to combat online piracy and have sustained their efforts to deny access to piracy websites, taking down infringing content on domestic sites and conducting raids and arrests of Malaysians either operating or posting links to sites with pirated content. The Ministry of Domestic Trade, Cooperatives and Consumerism (MDTCC) is responsible for IPR enforcement.

In the World Bank's global Doing Business report, Malaysia ranked 18th place among the 189 economies covered in the survey. The ranking is a slight decrease from previous years. In the past Malaysia ranked 17th out of 189 economies. Malaysia's lowest ranking is in "registering property" (38th), "enforcing contracts" (44th), "trading across borders" (49th), and "resolving insolvency" (45th). Many of the market challenges will be resolved or improved under the TPP. Under the TPP, Malaysia has committed to eliminate tariffs or substantially improve market access on imports from the United States through tariff reductions and tariff-rate quotas. Furthermore, the TPP Agreement sets strong and balanced standards on IPR protection and enforcement. Under TPP, Malaysia will also make significant improvements to its service markets.

Even though the Malaysian economy is facing some turbulence Malaysia has solid growth prospects and a rising middle class. In 2019, Malaysia's per capita GDP was USD $12,110; its purchasing power is among the third highest in ASEAN, after Singapore and Brunei. Malaysia's level of economic development also drives both consumer and business demand for products and services. Its consumers, though price sensitive, are accustomed to several decades of strong growth. As a result, they are attracted to and are familiar with international branded products, better education and quality healthcare products and services. The World Bank classifies Malaysia as an upper-middle income nation. In terms of manufacturing sector, the value of gross output rose 5.7% per annum to RM 1275.8 billion in 2017 as compared to 2015 (RM 1142.0 billion). Value added improved 6.9% per annum to RM 294.0 billion in 2017 (2015: RM 257.1 billion). The number of persons engaged grew 2.2% to 2,214,883 persons in 2017 as compared to 2,119,158 persons in 2015. Throughout 2015–2017, the value added of the Manufacturing sector increased from RM 257.1 billion to RM 294.0 billion with a growth rate of 6.9% per annum. The Petroleum, chemical, rubber and plastic products sub-sector remained as the dominant contributor with the value of RM 89.6 billion (30.5%) in 2017. The second largest contributor was the Electrical, electronic and optical products sub-sector which amounted to RM 78.6 billion (26.7%), followed by the Non-metallic mineral products, basic metal and fabricated metal products sub-sector with RM 38.1 billion (13.0%) Through the Economic Transformation Program (ETP) the Malaysian government remains committed to reaching a high-income status by 2020. This initiative includes a commitment to attract investment in "National Key Economic Areas" (NKEA) and a commitment to improving Malaysia's infrastructure, especially its transportation infrastructure in East Malaysia (Sabah and Sarawak). Planned projects include the below:

- Development and upgrading of the 2083 km Pan Borneo Highway that connects Sabah, Sarawak, and Brunei. Estimated value: RM 16.6 billion; estimated completion date: 2021.
- Sungai Besi-Ulu Klang Expressway (SUKE), a 31.8 km expressway linking Sg. Besi, Alam Damai, Ampang-KL Elevated Highway and KL Middle Ring Road. Estimated value: RM 5.3 billion; estimated completion date: unknown.
- The Bandar Utama-Klang Valley light rapid transit (LRT) line is slated to be the third LRT system in Klang Valley. The LRT is currently in the planning stage and will stretch 36-kilometers with 25 stations. Estimated value: RM 9.3 billion; estimated completion date: 2020.
- The MRT Sungai Buloh-Serdang-Putrajaya Line (MRT2) is the mass rapid transit line servicing the Sungai Buloh-Serdang-Putrajaya area. The line is part of a larger mass transit project aimed at connecting the Klang Valley. Construction commenced in 2016. Estimated value: RM 28 billion; estimated completion date: 2022.
- Development of the Cyber City Centre in Cyberjaya, with an investment of RM 11 billion over a period of 5 years.
- A 1300-ha Aeropolis KLIA to be developed that is expected to attract RM 7 billion in investments.

External trade (RM millions)	2000	2005	2010	2015	2018
Exports, fob	373,270	536,234	638,822	777,355	998,278
Imports, cif	311,459	432,871	528,828	685,778	877,761
Trade balance	61,811	103,363	109,994	91,577	120,518

Source Asian Development Bank (ADB, 2019)

Main commercial partners (USD millions)	2000	2005	2010	2015	2018
Exports					
1. Singapore	18,050	22,010	26,544	27,808	32,801
2. China, People's Rep. of	3028	9303	24,912	25,987	36,404
3. United States	20,162	27,763	18,987	18,880	21,970
4. Japan	12,780	13,181	20,782	18,999	20,201
5. Thailand	3550	7585	10,587	11,403	12,755
6. Hong Kong, China	4440	8241	10,088	9482	16,313
7. India	1925	3955	6517	8128	8208
8. Indonesia	1707	3322	5616	7473	7963
9. Australia	2426	4766	7472	7214	7949

(continued)

(continued)

Main commercial partners (USD millions)	2000	2005	2010	2015	2018
10. Korea, Rep. of	3235	4737	7555	6475	10,133
Imports					
1. China, People's Rep. of	3237	13,177	20,682	33,155	44,203
2. Singapore	11,763	13,424	18,761	21,052	23,627
3. Japan	17,331	16,634	20,726	13,785	16,512
4. United States	13,668	14,789	17,526	14,194	15,678
5. Thailand	3176	6045	10,263	10,691	12,387
6. Korea, Rep. of	3663	5706	8933	7968	7822
7. Indonesia	2269	4375	9151	7950	8715
8. Germany	2441	5088	6648	6009	6141
9. Taipei, China	4611	6331	7422	9373	–
10. India	725	1100	2485	3901	6790

Source Asian Development Bank (ADB, 2019)

Finance and Taxation

Tax

Corporate Income Tax

Corporate tax rates for company resident's in Malaysia is 24% from.

Companies resident in Malaysia receive special tax rates if they have paid-up share capital of MYR 2.5 million or less from the beginning of the basis period for a year of assessment. This is conditional upon the basis that no more than 50% of the ordinary paid-up share capital of the company is directly or indirectly owned by (or linked to) a related company which has an ordinary paid-up share capital of more than MYR 2.5 million at the beginning of the basis period for a year of assessment):

- 17% on the first MYR 500,000 (currently 18%).
- 25% on every ringgit exceeding MYR 500,000.

Residence

A company will be a Malaysian tax resident if at any time during the basis year the management and control of the company's business or any one of its businesses are exercised in Malaysia.

Compliance Requirements

- Assessment system—Self assessment.
- Estimate of tax payable must be made 1 month before the commencement of a year of assessment.
- Monthly instalments must be paid based on an estimate of tax payable.
- Filing due date—7 months from the date following the close of the accounting period.

International Withholding Tax Rates

- Dividends paid to non-residents are not subject to withholding tax.
- Royalties paid/credited to non-residents are subject to withholding tax at 10%. The rate may be lowered by the relevant Double Taxation Agreement (DTA).
- Interest paid/credited to non-residents is subject to withholding tax at 15%. The rate may be lowered by the relevant DTA.

Holding Rules

There are currently transitional rules in place prior to the full implementation of the single-tier dividend system, which became effective from 1 January 2014. The transitional rules affect dividends paid by a resident company to its shareholders. The dividends will be regarded as franked dividends provided:

- They are paid in cash on ordinary shares; and
- The ordinary shares have been held continuously for 90 days or more (this condition does not apply to dividends paid by publicly listed companies).
- There is no capital gains tax in Malaysia. However, there is real property gains tax (RPGT).

RPGT is levied on the disposal of real property situated in Malaysia as well as the disposal of shares in a Real Property Company (RPC). An RPC is a controlled company which owns real property or shares or both in another RPC which have a defined value of not less than 75% of the value of its total tangible assets.

Tax Losses

Business losses may be offset against income from other sources for that year. Tax losses may be carried forward indefinitely to offset against future business income only unless the company does not satisfy the continuity of ownership test.

Tax Consolidation/Group Relief

There are no consolidation provisions in Malaysia. However, resident companies within a 70% owned group can surrender up to 70% of their current year's adjusted business losses to other related resident companies, provided certain conditions are met.

Transfer of Shares

Stamp duty of 0.3% (of the price or value of the shares, whichever is higher) is payable on the transfer of shares.

Transfer of Assets

On the transfer of land and buildings, ad valorem stamp duty rates from 1 to 3% on the transfer consideration or the market value of the property, whichever is higher, is payable.

Stamp duty relief is available in certain circumstances such as transfers within 90% groups provided certain conditions are met.

Transfer Pricing

Malaysia's transfer pricing regime is largely based on OECD guidelines. Documents pertaining to transfer pricing does not need to be submitted with a taxpayer's annual income tax return but they should be made available to the tax authority upon request.

Advance pricing agreements (APA) are governed by the Income Tax (Advance Pricing Agreement) Rules in 2012. The Rules establish the process and expected timeline for the application of unilateral, bilateral and multilateral APAs.

Thin Capitalization

Malaysia has thin capitalization legislation. However, the implementation of the regime has been deferred to the end of December 2015.

General Anti-avoidance

There are general anti-avoidance rules in Malaysia which allow the tax authority to disregard any adjustment if there is reason to believe that any transaction has the effect of evading, avoiding or altering the incidence of tax.

Anti-treaty Shopping

There are no specific anti-treaty shopping provisions. However, the general anti-avoidance provisions can be used.

R&D Incentives

Malaysia's R&D tax incentive scheme includes tax exemptions and double deductions for certain R&D expenditure incurred in Malaysia.

Other Incentives

Tax incentives are available for a wide range of companies in Malaysia such as: Operational Headquarters, International Procurement Centers, Regional Distribution Centers and Treasury Management Centers operating in Malaysia.

Additionally, incentives are available in Malaysia for investments in promoted products and activities in the manufacturing, agricultural, hotel and tourism industries as well as training activities and specific business activities promoted by the Malaysian Government. Generally, the incentives provide partial or total relief from income tax or an incentive based on capital expenditure which could last for a duration of five or ten years.

Special Tax Regimes for Specific Industries or Sectors

Foreign-sourced income received in Malaysia by a resident company (other than a resident company carrying on the business of banking, insurance, shipping or air transport) is exempt from tax.

Indirect Taxes

Service tax is chargeable on the value of taxable services provided by a taxable person. Examples of taxable services include: operators of hotels, operators of restaurants, bars and coffee houses, insurance companies, telecommunication companies, consultants and professional firms. There is a limited exemption for services provided within a group. Sales tax is a form of consumption tax levied on taxable goods manufactured in Malaysia or imported into Malaysia for local consumption. Exports are exempt.

Standard Rate

- Service Tax: 6%.
- Sales Tax: Generally, 5% or 10%.

GST Reforms

A goods and services tax (GST) introduced in Malaysia from 1 April 2015 and replaced the previous sales and service taxes. The standard rate of GST will be 6% although some supplies will be zero-rated or exempt. Businesses with an annual taxable sales value of MYR 500,000 and above will be required to register for GST purposes. Businesses below the threshold may register on a voluntary basis. The widely-anticipated “digital tax” will be implemented with effect from 1 January 2020. Foreign service providers providing digital products and services to consumers in Malaysia in B2C transactions will be required to register with Customs and charge and account for service tax on the same.

Personal Income Tax

The top rate of personal income tax in Malaysia is 26% and applies to income greater than MYR 100,000. The maximum income tax rate will reduce to 25% and it will apply to chargeable income of MYR 400,000 or greater.

Non-residents are taxed at a flat rate of 26% (pending issuance of the Finance Bill) on gross income from all sources.

There is no general social security framework in Malaysia. However, mandatory contributions are made monthly by both the employer and the employee to the Employees' Provident Fund, which serves as a compulsory savings and retirement plan. In addition, where an employee earns less than MYR 3000 per month, both the employer and the employee must make monthly contributions to the Social Security Organization, which serves to provide certain benefits to employees in cases of employment injury.

Property Taxes

Local councils may impose a levy rate (commonly known as land tax) on residents in respect to the services provided by the local council. The amount varies from council to council and is dependent on the value of the property. Quit rent is a form of tax imposed by the State Government. It is imposed on owners of landed property (as opposed to units in high-rise building). The amount of quit rent imposed varies from state to state and will depend on the locality and category of land in use.

Import Duty

Import duty is generally payable on imported goods at the time of clearance from Customs' control. The rates of import duty will generally range from 0 to 60% depending on the category of goods imported. Malaysia is committed to ASEAN and as such import duties imposed on most manufactured goods of ASEAN origin have been reduced to a range of 0–5%.

Export Duty

Export duty is generally imposed on depleting resources to discourage exports of such commodities.

Excise Duty

Excise duty is a domestic tax imposed on a limited range of locally manufactured goods or goods imported into Malaysia. The rate of tax to be levied varies and would depend on the nature of the goods manufactured or imported. Excise duty is generally levied on alcoholic beverages, tobacco products and motor vehicles.

Nicknamed "soda tax", excise duty of RM 0.40 L^{-1} imposed from 1 April 2019 on specified beverages which exceed the specified limit on sugar content, ostensibly to curb diabetes.

Tax rate	%
Corporate tax	24
Personal income tax	28
Sales tax	10

Source Trading Economics (2019)

Audit and Accounting

Audit cases can be selected based on several factors, such as:

- risk analysis criteria;
- information received from a third party;
- industry type;
- a specific issue concerning a certain group of taxpayers;
- location.

There are two types of audit—a desk audit which is carried out at the IRBM's office and a field audit which is carried out at the taxpayer's business premise.

A typical tax audit commences with a letter of notification which will indicate the records that should be made available for audit, the years of assessment to be audited and the names of the relevant audit officers. This is followed by an examination of the relevant documents. The IRBM will then issue an audit finding report which will contain details of any proposed tax adjustments and the rationale for those adjustments. If the taxpayer disagrees with the adjustments an official objection must be submitted. If there are no objections to the adjustments made the IRBM will issue a notice of additional assessment.

The timeframe for settlement of a tax audit should be 3 months from the commencement of the audit but can take longer to reach a resolution in more complex cases.

Key focus areas for the IRBM in tax audits conducted in recent years have included transfer pricing.

Risk Assessment

Political Risks

Malaysia's political risk ranks amongst the lowest in Asia. This robustness is due to macroeconomic stability and a great economic openness in an extremely dynamic South-East Asian region. This is also due to low foreign debt, a current account surplus, achieving controllable inflation and maintaining strong average growth. The sharp deterioration of public finances in the period after 2008 has intensified the political risk, prompting the government to launch a budget consolidation program, which is still under way. The current tightening of monetary policy aims to maintain stability at the expense of greater growth.

Overall, the macroeconomic forecasts and the business environment are favorable. Malaysia has a short-term political risk rating of 1/7 and a systemic commercial risk of (A). In the future, however, structural reforms and diversification of the economy will be critical to avoid the middle-income trap.

The beginning of the establishment of the one-party government policy is one of the key factors of the reduced size of the Malaysian political risk which has also contributed to the economic development of the country. Since opposition protests occurred because of strong polarization of last year's election result, the risks of internal instability have increased. The country faces growing democratic aspirations and demands of a young population that want liberal reforms and good governance. Furthermore, ethnic issues continue to fuel tensions especially since many Malay citizens still enjoy preferential treatment.

Prime Minister Najib also lost the support of the population due to deteriorating economic conditions and lower consumer confidence after heavy criticism of state institutions for the bad management of the accident which affected the Malaysia Airlines flight MH370 in March. In addition to increasing dissatisfaction due to the level of corruption, alleged electoral fraud, ethnic and economic policy measures the government have lost a large amount of popularity. Yet, Najib, the main unified force within UMNO, should be able to maintain the position of Prime Minister in future years.

The five years prison sentence of the political leader Anwar Ibrahim (for sodomy) also impacted the political landscape of the country. This is because many political leaders disagree with his imprisonment and therefore protests and fighting have occurred due to many leaders now wanting to lead the party. This will eventually destabilize and weaken the opposition in Parliament and potentially damage his election prospects in future. As a result, the world may have to wait to see Malaysia's first peaceful and democratic transfer of power.

It must be stated that ethical tensions, political corruption and bad governance are the main risks facing political stability. The change in the political landscape is explained by the evolution of the Malaysian society which has become increasingly urban. The BN coalition is backed by tradition from the rural population, elderly and poor. But the PR is increasing amongst the urban middle class and young people who are tired of corrupt systems which are based on nepotism and privileges of divisive ethnic groups.

Ethnicity is a sensitive point in Malaysia. This is evidenced by sporadic ethnic tensions between many Malaysians and Chinese. To meet the advancement of PR Najib intends to change the political and socio-economic system by making it more inclusive under the ethnic profile. This is however opposed by the radical fringes of the party and the judicial system (as evidenced by the conviction of Anwar).

Malaysia is highly exposed to the risk of riots and inter-racial clashes. In 2013, there were mass protests and alleged electoral fraud that altered the election results. However, since then, the country has stabilized. Nevertheless, growing discontent from supporters of the opposition towards the government must also be noted. As this will lead to an increase in demonstrations, especially in the run-up to the next elections. Another potential risk is the repatriation of Muslim militant radicals who fought in Syria and in Iraq. Malaysia, however, has always promoted Islam, its state organs and the intelligence services. This should be able to mitigate the domestic threat of Islamist attacks.

Economic Risks

Malaysia is no longer in the "economic tiger" era of the pre-Asian financial crisis of 1997–1998. However, the country has achieved a high rate of growth due to the benefits which it has accumulated over time. The country is still very export-oriented and Malaysia's main trading partner is China. Although, from 2006 onwards the share of foreign trade on total economic activity has declined steadily. Despite the obvious tendency to depend less and less on foreign markets it should be noted that exports of goods still account for 70% of Malaysia's GDP and strongly influence economic developments. Malaysia's economic openness exposes the country to external shocks as seen during the Asian financial crisis and the global crisis of 2009. In both cases, the country entered a recession before recovering quickly.

The average GDP growth rate gradually declined from 8.5 to 5% prior to the Asian crisis. Last year, the country recorded a GDP growth rate at 4.7%, which has been the lowest value over the last four years. The country also experienced a decline in commodity prices, which accounts for over 1/5 of total exports, which are dominated by oil and gas. The country's reduced growth rate can also be attributable to reduced foreign demand, especially from the United States and the European Union. In 2014, the country recorded a strong growth rate of 6.2% in the first half of the year, despite an uncertain global environment. Most of this growth has been supported by a resilient export sector. The main exporting goods are within electronics, commodities, services and industrial production.

The Malaysian economy is driven by exports, continued increase in domestic demand and private consumption. The populous middle class supports the measures for increasing economic growth, but has also fueled a large private debt. In addition, Malaysia is moderately vulnerable to external shocks, such as the slowing of the Chinese economy, which also has repercussions on other export markets of Malaysia. Furthermore, the weakening of the US/EU demand and output from the Fed's quantitative easing program also impacts the economy. Risks to the outlook tilt downward. Any escalation of trade tensions between the US and People's Republic of China could derail Malaysia's highly trade-dependent economy.

Consumer demand is also strong due to a growing urban middle class. Although the spending on private consumption could be hindered by the presence of less favorable conditions. For example, the rise in consumer prices and the persistence of the high level of household debt servicing mortgage loans by half. This contributes to more than 85% of GDP and represents a risk to internal stability. However, this can be mitigated by having a greater level of consistency of financial assets of households, which in the case of a negative shock, could act as a buffer. Given the acceleration of the tapering of the Fed, the country looks vulnerable to capital outflows from emerging markets. This occurred in 2013, which resulted in the value of the ringgit falling to approximately 10%.

Overall, Malaysia should be able to resist this risk of heightened volatility of short-term capital due to the strength of domestic demand, the economic rebalancing and the strength of the financial sector. It is also important to note that the central bank has a wide margin of foreign exchange reserves, which accounts for around 6 months of imports, representing more than twice the short-term debt and it is likely that this availability will maintain the confidence of investors in the country. This is evidenced by the gradual appreciation of the ringgit in the current year.

Policies to Amend the Economic Imbalances

In the future, Malaysia will continue to adopt austerity policies, which could be harmful to the growth of the economy over the medium term. For the first time since 2011, the central bank has raised interest rates because of the rapid growth the country has experienced as well as the high inflationary pressures, which have risen from 3.5 to 4%.

The Government have cutback heavily on grants and have introduced a tax on goods and services (GST, goods and services tax) from 2015. This will increase the Government's revenues.

Furthermore, Kuala Lumpur has had to face severe budgetary imbalances and heavy deficits which have persisted since 2008. These have also fueled the public debt. In fact, the aggressive fiscal policy adopted to stimulate domestic demand after the global crisis has ended up deteriorating the public finances of the country. As a result, Malaysia's fiscal debt is one of the worst in Southeast Asia.

The austerity budget, which has been created, will drastically impact the economy, especially due to the reduction of subsidies such as fuel, electricity, food and the introduction of the GST.

Consequently, the Government budget deficit is expected to gradually decline from a record low of 6.8% of GDP in 2013 to less than 5% in 2016. The public debt, which has reached a record level of 57% of GDP, is one of the highest in the region and is expected to decline. This means that the data will be monitored by investors who will want to ensure that fiscal consolidation is not rejected. The fact that the debt is mainly held by domestic investors as part of a deeper internal market for capital, mitigates the risks associated with currency crises or external financial shocks.

The Economic Transformation Plan (ETP) aims to improve the competitiveness of the country and has already yielded an increase in investment. The Government's restrictions on the exportation of commodities has dramatically reduced the surplus which started from 2011. The surplus declined from 11.6% of GDP to 4% of GDP. This is similar to the forecast predicted for the medium term. The ultimate objective of the Prime Minister is to transform Malaysia into a high-income country by 2020 moving it away from the upper-middle income category. The per capita GDP of Malaysia which exceeds USD 10,000, is significantly lower than that of neighboring countries, such as Taiwan.

Malaysia's economic diversification has not been successful. Its manufacturing must fight against strong regional competition, particularly in the electronics industry, which also attempts to achieve higher levels of income. The commodities sector contributes to the majority of trade growth. To improve the economic outlook and to avoid citizens getting stuck in an income trap, which threatens both Malaysia as neighboring Thailand, it is necessary to address the shortcomings in the areas of productivity and research and development. (R&D) To achieve this goal, there needs to be a larger pool of highly skilled workers and the service sector needs to be further developed. It is also important that the country improves their institutional and political framework. However, the new government's continuing reexamination of many large infrastructure projects approved by the previous administration creates uncertainty for foreign and domestic investors alike. The new government's decision to cancel or postpone investment projects is a tacit admission that the return on many public projects is low and will only add to the nation's indebtedness. It is thus highly likely that public investment will continue to slow in the coming years.

Overall, the outlook for medium-term growth still appears promising, due to several planned infrastructure projects, the attractiveness of the investment climate for foreigners and a favorable demographic profile. The success of the Malaysian economy will depend on the country taking full advantage of the resources that it has including its young working population, despite the decline in the fertility rate.

In addition, Malaysia has a thriving business environment, which is one of the best in Asia. This is mainly because Malaysia has a politically stable environment which acts as an incentive for business investment in this country. Furthermore, Malaysia has a strong rule of law, the country also has a flexible labor market, the economy is open and competitive and the country's infrastructure is sufficiently developed. It must, however, be noted that the main obstacle facing Malaysia is being able to attract more investment into the country.

MYANMAR

Official name

Republic of the Union of Myanmar

Capital

Naypyidaw

Area

676,578 sq. km

Population

54.3 mln

Languages

Burmese (official)

Main ethnic groups

Burman 68%, Shan 9%, Karen 7%

Main religions

Buddhist 88%, Christian 6%, Muslim 4%

Government type

Parliamentary Republic

Urbanization

30.6%

Life expectancy ratio

67 years

Fertility rate

2.1 children born/woman

Currency

Kyat MMK

Myanmar

Population, Location, Geography, Climate

Myanmar was previously known as the Republic of Burma before it won its independence from Great Britain in 1948. However, many foreign governments still refer to the country as Burma. The country is primarily agrarian and has a population of more than 54 million with 90% of people residing in rural areas. Myanmar's population density is 80.0 people/km^2. 27.5% of the population are under the age of 15 years, 67.5% of the population are between the ages of 15–65, which is the productive sector of the population, and 5% of the population are above the age of 65 + years. As a result, Myanmar's dependency ratio is relatively low.

The country's population consists of several ethnic communities, which can be traced back to three surges of migration. The first rise in migration occurred by the Hmon people which are currently referred to as Cambodian. The second was by the Mongol people from the Eastern Himalaya, and the third was by Thai people from Northern Thailand. As a result, there are now over 100 different countrywide groups living within the country's borders. The ethnic demographics are made up of 68% Bama or Myanmar, which are the majority group living in the central zone. 9% are Shan, 7% are Karen, 4% are Rakhine, 3% are Chinese, 2% are Indian, 2% are Mon and 5% are of other sub-groups, which live in mountainous regions closer to the borders or along the coast. The official language is Myanmar (Burmese), however many other dialects and languages are spoken throughout the country. However, within business environments, English is widely spoken. It is taught as a second language in Government schools.

Like in many other Asian economies, religion plays a large part in defining the local way of life. In Myanmar 89% of people practice the religion of Theravada Buddhism. The remaining 11% consist of Hindu's, Muslim's, Christian's and animists. Interestingly, the majority of Buddhists have some animist beliefs, including worship of nats (spirits) which are rationalized as being disciples of the Buddha. Local traditions such as removing socks and shoes before entering a religious building, must always be done as a sign of respect towards the religion.

Geographically speaking, Myanmar is the largest country in Southeast Asia, which has a total area of 678,500 km^2 (262,000 mi^2), and the 40th-largest in the world. Myanmar's population density on average has 76 people/km^2. The most densely populated region is Yangon, which was previously Myanmar's former capital, which has 716 people/km^2. Yangon also has the highest urban proportion of 70%.

The country is bordered by several countries, those of which include China, Laos, and Thailand in the east, Bangladesh and India in the north and the Indian Ocean in the west and south. Its shape can be described as roughly diamond with a long southeastern 'tail' and extends 925 km from east to west and 2100 km from north to south. Southern Myanmar consists of the western slopes of the Bilauktaung Range. Northern Myanmar covers majority of the country's area and consists largely of the broad river valley called the Irrawaddy. The river is Myanmar's main river artery and often referred to the Ayerawady. It starts high up in the Himalayas and runs down mountains in northern Myanmar before spreading out into one of the largest river deltas in Asia on the south coast. Both of Myanmar's main cities, Rangoon and Mandalay are located along the river Irrawaddy. North of the delta lies the Irrawaddy basin and the arid plains of central Myanmar, which are protected by a horseshoe of mountains rising to over 3000 m. To the west are the Arakan mountains and the Kachin Hills are to the north; to the east lies the Shan Plateau. The Kachin range includes Southeast Asia's highest mountain, Hkakabo Razi which reaches 5881 m.

Myanmar lies in the monsoon region of Asia, which has three main seasons. The hottest period is between February and May, when there is little or no rain, and temperatures can rise above 40 °C (104 °F). The rainy season is generally from May to October, the dry, cooler weather occurs from October to February. The coast and the mountains have significantly more rainfall than the arid central plains, receiving over 5000 mm (196.9 in) of rain annually. Annual rainfall in the delta region is approximately 2500 mm (98.4 in), while the average annual rainfall in the Dry Zone, which is in central Myanmar, is less than 1000 mm (39.4 in).

Majority of Myanmar's land is covered by subtropical forest; however, this has been significantly reduced by extensive logging for teak. Myanmar's fertile land is crossed by several rivers that are used for transportation, irrigation and as a source of food. Myanmar's top natural resources include arable land, forestry, minerals, natural gas, freshwater and marine resources, gems and jade. Mining, which is extremely widespread in Myanmar, have produced some of the world's finest rubies and imperial jades. The country's natural resources also include flora and fauna, rare birds and butterflies, many of which are protected by Myanmar's system of national parks and wildlife sanctuaries.

Internal Policy

Since Myanmar's independence the country is governed as a parliamentary system. The chief of state includes the President and two vice-presidents. The President is the head of Government who is elected by the Parliament from three Vice Presidents. Each Vice President is nominated by the upper house, lower house and military members of Parliament. The cabinet members are appointed by the President and only formally ratified by parliament. Following the start of the new Government, the number of ministries has been reduced from 36 to 21. Both the president and the cabinet can only be removed through conducting unlawful activity. This structure and system of the government is stated in Myanmar's constitution, which has been its third since its independence in 2008 after the country's referendum.

The parliament has a two-tier legislature called the Pyidaungsu Hluttaw. The two-tier structure is made up of two houses. The upper house also called Amyotha Hluttaw (House of Nationalities) sits 224 members, 168 of which are directly elected and 56 are appointed by the Burmese Armed Forces. The lower house also called Pyithu Hluttaw (House of Representatives) sits 440-seat members, of which 330 are directly elected and 110 are appointed by the military.

In the executive branch, the President is accountable to the legislature. A small number of legislators are appointed by the military, and others are elected in general elections.

In the judiciary branch, a mixed legal system of common and customary law is in place. It is interesting to note that the president, two vice presidents, and speaker of the lower and upper houses of parliament were all former military officers. As a result, this has led to numerous concerns about continued military dominance.

International Relations

International relations between Myanmar and other world countries have been shaky. However, due to the formation of a new Government in 2015 and the transition of the country to become a market orientated economy in which many reforms have taken place. Myanmar has become increasingly integrated into the world economy and global powers have begun to re-establish ties with Myanmar.

For example, the United States, lifted its sanctions on the county. Furthermore, President Obama's visit to Yangon in November 2012 and President Thein Sein's visit to Washington in May 2013 has led to an enhanced relationship between the U.S. and Myanmar. Additionally, the European Union, Australia, and Japan have all dropped some of their economic sanctions on the country.

Myanmar is a member of a number of organizations, which is beneficial for the country's economy. For example, in 2014, Myanmar acted as the rotating chair of ASEAN for the first time after joining ASEAN in 17 years. As a member of ASEAN, Myanmar is involved in a number of partnerships. This includes The ASEAN-China Free Trade Agreement, under which a zero—tariff market took effect in 2010 and the ASEAN-Korea Framework Agreement on Comprehensive Economic Cooperation, under which tariffs on 90% of the products were eliminated from 1 January 2009. Myanmar is also a part of the Asian Development Bank (ADB) which it joined in 1973.

Myanmar's relationships seem to be the most thriving with other South East Asian Economies due to the close economic and political ties. For example, most of Myanmar's partnerships are with its neighbors. These partnerships are for major projects within sectors such as oil and gas, power, transport, manufacturing, telecoms, real estate, mining, tourism and hospitality, industrial estate, livestock, healthcare, agriculture, consumer retail, technologies and banking and finance.

It must however be noted that although Western countries have welcomed Myanmar's transition towards a democratic society, the country's continued oppression of the Rohingya Muslims, has led to an outcry from the international community, with many foreign Governments condemning the acts and the United Nations Refugee Agency arguing that the Rohingya are victims of "crimes against humanity". This of course, is damaging Myanmar's international reputation and may dampen Myanmar's democratic transition. Myanmar's neighbors have also condemned the acts.

Economy

Macroeconomic Overview

Myanmar's economic development has been hindered by political instability and social obstruction. As a result, social, political and economic reform has been slow, which has led to a slow transition towards a democratic society.

Myanmar has effectively improved its involvement in regional and global activities and has established trading relationships with various partners such as the Asian Development Bank, ASEAN group and the World Bank. Since the Government's transition, several multinational companies have shown interest in investing in the country. Myanmar received its highest level of Foreign Direct Investment (FDI) in 2015/16 for approximately USD 9.4 billion. In March 2015, the government announced that FDI hit more than $8 billion, which was twenty-five times the amount received the year before the military gave up power in 2010.

	Unit	2000A	2018	2020F
GDP, current prices	USD (billions)	10.26	68.56	71.40
GDP per capita, current prices	USD	221.19	1297.67	1337.69
GDP based on PPP per capita	Current International dollar	1198.53	6511.29	7598.00

Source IMF Outlook (2019)

This upsurge in investment can also be attributed to Myanmar's economic reforms. Examples are establishing a managed float of the Burmese kyat in 2012, re-writing the Foreign Investment Law in 2012 to allow more foreign investment participation, granting the Central Bank operational independence in July 2013, enacting a new Anti-Corruption Law in September 2013, and granting licenses to operate to nine foreign banks in 2014 and four more foreign banks in 2016.

The most receiving sectors of FDI are energy, garment, information technology, and food and beverages sectors. FDI is also expected to increase due to factors such as Myanmar's abundant natural resources and young labor force. Despite this positive increase in FDI, Myanmar still receives significantly less investment than its Asian neighbors.

Structure of output (% GDP)	2000	2005	2010	2015	2018
Agriculture	57.2	46.7	36.8	26.8	23.3
Industry	9.7	17.5	26.5	34.5	36.3
Services	33.1	35.8	36.7	38.8	40.4

Source Asian Development Bank (ADB, 2019)

Myanmar has had a truly remarkable growth rate during the last decade. Myanmar's growth rate averaged 6.4% in 2019, which is one of the highest growth rates in South East Asia, despite the country's inflation rate of 8%. This was however a contraction in growth from the 8.5% growth rate achieved in 2015. The reduced growth was a result of a supply shock from heavy flooding, a slowdown in new investment during an election year, and a more challenging external environment. This external environment included lower commodity prices which ultimately affected Myanmar's main exports.

Myanmar's economy has become increasingly diversified. The most important sector of the economy is services, which has been growing steadily in the last few years, and now accounts for over 38% of GDP. The share of agriculture in the economy has been declining, and now represents only 36% of GDP. The industry sector contributes the remaining 26% of GDP.

Myanmar exports several products, which has revealed a comparative advantage to economies its size. As a result, the country's share of global exports is larger than what would be expected from the size of its export economy and from the size of its product's global market. Myanmar's top exports include Petroleum, Gas and Dried Legumes, which represents 37.7 and 8.89% of the total exports of Myanmar respectively. Despite Myanmar's progress in exporting, the country has a negative trade balance due to a substantial amount of imports needed for its investment projects and sustained consumption. Myanmar's trade balance was negatively affected by the decline of oil prices in 2015, which negatively influenced its exports.

The country's main exporting and importing countries are all from Asia, which may be due to the close economic and political ties. Myanmar's top exporting partners are China, Thailand, Singapore and India. They are also Myanmar's top importing partners as well as Japan. During the last five years the imports of Myanmar have increased at a rate of 28%. Myanmar's main import is Refined Petroleum which represents 9.3% of the total imports of Myanmar.

Myanmar's key sectors include the manufacturing, power, transport, agriculture, and tourism industries. Agriculture is the main industry in Myanmar, employing approximately 60% of the labor force. The country previously claimed the status of being Asia's largest exporter of rice, nevertheless rice continues to remain the country's most crucial agricultural commodity. Other main crops include beans, groundnuts and sugarcane. Unfortunately, Myanmar is extremely vulnerable to bad weather, which has a detrimental impact on the agricultural sector. The country experienced heavy monsoonal rains and flooding in both 2015 and 2016, which has caused growth to contract in the agricultural sector. The flooding combined with a slowdown in new investment flows and a more challenging external environment have all contributed to the slower rate of growth.

Tourist arrivals have had a positive impact on the country, especially since Myanmar's transition and its willingness to improve its relationship Western countries. Tourist arrivals hit 6 million in 2016, and the value is continuing to increase. Over 2.84 million tourists visited Myanmar till at the end of October 2018 and the number of tourists' arrivals in that period is increased a little more than one per cent of the tourists' arrival in the same period last year, according to the

Ministry of Hotel and Tourism. The Ministry of Hotels and Tourism expects this to rise to 7.5 million by 2020. Myanmar's garment sector is also improving due to factors such as lower labor costs. In 2012, Thailand's largest garment manufacturers announced that they would move production to Myanmar, specifically due to lower labor costs. Cheaper labor costs in Myanmar compared to its neighbors have been a contributing factor to the country receiving an increase in FDI.

Despite these factors, Myanmar is still one of Asia's poorest countries with approximately 26% of the population still living in poverty and over half of Myanmar's population do not have access to electricity. Myanmar must do more to develop its economy and increase its economic growth. This should include focusing on macroeconomic policies that has a focus on fiscal stability and avoiding unsustainable budget deficits.

Structure of expenditure (% GDP)	2000	2005	2010	2015	2018
Final consumption	87.7	86.9	67.3	74.0	71.3
Gross capital formation	12.4	13.2	23.2	34.8	34.1
Exports of goods and services	0.5	0.2	19.6	17.4	20.0
Imports of goods and services	0.6	0.1	15.1	27.9	28.0
Statistical discrepancy	0.0	−0.2	5.0	1.8	2.7

Source Asian Development Bank (ADB, 2019)

Economic Policy

Economic Policy in Myanmar before its transition towards a democratic society was aimed at isolating itself from the rest of the world. This included the use of a type of central planning, which was rather inefficient to its earlier status as an agrarian society. Although these policies were ended over a decade ago, there are still signs of the old system in place.

Due to the interlinking nature of the economic, political, and social aspect of the economy, economic policy reform is likely to change in correlation with political and social reform to achieve liberalization and stability. This is evidenced by the transformation of Thein Sein's parliament, in which the country has attempted to become increasingly integrated into the world economy. The Government's economic policy lays its foundation on developing a market-orientated system and establishing an economic framework in support of national reconciliation. The Government led several economic reforms, including the pardon for most political prisoners, relaxation of censorship, establishment of the National Human Rights Commission, and efforts toward peace with ethnic rebel groups.

The government is also seeking to reform economic policy to ensure that natural resource extraction is transparent and sustainable and will extend the Extractive Industries Transparency Initiative to include the mining industry. The Government has also shown a commitment to support competition in the private sector. This can be shown by removing bureaucracy, expanding access to credit and limiting monopolies. Strengthening public financial management and work on fiscal and macroeconomic stability is also an economic policy reform priority. This includes making public spending more efficient, improving budget transparency and privatizing suitable state-owned enterprises that act as a constraint on the Government's budget.

It must be stated that economic policy reform in policies and laws for land management, environmental protection, decentralization, and urban planning and development are limited.

Banking System

The financial sector of Myanmar is made up of the Central Bank of Myanmar (CBM), the newly formed Ministry of Planning and Finance, state owned banks, private banks, finance companies, branches and representative offices of foreign banks, Yangon Stock Exchange (YSX), Securities Exchange Commission of Myanmar (SECM), securities companies and insurance companies.

The bank system in Myanmar includes: 9 semi-state-owned banks, 11 private banks and 33 foreign bank representative offices and 863 bank branches. Myanmar's banking sector has struggled to recover from the 2003 banking crisis, as a result the banking sector is lagging behind neighboring countries. The banks have been limited in their availability of banking credit due to the very small deposit base and conservative lending approach. For example, there is a cap of 13% per annum on lending rates, average deposit rates are very close to the specified minimum of 8%.

In 2014, the Central Bank of Myanmar (CBM) granted nine foreign banks their first operating licenses, specifically aimed at liberalizing Myanmar's banking sector. These licenses allow the banks to participate in services which were previously restricted in the country like providing credit to foreign companies and local banking institutions.

To open a bank account with the Myanmar Government or private banks the investor is required to forward money from the foreign country to a Myanmar bank in a "suspense account" intention to company name with the description of the "capital brought into Myanmar". After the bank receives the remittance money, the bank will issue a "credit note" concern with remittance money. The investor is required to submit a copy of the credit advice in order to submit the forms of the company required. When the investor has submitted the necessary forms, the investor can open a bank account with the name of the company. Then, the investor is then required to apply to the bank to transfer the money from Myanmar Bank's suspense account to the investor's company account.

The Kyat is Myanmar's official currency. The import and export of local currency is prohibited. The US dollar is widely used throughout the country, as an alternative, particularly for larger purchases. In general, if companies in Myanmar want to deal with foreign exchange in relation to borrowing abroad, repaying necessary interest, making payments abroad, opening accounts in foreign banks abroad and the remittance of profits, they must obtain permission from the Foreign Exchange Management Board (FEMB).

Investment Area

The investment area in Myanmar has been hugely influenced by the political nature of the economy. The country has undergone a smooth and peaceful political transition into 2016. Also, Investor confidence has increased, which has been evidenced by an increase in FDI, which quadrupled from USD 1.9 billion in 2011/12 to USD 8.1 billion in 2014/15, and it is still growing up.

The substantial increase of FDI can also be attributed to the Development of three Special Economic Zones (SEZ), which all opened in 2015. The first zone to open was Thilawa, which is a Myanmar-Japan consortium. The second SEZ is Dawei, is a consortium formed by Italian-Thai Development, Rojana Industrial Park, the Myanmar government as well as the Japanese Government. The third is Kyaukphyu, which is in Rakhine State, in which China's conglomerate CITIC will hold an 85% stake in the SEZ.

The lifting of sanctions by the European Union and the United States has also led to an increase in investment in Myanmar. Specifically, the 1996 ban on entry visas to the former Myanmar's military rulers, their business partners, and immediate families was lifted by President Obama in 2013. Myanmar has also benefited from being readmitted to the EU's Generalised System of Preferences to benefit from lower duties on exports. Furthermore, as Myanmar is a member of the ASEAN Free Trade Area (AFTA), the country benefit from the elimination of tariff barriers among ASEAN countries.

The introduction of the Myanmar Foreign Investment Law (MFIL) in November 2012, has led to an improved regulatory environment for foreign investors across various sectors, increasing investor confidence. A new draft of the Myanmar Investment Law (MIL) is being put in place, which demonstrates the government's commitment in supporting direct investments. The establishment of the Yangon Stock Exchange, with the first share traded in March 2016, has also led to improved local businesses' access to capital markets.

In 2019, the top four investors in the country were all Asian countries. This include Singapore, China, Thailand and Hong Kong. At a meeting on streamlining investment in Nay Pyi Taw last week, U Aung Naing Oo, the ministry's permanent secretary underlined that the top investor in Myanmar through December 2018 was China, but Singapore has overtaken it since January. U Aung Naing Oo said that some investors from Singapore may not be Singaporean but are based in the island-nation. Many companies investing in Myanmar from Singapore are multinationals that set up regional headquarters in the Lion City. The UK, the Netherlands, France, Canada, and the United States are the only countries outside of Asia who are in the top 10 of foreign investors in the country. The heavy investment of Asian countries may be due to the close economic and political links that exists between the countries.

The main sectors receiving the largest amount of investment include oil and gas and infrastructure (including power plants, transport, and telecommunications) which obtains 35% and 31% of investment respectively. The sectors receiving the smallest amount of investment include industrial estate and construction which receives 0.32% and 0.06% respectively.

The reform for foreign investment is the Foreign Investment Law ("FIL"), approved in November 2012 by President Thein Sein. The key guarantees and incentives are as follows:

- foreign investors are permitted to own 100% of businesses which are not in the restricted or prohibited lists;
- businesses set up under the FIL enjoy an initial 5-year tax holiday;
- foreign investors may lease land for their business;
- repatriation of profits after taxes and relevant funds is allowed through banks prescribed by the Myanmar Investment Commission ("MIC") in the relevant foreign currency and at the prevailing official exchange rate. Further approval for repatriation is required from the Central Bank of Myanmar.

The stated objectives of the 2012 Foreign Investment Law are to support:

- the extraction/export of the rich natural resources of the state for the benefit of the people;
- the creation and accumulation of jobs for the people;
- the development of human resources;
- the development of infrastructures like banking and finance, modern roads, interstate highways, production of electricity and energy, and modern information technology;
- transportation of rail, water and air via an international standard to enable citizens to do business throughout the world; and
- the advent of businesses and investments which are in line with established international practices and norms.

There are two steps companies can go about investing in Myanmar. The first includes the MIC route with a permit. This is regulated under the Foreign Investment Law, Reserved sectors/industrial, Long-term lease, Import licence, Tax incentives/guarantees, and a minimum capital requirement. The foreign investor must invest a minimum capital between approximately USD 50,000 to USD 167,000, depending on the type of business activity.

The second is by the Companies Registration Office (CRO) route (without MIC Permit), which is under the companies act, service companies/branches, one-year lease, no import license, no tax incentives/guarantees, minimum capital requirement.

Domestic Market

Myanmar's domestic investments are highly concentrated within the manufacturing, real estate, transport and tourism. Following the successful political transition, the Ministry of Hotel and Tourism foresees that the number of foreign visitors will continue to grow up during next years. In addition, domestic investments will continue to play an important role in both real estate development and infrastructural improvement. Other domestic markets may also see growth as other destinations in Myanmar open to tourism and new business opportunities.

The Myanmar government's program to privatize state-owned enterprises (SOEs) started in 2010 and provides another source for domestic investments. For example, in 2013, local conglomerate KBZ Group announced its intention to take full control of Myanmar Airways International (MAI) by buying the remaining 20% stake from the government.

In 2012, partial lifting of sanctions imposed by the United States and the European Union has also benefited the economy. Furthermore, customs duties have been reduced, and there are few non-tariff trade barriers. Import licenses have been partially abolished and taxes on exports decreased.

Consumption in the agricultural sector is expected to rise due to increased consumer and animal feed demand. Domestic corn consumption is expected to grow in 2016/17 in line with the growth of Myanmar's livestock industries, especially poultry. The key players in the domestic wheat industry are the U Kyu Family Group, Capital Diamond Star and Htun Myittar companies, which together have a 90% share of the Myanmar wheat market. However, local wheat production is still expected to be insufficient to meet domestic demand. As a result, it is likely that Myanmar will have to rely on imports to meet its growing domestic consumption. Strong export demand, particularly from India and China, led domestic prices for all types of beans and pulses to increase sharply in 2020.

Since Myanmar opened its economy to the outside world, Myanmar has seen large growth due to internet penetration and mobile phone adoption. Within the country the mobile phone penetration rate has now reached around 50% of its estimated 54 million population last year. A report in 2015 by the telecom equipment supplier Ericsson suggested that 6% of the world's new mobile subscribers came from Myanmar, which would make the country the fourth fastest-growing mobile market in the world.

External trade (USD millions)	2000	2005	2010	2015	2018
Exports, fob	1756	3836	8872	11,432	16,672
Imports, cif	2407	1934	4866	16,743	19,345
Trade balance	−651	1902	4006	−5311	−2673

Source Asian Development Bank (ADB, 2019)

Main commercial partners (USD millions)	2000	2005	2010	2015	2018
Exports					
1. China, People's Rep. of	113	249	874	4831	4763
2. Thailand	233	1623	2590	3359	3233
3. Singapore	678	695	276	670	1275
4. India	200	471	958	1014	430.6
5. Japan	85	145	215	487	1122

(continued)

(continued)

Main commercial partners (USD millions)	2000	2005	2010	2015	2018
6. Korea, Rep. of	20	49	125	293	335
7. Germany	–	–	–	79	538
8. Hong Kong, China	81	183	1612	314	148
9. Malaysia	60	115	163	186	224
10. United States	489	2	2	69	376
Imports					
1. China, People's Rep. of	310	616	1128	6432	7225
3. Thailand	343	338	473	3659	2294
2. Singapore	683	712	1122	1957	3412
4. Japan	304	117	219	1534	901
8. Korea, Rep. of	306	105	252	474	482
6. Malaysia	407	199	134	530	1021
5. India	73	126	164	587	1045
8. Indonesia	74	176	203	412	706
10. Viet Nam	5	42	38	103	499
9. United States	75	11	25	269	727

Source Asian Development Bank (ADB, 2019)

Finance and Taxation

Tax

There are 15 types of taxes and duties in Myanmar, which are: Taxes levied on domestic production and public consumption, taxes levied on income and ownership, customs duties, and taxes levied on utility of State-owned properties.

Taxpayers are classified as resident or non-resident companies. A resident company is defined as a company formed under the Myanmar Companies Act or any other existing law of Myanmar. Resident companies are taxed on a worldwide basis, and as such, income from sources outside of Myanmar is taxable. A resident is somebody who has lived in the country for 183 days during the income year. Individuals working for Myanmar Foreign Investment Law (MFIL) companies are treated as foreign residents, regardless of their period of stay in Myanmar. A Non-resident Company (NRC) is defined as a company that is not formed under the Myanmar Companies Act or any other existing law of Myanmar. This includes the majority of foreign companies.

Companies registered under the MFIL are treated as resident companies. Resident companies are taxed on their worldwide income. However, resident companies registered under MFIL are not taxed on foreign income. NRC's are taxed only on income derived from sources within Myanmar. Income received from any capital assets within Myanmar and from any source of income within Myanmar is income received within Myanmar. The income is generally subject to tax under the normal rules for residents, except that different tax rates apply.

Corporate taxable income includes any income from a business, profession, property, other sources, and income that was not assessed, as well as capital gains. Taxable income is calculated after deduction of allowable expenses and depreciation.

Corporate tax rate is 25% for all enterprises that do not benefit from tax incentives. This applies for the companies under the Myanmar companies, companies under the MFIL, foreign organizations that operate under state sponsored projects or enterprises and a branch of a foreign company. A 2% advance corporate income tax is levied on the import and exports of goods.

Companies registered under the Myanmar Foreign Investment Law can be granted a wide range of tax incentives, including all of the following:

- Tax holiday from corporate income tax of 5 years or more for enterprises engaged in the production of goods or services.
- Tax exemption for profits maintained in a reserve fund and reinvested within 1 year.
- Accelerated depreciation on certain assets.
- Customs duty relief and/or exemption for certain imports.
- Deductions for certain research and development expenditure.
- Relief from income-tax up to 50% on the profits for goods produced and exported.

Further incentives can be received for foreign investors carrying out business in one of the Special Economic Zones.

Personal Taxation

The personal taxation rates follow a progressive tax system from 0 to 25%. The following rates are:

- Income from salary (Progressive rate from 0 to 25%).
- Income that escaped assessment (Progressive rate from 15 to 30%).
- Other income (0 to 25%).
- Capital Gains (10%).

No tax is payable if total income under salaries does not exceed MMK 4,800,000 in a year. Employers are required to withhold income tax from employees' salaries, with the tax being payable to the tax authority in monthly instalments.

For an individual, the taxable period of a company is the same as its financial year (income year), which is from 1 April to 31 March. Income earned during the financial year is assessed to tax in the assessment year, which is the year following the financial year. Income tax returns must be filed within three months from the end of the income year. Tax returns for capital gains must be filed within one month from the date of disposal of the capital assets.

Myanmar does not levy a VAT. However commercial tax is levied as a turnover tax on goods and services. The commercial tax applies to all service transactions, unless the transactions are listed as exempt. The rate may be 5% or may range between 5 and 120%, depending on the types of products and services.

Commercial tax registration applies only for Myanmar resident entities. Registration for commercial tax is required when the amount of income from sales and services for an income year is MMK 20 million or more. Commercial tax returns are submitted on a quarterly basis on 30th April, 31st July, 31st October and 31st January, and the payment for commercial tax is due by the 10th day of the following month.

Customs duty is levied at rates ranging from 0 to 40%. Companies registered under the MFIL and which have obtained permits from the MIC may, at the discretion of the MIC, be given relief from customs duty depending on certain items. This includes but are not limited to items such as: machinery, equipment and instruments, materials for the first three years of commercial production. Special Goods Tax Law is imposed on a number of goods, which include but are not limited to: cigarettes, tobacco leaves and alcoholic beverages. The tax rates range from 5 to 120%.

Myanmar has also negotiated a number of Double Taxation Avoidance (DTA's) with countries, all of which are Asian countries except from the United Kingdom.

Tax rate	%
Corporate tax	25
Personal income tax	25
Sales tax	5

Source Trading Economics (2019)

Audit and Accounting

Myanmar has adopted International Financial Reporting Standards (IFRS) for all publicly accountable entities. Those standards are known as Myanmar Financial Reporting Standards (MFRSs). In addition, audited financial statements must be filed with the corporate income tax return within 3 months from the fiscal year.

The Myanmar Accounting Council (MAC) is formed under the Myanmar Accountancy Council Law, which is renewed every four years. The MAC is responsible for setting the rules for accounting standards, auditing standards and ethical standards for practicing accountants in Myanmar. The MAC sets the criteria required to qualify as an auditor, requiring that all auditors be either a Certified Public Accountant (CPA) or hold an accountancy certificate or degree conferred by any foreign country recognized by the Myanmar Accountancy Council. Additionally, auditors had to be citizens of Myanmar and registered with the MAC to obtain a Certificate of Practice.

The following types of entities use Myanmar Accounting Standards:

- Public companies.
- Securities companies.
- Companies whose securities trade in an over-the-counter market.
- Stock exchanges.
- Persons who serve as a responsible person, member, staff and agent of the above categories.
- Entities that hold a license as a lawyer or auditor, or agent of such license-holder.

Companies in Myanmar must appoint one or more auditors, and the first auditor may be appointed by the company's directors. Subsequent auditors may be appointed by the shareholders at the annual general meeting. The directors of a company are required to submit a set of audited financial statements at each annual general meeting. A company is required to hold its first annual general meeting no later than 18 months from the date of its incorporation, and in subsequent periods at intervals of no more than 15 months but shall not exceed its calendar year.

Risk Assessment

Economic growth contracted in 2015/16 due to bad weather and a slow-down in investment due to uncertainty from the recent political transition, ongoing structural changes, short-term exchange rate pressures and rising inflation, which peaked at 16% in October 2015. Myanmar still however remains a fast-growing economy with GDP growth at 7% in 2015/16. The future growth forecasts for the country, remain positive with growth expected to reach 8–9% over the next 5 years. This growth will largely be driven by a rise in FDI within the industrial estates, energy and transport industries. Public-private partnerships (PPI) will be vital in the development of many projects. Sustaining this economic growth will rely on the country's young labor force, and the country's willingness to further integrate into regional and international activities. Myanmar also has to take advantage of its strategic location in between the world's fastest emerging economies.

Myanmar ranks 137 out of 144 in terms of its global competitiveness ranking, which is significantly lower than the rest of its South East Asian neighbors. The World Bank's Myanmar Economic Monitor found that exports declined by 12% in nominal terms in the first three quarters of 2015/16 compared to the same period last year due to the agriculture supply shock and declining commodity prices. This contributed to a growing trade deficit that has put pressure on the exchange rate. In an effort to boost trade, Myanmar has introduced cuts to trading taxes since 2013.

Myanmar recorded a trade deficit of 1.05 billion USD in June 2019. Myanmar's standing on the Ease of Doing Business ranking has slightly improved to 170th in 2016 (from 171st). Investment opportunities are also expanding in sectors such as tourism and telecommunications. Businesses operating in Myanmar however still face major challenges due to the underdevelopment of a legal and regulatory system, recurring natural disasters and underdeveloped infrastructure such as weak transportation links.

The most significant risks affecting the country are both economic and political. The disputes arising from the Government and the Rohingya community who are no longer classified as a citizen of Myanmar must prove their family has lived in Myanmar for at least 60 years to qualify for citizenship or they face the risk or being put in detention camps and face deportation. The risks associated with the role of the military in domestic affairs and the government's treatment of ethnic minorities, will surely influence the progress of the economy. Furthermore, the political tensions towards China because of China's strong presence in the country acts as a threat towards the Myanmar's development.

Economic Risks

Myanmar faces significant economic challenges. According to a recent report by the International Monetary Fund (IMF) the country's macroeconomic imbalances persist, inflation remains high, the fiscal deficit has increased significantly, and the external current account deficit continues to widen. Furthermore, the country is at risk of overheating.

"Therefore, safeguarding macroeconomic stability remains a top priority, which means bringing down inflation, strengthening Myanmar's external position, and fortifying the banking system" states International Monetary Fund (IMF) staff team led by Yongzheng Yang. "The fiscal deficit needs to be kept in check, monetary conditions tightened, and the exchange rate allowed to move more flexibly in line with market conditions. Phasing out central bank financing of fiscal deficits is a priority. To safeguard financial stability and improve financial inclusion, prudential regulations should be issued soon, and state-owned banks reformed to reduce risks to public finance and the financial system."

It must be stated that Myanmar's increasingly integrated relationship into the world economy can also have a negative impact on the economy. This is because the country will be exposed to external shocks, which can restrain growth. However, policies such as a stable financial system can be put in place to protect the economy from external shocks.

Despite these economic challenges many Economists argue that if Myanmar's economy continues to have a high level of labor productivity growth, improves its use of capital, innovates, and gains operational efficiency through increased competition, then the size of the economy could quadruple by 2030.

"For much of the twentieth century, Myanmar largely missed out on the spectacular growth seen across most of the global economy and most recently in its Asian peers. It now has the potential to be one of the fastest-growing economies in emerging Asia," said Richard Dobbs, a director of McKinsey & Company and MGI.

"To support this higher growth rate, Myanmar has to get all the fundamentals right—political and macroeconomic stability, the rule of law, and enablers such as skills and infrastructure," according to the report by Mckinsey Global Institute.

BMI research states that "Myanmar remains a very high-risk location for investment despite generating much investor interest due to its economic potential. Foreign businesses must be aware that, in order to reap the rewards of the country's largely untapped market, they must navigate a series of severe operational risks, largely stemming from an underdeveloped logistics network, a weak rule of law, an unclear environment for foreign direct investment and numerous layers of red tape. Myanmar remains one of the world's least developed states, and essential investment in infrastructure and education, as well as an improvement in political stability and security, will take many years to achieve. Investors must therefore be prepared to hedge against substantial risks when considering Myanmar as a base for investment".

Political Risk

Myanmar's political shift has not been a smooth and easy road. It has been hindered by violence issues like ethnic differences existing throughout the country. In October 2015, a nationwide cease-fire was signed by the Government between eight armed ethnic groups. Many policymakers however argue that this agreement didn't coincide with expectations as no agreement was forged between the fifteen participating rebel groups. Joshua Kurlantzick, CFR Senior Fellow for Southeast Asia states that any future conflict between the army and the larger armed ethnic groups "would be disastrous for Myanmar's nascent political reforms."

One of the central political problems in Myanmar is that Rohingya Muslims, living in Rakhine State, Burma's main group of stateless people; however, the Myanmar Government does not recognize the Rohingya as a "national race" and stripped them of their citizenship under the 1982 Citizenship Law, categorizing them as "non-national" or "foreign residents"; under the Rakhine State Action Plan drafted in October 2014. According to a United Nations refugee agency, the Myanmar military and border police are "engaging in collective punishment of the Rohingya minority", yet the Myanmar government denies the allegations.

The Office of the United Nations High Commissioner for Human Rights stated in November 2016 that "Protection of civilians and unfettered humanitarian access to conflict affected areas is critical," underscored the UN rights chief. "Measures that may heighten the vulnerability or pose threats to the safety and security of internally displaced people—such as requiring internally displaced persons (IDPs) to cross conflict lines—must be avoided," he added. The UN rights Office also stressed that the authorities must respect international humanitarian law and the rights of IDPs, pointing out that continued failure to do so would draw a sharp response from the international community.

A senior United Nations official accused Myanmar of seeking to ethnically cleanse the country of its Muslim minority, as Bangladesh stepped up border patrols as constant discrimination and current persecution have forced many Rohingya to flee from their homes to camps in Bangladesh. Bangladesh has also formally requested that Myanmar make efforts to "ensure the integrity of its border" through the ambassador's office.

The United Nations Special Adviser on the Prevention of Genocide, Adama Dieng however states that the new Government of Myanmar "needs to demonstrate its commitment to the rule of law and to the human rights of all its populations. It cannot expect that such serious allegations are ignored or go unscrutinised. Wherever and whenever these types of allegations are reported in the world, it is the duty of the international community to remind States of their responsibilities to their populations and their obligations under international law. Myanmar is no exception." Adama Dieng also advised the Government of Bangladesh not to close its borders to refugees fleeing Myanmar. "Closing the border, deporting refugees or failing to provide assistance, exposes these populations to further violence that could, in the worst case, constitute international crimes".

Political tension inside the country has a negative knock on effect in other areas of the economy such as investment. However, Myanmar's political disputes with other countries are just as damaging to the economy. Political reforms are taking place within the country, however the political reforms that will be brought into effect will only be successful if they are combined with economic reforms.

Corruption Risk

Corruption in Myanmar is widespread like many of its South East Asian neighbors. The Government has pursued several anti-corruption initiatives such as the introduction of The Anti-Corruption Law in 2013 (ACL). This law prohibits public sector bribery, abuse of office and attempted corruption. The law, states that the maximum punishment for corruption is fifteen years imprisonment and a fine. Furthermore, in 2006, Myanmar was removed from the International Financial Action Task Force's (FATF) list of "Non-cooperative Countries and Territories" with its implementation of controls in accordance with the IMF's Anti-money Laundering/Combating and Financing of Terrorism guidelines (AML/CFT).

It must be noted that many officials have been prosecuted for corruption, the most recent case occurred in 2015, when two major judges were dismissed for participating in illegal activity. As a result, corruption and the prosecution of abuses of major officials are gaining attention and therefore, should act as a deterrent against officials participating in corruption practices.

Corruption in Myanmar's is ultimately due to the country's lack of a transparent regulatory and legal framework. This has caused the country to suffer from environmental corruption in the Mekong River Basin such as logging in conservation zones. Furthermore, Myanmar's multiple exchange rates and currencies also make conversion and repatriation of foreign exchange very complex, and easy for corruption.

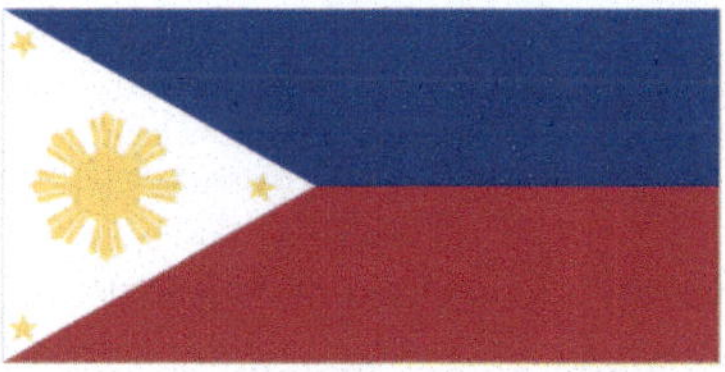

PHILIPPINES

Official name
Republic of the Philippines

Capital
Manila

Area
300,000 sq. km

Population
106.6 mln

Languages
Filipino Tagalog (official), English (official)

Main ethnic groups
Tagalog 28%, Cebuano 13%, Ilocano 9%

Main religions
Catholic 83%, Muslim 5%

Government type
Presidential Republic

Urbanization
51.2%

Life expectancy ratio
70 years

Fertility rate
2.8 children born/woman

Currency
Peso PHP

Philippines

Country Introduction

Population, Location, Geography, Climate

The Philippines officially known as The Republic of the Philippines is in Southeast Asia and is one of the world's largest English-speaking nations. It is the 12th most populated country with approximately 106 million people. Almost 60% of the population are below 29 years old, about 62.1% of the population are between the ages of 15–64 years old and those below the ages of 14 years and older than 65 years old add up to 37.6% of the population.

The capital city is Manila, which has a population of approximately 1,780,000 citizens, this accounts for 2% of the Philippines' total population. The most populated city is Quezon City which has 2,936,000 citizens. Caloocan is also an extremely populated city, which has 1,490,000 citizens, which means 22.71 million people are in an area of about 1500 km^2. This is larger than the national capital region.

Many Philippine citizens are of Malay-Polynesian origin, although there are also many other ethnic groups. This consists of Tagalog (28%), Cebuani (13%), and Ilocani (9%). Furthermore, there are over a hundred tribal groups, which comprise less than 3% of citizens. These are in the mountainous areas.

Interestingly, the Philippines is the only predominantly Christian country in Asia. Much of the population practice the Catholic religion (81%). This is followed by Protestants or members of other Christian denominations (12%), Muslims (5%) and Buddhists (2%). The majority of Philippine's are bilingual, speaking English and Filipino. However, there are around 168 dialects or native languages like Ilocano or Cebuano. Furthermore, a small percentage of the population speaks Chinese or Spanish.

The Philippines is divided into 17 regions. There are two special regions: The Capital District and the Autonomous Region in Muslim Mindanao. The urbanization rate is 49% with an even distribution between urban and rural population at the country level. However, some islands can be more urbanized than others. The country is an island and borders China, Indonesia, Japan, Malaysia, Taiwan, Vietnam and Palau by sea. The country is located around 800 km from the Asia mainland and is one of the largest archipelagos in the world. The archipelago, which extends 1770 km north to south, is roughly triangular. There are 7107 islands (to be precise) of which nearly 4000 do not have an official name and eleven islands constitute over 90% of the total land area.

The country's coastal development goes beyond 36,000 km. Luzon, is in the north and is the largest island. It is 104,688 km^2. Mindanao is the second largest island in the south east with an area of 94,630 km^2. The two coasts are similar in size and make up 67% of the total area of the nation. The islands are also well known for being the major islands in Asia ranking 6th and 7th place respectively. Between the two islands are scattered a range of islands including those of the

Visayas group. These include Samar (13,080 km^2), Negros (12,705 km^2), Panay (11,515 km^2), Mindoro (9735 km^2), Leyte (7214 km^2), Cebu (4422 km^2) and Bohol (3865 km^2). Palawan (11,785 km^2) is another major island, but it occupies the western part of the country and is not located between the two main islands.

The Philippines is largely mountainous, however, there are also low-lying areas in the inland river valleys. The main mountain is located on the island of Mindanao, which reaches almost three thousand meters. The island of Mindanao also has two highest peaks in the country. This includes Mount Apo, which has a height of 2954 m and Mount Dulang-Dulang, which reaches a height of 2941 m.

The Philippines consists of numerous rivers. The Cagayan is the longest reaching a length of 505 km and flows in the northern part of Luzon. Mindanao is the second longest, reaching a length of 373 km. The Philippines also has several lakes. The longest is Laguna de Bay at 900 km ^{2}, which is in the south-east of the capital city of Manila. The second longest is the Lanao, which is 347 km^2, and is also the largest lake in Mindanao.

The Philippines has a tropical climate with has three seasons. Summer, which is also the hot and dry season is from March to May. The rainy season is from July to November and the cool dry season is from December to February. The climate is heavily influenced by monsoons which is like other Asian countries. The rainy season is when the Philippines are regularly hit by typhoons, which are more violent in the center of the country. The average annual temperatures are about 26°–28° without significant variations from month to month.

Internal Policy

The Philippines gained its independence from American forces in 1946 and in 1972 a democratic Government was established. This is modeled on the United States system. The Government of the Philippines is a democratic republic where the President of the Philippines is limited to a single six-year term but also serves as both the head of state and head of government within a multi-party system.

The Philippines political structure consists of 19 departments in the executive branch, more than 200 congressman, 24 senators in bicameral legislative branch and 15 justices in the Supreme Court. The government has three interdependent branches. This includes the legislative branch, the executive branch and the judicial branch. The powers of the branches are vested by the Constitution of the Philippines. Legislative power is vested in the two-chamber Congress of the Philippines. The Senate is the upper chamber and the House of Representatives is the lower chamber. Executive power is exercised by the government under the leadership of the President. Judicial power is vested in the courts with the Supreme Court of the Philippines as the highest judicial body.

The local Government in the Philippines are divided into provinces, municipalities and chartered cities each enjoying a certain degree of local autonomy. The Barangay is the basic political unit. Local governments have been given more powers, authority, responsibilities and resources through a system of decentralization. Each unit can levy and collect taxes and other fees in accordance to the power delegated to them under the Local Government Code of 1991.

The Philippines political scene is experiencing a period of relative stability. The Administration has made good progress in implementing its 10-point Economic Agenda which aims to continue the factors that have led economic growth in the Philippines. These factors include maintaining a stable fiscal balance, investing in human resources and capital development along with many others. Furthermore, the implementation of programs such as the fight against poverty, overcoming corruption, providing greater transparency in administrative procedures and improving the business environment has significantly stabilized the political environment and has contributed to the popularity of the President.

The Government have recently gone through a general election in May 2019. The next general elections will take place in 2022.

International Relations

The Philippines has continued to integrate with other ASEAN countries. The Philippines became a member of the ASEAN Economic Community in 2015. At the same time a single market was established.

The Philippines has excellent relations with the United States which the country views as vital to its success. As a result, this relationship is likely to remain strong going into the future. Although, both countries have former colonial ties the relationship has improved as the United States is now a major trading partner of the Philippines. The two countries also have a strong military relationship. For example, the US military have supported the Government of the Philippines for their campaign against Muslim separatists in Mindanao. There are also signs that point to a further strengthening of bilateral relations. This is evidenced by a greater defense cooperation including maritime safety. This increasing cooperation between the two countries is part of a new foreign policy plan, which is being implemented by the United States in East Asia.

The Philippines also has a strong relationship with China. For example, China has been a major trading partner and source of investment for the Philippines. Chinese investment has also continued to grow between 2012 and 2016. This relationship continues to be strongly maintained by the Philippine's President Rodrigo Duterte's state visit to China in October 2016. This was his first official trip outside South East Asia as head of state. Although the Philippine-China relationship appears to be flourishing, it must be noted that there are still tensions between the two countries due to the conflicting territorial claims in the South China Sea especially for disputes involving the Spratly islands. Furthermore, tensions have arisen due to competing demands for sovereignty on the Scarborough Shoal which is a maritime area located to the west of the island of Luzon. The Philippines has stated this as a dispute to the International Tribunal for the Law of the Sea (ITLOS).

It must also be noted that since the start of Duterte's Presidency in 2016 the Philippines foreign policy has taken a shift. For example, the president announced a separation from the US on his third day visit to China. This of course marks a complete reversal of the Philippines' diplomatic stance under Duterte's predecessor Benigno Aquino (2010–2016). This will have important consequences for the US's geopolitical strategy in Asia as well as economic, investment and trade opportunities between China and the Philippines. Duterte's independent foreign policy appears as if he wants Russia as an ally, China as an economic partner and to have Japan compete with China to provide economic benefits and regional security for the Philippines.

Among the bilateral relationships that the Philippine has its relationship with Australia has been growing the fastest. Australia are providing the security that the Philippines require. However, the Philippines relationship with Australia is being impacted by the government's dislike regarding the criticism faced by Australia and the United States about their views on human rights. This relationship is also being affected by the Philippines President Duterte's skepticism of Australia and the United States not wanting to support the Philippines.

Furthermore, the Philippines also has strong relationships with the UK economy. Last year, the UK was the Philippines third largest investor and has consistently remained the Philippines largest EU investor. Major British investors including HSBC, Glaxo Smith Kline and Shell. British exports to the Philippines grew by 38% last year. Furthermore, UK goods and services are making a difference to high-value sectors such as: energy, education, Smart Cities and science.

Economy

Macroeconomics Overview

	Unit	2000A	2018	2020F
GDP, current prices	USD (billions)	81.02	330.85	389.05
GDP per capita, current prices	USD	1055.12	3103.62	3507.88
GDP based on PPP per capita	Current International dollar	3400.54	8935.92	10,130.10

Source IMF Outlook (2019)

On the 30th June 2016 a new administration entered the office in the Philippines whilst the economy had the fastest growth compared to its East Asian peers. The country has sound economic fundamentals a globally recognized competitive workforce and is one of the most dynamic economies in the East Asia region. For the past five years the Philippines has had robust growth, which has averaged at 6.2% from 2010 to 2015. This has been much higher than the average of 4.5% annual growth achieved from 2000 to 2009. Unlike its regional neighbors the Philippines was not significantly impacted by the 2008–09 global recession. This was due to the country's small amount of exposure to securities issued by global financial institutions, lower reliance on exports and relatively resilient domestic consumption. Furthermore, this was supported by large remittances from approximately four million overseas Filipino workers and a growing business process outsourcing industry. Growth was further strengthened by strong election spending.

For the first half of 2018 the annual growth rate of the economy was 6.2% compared to 6.1% from 2015. This exceeded the growth rate of China, Malaysia, Thailand and Vietnam. Among the major economies the Philippines is behind China and Vietnam only. The growth performance translates to an estimated annual per capita income of about USD 2450 putting the Philippines among the middle income developing Asian economies. This growth has been due to strong private consumption and fixed investment. Furthermore, the Philippines benefits from today's low energy prices and growing consumer demand.

The country's demand for imports was weak in July and slightly declined. Growth in retail sales also slowed in July but then accelerated in August. According to Standard and Poor the country's credit rating was "BBB" on the 21st September. The country has a sound monetary policy, improved banking supervision and robust external position. However, current president Rodrigo Durterte's government's unpredictability, instability and possible weakening of the rule of law has caused concern for the rating agency. Overall, however, it is expected that the new government will broadly continue the pro-development approach inherited from the previous administration.

The main engines of growth continue to be the service and industry sectors for production. The negative effects of El Nino, which is the warming of sea surface temperature over the Pacific Region, have led to a weakening of agriculture. The demand in growth has been driven by robust private consumption, capital formation and a 10% expansion in public spending. External demand was weak causing a negative effect on net exports.

Cash remittances from Overseas Filipino Workers (OFW) grew 16.3% to USD 2.3 billion in August this year. This marked the sharpest growth rate since March 2014. In contrast it fell by 5.4% in July. In the 12 months before August, cash remittances totaled USD 26.4 billion. This was an improvement in the overall trend from July's USD 26.1 billion. In August, remittances mainly came from the United States, Saudi Arabia, the United Arab Emirates and Singapore. For many Philippine families' remittances are an important source of income and therefore, one of the main drivers of private consumption. In 2015, they accounted for approximately 9.8% of GDP.

The external debt is at an acceptable level. Foreign exchange reserves are significant covering close to 10 months of imports. The goods trade deficit remains the main hurdle with a weak export performance compared to imports.

Due to weak demand from Japan, Hong Kong and the USA the Philippines have seen a fall in exports for seventeen consecutive months up to August this year. The annual drop in exports went from 13% in July to 4.4% in August. Looking ahead, GDP growth is forecast to decelerate slightly. Net exports will continue to underperform due to strong growth of imports and limited growth of exports. Private consumption is set to moderate. A rise in inflation is to be blamed as it hinders purchasing power. Fiscal policy should remain supportive with spending focusing on infrastructure and social services.

Structure of output (% GDP)	2000	2005	2010	2015	2018
Agriculture	14.0	12.7	12.3	10.3	9.3
Industry	34.5	33.9	32.6	30.9	30.8
Services	51.5	53.5	55.1	58.8	59.9

Source Asian Development Bank (ADB, 2019)

Structure of expenditure (% GDP)	2000	2005	2010	2015	2018
Final consumption	83.6	84.1	81.3	84.7	85.8
Gross capital formation	18.4	21.6	20.5	21.12	26.9
Exports of goods and services	51.4	46.1	34.8	28.4	31.7
Imports of goods and services	53.4	51.7	36.6	34.3	44.4
Statistical discrepancy	0.0	0.0	0.0	0.0	−0.4

Source Asian Development Bank (ADB, 2019)

Economic Policy

The new administration has not changed any macroeconomic policies; however, the tax collection system has been reformed. The Government's 10-point plan highlights the main areas that it will focus on into improve the economy. This includes equitable tax reform enhanced public spending, greater transparency, accountability, improved ease of doing business, continued investment in education, skills, health and social assistance to the poor. From 2014 to 2018 the administration was focused on improving public finances and targeted a budget deficit equivalent to 2% of GDP in 2018.

Additionally, numerous legislations have been put in place by the Government to deregulate and dismantle monopolies within the following sectors: domestic shipping, banking, telecommunications, power, mining and downstream oil industries. Monopolies, mergers or business combinations that restrain trade or create unfair competition are prohibited by the constitution. However, the limited domestic market means that there are several cartels. To control inflation or ease social tension price controls are levied on a list of basic commodities via The Price Act. Foreign exchange regulations have also been liberalized by the central bank. In 2016 to 2018, the tariff-cutting program, has been enforced and is expected to continue. However, political pressures mean that some areas may liberalize faster than others.

Free retail competition and open access was introduced in the electricity sector in 2014–2015. Tax incentives will be rationalized and the disposal of state assets are set to continue for 2016–2018. The Foreign Direct Investment (FDI) Act of 1991 limits foreign equity in companies from certain sectors which has resulted in the Philippines FDI levels being amongst the lowest in Southeast Asia. On the other hand, government reforms to remove large-scale corruption and maintain fiscal discipline have led to increased FDI in recent years. The Philippines is becoming a more attractive place in which to do business due to these developments.

Many exporting companies view the Philippines as a favorable place to invest due to the country's medium cost, strategic location and safe manufacturing base due to its highly skilled and English-speaking labor force. Furthermore, special economic zones use various tax and non-tax incentives to attract export enterprises.

Bank System

Volatilities in the local and global markets, have posed numerous challenges to the Philippines banking system, which has led to falling investment yields. Banks have reverted to lending activities, which resulted in a net profit of 2014, which was highly driven by interest income. Universal/commercial banks (U/KBs) have expanded their reach in areas considered as the home turf of rural banks. Indicative banks' support inclusive growth by providing access to finance for all Filipinos regardless of their socio-economic status. The industry additionally continues to capitalize on its technology-enabled services such as electronic banking (e-banking) to cater to the needs of a diverse and increasingly sophisticated market.

Overall, the banking system landscape remains streamlined on the back of continued industry mergers, consolidation and several small bank closures. For many banks, the option to consolidate or acquire other banks is driven by the need to grow their market and accelerate network expansion. As a result, even though there was a noted decline in the number of head offices this was offset by the increase in the number of newly established regular branches and so-called "light branches" or other banking offices (OBOs)/micro-banking offices (MBOs) that served as additional financial access points. Furthermore, credit remains skewed to the real estate sector.

Interest Rates (% per annum; period averages)	2000	2005	2010	2015	2018
On deposits					
Savings	7.4	3.8	1.6	0.7	0.9
Time: 6 months	7.2	5.4	3.1	1.5	2.8
12 months	10.5	6.0	2.1	3.1	3.5

Source Asian Development Bank (ADB, 2019)

Investment Area

The Philippines is becoming increasingly attractive to foreign investors. The country has opened its economy to foreign markets and established a network of free trade agreements with several countries. The country has a competitive advantage in the exports of consultancy. Its main exports include: electronic products which are primarily semiconductors, woodcraft, furniture, metal components, apparel and clothing accessories. On the other hand, its main imports are electronic products, mineral fuels and lubricants, transport equipment, industrial machinery and equipment. The country's major trading partners are Japan, the United States, China, Hong Kong and Singapore.

The Philippines has a commitment to open free trade. This is evidenced by the organizations that the Philippines are a part of. This includes the World Trade Organization (WTO), participation in the ASEAN Free Trade Agreement (AFTA) and the General Agreement on Tariff and Trade (GATT). The country received its first World Bank loan in 1957 and since then has financed irrigation and other agriculture-related infrastructure and rural development needs. This has produced significant results for its citizens. Over the last thirty years, the Bank has increased the amount of support it offers to a wide range of projects and analytical work, policy advice and capacity development in aid of the country's development agenda.

The Philippines is classed as an emerging market economy and is one of Goldman Sachs Next Eleven economies. The country's strategic location, which is placed at the center of international shipping and airlines is a critical entry point to over 500 million people in the ASEAN Market and is a natural gateway to the East-Asian economies. A surge of investment within the economy as well as strong consumption has had a major impact on increasing the growth of the economy at the start of the year.

Furthermore, the devaluation of the country's currency in 1997, led the International Monetary Fund (IMF) to provide the Philippines with around one billion dollars in assistance. Many foreign investors particularly from Japan and Taiwan have turned to the Philippines as a country that they would increase investment in. This is since the Government of the Philippines (GPH) actively encourages foreign investment to promote economic development within the country. The advantages for foreign investors include but are not limited to the following:

- free trade zones, including the Philippine Economic Zone Authority (PEZA);
- tax exemptions e.g. income tax holidays (ITH);
- opportunities in business process outsourcing (BPO), which is one of the fastest growing industries in the world—one in which the Philippines remains a world leader;
- right to repatriate the entire proceeds of the liquidation of the investment;
- right to remit earnings from the investment;
- right to remit sums as may be necessary to meet the payments of interest and principal on foreign loans and obligations arising from technological assistance contracts;
- freedom from expropriation except for public use or in the interest of national welfare or defense and upon payment of just compensation.

Furthermore, the Philippine law provides numerous incentives for multinational enterprises to establish regional or area headquarters and regional operating headquarters in the Philippines. For example, multinational corporations such as Toyota, Intel and IMB have all taken advantage of the Philippines attractive investment climate. This includes lower costs of operating including lower domestic wages and a highly educated English-speaking workforce. It must also be stated that the Philippines has a large mineral and geothermal resource producing more geothermal energy than all other countries except the United States.

The UK continues to be one of the Philippines biggest European investors, particularly in the power industry, electrical machinery and pharmaceuticals. There are many opportunities, which exist for British companies in the energy sector, retail, business process outsourcing (BPO) and health as there is potential for collaboration with the Philippine governments towards public-private partnership (PPP) projects.

International metrics highlighted the improvement in the investment climate under the Aquino Government. The Philippines also experienced increased rankings in competitiveness and ease of doing business in the following global economic surveys:

- 64th in the Global Competitiveness Index 2019 (published in August 2019).
- 124th (out of 190 countries) in the World Bank's Ease of Doing business report.

In 2013 and 2014, the international credit rating agencies, including Moody's, Standard and Poor's and Fitch, raised the country's investment grade. Some key factors that make the Philippines attractive to investors include: an expanding consumer base driven by an emerging middle class and inflow of overseas remittance amounting to USD 28.9 billion in 2019. The Philippines is one of the largest markets in South East Asia. The country has a labor force with a large youth demographic (45% labor force participation rate of workers between ages 15–24) and women (50% labor force participation rate of women).

It must also be stated, although the Philippines has an attractive investment climate, due to its strategic location, English speaking and skilled workforce and a stable democratic Government, the country was ranked by the IMD as 43rd out of 59 in terms of Competitiveness. As a result, the country still has a lot of room for improvement to become a successful investment climate. Legal restrictions, regulatory inconsistency and a lack of transparency hinder foreign investment. In many sectors of the economy, GPH regulatory authority remains ambiguous and corruption is a significant factor. In addition, a complex and slow judicial system inhibits the timely and fair resolution of commercial disputes.

Domestic Market

After the Philippines gained independence, the country started to face an economic slow-down and a difficult transformation through land reform and the establishment of some related industries. Nonetheless, the economic structure of the Philippines preserves the mark left by the United States, particularly in the productive activities of the cultivation of sugarcane, which has received a strong boost.

However, it must be noted that compared to most third world countries, the Philippines has quietly developed its economy. The encouraging trends of the seventies even recorded average growth rates of 6%. The achievement of self-sufficiency in rice production in the eighties was severely penalized by heavy foreign debt, which was accumulated by the Marcos regime.

The beginning of the Corazon Aquino presidency (11th President of the Philippines) sought to boost the agricultural sector by launching a new reform. However, this Government faced many obstacles such as: promoting privatization and private investment and fighting corruption to reduce the foreign debt. In 1998 many Asian markets suffered by the crisis that had little impact on the Philippines especially in comparison to the neighboring states. This is due to large inflows of remittances coming in from Philippine citizens abroad and the support of international organizations. The slowdown in growth, in 2000, was largely due to the decline in foreign investment, which was caused by the unstable political environment.

The fastest growing industry was the manufacturing sector, which includes the production of textiles, chemicals and building materials. Furthermore, the growth of the electronic and electro-mechanical components sector. The latter industry is becoming increasingly successful due to the use of both cheap and skilled labor. The country's main exports include Integrated Circuits (USD 32.2 billion), Computers (USD 5.19 billion) and Office Machine Parts (USD 10 billion). The country's top exporting destinations include China, Japan, the United States, Singapore and Hong Kong.

It must also be noted that the country's Information Communications Technology (ICT) sector is experiencing a boom particularly regarding call centers, business processing, animation, medical and legal transcription, engineering software and design. The global demand for information technology (IT), BPO and global in-house center (GIC) services are expected to double to approximately USD 270 billion by 2016. Companies that provide such services in the Philippines can grow to USD 25 billion in revenue, employ more than 1.3 million Filipinos directly and contribute to 10% of the country's gross domestic product (GDP).

Overall, the Philippines economy is becoming increasingly important among all world markets. Furthermore, the medium-term development plans launched by the government aims to address the most pressing issues to facilitate economic change. These issues include privatization, outsourcing and liberalization, tax reform, infrastructure improvement and continuation of agrarian reform. Additionally, an increase in industrial production, achieving energy independence, reforming social and domestic policy is included in the Government's agenda.

The current Government has aimed at encouraging several sectors. This includes enhancing the mining, metallurgical industry as well as the offshore extraction of oil and natural gas. The Philippines is the 37th largest exporting economy in the world and the 61st most complex economy according to the Economic Complexity Index (ECI).

External trade (USD millions)	2000	2005	2010	2015	2018
Exports, fob	38,078.2	41,254.7	51,497.5	58,827	69,307
Imports, cif	33,807.4	49,487.4	58,467.8	71,067	112,842
Trade balance	4270.8	−8232.7	−6970.3	−12,240	−43,533

Source Asian Development Bank (ADB, 2019)

Main commercial partners (USD millions)	2000	2005	2010	2015	2018
Exports					
1. Japan	5609	7203	7827	12,381	9474
2. United States	11,406	7429	7568	8811	10,550
3. Hong Kong, China	1907	3339	4334	6199	9554
4. China, People's Rep. of	663	4077	5701	6393	8669
5. Singapore	3124	2706	7331	3650	4234
6. Germany	1329	1346	2657	2646	2809
7. Korea, Rep. of	1172	1391	2228	2512	2542
8. Thailand	1206	1169	1784	2263	2717
9. Taipei, China	2861	1886	1752	2177	2474
10. Netherlands	2982	4032	2429	1772	2481
Imports					
1. China, People's Rep. of	786	2973	5070	11,915	22,579
2. Japan	6511	8071	7422	7023	11,397
3. United States	6413	9105	6452	7940	8297
4. Korea, Republic of	2754	2294	4210	4771	11,503
5. Thailand	879	1583	4253	4664	7948
6. Singapore	2325	3727	5703	5146	6311
7. Taipei, China	2255	3549	4045	5787	5412
8. Indonesia	693	1003	2459	3222	6789
9. Malaysia	1307	1779	2682	3481	4286
10. Germany	771	1131	1223	2761	2493

Source Asian Development Bank (ADB, 2019)

Finance and Taxation

Tax

The Philippine Constitution mandates that the rule of taxation should be uniform and equitable and the Government should conduct a progressive system of taxation. Both the national Government and the local Government impose business taxes. For income tax purposes companies are classified as domestic or foreign depending on the place of incorporation or organization.

A domestic corporation is organized under the Philippine laws. It is taxed based on net worldwide income. A foreign corporation is organized under the laws of another country and is further classified as a resident or non-resident. It is considered a resident of the Philippines if it is engaged in trade or business in the Philippines (e.g., through a branch). A resident foreign corporation is taxed on net Philippine-source income while a non-resident foreign corporation is taxed on gross Philippine-source income.

The rates vary depending on the type of business. Corporate tax rates for both domestic and foreign corporations are subject to either of the following:

- Regular corporate income tax of 30% of their taxable income (gross income less allowable deductions).
- Minimum corporate income tax equivalent to 2% of gross income during the taxable year.

Non-resident foreign corporations are taxed at 30% of their gross taxable income. However, this is only on Philippine-source income. Certain types of income and corporations are subject to special tax rates. For domestic corporations they are subject to taxes which are not limited to the following:

- 10% of taxable income for proprietary educational institutions and hospitals;
- 20% interest from deposits and yields or any other monetary benefit from deposit substitutes and from trust funds and similar arrangements and royalties.

Examples of taxes for resident foreign corporations:

- 2.5% of gross Philippine billings for international carriers doing business in the Philippines;
- 10% for interest income derived by offshore banking units from foreign currency loan transactions with residents.

Examples of Taxes for non-resident foreign corporations:

- 25% on gross income for owners, lessors or distributors of motion pictures;
- owners of vessels—4.5% of gross rentals, lease or charter fees from leases or charters to Philippine citizens or corporations as approved by the Maritime Industry Authority.

Taxable income must be calculated in accordance with International Accounting Standards which is subject to adjustments as required by provisions in the tax law. These adjustments mean that the amount of taxable income frequently differs from the amount of income for financial reporting purposes. Normal business expenses may be deducted in computing taxable income. A corporation can choose the fiscal or its calendar year for its taxable year depending on which would reflect its taxable income more accurately.

Philippine tax law does not allow nor require the filing of amalgamated tax returns or the relieving of losses within a group of companies. Each company is an independent unit that must file its own tax returns.

Transfer pricing regulations set in 2013 state how related companies must transact. Attribution of revenue and expenses between branches and head office is subject to certain conditions. Companies are not allowed to use interest as a deduction for income tax purposes if paid to related entities such as:

- an individual owning, whether directly or indirectly, more than 50% of the outstanding stock of the corporation;
- a common individual shareholder owning more than 50% of the value of the outstanding stock of between two corporations. If either one of the corporations is a personal holding company or a foreign personal holding company.

Tax rate	%
Corporate tax	30
Personal income tax	35
Sales tax	12

Source Santander Trading Economics (2019)

Personal Income Tax

The personal income of residents in the Philippines is taxed progressively up to 32%. Resident citizens are taxed according to their net income. Net income can be derived from sources within and without of the Philippines. However, for non-residents income is taxable only on income derived from sources within the Philippines.

The above rates apply to individuals who derive income from business (including capital gains from the sale transfer or exchange of shares in a foreign corporation) or from the practice of a profession. Individuals holding managerial and highly technical positions employed by multinational companies and offshore business units are taxed at 15% on their gross income.

Income in the Philippines is divided into the following three categories. These are taxed separately as summarized below.

- Compensation employment income: this income is taxed at progressive rates on gross income after deduction of personal and additional exemptions but without deductions for expenses.
- Passive income: this income, including dividends and interest, is subject to tax at 7.5%.
- Business income and professional income: this income is taxed at progressive rates on net business income after deduction of certain specified expenses.

Taxable income (PHP)	Tax rate (%)
0–250,000	0
250,000–400,000	20
400,000–800,000	25
800,000–2 million	30
2 million–8 million	32
Over 8 million	35
Fringe benefit tax (Levied on benefits furnished to managerial and supervisory-level employees)	35 (25 for non-resident alien not engaged in trade or business)

Source Santander Trade (2019)

Tax Incentives for SMEs

1. Direct Tax.
   Tax incentives for importers and exporters.

   - Tax credits are available for taxes and duties paid on purchases of raw materials of products for exports, domestic capital equipment, domestic breeding stock and genetic materials.
   - A tax credit of 25% of the duties paid on raw materials and capital equipment and/or spare parts.

   Tax incentives are also available to enterprises registered with the Philippine Economic Zone Authority (PEZA). These incentives are shown below:

   - 4–8 years income tax holiday. A 5% tax on the modified gross income is imposed after the end of the income tax holiday;
   - tax and duty exemption on imported capital equipment and raw materials;
   - national and local tax exemption;
   - tax rebate for the purchase of domestic capital goods.

2. Indirect Tax.
   Under the Investment Priority Plan (IPP), SME owners are eligible for the following incentives:
   - an exemption from export taxes, duty imports and fees;
   - additional deduction for labor expense (ADLE);
   - additional deduction for necessary and major infrastructure works.

Goods imported into the Philippines are generally subject to customs duty (aside from 12% VAT and excise tax on certain goods). For customs purposes, the value of imported goods is based on their transaction value, i.e., the price paid or payable for the goods when sold for export to the Philippines, with certain specified adjustments. Excise tax on exported goods produced or manufactured locally can be credited or refunded upon submission with the proof of actual exportation upon receipt of the corresponding.

Audit and Accounting

Accounting standards in the Philippines are adopted by the Philippines Financial Reporting Standards Council (PFRSC) and approved by the Securities and Exchange Commission (SEC). The PFRSC has formed the Philippine Interpretations Committee (PIC), which issues implementation guidance on PFRSs.

The PFRSC has adopted most IFRSs, in some cases with modifications, and in some cases the most recent amendments to IFRSs have not been adopted. These standards are known as the Philippine Financial Reporting Standards (PFRSs) and Philippine Accounting Standards (PASs). Philippine standards apply to all entities with public accountability. That includes: entities whose securities are listed in a public market or are in the process of listing; all financial institutions including banks, insurance companies, security brokers, pension funds, mutual funds and investment banking entities.

Depending on the category that the companies falls into, there are different financial reporting frameworks for which a company must follow according to the Securities Regulations Code Rule 68:

- large and/or publicly-accountable entities should use the Philippine Financial Reporting Standards (PFRS);
- small and medium-sized entities (SMEs) should use PFRS;
- micro entities have the option to use PFRS for SMEs, the income tax basis of accounting standards.

Risk Assessment

The Philippine economy has robust economic growth year-on-year with an average of 6% in the last five years. From 2012 to 2014 the Philippines was a top regional performer and had the second highest growth rate, behind China in the East Asia region. Macroeconomic fundamentals remain positive with low inflation rates and a stable Philippine peso set against foreign currency. According to the International Monetary Fund, "growth is expected to remain robust, underpinned by resilient domestic demand." Furthermore, the country has benefited from solid monetary and fiscal policies in recent years, continued current account surpluses since 2003, relatively low external debt, large foreign exchange reserves and strong remittances inflows.

Public finances have improved to a large extent over the past ten years. Public debt has decreased to around 45% GDP in 2015 (down from 68.5% GDP in 2005) and should remain broadly stable over 2019–2020. The fiscal deficit remains acceptable despite an increase in spending in 2016.

Nonetheless, the country faces several risks to its economy. These risks include economic, political and corruption risks all of which can act as a hindrance to the success of the economy. These issues will be discussed below.

Economic Risks

The main areas of economic risk in the Philippines are linked to the political and security risks in the country. Furthermore, key economic risks include uneven recovery of high-income economies, slower than anticipated growth of large emerging market economies, financial market volatilities, slower remittance growth from oil exporting economies and the continuation of El Niño in 2016. The key economic challenge is to sustain growth despite changes in the political administration and to further boost foreign direct investments, which, currently, does not contribute a significant amount to the country's national income accounts. Furthermore, the country will be impacted by the risk of large income disparities, a high dependency on electronic, electrical exports, tourism and a weak business environment.

The country's weak business environment is evidenced by the countries ranking. In the World Bank's latest business survey, it ranked 124 out of 190 countries. This survey highlights the difficulties in legal procedures to start companies and to protect minority investors.

IMF resident representative Shanaka Jayanath Peiris states that "the economic outlook is one of the strongest in the region but subject to increased downside risks, including lower growth in China and the region, higher global financial volatility, capital outflows and weather-related disruptions."

The rise in food prices is also an issue, which could potentially pose an even bigger challenge for the government than corruption scandals. Cost pressures are likely to drive even more Filipinos to leave the country in search of better paying jobs abroad, while at home there will be pressure to offer relief to the poorest Filipinos, relief that government really cannot afford in economic terms, but which it might feel, it has no choice but to provide due to political pressures.

For the Philippines to overcome these risks the country needs to focus on stabilizing its macroeconomic fundamentals and significant fiscal space. This will allow the Philippines to accelerate the reforms needed to achieve more inclusive growth to reduce poverty and boost shared prosperity.

Political Risks

The previous administration under President Benigno "Noynoy" Aquino is now nearing the end of his six-year term. Following his election in 2010, Aquino pledged to introduce a good governance agenda with reforms to counter corruption, boost the economy and improve the business and investment climate in the Philippines. Progress has been made in the basic services provision which streamlines government efforts to ease economic activity and increase fiscal transparency which the International Monetary Fund (IMF) assessed in 2015 as "generally good".

Despite reforms to ease economic activity, political risks that affect the business environment remain prevalent. The main political risks include: a weak judicial system with a poor record in case disposition with procedural delays and technicalities. Additionally, the inconsistent application of laws and regulations on procurement, taxation and land use and inefficient public financial management also increases the political risks in the country. Government procurement can be relatively slow and bureaucratic, and business to business deals can often progress much more quickly.

Separatist movements in Mindanao and a communist insurgency in rural areas present security risks to investors and business groups, but optimism remains in the Comprehensive Agreement on the Bangsamoro (CAB) which was signed in 2014 between the Philippine government and the Moro Islamic Liberation Front (MILF) and established lasting peace in Muslim Mindanao.

Furthermore, the current political landscape raises uncertainties. The government's controversial 'war on drugs' has evoked criticism from international institutions (e.g. U.N.) and denunciations of human rights abuses. Intemperate remarks by the country's president against key allies (U.S.) could hinder the private sector sentiment, trade and investment flows.

According to BMI Research the country is expected to worsen due to the Duterte administration's heavy-handed approach on crime and drugs as well as the military's conflict with the Abu Sayyaf militant group in the South. The government's crackdown on these outlaws is likely to lead to greater reprisals and an increase in frequency of terror attacks. As a result, the Philippines's short-term political risk index score has previously ranked from 64.6 to 66.3. The following risks will affect the Philippine's political system:

1. Continued graft and corruption in key agencies
2. Lack of transparency and accountability in governance
3. Regulatory capture—agencies captured by vested interests
4. The weakness of the electoral processes—prone to cheating and manipulation of results
5. Dynasties and traditional politics
6. Armed conflict
7. Worsening human rights situation particularly extra-judicial killings of journalists and activists of the left
8. Apathy or withdrawal from political engagement especially at the national level.

As a result of these future risks the Government should focus on electoral reforms, advocacy for Human Rights, advocacy for Peace and Development and anti-Corruption Advocacy.

Corruption Risks

In 2014, the Philippines improved its ranking (85th out of 175 countries) in the Transparency International's corruption perception index (CPI), which is an improvement of 44 places from 2011 (129th). However, corruption remains a pervasive and longstanding problem in the Philippines. Although President Aquino, who assumed the presidency in July 2010 on a good governance platform, vowed to combat corruption as critical to inclusive growth and poverty reduction. Early efforts to reign in corruption by the administration have improved public perception but are frequently overshadowed by high-profile cases reported in the Philippine media.

As a high political priority, anti-corruption measures were enforced in 2010 through legislation and institutionalization of inter-agency monitoring bodies. The government has formulated a national action plan on transparency and good governance that includes measures both at the national and at the local levels. An Inter-agency, Anti-graft Coordinating Council comprised of independent anti-corruption agencies have been revived to collaborate in both the investigation and prosecution stages. The government has further attempted to increase transparency and mitigate corruption by investigating and convicting corrupt officials as well as implementing e-governance systems in the country.

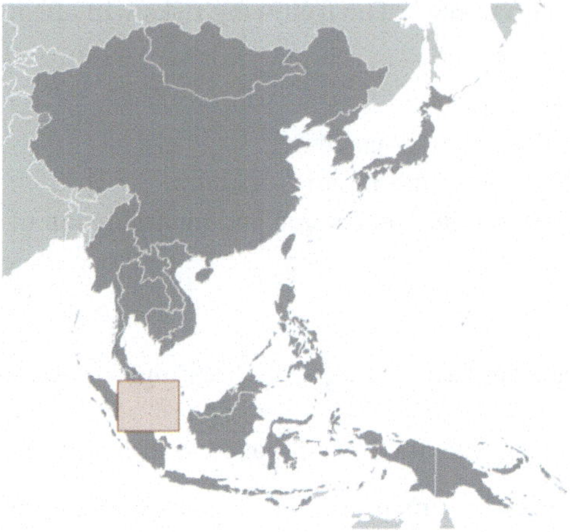

SINGAPORE

Official name
Republic of Singapore
Capital
Singapore
Area
697 sq. km
Population
5.6 mln
Languages
Mandarin (official), English (official) Malay (official)
Main ethnic groups
Chinese 74%, Malay 13%, Indian 10%
Main religions
Buddhist 34%, Muslim 14%, Taoist 11%
Government type
Parliamentary Republic
Urbanization
100.00%
Life expectancy ratio
84 years
Fertility rate
1.3 children born/woman
Currency
Singapore dollar SGD

Singapore

Country Introduction

Population, Location, Geography, Climate

Singapore is a city-state made up of a main island and other fifty smaller islands. It is located at the southern end of the Malay Peninsula and is separated from Malaysia by a narrow strait. The strategic location at the mouth of Malacca has made Singapore one of the major trading centers in Asia. Given the paucity of land and high population Singapore has one of the highest population densities on the planet.

The territory has a maximum altitude of 164 m and is separated from Malaysia by the Straits of Joho. However, the nearest Indonesian island, Batam Island is located about 15 km from the southern coasts of the country with some others closer islets.

The coasts are generally low and sandy and stretch for 193 km. In recent decades, the total area of the country has increased to 582 km^2 as some islands have combined together.

The main island of Singapore, Pulau Ujong, is 640 km^2 which constitutes 89% of Singapore's territory. The other main islands are Jurong (32 km^2), Tekong (24.5 km^2) and Ubin (10 km^2).

Given the small size of the territory there are only short streams for example Seletar Major (15 km) and limited lakes many of which are artificial.

The climate is equatorial with abundant rainfall all year round. However, the peak season for Singapore is between November and January as this is when the monsoon blows from the north-east and the difference between the average monthly temperature is minimal.

Officially, the urbanization rate is 100% but you can find the most rural areas in the north and in the smaller islands.

The Chinese (74%) make up most of the population, followed by Malaysia (13%) and Indians (9%) and these should be added to the 1.554 million of non-residents, workers or students with temporary permits, which overall are 29% of the total population.

In Singapore there is freedom of worship and a multi-ethnic culture means many religions are practiced. The most common ones are Buddhism (33%), Christianity (18%), Islam (15%), Taoism (11%) and Hinduism (5%) while 17% are not religious.

Internal Policy

Singapore enjoys a political and institutional system characterized by strong stability. This helps to create a long-term security framework for economic activity in the country.

The Republic of Singapore is the constitutional parliamentary whose principles are based on the Westminster model. The executive branch of the government comprises the Cabinet, the Attorney-General and a democratically elected President. The Cabinet is responsible for the direction of the Government, which is headed by the Prime Minister, which represents the effective head of the executive branch. The one who has the most seats in Parliament is elected as Prime Minister. Prime Ministers serve for five years or less after which the Parliament of Singapore must be dissolved. The President holds a largely ceremonial position with discretionary powers which serve as a check on the Cabinet. Presidents serve for six-years and represent the nation in internal and foreign affairs.

The parliament is dominated by the People's Action Party. These have retained a majority in parliament since self-governance was established in 1959. The legislative branch is the parliament. The Members of Parliament (MPs) can either be elected, non-constituency or nominated members. Most of the members are elected through votes and will serve for five-year period. The Constitution will also provide the appointment of non-elected MPs and while there up to nine Non-constituency Members of Parliament (NCMPs) from political parties the opposition can be appointed. Additionally, since 1990, a constitutional provision has permitted the appointment of up to nine Nominated Members of the Parliament (NMPs) to ensure that a wide range of community views are represented. Legislation are passed by the parliament and assented by the President. The legal foundation is the Constitution of the Republic of Singapore. Which is the Singapore's supreme law. The legal system is based on the English common law system although there are key differences. The most notable is abolition of the jury in favor of resting decisions exclusively with judges.

The judicial branch consists of the State Courts and the Supreme Court. The State Courts (District Courts, Magistrates' Courts, Family, Juvenile, and Coroner's Courts and a small civil claims court called the Small Claims Tribunal) form the first tier in the judicial hierarchy. They hear civil matters where disputed amounts which do not exceed SGD 250,000, SGD 60,000 and SGD 10,000, respectively. It must also be noted that the Small Claims Tribunal can hear claims of up to SGD 20,000 however only if both parties agree. The Supreme Court is formed by the High Court and the Court of Appeal (the highest court in Singapore). The High Court hears criminal cases (including those appealed from the State Courts) and civil claims of more than SGD 250,000 and the Court of Appeal will hear appeals from the High Court.

Singapore operates a famously comprehensive and strict criminal justice system under which punishments may include death, imprisonment, forfeiture of property, fines and caning. Since its independence in 1965, Singapore has seen the government the People's Action Party (PAP), led by the Lee family. The PAP has managed to maintain its power through its ability to ensure the country sees a rapid and steady economic growth as well as control in many areas of people's social life.

The general elections in 2011, while confirming the hegemony of the PAP with 60.1% of the votes, they recorded a decline in votes. However, the PAP still maintained a parliamentary majority. The last round of elections was on September 11 in 2015 however reported the PAP at very high levels of consensus as they retained almost 70% of the votes. The elements favored were in the wake of the founding father of Singapore, Lee Kuan Yew, who was the undeniable economic success of the city-state in the openings toward greater pluralism and greater social spending favor of average bands.

The new government, Prime Minister Lee Hsien Loong, took office on the 1st October and saw confirmation of some historical personalities of the party and the inclusion of younger elements. It has announced the start of a process of constitutional reform to be completed by 2019.

Although they face some important challenges such as: the slowdown in economic growth, the increase of foreign workers and the strong upward pressure on prices, especially in real estate sector. The country remains very stable, with a per capita GDP among the highest in the world and a business-friendly environment characterized by markedly and open to international trade.

International Relations

The ongoing commitment of the Singaporian Government to favor the liberalization of international trade, both at the multilateral level and at the bilateral, is due to Singapore's economic growth based on free trade and inward investment.

Singapore is one of the founding countries of ASEAN and is aware of the importance of continuing the path of integration, the need to confirm the role of the organization within the region and intensify relations with third countries.

Singapore is also an active member within the framework of ASEM which is the main multilateral forum of Euro-Asian relations.

Singapore has promoted Asia-Middle East Dialogue: a dialogue forum between the countries of these two areas of the world. It is created to deepen ties and of already existing forms of co-operation based on the principles of voluntariness, informality and flexibility as well as on the principles of international law.

Relations with the European Union

Singapore has signed with the EU within a free trade agreement on 16.12.2012. The agreement covered the sector of financial and banking services, the communications sector, import fees, standards of quality awards, intellectual property, certificates of origin, investment, sanitary and phytosanitary standards recognition, market access, professions and titles professional, alternative energy, movement of persons, recognized legal texts, state supplies, legal and trade disputes, environment and sustainable development. The agreement, however, is still awaiting ratification.

Trans-Pacific Partnership

It is also worth noting the accession of Singapore to the TPP (Trans Pacific Partnership), signed in Atlanta in October 2015. This was the promoter from the start. In addition, to the potential links to trade the intensification of traffic should reinforce the pivotal role in the Asia-Pacific of the city-state for its advanced logistics infrastructure.

Economy

Macroeconomic Overview

Indicator	Unit	2000A	2018	2020F
GDP, current prices	USD (billions)	95.84	361.11	391.88
GDP per capita, current prices	USD	23,793.28	64,041.42	68,487.46
GDP based on PPP per capita	Current International dollar	40,928.21	100,344.70	107,604.80

Source IMF Outlook (2019)

Singapore is an open market economy. In the late nineties it was considered one of the four Asian tigers along with Hong Kong, South Korea, and Taiwan. The economy depends heavily on exports, particularly in the manufacturing sector, which constituted 26% of GDP in 2005. This included the electronics, petroleum refining, chemicals, mechanical engineering and biomedical sciences. Singapore has one of the busiest ports in the world and is the fourth main square for trade after London, New York and Tokyo. In 2007 the World Bank ranked Singapore as the most important hubs for logistics. The economy of Singapore is also ranked among one of the ten most open economies in the world. Singapore also involved hundreds of thousands of foreign workers, including Indians, Indonesians, Chinese and those from other continents.

Due to the recession in the early 2000's the technology sector collapsed and in 2001 the country's GDP contracted by 2.2%. The Economic Review Committee (ERC) was established in December 2001 and this recommended a new policy of innovations to revitalize the economy. The economic recovery of Singapore driven by the global growth of the period, led to 8.3% growth in 2004, 6.4% in 2005 and 7.9% in 2006.

As part of the 2007–2009 economic crisis the Singapore Sovereign Fund allocated funds for more than 35 billion US dollars for the recapitalization process despite the write down in major financial intermediaries.

As cyclical factors put a dampener on economic growth recent trends have displayed a slow growth environment is expected to continue for Singapore's economy. In the latest economic review the Monetary Authority of Singapore (MAS) noted a softening growth among Singapore's key trading partners and this would affect externally-oriented industries. Growth in capital formation is expected to be lower than the G3 economies and this will affect trade-related sectors such as precision engineering. Key prospects for China also remain subdued. The report also noted growth in the US weakened towards the end of 2015. This can be explained through the moderation in personal consumption and weak exports. While the US is still expected to grow at a modest pace Singapore may not be able to fully capitalize on it as most of the US growth will be driven by domestic spending. Meanwhile, India could be a bright spot with a tepid growth outlook driven by private consumption and public infrastructure spending. On a national scene, while domestic-facing sectors are expected to generally be more resilient, the central bank observed economic activity weakening among corporates, which saw more firms undertake consolidation activities in 2018. This has included a slow growth in business loans and an uptick in redundancies. However, it added the corporate adjustments appear to be less severe compared to past periods of outright recession and seems to be confined to specific pockets of industries.

Looking ahead MAS said the long-term prospects for regional service trade is still bright as China's on-going rebalance towards a consumption-based economy is expected to fuel demand for imported services. In a review, MAS highlighted opportunities for service firms in the areas of transport and communications as well as healthcare and medical. Overall, MAS said Singapore's economy is expected to grow between 0.5 and 1% in 2020.

Structure of output (% GDP)	2000	2005	2010	2015	2018
Agriculture	0.1	0.1	0.0	0.0	0.0
Industry	34.8	32.4	27.6	25.8	26.6
Services	65.1	67.6	72.3	74.2	73.3

Source Asian Development Bank (ADB, 2019)

Structure of expenditure (% GDP)	2000	2005	2010	2015	2018
Final consumption	52.3	49.3	45.7	14.1	45.5
Gross capital formation	34.9	21.4	27.9	−8.6	26.6
Exports of goods and services	189.2	226.1	199.3	5.0	176.4
Imports of goods and services	176.9	196.3	172.8	3.4	149.8
Statistical discrepancy	0.5	−0.5	0.0	0.0	1.3

Source Asian Development Bank (ADB, 2019)

Economic Policy

Singapore's economic policy has traditionally been interventionist. The government is directly involved in the management of the economy, not only through micro and macro-economic policies, but also with the direct ownership of several companies operating in various sectors. Under the long rule of Lee Kuan Yew (1959–1990), Singapore has been able to combine an authoritarian political model to a capital attractive approach. In a few years the multinationals, encouraged to expand and prosper through favorable tax rates, found a natural hub in Singapore in which to invest. The authoritarian nature was seen by the same founding father as an essential element of success, and it was justified in the historically hostile nature of neighboring countries. The dependence of the City-State from international trade meant that it was mostly suffering from the recent international financial crisis. However, unlike other Asian countries Singapore promptly resumed from that crisis. From 2011 the government started a plan to reform the tax structure, reducing inequality and significantly increase productivity. The medium to long-term objectives would on the one hand change their growth pattern, decrease the dependence on foreign labor and repurpose skills at all levels of the working chain. Secondly, the redevelopment of skills (at all levels of the working chain) would obtain an increase of 30% in productivity over the next decade. Thus, this would allow Singapore to exceed even the advanced economies such as the US, Japan, and Scandinavian countries.

The government boards that implement the economic and development policies are the following:

- Economic Development Board (EDB). Established as one of the earliest Statutory Boards in the country. The EDB is Singapore's primary agency which formulates and implements policies to attract private sector foreign investments. It maintains international offices in over 12 countries to promote Singapore to foreign companies and investors and to facilitate their eventual business start-up in Singapore.
- Standards, Productivity and Innovation Board (SPRING Singapore). SPRING Singapore is charged with the mission of growing Singapore's small and medium enterprises (SME) through productivity improvement, capability and management development and access to technology, innovation, and markets. SPRING also oversees the development and promotion of national standards and quality assurance programs.
- Agency for Science, Technology and Research (A*STAR). A*STAR directs the implementation of the National Science, Technology and Enterprise Plan, oversees several research institutes conducting research ranging from Microelectronics to Immunology and is responsible for developing the scientific talents needed to support Singapore's knowledge-based economy. Within A*STAR, the Biomedical Research Council coordinates public sector biomedical sciences research and development activities through funding opportunities and oversees several research institutes, research consortia and research programs.

- JTC Corporation (JTC). JTC oversees the planning and development of industrial parks and facilities in Singapore to support the growth of key target industries. It developed the Jurong Industrial Estate in the late 1960s, the Science Parks in the 1980s and 1990s and more recently the Biopolis, Tuas Biomedical Park and the Medtech Hub.
- International Enterprise Singapore (IE Singapore). IE Singapore promotes the internationalization of Singapore-based enterprises and the export of Singapore goods and services. With offices around the world, IE Singapore provides business advisory services to help Singapore companies identify overseas markets, develop international trade capabilities, and expand into the region using Singapore as a base.

An Economic Strategy Committee (ESC) was convened by the Singapore government in 2009. This was deriving new economic strategies and make Singapore 'future ready' for the next decade to be driven by sustainable and inclusive economic growth. The resultant ESC report broadly recommended Singapore focus on productivity-driven growth. It called for a qualitative re-structuring of the economy towards higher value activities and to become one that is rooted in innovation and skilled labor. Furthermore, the biomedical sciences sector was singled out as a new growth area. The Committee put forth a total of 7 key economic growth strategies:

- Growing Through Skills and Innovation.
- Anchor Singapore as a Global-Asia Hub.
- Build a Vibrant and Diverse Corporate Ecosystem.
- Make Innovation Pervasive and Strengthen Commercialization of R&D.
- Become a Smart Energy Economy.
- Enhance Land Productivity to Secure Future Growth.
- Build a Distinctive Global City and an Endearing Home.

Bank System

Singapore has a prosperous financial system. The Singapore Stock Exchange (SGX) hosts many foreign listings allowing investors to access shares from a wide range of companies from the Asia Pacific Region. Forex market is also very developed with a daily FX turnover of over USD 633 billion registered in April 2019. This large FX market is a key facilitator of Singapore's position as a global trading hub. Singapore also has a large OTC derivatives market.

With regards to the banking system the Monetary Authority of Singapore (MAS) is the Central Bank. Its main task is to ensure monetary stability as well as manage credit and exchange policies to promote growth. After having merged with the Board of Commissioners of Currency in 2002, MAS also manages currency issuance. The banking system benefits from a pro-business environment maintained by careful but minimal regulation. There are over 200 banks operating in Singapore.

Banks in Singapore are separated based on the licenses they hold. There are different licenses corresponding to different range of services the holder can offer. Full banking licenses allow for the greatest range of services and allow business to hold both corporate and retail clients. Foreign full banks with 'Qualifying Full Bank' licenses apply only to non-Singaporean banks and serve to expand their capability to open branches and operate ATM networks. In addition, there are seven banks designated by the MAS as Domestic Systematically Important Banks (D-SIBs). D-SIBs are banks which are assessed to have a significant impact on the stability of the financial system and therefore they need a more careful supervision. There are no restrictions imposed on resident or non-resident companies to hold bank accounts nevertheless saving accounts are not generally offered to companies. The process of opening and using a bank account is reasonably simple subject to 'Know Your Customer' practice. Through their bank accounts investors generally gain access to a wider range of credit facilities. Commercial banks, merchant banks and finance companies all offer forms of credit. The Monetary Authority of Singapore (MAS) announced the formation of a new FinTech & Innovation Group (FTIG) within its organization structure with effect from 1 August 2015. FTIG is responsible for regulatory policies and development strategies to facilitate the use of technology and innovation, enhance efficiency and strengthen competitiveness in the financial sector. FTIG comprises:

- Payments & Technology Solutions Office, which develop strategies for secure payments and other technology solutions for financial services.
- Technology Infrastructure Office, which is responsible for regulatory policies and strategies to develop efficient technology for the financial sector.
- Technology Innovation Lab, which works with the relevant industries to test and launch innovative ideas.

Interest rates (% per annum; period averages)	2000	2005	2010	2015	2018
On deposits					
Savings	1.28	0.26	0.13	.014	0.16
Time: 6 months	2.04	0.66	0.28	0.24	0.23
12 months	2.42	0.86	0.45	0.34	0.45

Source Asian Development Bank (ADB, 2019)

Investment Area

The Government is focusing on an economic model that will help Singapore sustain it is a competitive advantage over other countries in the region. This has made Singapore the first choice for investors who want to invest in Southeast Asia. The objective is to organize a technology advanced economy which is able create value through highly specialized services. While manufacturing will have to be concentrated on forefront sectors such as: pharmaceutical and applied technology to medicine, information technology, aerospace, renewable energy, maritime engineering and precision. In this context foreign investments are welcomed providing they offer knowledge, technology and stimulate the growth of innovative start-ups. There has been continuous growth in investments with applied scientific research and in support services for the sector of innovative start-ups. Public funds will be very heavy destined, in upcoming years, to the digital economy. The sector of information technology is indeed important in Singapore where limitations in terms of territory and natural resources impose a constant modernization of promoting sustainable growth. A lot of investments are made in the so-called "internet of things", the development of a sophisticated urban infrastructure connecting sensor systems to monitor the environmental situation, the conditions of traffic, lighting systems, energy conservation, waste management and water consumption.

Transportation

Singapore's Government plans in the next ten to twenty years to double the subway line, build airport terminals and shift and expand the port despite (already being among the first in the world for flow of ships and moving loads). Recently, Singapore has also signed an agreement with Malaysia to build a high-speed rail line connecting Singapore and Kuala Lumpur. This plans to be operational by 2026. As for storage there is an exciting opportunity for operators in Singapore, especially at the port and the Changi airport, as some sites are subject to an exemption from import duties (so-called Free Trade Zones). In these zones companies can store the products for re-export and sell to third parties without the payment of customs duties or GST (the corresponding local VAT). These taxes will be due once the goods are brought out by the Free Trade Zones for entry into the territory of the City-State.

Utilities and Renewable Energy

In the field of renewable energy and environmental services Singapore is at the forefront for treatment of clean energy, wastewater and emphasizing research and development. Regarding environmental issues, Singapore is proposed as a model of sustainability in the energy and chemical sector and it supports those companies innovating in energy efficiency and carbon emissions reductions.

Food and Beverage

The food industry in Singapore is flourishing. Being a high-income country there is an extensive demand (but also offering) of high-end products. Once it enters force, the FTA between the European Union and the City State, the killing of numerous non-tariff barriers will facilitate imports of certain typical European products, particularly appreciated in the world. However, it is worth noting that large retailers impose substantial costs for the marketing of food products and that it is a "mature market" so, in some sectors, such as wine, the substantial offer may leave little room for new products which are not particularly competitive or of the highest quality.

Establishing a Company

The most common business structures in Singapore are:

- companies;
- sole-proprietorship;
- branch of a foreign entity;
- partnership.

A Company (or Limited Liability Company—LLC) is the most popular type of business. A company has a separate legal entity to its shareholders, can hold property in its own name and can sue, and be sued. Most companies in Singapore are private companies limited by shares and bear the suffix 'Pte Ltd' or 'Private Limited' to their name. A private company which wishes to maintain more than 50 shareholders must be converted to a public company. An Exempt Private Company (EPC) is one with less than 20 individual shareholders, and has no corporate shareholders. An EPC does not need its accounts to be audited if revenue is less than 5 million SGD for the financial year. A Public Company Limited by Shares must have at least 50 shareholders. The company may raise capital by offering shares and debentures to the public. The registration of a Singaporean company involves the name approval and incorporation. Before incorporation, the company must have:

1. Drawn up the Constitution;
2. A local address.

Any company wishing to do business in Singapore should consult the relevant regulatory body to establish whether additional licenses are necessary. Once the company has provided the directors' and obtained the Singapore Standard Industrial Classification (SSIC) investors can submit an online application via BizFile or choose the services of a professional firm to do this on their behalf. The application may take between 14 days and two months for approval. This will depend on whether it needs to be referred to other authorities or not.

A sole-proprietorship is the simplest and most flexible business structure. It must be owned by a local resident (who is at least 18 years old). If the owner is not a resident in Singapore, a local manager must be appointed. The appointed manager must be a person of at least 18 years of age. There are no capital requirements for a sole-proprietorship but the owner is personally accountable for all liabilities incurred during business.

A partnership is a business firm owned by two and 20 partners. The partners can be individuals or companies. If there are more than 20 partners, the business must be registered as a company under the Companies Act. Most partnerships do not constitute a separate legal entity and therefore the partners are liable for the losses and obligations of the firm. An LLP (Limited Liability Partnership) is a business structure that offers all its members limited liability while allowing them to retain the flexibility of operating the LLP as a traditional partnership. Unlike other forms of partnership, LLP is a separate legal entity. Partners are personally liable for their own negligence and personal misconduct. The LLPs are commonly used by professional firms and start-ups. The LLP structure would appeal to investors who wish to be 'silent partners' in a business and whose liability is limited to the extent of their investment. An LLP can be set up with a minimum of two partners and there is no maximum limit. An LP is a hybrid of partnership and a LLP, which includes one or more partners and one or more limited partners. Limited partners of an LP enjoy limited liability but are unable to take part in the management of the firm while one or more general partners may have unlimited liability.

Foreign companies may conduct business in Singapore by establishing a branch office. Any foreign company wishing to register a branch office can engage a professional firm such as a corporate secretarial firm or a legal firm to assist in the application. A branch of a foreign company is not a separate legal entity, it is only an extension of its head office and therefore its debts and liabilities are part of the liability of the head office.

Domestic Market

Singapore has a relatively small domestic market and thus, must open its economy to external markets for the economy to thrive.

Singapore is a highly developed trade-oriented market economy. Its economy has been ranked as the most open in the world, 7th least corrupt, most pro-business, has low tax rates (14.2% of Gross Domestic Product, GDP) and has the third highest per-capita GDP in the world in terms of Purchasing Power Parity (PPP). APEC is headquartered in Singapore. Government-linked companies play a substantial role in Singapore's economy which are owned through the sovereign wealth fund Temasek Holdings. Singapore's economy is a major Foreign Direct Investment (FDI) outflow financier. Singapore has also benefited from the flow of FDI and from the global investment and institutions. This is due to its attractive investment climate and stable political environment. Exports particularly in electronics, chemicals and services, including Singapore's position as the regional hub for wealth management, provide the main source of revenue for the economy, which permit Singapore to purchase natural resources and raw goods, which it is, currently, lacking. Moreover, water and the scarcity of land is defined as a precious resource in Singapore. However, Singapore has limited arable land. This means Singapore must rely on the agrotechnology park for agricultural production and consumption, what is more underlining, that the lack of human resources is also an issue for the health of the Singaporean economy. In 2014, the economy of Singapore ranked 2nd in the Scientific American Biotechnology, with the featuring of Biopolis. Thus, Singapore could be said to rely on an extended concept of intermediary trade, by purchasing raw goods and refining them for re-export, such as in the wafer fabrication industry and oil refining. Singapore also has a strategic port. This makes Singapore more competitive than many of its neighbors in carrying out such entrepot activities. Singapore also has one of the highest trade GDP ratios in the world. This averaged around 400% during 2008–11 and in 2017 it registered a trade-to-GDP ratio of 322.4%. The Port of Singapore is the second-busiest in the world. In addition, Singapore's port infrastructure and skilled workforce, which is due to the success of the country's education policy in producing skilled workers, is also fundamental in this aspect, as they provide easy access to markets for both importing and exporting, and the skills needed to refine imports into exports.

The petroleum and petrochemicals industry in Singapore are two of the biggest in the world. Singapore imports oil from other countries before refining them for further use to other countries. The Singapore Petroleum Company (SPC) is also a leading player in the petroleum industry and is engaged in exploration, production, refining and distribution. Manufacturing is another major industry in Singapore. Although Singapore has specialized in digital and electronics manufacturing for the past forty years the country has diversified into other forms of manufacturing. Thanks to government initiatives and subsidies, biomedical and pharmaceutical manufacturing are seen to be the future for Singapore industries.

Singapore is also a global leader in services, particularly in finance. Singapore's banking system is considered to be the strongest in the world. Singapore has the fourth largest foreign exchange market in the world after London, New York and Tokyo. The Singapore Government Securities is the only Asian market, besides Japan, to be part of the Citigroup World Bond Index. The Singapore Exchange (SGX) was also the first demutualized, integrated securities and derivatives exchange in Asia-Pacific. Singapore is recognized as one of the premier asset management centers in Asia with more than 200 international asset management firms. Finally, the Asian Dollar Market in Singapore has become an influential element to the economic development of the whole of Asia.

Apart from finance, tourism is the other major service industry available in Singapore. Thanks to government initiatives tourism has diversified into niche markets such as medical tourism, the gaming industry and the MICE (Meetings, Incentives, Conferencing and Exhibitions) industry. In 2018, tourism receipts rose 1.0% to S$27.1 billion, mainly due to growth in visitor Arrivals across almost all of the top 15 markets and higher visitor spending from all top five TR markets. Record arrivals from seven markets helped boost overall visitor arrival by 6.2% to 18.5 million.

To preserve its international standing and further its economic prosperity in the twenty-first century Singapore took measures to promote innovation, encourage entrepreneurship, re-train its workforce and even attract foreign talents. Singaporean government issues Employment Pass (EP) under three categories attracted foreign talents. P1 Employment Pass for those individuals with monthly income of $8000 and above, P2 Employment Pass for individuals with monthly income of $4500–7999 and Q1 Employment Pass individuals with a monthly income of at least $3000. The Ministry of Manpower (MoM) oversees the matter related to immigration of workers. These measures aim to boost Singapore's productivity so Singapore remains competitive and ready for the challenges of an information-driven global economy.

External trade (USD millions)	2000	2005	2010	2015	2018
Exports, fob	237,826	283,683	480,709	491,816	555,665
Imports, cif	232,175	334,314	426,327	423,403	500,194
Trade balance	5651	49,370	54,383	68,414	55,471

Source Asian Development Bank (ADB, 2019)

Main commercial partners (USD millions)	2000	2005	2010	2015	2018
Exports					
1. China, People's Rep. of	5377	19,752	36,495	48,254	50,619
2. Hong Kong, China	10,841	21,570	41,326	40,337	48,633
3. Malaysia	25,041	30,405	41,913	37,841	44,895
4. Indonesia	N/A	22,109	33,091	28,906	33,018
5. United States	23,891	23,880	23,005	24,115	31,890
6. Japan	10,404	12,536	16,412	15,281	20,036
7. Taipei, China	8225	8970	12,820	14,449	16,991
8. Korea, Rep. of	4916	8053.2	14,398	14,510	15,681
9. Thailand	5872	9431	12,701	13,807	15,561
10. Vietnam	2091	4421	7387	12,667	12,059
Imports					
1. China, People's Rep. of	7116	20,526	33,666	42,191	49,666
2. Malaysia	22,848	27,347	36,358	33,143	42,821
3. United States	20,270	23,482	35,633	33,371	42,120
4. Taipei, China	5965	11,835	18,517	24,670	31,400
5. Japan	23,189	19,244	24,454	18,589	22,264
6. Korea, Rep. of	4822	8599	18,029	18,193	14,199
7. Indonesia	N/A	10,452	16,839	14,377	15,279
8. Saudi Arabia	4338	8958	11,241	7939	12,624
9. United Arab Emirates	1506	2538	6371	8173	9775
10. Germany	4235	5955	8904	8950	10,140

Source Asian Development Bank (ADB, 2019)

Finance and Taxation

Tax

In Singapore taxes are levied based on the income of companies and individuals. In addition, there are Goods and Services Tax (tax on consumption) and property tax

(tax on the ownership of property). There is, however, no capital gains tax in Singapore.

Taxation of Companies

Singapore's taxation system is territorial; this means companies in Singapore are subject to pay tax on income accruing or derived from Singapore. This is also the case for foreign income received in Singapore. Foreign-sourced dividends, foreign branch profits and foreign-sourced service income received in Singapore by a Singapore-resident company, are exempt from income tax under the foreign-sourced income exemption scheme if the following conditions are met:

- the headline tax rate of the foreign jurisdiction from which the income is received is at least 15%;
- the income is subject to tax in the foreign authority from which it is received; and
- the Comptroller of Income Tax is satisfied that the tax exemption would be beneficial to the person resident in Singapore.

If the above conditions are not met, it is possible to apply for an exemption to the Comptroller of Income Tax, who would consider the applications on a case-by-case basis. Where the Singapore-resident recipient of the income is not entitled to the foreign-sourced income exemption scheme (discussed above) he may nevertheless claim bilateral or unilateral tax credits for the foreign tax suffered on such foreign-sourced income.

Corporate Income Tax

The prevailing headline corporate tax rate in Singapore is 17%. However, like many other jurisdictions, this headline corporate tax rate does not accurately reflect the effective corporate tax rate. Singapore's effective tax rate can be significantly lower due to applicable tax exemptions or tax incentives. For example, the partial tax exemption (where the first $10,000 benefit of 75% exemption and next $190,000 of chargeable income is exempt from tax for 50%) is available to companies and generally the first $300,000 of their taxable income would reduce significantly the effective tax rate for small-to-mid sized companies in Singapore.

For newly incorporated companies which meet certain conditions tax exemption will apply. For the first three consecutive years of assessment (YA) the first $100,000 of chargeable income is charged 50% tax. This is also the case for the next $200,000 of chargeable income. Singapore also provides several incentive schemes which, if applicable, could reduce the effective corporate tax rate on income from qualifying activities to as low as 5% or 10%. The effective corporate tax rate for an existing company of taxable profits up is to $300,000 and can be as low as 5.9 and 4% for a newly incorporated Singaporean company after considering the corporate income tax rebate.

Dividends

Under Singapore's one-tier corporate tax system, corporate profits are taxed at a corporate level. The corporate tax paid is a final tax and dividends distributed by Singapore tax-resident companies. Tax exemption is in the hands of their shareholders in Singapore. In addition, Singapore does not impose withholding tax on dividends.

Capital Gains

Singapore does not have a capital gains tax regime. Singapore income tax is imposed based on the gain of disposal of shares/investments however only if the gain is regarded as a revenue gain sourced in Singapore. To provide more tax certainty on divestment of equity investments, gains derived from equity investments disposed by a company during the period 1 June 2012–31 May 2017 will also be exempt if the following conditions are met:

- the shares divested are ordinary shares;
- prior to the date of disposal, the divesting company had held at least 20% of the ordinary shares in the investee company for a continuous period of at least 24 months.

However, this exemption would not apply to:

- A divesting company which is an insurer where gains or profits from the disposal of shares are included as taxable profits under Section 26 of the Income Tax Act;
- gains from disposal of shares in an unlisted investee company that is in the business of trading or holding Singapore immovable properties (including property development);
- disposal of shares by a partnership, limited partnership or limited liability partnership where one or more of the partners is a company or companies.

Tax Incentives

Singapore is well-known for its extensive suite of tax incentives available to incoming investors. There are two main categories of tax incentives. There are those administered by:

- the Singapore Economic Development Board under the authority of the Economic Expansion Incentives (Relief from Income Tax) Act;
- various other government bodies and those granted under the Singapore Income Tax Act itself.

Examples of Singapore's tax incentives include the:

- Financial Sector Incentives Scheme;
- Headquarters (HQ) Program which comprises the Regional Headquarters (RHQ) tax incentive and International Headquarters (IHQ) tax incentive;

- Global Trader Program, where qualifying income is taxed at concessionary income tax rates of 5% or 10% for a renewable 5-year period on qualifying trading income.

Taxation of Individuals

Singapore's personal income tax rates are competitive which attract talent from around the world to Singapore. Personal tax rates start at 0% and are capped at 22% (for chargeable income above $320,000) for tax residents. The employment income of non-residents is taxed at 15% or at the applicable resident rate, whichever gives rise to a higher tax amount.

Administration

The tax year, known as the year of assessment, runs from 1 January to 31 December. The period for which the profits are identified for assessment is called the basis year. The basis year is generally the year preceding the year of assessment (YA). Therefore, income earned during the 2019 basis year is assessed to tax in the year of assessment 2020. An estimate of chargeable income (ECI) must be filed within three months from the end of their financial year. As a concession, Singapore operates a single tier tax system, with a flat rate of 17%. Companies with revenues of not more than SGD 1 million for the financial year and nil ECI for the YA are not required to file an ECI. The statutory deadline for filing income tax returns is 30 November (paper file) and 15 December (e-file) of the YA. No extension of time is allowed.

Income tax payable is due within one month from the date of notice. A late payment penalty of five percent of the tax due is applicable, if it is not paid by the due date. An additional one percent is added for every subsequent month that the tax remains unpaid up to a maximum of 12%. In Singapore, it is an offence not to file an income tax return with the tax authority.

Taxable Income

For a company based in Singapore, the taxable income is the book profits reported in the audited financial statements adjusted according to the relevant Singapore tax rules. Financial statements must be prepared under the Singapore Financial Reporting Standards unless otherwise approved. Expenses can be deducted if they are:

- incurred wholly and exclusively to produce taxable income;
- not prohibited under the tax law;
- revenue in nature.

Special rules apply on the deductibility of expenses for investment holding companies. Allowable expenses attributable to foreign-source income can be deducted against income received in Singapore in the year the expenses are incurred and subject to tax in Singapore. If the taxpayer has opted for the liberalized tax treatment, the deduction will be allowed in the year of receipt. While book depreciation of fixed assets is not required, capital allowances are granted according to statutory rates.

Tax Losses

Trading losses can be offset against chargeable income for the same year. It is possible to carry forward unused losses indefinitely. Additionally, capital allowances can be offset against other chargeable income of the same year and carried forward indefinitely. A one-year carry back is permitted for an amount up to SGD 100,000 of the current year unused capital allowances and trade losses. For the carry back to be permitted it is necessary to comply with various administrative procedures. Both the carry forward and carry back of losses are subject to the 'shareholder test'. The shareholders must remain substantially (50% or more) the same at the relevant comparison dates. However, companies with a substantial change in ownership may be granted a waiver from applying the shareholder test by the IRAS to deduct their unused tax losses and capital allowances if the change in ownership was not tax-motivated.

Unutilized capital allowances can be carried back to the tax year immediately preceding the year in which the capital allowance arose. Unutilized capital allowances can also be carried forward indefinitely. The utilization of carry back and carry forward of capital allowances is subject to the 'shareholder test' and the same trade test, i.e. there is no change in the company's principal activities during the relevant comparison dates.

Groups

In Singapore, groups of companies are generally formed by a Singapore-incorporated parent company and all its Singapore-incorporated subsidiaries. It is considered that two Singapore-incorporated companies are members of the same group when one owns 75% of the other or if both are 75% owned by a third Singapore-incorporated company. Under certain conditions, groups have access to group-relief measures that allow them to transfer between the members of the group current-year unused losses, capital allowances and donations. Nevertheless, consolidated returns are not required and each company must file its own tax return.

Transfer Pricing

The IRAS has published specific transfer pricing guidelines consistent with the arm's length principle' outlined in the Organization for Economic Cooperation and Development (OECD) Transfer Pricing Guidelines for Multinational Enterprises and Tax Administrations. There is a specialized transfer pricing consultation process in place where taxpayers are interviewed to ascertain compliance levels with transfer pricing guidelines. The IRAS expects companies to assess their transfer pricing risk and prepare sufficient and contemporaneous transfer pricing documentation to support their transfer pricing practices. To ease compliance burden, the IRAS has announced thresholds for which the full transfer pricing documentation is not required.

Tax rate	%
Corporate tax	17
Personal income tax	22
Sales tax	7

Source Trading Economics (2018)

Audit and Accounting

Singapore has an excellent accounting and audit regime, which draws heavily from the International Financial Reporting Standards (IFRS), and as such maintains high quality and international recognition. The accounting regime is regulated by the Accounting and Corporate Regulatory Authority, which maintains the standards described in the following laws:

- Singapore Companies Act, Cap 50 (applicable for all companies);
- Singapore Exchange Listing Manual (applicable for public companies);
- Charities Act, Cap 37 (applicable for institutions of public characters);
- Societies Act, Cap 311 (applicable for societies).

Accounting Standards

Accounting standards in Singapore are prescribed by the Accounting Standards Council (ASC). In Singapore, Accounting standards are known as Singapore Financial Reporting Standards (SFRS) and are based on IFRS. Accounting is done on an accrual basis and transactions are recorded as they occur. Future cash receipts and obligations are also recorded.

Following the addition in 2009 of a separate IFRS for Small and Medium Sized Enterprises (SME), the ASC released a SFRS for Small Enterprises (SE) in 2010. This SFRS is an alternative framework to the full SFRS. This provides SEs with a relief from the stress of full compliance, while maintaining transparency and quality. Companies can qualify for the SFRS for SEs if:

- they are not publicly accountable;
- they publish general-purpose financial statements for external users;
- they are a small entity with total annual revenue of not more than SGD 10 million, total gross assets of no more than SGD 10 million and there are less than 50 employees.

Accounting Records

Every incorporated company must keep records to a certain standard, including a profit and loss account. These records must be kept in a place which the directors see fit. If this place is outside Singapore, then the statements and returns must be sent and kept at a place in Singapore where directors can inspect them. Accounting records must be kept for five years following the end of the business year in which the relevant transaction occurred. Though some companies are exempt from the requirement to file audited accounts, they are still required to keep sufficient accounting records including a profit and loss account. Accounts are available to inspection from the public for a small fee. Audited accounts must be filed with ACRA on an annual basis but firms are free to choose their tax year. All private and public companies must appoint auditors within three months of incorporation. Accounts must generally be placed before members at an annual general meeting, no more than six months after the end of the financial year. These accounts must then be submitted to ACRA with a statement from two directors and an auditor's report where applicable. A Singapore-incorporated company must have at least one director who is ordinarily resident in Singapore.

Every company must lodge an annual return with the registrar within a month of its annual general meeting which, in turn, must be held no later than 18 months from the date of incorporation (in respect of the company's first annual general meeting), or 15 months from the date of the last annual general meeting. The accounts laid at the annual general meeting must be not more than six months old. For a public company listed or quoted on a securities exchange in Singapore, the accounts presented at the AGM shall be made up to a date not more than four months before the AGM.

Audit Requirements

All companies, including foreign branch offices, except those specifically exempted, must appoint an independent certified public auditor to audit their annual financial statements. Financial statements must be audited according to the Singapore Standards on Auditing (SSA) or the International Standards on Auditing (ISA). To reduce the regulatory burden on small companies, a new small company exemption from the audit requirement was introduced for financial years commencing on or after 1 July 2015.

To qualify as a small company, the company must qualify the following criteria:

- it must be a private company;
- for the past two financial years, meeting at least two of the following criteria:
  - total annual revenue: SGD 10 million or less;
  - total assets: SGD 10 million or less;
  - number of employees: 50 or less.

Sole-proprietorships, partnerships and representative offices are not required to prepare audited financial statements.

Risk Assessment

The country has the following strengths:

- Stable political system and effective policymaking.
- High income country serving as a regional and global hub for trade and financial services.
- Track record of sound and flexible economic policies.
- Strong external position with a long history of current account surpluses, ample foreign exchange reserves and low public external debt.
- Very strong business environment and banking sector.

At the same time there are also some weaknesses:

- Very high export dependency.
- Economic growth volatility associated with lower global trade and volatile financing conditions.
- Shortage of high skilled professionals.
- Very high old age dependency ratio (number of elderly people as a share of those of working age).

Data Protection

The Personal Data Protection Act (PDPA) is the main legislation that protects consumer and personal data although there are several other laws that may relate to the processing of personal data. This includes:

- The Computer Misuse and Cybersecurity Act.
- The Official Secrets Act.
- The Statistics Act.
- The Statutory Bodies and Government Companies (Protection of Secrecy) Act.
- The Electronic Transaction Act.
- The Banking Act.
- The Telecommunications Act.
- The Law of Confidence.

These laws cover individuals, companies and government organizations. They apply to any personal data that is collected, used, or disclosed in Singapore. Personal data is defined as data about an individual who could be identified by that data or about other data held by an organization. This does not include business contact information, data that has been in existence for 100 years or more or data regarding individuals who have been deceased for 10 years or more. The key provisions for those holding personal or consumer data are:

- individuals must consent to the collection and use of their data by an organization;
- organizations must obtain data for a specific purpose and must inform the individual of this purpose;
- data retained must be accurate and complete;
- organizations have a responsibility to keep data secure;
- personal data cannot be kept longer than necessary and must be deleted once no longer useful;
- individuals have the right to access and correct their own personal data;
- organizations may not transfer personal data outside Singapore unless the recipient meets the same standards of data protection;
- organizations must be open and transparent about their data protection practices.

Although PDPA stipulates consent is required to gather personal data, it provides for 'deemed consent'. An individual is deemed to consent on the collection of data if the individual voluntarily provides the personal data to an organization and it is reasonable that the individual would voluntarily provide the data. The PDPA provides for the existence of a 'Do Not Call' (DNC) registry which allows consumers to opt out of receiving marketing material. In accordance with DNC provisions, organizations must not send marketing material to any individuals who are registered in the National DNC Registry unless clear and unambiguous consent has been provided. Certain exemptions apply, wherein organizations are exempted from specific provisions of PDPA under certain circumstances such as; emergencies, national interest, historical or statistical research or for the provision of legal services.

The regulatory body that supervises adherence to PDPA is The Personal Data Protection Commission (PDPC) which has the authority to investigate potential breaches of regulation and direct companies to change policy to comply with the PDPA. If an organization is in breach of the data protection provisions in the PDPA, the PDPC can demand that the organization:

- stops collecting, using or disclosing personal data in contravention of the Act;
- destroys personal data collected in contravention of the PDPA;
- provides access to or correct the personal data;
- pays a financial penalty of an amount not exceeding SGD 1 million.

Money Laundering Regulations and Exchange Controls

There are no official exchange controls in place in Singapore. Singapore operates a strict anti-money laundering (AML) and counter terrorist financing regime, through a broad legal and supervisory framework. Singapore is a member of the Financial Action Task Force (FATF) and an active participant in international discussion on the matter. The main anti-money laundering legislation in Singapore is the Corruption, Drug Trafficking and Other Serious Crimes (Confiscation of Benefits) Act (CDSA). Additionally, the Terrorism (Suppression of Financing) Act (TSOFA) was enacted in 2002 to counter terrorism financing in Singapore.

The Monetary Authority of Singapore (MAS) is the primary regulatory authority. However, investigation and enforcement of AML regulations are managed by The Financial Investigation Division (FID) which is part of the Commercial Affairs Department. The FID has three subsidiary departments:

- The Financial Investigation Branch, which is responsible for investigating money laundering offences under CDSA as well as the TSOFA.
- The Proceeds of Crime Unit, which identifies and forfeits illegally held or obtained assets.
- The Suspicious Transaction Reporting Office, which receives and analyses reports from institutions, and provides financial intelligence for the detection of money laundering, terrorist financing and other offences.

The Cash Enforcement Branch, which also operates under the Commercial Affairs Department, is tasked with investigating infringements of cross border cash movement reporting requirements.

All companies must comply with the CDSA, which places several responsibilities and restrictions on businesses. These include the reporting of suspicious transactions. Under the CDSA, companies are required to file a Suspicious Activity Report (STR).

All financial institutions are required to keep Financial Transaction Documents (FTDs) for a minimum period of five years. FTDs include any documents relating to opening, closing and withdrawing from accounts. Failing to keep necessary documentation can result in a fine of up to SGD 10,000.

The penalties for money laundering are imprisonment for up to 10 years and a fine of up to SGD 500,000 for natural persons and a maximum of SGD 1,000,000 for offences committed by institutions or corporations.

Intellectual Property Rights

Singapore recognizes the importance of Intellectual Property Rights (IPR) for maintaining a productive and incentivized knowledge economy.

IPR protections offered include copyright, trademarks, patents and registered designs as well as other specialized protections for innovations such as printed circuits.

THAILAND

Official name
Kingdom of Thailand

Capital
Bangkok

Area
513,120 sq. km

Population
66.5 mln

Languages
Thai (official)

Main ethnic groups
Thai 96%, Burmese 2%

Main religions
Buddhist (official) 94%, Muslim 5%

Government type
Constitutional Monarchy (Military Junta de facto)

Urbanization
49.9%

Life expectancy ratio
76 years

Fertility rate
1.4 children born/woman

Currency
Baht THB

Thailand

Country Introduction

Population, Location, Geography, Climate

Thailand is the most developed country of the Indochinese Peninsula, considering it was not developed under colonial rule. The southernmost part of the country is covered by beaches, while the northern territory is quite mountainous. The central part of the frame is almost all flat, and numerous islands fringe the coast, especially along the Andaman Sea.

The heart of Thailand is made up of the central plains, which is about 1/3rd of the territory. However, there are many mountainous areas, where there are peaks of over two thousand meters high.

The major peaks, as mentioned above, are located in the northern region. The Doi Inthanon (2565 m.) is the highest point of the Nation.

Coastal development is over 3200 km, in particular the coast of the Andaman Sea is quite rugged, more than the Gulf of Siam; there are numerous islands in both seas around the country, some very famous for tourism, such as Phuket (543 km^2), the largest of Thailand, Ko Samui (229 km^2), and Ko Chang (217 km^2).

There are two major river systems, one of that is Chao Phraya River (1112 km, including its longest tributary, the Nan), which affects the central northern area of the country. Secondly, is the Mekong (4350 km), which is located in the eastern part. However, this river never goes into Thai territory but rather marks the border between Laos and Thailand.

Songkhla Lake (1040 km^2), a system of lagoons in the southern part of Thailand, is the largest natural lake basin of the nation. It is then followed by Bueng Boraphet (212 km^2) and Nong Han (125 km^2).

The climate is tropical, with slight differences in temperatures throughout the year. A rainy season happens, on average, from May to October. Given the north-south extension of the country, there are some regional differences. The coastal zones are the rainiest, while the northern mountainous areas are suffering cooler temperatures. In the south there are equatorial conditions, resulting in rainfall throughout the year; having the most rain in the fall.

Thailand is divided into 77 provinces (changwats), with two special local areas corresponding to the cities of Bangkok and Pattaya. About 2/3rds of the population lives in rural areas. Yet, the urbanization rate is 34%.

Bangkok (8,305,000 inhab., 14,910,000 Aggl. Urban), the capital, is known as Krung Thep in local language, which includes the city of Samut Prakan (389,000 pop.) and Nonthaburi (292,000 abs.); four centers exceed two hundred thousand inhabitants, Udon Thani (247,000 pop.), Chon Buri (219,000 pop.), Nakhon Ratchasima (209,000 pop.) and Chiang Mai (201,000 pop.).

The Thai make up 96% of the population, of which about 14% are of Chinese origin, the most substantial minority is of Burma (2%). Theravada Buddhism is the national religion, making up 93% of the population. A small minority of 5% are Islamic.

Internal Policy

After the coup of May 2014, which put an end to six months of severe internal political instability, the situation of public policy was quiet and business activity continued without difficulty. To guide the country, the current military junta presented a second draft of the new Constitution, at the end of March 2016, after a first version failure of last September. The Thai citizens were called to express themselves on it in a referendum in August 2016.

The Thai government is focusing on economic policies to promote growth, especially on the demand side through massive infrastructure development plans. Particular attention is made to maintain the image of Thailand as a tourist destination and foreign direct investment.

International Relations

Thailand is a partner of great interest because of its political and economic weight within South-East Asia. It is a part of a region of growing importance and within an international geopolitical center because of constant and sustained economic growth.

After the coup of May 2014, the new government was committed to re-establish relations with key partners—most importantly, ASEAN. Negotiations with the European Union to conclude a Free Trade Agreement (FTA) has suffered an inevitable slowdown due to the recent troubles of domestic policy. The EU's common position, currently, includes the maintenance of diplomatic and economic relations but freezes high-level political relations. Japan and China are interested to enhance their partnership with the Asian country because of the commercial potential generated by the newly formed ASEAN Economic Community, of which Thailand is a strategic member. Furthermore, the United States, Australia, New Zealand, Russia, and India hope to maintain profitable relationships.

Economy

Macroeconomic Overview

	Unit	2000A	2018	2020F
GDP, current prices	USD (billions)	126.39	487.24	547.43
GDP per capita, current prices	USD	2028.08	7187.19	8048.58
GDP based on PPP per capita	Current International dollar	7358.20	19,476.48	21,610.49

Source IMF Outlook (2019)

After a military coup, which has allowed Prayuth Chan-Ocha to take the power, the economic situation has considerably improved. The new government has focused its attention on the lowest class. Once completed the first project, it has turned the priority on infrastructure needed for the country. To further its development, Thailand has participated in international and regional organizations. It has developed the cooperation with other ASEAN members: Indonesia, Malaysia, the Philippines, Singapore, Brunei, Laos, Cambodia, Burma, and Vietnam—whose foreign and economic ministers hold annual meetings. Regional cooperation is progressing in economic, trade, banking, political, and cultural matters.

Over the last four decades, Thailand has made considerable progress in social and economic development—moving from a low-income country to an upper-income country in less than a generation. The government has embarked on an ambitious reform program to raise Thailand's long-term growth path and achieve high-income status.

Thailand's economy grew at an average annual rate of 7.5% between 1986 and 1996, and 5% following the Asian crisis during 1999–2005. This created millions of jobs that helped millions of people.

Poverty has declined substantially over the last 30 years, from 67% in 1986 to 11% in 2014 during periods of high growth and rising agricultural prices. However, poverty and inequality continue to pose significant challenges, as poverty in Thailand is primarily a rural phenomenon. Although inequality has declined over the past 30 years, the distribution in Thailand remains unequal compared to many other countries in East Asia.

There are some opportunities, including expanding trade through a full integration with the global economy, implementing public investments in private capital and improving the quality of public services. This will support a more balanced resumption, trying to eliminate extreme poverty.

Almost two years after the coup, the situation in the country appeared healthy and worthy of interest. In 2014, Thailand recorded an average +0.7% growth, caused by the political crisis that had blocked public spending and generated fears about the stability of the country. However, in 2015 the economy returned to acceptable levels, with an increase of 2.9%. Thai economics has grown from the most important cities: Bangkok, Chiang Mai, and Phuket, where the size of the upper-middle class is increasing.

GDP grew at a rate of around 4% per year in 2017 and 2018.

Structure of output (% GDP)	2000	2005	2010	2015	2018
Agriculture	8.5	9.2	10.5	8.9	8.1
Industry	36.8	38.6	40.0	33.4	32.4
Services	54.7	52.2	49.4	57.7	59.5

Source Asian Development Bank (ADB, 2019)

Structure of expenditure (% GDP)	2000	2005	2010	2015	2018
Final consumption	67.7	69.5	68.0	67.1	63.9
Gross capital formation	22.3	30.4	25.4	22.4	25.0
Exports of goods and services	64.8	68.4	66.1	68.7	2.1
Imports of goods and services	56.5	69.5	60.6	57.2	66.8
Statistical discrepancy	1.6	1.1	1.1	−2.0	56.5

Source Asian Development Bank (ADB, 2019)

Economic Policy

During the 1960s, Thailand followed a policy of industrialization, under the government act named as a promotion of industrial. The Government encountered many problems with the small-scale domestic market and a growing trade deficit owing to increased imports of capital. The government needed to find a solution. To do so, it introduced a measure to promote exports. Following the attempt to ignite the economy, the 1970s were a period of nationalism, when Thailand restricted foreign capital and limited the types of jobs foreigners could obtain. By which, during the 1970s, Thailand began to adopt export promotion policies, while continuing to import substitution towards the promotion of heavy industry.

In the early 1980s, the country entered into a recession caused by the effects of the second oil-shock. It ultimately caused Thailand to run into a problem with the balance of payments. In response, the Thai government adopted a structural adjustment program and set up further export promotion measures. In fact, it has promoted liberalization policies due to the growing demands of the domestic market. By following trade liberalization to integrate into the world market, Thailand abolished protection and regulatory measures in order to stimulate trade and investment. In this period, foreign investment, in particular from Japan and Taiwan, played an important role in economic growth.

Right now, according to a World Bank report, economic development in Thailand is characterized by macroeconomic stability, but also by a series of badly managed sectoral interventions. In Thailand, however, there has been little state direction of credit or financial allocation. Unlike governments in other East Asian, the Thai government has always focused on conservative fiscal and monetary policies and infrastructural investments.

It is possible to assert that Thai Economy is quite steady. During 2016, the GDP grew by 0.8%. In addition to cutting interest rates, the Bank of Thailand facilitated transactions in foreign currency, promoting a Baht depreciation. This policy has supported the encouragement of exports but is challenged by the growing price of raw materials.

Even if the growth did not reach the forecasts, Thailand can be considered, as one of the most important Asian markets. According to Minister of Finance, unemployment is stuck at 0.87%, due to agro-industry which represents 8% of GDP, and employs 40% of the population.

Bank System

During the 1980s and early 1990s, the financial institutions in Thailand, particularly the largest, as the Bank of Thailand, were under financial liberalization. Liberalization included the deregulation of international capital flows, movement towards a more flexible exchange rate system, and financial innovation.

The Financial Institution Act, introduced in 2008, had the task of regulating commercial banking and establishing the types of businesses, which a bank can participate in.

The financial industry is controlled and regulated by the Ministry of Finance and the Bank of Thailand.

The Ministry formulates fiscal policy and oversees the nation's finances, including the development of taxation plans, printing of money, banking industry, and control of foreign currency reserves. The Bank of Thailand is responsible for implementation of Ministry of Finance plans, including issuing bank notes, advising the government on monetary policies, supervising financial institutions, and maintaining monetary stability.

The Thailand financial sector is relatively large, with assets close to 180% of GDP.

Foreign banks play an important but limited role. Foreign banks account for about 18%, in line with many emerging market countries. In accordance with Bank of Thailand rules, they operate mostly as single branches, with only two full-service foreign commercial banks.

Most foreign banks are focused on the wholesale market. Otherwise, domestic banks do not have a major presence abroad.

Since the financial crisis, banks have diversified their revenue—which has helped improve their risk profile. Banks have focused on expanding their services to retail customers, small-sized enterprises, medium-sized enterprises. This has helped them diversify their loan and revenue base.

There are several actions, some of which the BOT is already implementing, that could both address the current overhang of NPAs and reduce the likelihood of a recurrence of this problem in the future.

By applying IAS 39, the clarity in the financial statements of banks has increased. This has encouraged banks to manage problematic loans more easily, further promoting their level of sophistication.

Furthermore, it is necessary that the Bank of Thailand strengthens many parts of its supervisory team, while holding management fully accountable for distressed assets. The management of the banks should not have to rely on the supervisory team to discover problem loans.

The Bank of Thailand should also continue to promote conservative guidelines on restructured loans. This will further increase the level of Thailand's banks' level of sophistication.

Thai Financial System consists of 3 Operators Categories: Commercial Banking, Specialized Financial Institutions (SFI) and non-banking financial intermediaries (Financial, insurance companies, co-operative).

Currently, there are about 5000 financial institutions, including 30 commercial banks and 6 SFI. The financial system is dominated by Commercial Banks, which covers about 60% of total loans.

The Access to Credit by the Small and Medium Enterprises might be considered simple, even if the paperwork and requesting various documents sometimes might be excessive.

It is important to remind that the credit from banks and financial institutions should always be fully guaranteed, but this could represent a limit to access to credit. Yet, the rating of the assets by the banks might be considered excessively prudent. Successful business plan and good cash—flows are very important for the risk assessment. Required documentation is generally rather dense, and the procedure should go on over 30 days.

Interest Rates (% per annum; period averages)	2000	2005	2010	2015	2018
On deposits					
Savings	2.50	1.88	0.50	0.5	0.5
Time: 6 months	3.00	2.75	1.40	1.3	1.3
12 months	3.50	3.00	1.55	1.4	1.4

Source Asian Development Bank (ADB, 2019)

Investment Area

Under the Trade Competition Act of 1999, Thailand prohibited all trade practices that create or may create monopolies and/or reduce competition in the trade of goods and services. This included, price fixing, intervening in the operation of business of others, and mergers among business operators, which result in a monopoly or unfair competition.

To carry out any restricted practices, applicants must submit an application for permission to the Trade Competition Board, in addition to its procedures, criteria, and conditions. The application must state the business necessity for the restrictive trade practices, the details as to how the restrictive trade practices will be put into effect, and the time period within which the restrictive trade practices will continue.

In Thailand, foreign investors can gain a great deal of advantages, although there are many restrictions on certain industries.

A person, either from Thailand or foreign, may engage in business in the form of:

- single proprietorship
- limited company
- partnership
- joint venture
- branch of a foreign corporation
- representative/regional office.

The Accounts Act of 2000 authorizes the Director-General of the Department of Business Development and Ministry of Commerce to issue regulations regarding the books of accounts and supporting documents that must be maintained by business enterprises.

In accordance with the Accounts Act of 2000, all juristic companies, partnerships, branches of foreign companies, and joint ventures are required to prepare financial statements for each accounting period. The financial statements must be audited by and subjected to an opinion of a certified public accountant. There is an exception to the financial statements of a registered partnership established under Thai law whose capital, assets, or income, any one or all of them, are not more than that prescribed in the Ministerial regulations. Copies of the audited financial statements must also accompany the income tax returns that must be filed with the Revenue Department within 150 days from the closing date of each accounting period.

Accounting methods adopted by a company must be consistent; any changes need to be approved by the Revenue Department.

On March 3rd 2000, the Alien Business Act 1999 replaced the previous decree. Under this act, a foreign investor and a majority foreign owned company registered in Thailand are restricted from carrying on certain types of business activities, unless prior approval is granted by the authority.

According to Thai law, the principal forms of business are:

- proprietorship;
- partnership–unregistered;
- ordinary partnership;
- partnership and limited partnership;
- private limited company;
- public limited company;
- branch office of foreign company;

- representative office;
- regional office;
- joint venture.

The most common form of entity in Thailand is the private limited company. In general, foreign companies prefer to operate as a private limited company.

The BOI does not grant promotional privileges, including income tax incentives, to a branch office of a foreign company and for taxation purposes, the private limited company is treated as a separate legal entity. However, a branch office is considered the same legal entity as its head office, and accordingly, it is not possible to obtain a tax deduction for remittances to its head office for payments, such as interest, rent and royalties.

In addition, in most cases, it is not practicable to register a branch in Thailand.

It should take approximately three to four weeks to establish a private limited company after an application for the company's name is made. To establish a Thai limited company, the government fee is THB 5500 (US$169) per THB one million of registered capital.

Japan controls the most part of Thai manufacturing directly through joint ventures, but also indirectly through subcontracting and licensing agreements. Their presence is also strategic in relation to industrial choices of Thai companies, heavily influenced in the decisions on the technology and on the systems. In this context, it is worth mentioning the automotive sector which, dominated by Japanese and German industries, still offers interesting opportunities for "Business environment". Thailand is the world's second largest market for pick-ups and one of the largest markets in ASEAN for the production and assembly of automobiles. Nowadays, all the major industries like BMW, Mercedes Benz, Ford, General Motors, Volvo assemble cars locally. For decades, the automotive industry was a sector a priority for the Government's economic policy.

There could be more opportunities in the timber industry, the packaging sector, bottling, and the food processing industry—for farming equipment. Excellent opportunities can be found in the technology industries. The availability and efficiency of heavy network can offer the opportunity to speak with qualified represent a decisive factor of choice. These variables will have effects relevant on business opportunities, not only in the sector of technologies but also on the supply areas of consumables.

Other sectors, such as construction and infrastructure, can give excellent opportunities when the crisis economic and political will be over and when in the country will be re-established economics and social growth.

The construction sector has been constantly growing since 2003. The first signal of crisis has felt from the second half of 2008. This caused the prices growing down, which caused the blocking of some projects already started.

The development of the tourist and hotel facilities has been slowed by the crisis in the tourism sector, the most important projects concern the luxury sector, that the global crisis has slowed. The operators now expect a gradual improvement of flows and some signal shooting would seem to begin to emerge.

There were some signs of recovery in the construction sector since the cement and steel consumption has started to grow again. The development of infrastructure could offer good business opportunities, however, linked to the implementation of government investment programs. Infrastructure development is an important point for the modernization of the country and a stimulus for the economy.

Domestic Markets

Thailand is a newly industrialized country. The economy is classified as export-dependent; exports account for more than 2/3rds of the country's GDP.

The industrial and service sectors are the main sectors. Thailand's agricultural sector produces less than the trade and logistics and communication sectors. The construction and mining are another important sector. Other service sectors (including the financial, education, and hotel and restaurant sectors) represent a huge part of the country's GDP. The investment in telecommunication and service trade is expanding as the economy expands.

Following Indonesia, Thailand is ranked as the second-largest economy in the South-east Asia. Furthermore, it ranks second in external volume trade, after Singapore.

External trade (USD millions)	2000	2005	2010	2015	2018
Exports, fob	2773.8	4438.7	6113.3	7332	8148.9
Imports, cif	2494.1	4754.0	5856.6	6407	7430.3
Trade balance	279.7	−315.3	256.7	925	718.6

Source Asian Development Bank (ADB, 2019)

Main commercial partners (USD millions)	2000	2005	2010	2015	2018
Exports					
1. China, People's Rep. of	2806	9105	21,479	23,356	29,930
2. United States	14,706	16,950	20,243	23,682	27,785
3. Japan	10,164	14,979	20,317	19,743	24,745
4. Hong Kong, China	3474	6123	11,257	11,650	12,432
5. Malaysia	2813	5781	10,569	10,027	11,535
6. Viet Nam	838	2348	5846	8765	12,855
7. Australia	1615	3151	9372	9616	10,691
8. Singapore	5997	7641	9003	8614	9338
9. Indonesia	1338	3953	7347	7705	9985
10. Philippines	1082	2042	4888	5901	7831
Imports					
1. China, People's Rep. of	3377	11,153	24,526	40,902	48,806
2. Japan	15,315	26,026	38,320	31,126	35,077
3. United States	7291	8724	10,885	13,815	16,450

(continued)

(continued)

Main commercial partners (USD millions)	2000	2005	2010	2015	2018
4. Malaysia	3344	8092	10,857	11,872	12,860
5. United Arab Emirates	1766	5699	8886	8134	9644
6. Korea, Rep. of	2165	3888	8167	7013	8658
7. Taipei, China	2895	4501	6898	7502	8873
8. Singapore	3416	5375	6368	7141	8525
9. Indonesia	1299	3130	5759	6536	8063
10. Saudi Arabia	1159	4044	5892	4915	6933

Source Asian Development Bank (ADB, 2019)

Finance and Taxation

Tax

The principal taxation law of Thailand is the Revenue Code 1938. The Minister of Finance has the responsibility for implementing the Revenue Code. The Director-General of Revenue carries out the necessary administrative and enforcement functions of the Code. Royal Decrees, Ministerial Regulations, Ministerial Notifications and Board of Taxation Directives, and Rulings supplement the Code.

Thailand's tax operates through a self-assessment system. There are hefty penalties for non-compliance and fraud. Taxpayers who by willful neglect fail to file returns or fraudulently furnish false information with a view to avoiding payment of tax may be punished by imprisonment.

Both residents and non-residents who obtain an assessable income from employment or business through Thailand are subjected to the personal income tax—with the exception of the provisions of a DTA or other international/bilateral agreements. Residents are also subject to income tax on any income from foreign sources that is brought into Thailand in the same year it is received. Income tax is levied on "assessable income" as described under Section 40 of the Revenue Code. Each category of assessable income is subject to specific rules and regulations concerning computations, allowances, deductions, income tax rates and withholding tax rates.

Individuals are allowed various deductions and allowances in determining their assessable income. There are standard legislated deductions, fixed personal annual allowances, and deductions for expenses actually incurred. Expenditure of a private or capital nature, and expenditure incurred to produce income exempt from income tax, is not deductible. Individuals are subject to income tax at progressive rates. The income is also subject to withholding by the payer.

Companies and other legal entities, whether organized under Thai or foreign law, are referred to as “juristic companies or partnerships” in Thai tax legislation. Thai juristic companies or partnerships are subject to corporate income tax on their worldwide income. Entities incorporated under foreign law and carrying on business in Thailand are taxed on the net profits arising from their business activities in Thailand.

To reiterate, every person, resident or non-resident, is subject to Thai personal income tax.

Companies and other legal entities, whether organized under Thai or foreign law, are referred to as “juristic companies or partnerships” in Thai tax legislation. Thai juristic companies or partnerships are subject to corporate income tax on their worldwide income. Entities incorporated under foreign law and carrying on business in Thailand are taxed on the net profits arising from their business activities in Thailand.

The tax year normally follows the calendar year. In the case of a juristic company or partnership, however, the tax year is deemed to be the accounting year and it may, therefore, end on any date. However, once selected, this period must be used consistently unless permission to change it is granted by the Director-General of Revenue.

Thailand operates an extensive tax regime that is based on remittances within Thailand and abroad.

A number of documents and transactions are subject to stamp duty. Rates depend on the class of the instrument, but in general are between 0.1% and one percent. Flat rate duties range from THB 1 to THB 200 per instrument.

In Thailand, the principal taxes levied are:

- direct taxes;
- personal and corporate income taxes;
- petroleum income tax;
- indirect taxes value added tax;
- specific business tax;
- excise tax;
- customs duties;
- stamp duties.

Generally, income tax in Thailand is by self-assessment, and tax declarations and payments are assumed to be correct.

However, the Revenue Department has the power to audit taxes and taxpayer financial records.

Personal income tax varies between 5 and 35% among natural person, groups of people, and any unregistered ordinary partnerships.

Corporate income tax is imposed on companies and juristic partnerships at the rate of 20% of net profits. Reduced rates at the progressive rates of 15–20% are granted to SMEs with a tax exemption on the first THB 300,000 of net profits.

Under the Petroleum Act, there is a special petroleum income tax imposed on companies that are granted licenses to explore, produce, and export petroleum instead of corporate income tax.

Value-added tax (VAT) is collected upon consumption of goods and provision of services and is also levied on imported goods. VAT is imposed at the rate of 7%.

There is a Specific Business Tax (SBT) that is imposed on certain industries. Therefore, enterprises that are subject to SBT are exempt from the VAT. SBT is computed on monthly gross receipts at rates varying from 0.1 to 3%. When SBT is paid, an additional amount of 10% of SBT is levied as a municipal tax.

An excise tax is levied on selected goods (mainly luxury goods).

Customs duty is imposed mainly on imported and selected exported goods. Customs duty is levied in accordance with the Harmonized Commodity Description and Coding System or Harmonized System.

Stamp duty is levied on 28 classes of instruments specified in the Stamp Duty Schedule of the Revenue Code, such as powers of attorney, hire-of-work agreements, lease agreements, and loan agreements. The stamp duty rates vary according to the nature or content of the instrument.

The tax year normally follows the calendar year. In the case of a juristic company or partnership, however, the tax year is deemed to be the accounting year and it may, therefore, end on any date. Nevertheless, once selected, this period must be used consistently unless permission to change it is granted by the Director-General of Revenue.

A separate income tax law relates to companies involved in the exploitation of naturally occurring Thai oil and gas assets.

There are special annual tax incentives for companies that receive BOI promotion from the commencement of operations.

Thailand operates an extensive withholding tax regime that is based on remittances within Thailand and abroad.

VAT is levied on a wide range of goods (including capital items); of which, include services supplied in Thailand and also on the importation of goods and services. The present rate of VAT is 7%; however, it only applies to enterprises with annual gross sales revenue in excess of THB 1,800,000. The standard rate of VAT of 10% was reduced to seven percent on 1 April 1999. Certain businesses in Thailand are excluded from the VAT regime and are instead subject to SBT. These businesses are banking and similar businesses, finance, security and land credit insurance, factoring, and real estate business. The rate of SBT (after taking into account Municipal Tax) is generally 3.3% on gross receipts, but for life insurance businesses it is 2.75%.

A number of documents and transactions are subject to stamp duty. Rates depend on the class of the instrument, but in general are between 0.1% and one percent. Flat rate duties range from THB 1 to THB 200 per instrument. In Thailand, no state, provincial or city income taxes apply.

All realized gains are defined as income (including capital gains) regardless of the regularity of receipt of such gains. Thailand does not impose a separate tax on corporate capital gains. Gains that come from dispositions of assets, regardless of the purpose for which the assets were acquired, are treated as ordinary income subject to income tax.

Dividends

Dividends paid to another company; Thai company is subject to a 10% withholding tax, or are exempt if certain conditions are satisfied under investment promotion tax or the revenue code. Dividends, paid to a non-resident company, are subject to a 10% withholding tax. Dividends, paid to an individual (resident or nonresident), are subject to a 10% withholding tax that is considered as final tax. The withholding tax rate on dividend paid to a nonresident may be reduced under a tax treaty.

Dividends received by a juristic corporation are fully taxable unless the recipient has owned the shares, in respect of which the dividends have been received, for at least three months before and three months after the dividend is paid. If these criteria are met, the following treatment will apply:

- a company listed on the Stock Exchange of Thailand is exempt from income tax on all dividends received from other Thai-listed companies, ordinary or public companies and mutual funds;
- non-listed Thai limited companies organized under Thai law are not required to include as revenue, any dividends or share of profits received from another resident company, if the recipient company has held at least 25% of the total shares with voting rights, without any cross-shareholding by the paying company;
- non-listed Thai limited companies organized under Thai law must, if the condition of the preceding paragraph is not met, include as revenue only one-half of dividends, or share of profits, received from other resident companies, mutual funds or certain other financial institutions organized under Thai law.

Dividends themselves are not income tax deductible, but money borrowed interest, which enables dividends to be paid, is tax deductible.

Deductions

Generally, expenses incurred for the purpose of deriving profits or for conducting business in Thailand are deductible. Accordingly, usual business expenses, qualifying bad debts and depreciation at rates ranging from 5 to 100% (depending upon the nature of the item) are allowed as deductions. A full deduction may be claimed by commercial banks for provisions made for bad and doubtful debts where the provision is calculated in accordance with the Bank of Thailand's provisioning rules.

Certain expenditure is specifically non-deductible for corporate income tax purposes. Such expenditure includes reserves, provisions (with some exceptions), private expenses, income taxes, penalties, fines, donations to charitable institutions in excess of two percent of net profits, and entertainment expenses over and above the prescribed limit based upon the size of gross turnover.

In Thailand, surcharge (interest) and penalties for non-payment of income tax on a timely basis are not income tax deductible.

If head-office expenses are not expended exclusively in respect of a Thai branch's, operations cannot be deducted as a business expense of that branch. Expenses that pertain uniquely to the head-office (for example, office rental, utilities and stationery) will not be allowed as a tax deduction of the branch. This may cause difficulty if a portion of general head-office overhead expenses is recharged to the Thai branch. This is because for a deduction to be claimed, it is required to have a certificate from the head-office auditors to verify that head-office overhead expenses are recharged to the Thai branch and have been computed in compliance with Thai legislation.

Allowable expenses incurred are deductible in the accounting year in which they are accrued or incurred and must be reflected in the books of account.

Tax Losses

Tax losses incurred by juristic corporations in any accounting period may be carried forward for a maximum of five consecutive accounting periods and set off against assessable profits of whatever nature. No carry-back of tax losses is permitted in Thailand, nor is their provision for corporate group relief of losses.

Tax losses are not foregone upon a change in the ownership of the company or a change in the company's business.

Grouping/Consolidation

No corporate tax consolidation regime exists in Thailand. Each company has to prepare audited financial statements and file an annual tax return.

Tax Depreciation/Capital Allowances

Any generally accepted accounting method and depreciation rate can be used to calculate allowable depreciation charges, provided that the resultant depreciation charge does not exceed the permissible percentage of cost value or that the cost of the asset is not written off faster than it would have been using the officially prescribed depreciation rate.

Once a certain accounting method and depreciation rate are adopted, it must be applied consistently unless the Director-General of Revenue approves a change.

A Royal Decree came into force on 23 October 1999 that allows companies to adopt a depreciation rate of up to 40% for assets that are normally subject to a 20% rate limit. The rate must be applied using the diminishing value method and the remaining residual value of an asset may be claimed as depreciation expenses in the last accounting period of the asset's useful life.

However, if the rate of depreciation in the taxpayers' books of accounts for accounting purposes is less than the prescribed tax depreciation rate then that lesser rate must be used for tax purposes.

To be eligible for an additional depreciation write-off, the company must have fixed assets (excluding the cost of land) not exceeding two hundred million THB and not have more than 200 employees. Three years after the effective date of the law, the General Director of the Revenue Department may issue regulations on the eligibility criteria.

Special deduction allowances may be available for BOI-approved companies in respect of infrastructure installation or construction costs.

Assets acquired during an accounting period shall have their depreciation allowances apportioned.

Gains or losses on the disposal of depreciable assets are assessable/deductible. They are calculated as the difference between the sales consideration of the asset and the asset's tax written-down value.

Tax Rates

The corporate income tax rate, in general, is 20% of the net profits of a juristic corporation.

A corporate income tax rate of 10% on net profit applies in respect of the business of BIBFs.

The reduced tax rate of 10% on net profit also applies to the companies qualified with the Royal Decree issued under the Revenue Code and licensing to engage in oil trading business specifically for import and export out of Thailand, duty free zone or between duty free zones, for the includable income from oil trading not less than THB two billion per annum.

Royal Decree has been issued under the Revenue Code to reduce the tax rate for listed companies, i.e. companies listed on the SET, or the MAI, the trading board newly established by the SET.

SMEs are also granted reductions of corporate income tax rates. SME is defined as a juristic company or partnership with paid-up capital not exceeding 200 million Baht at the end of any accounting period.

The reduced tax rates applicable to Regional Operating Headquarters in Thailand are discussed under "Tax Incentives" below.

Profits that are remitted abroad are subject to a 10% withholding tax.

Foreign international transportation corporations under foreign jurisdiction must pay tax on the gross income before deducting expenses. The tax rate of the carriage of passengers is 3% of collectible fairs in Thailand. For the carriage of goods, the tax rate is 3% for each collectible freight in Thailand.

Tax Administration

All companies in the jurisdiction of Thailand must submit a corporate income tax return. Thailand operates a self-assessment system of taxation. No provision exists for consolidated group returns.

A juristic company may choose any 12-month period as its accounting period but, once adopted, can only be changed with the approval of the General Director.

Corporate income tax is payable in two installments each year and the taxes must accompany the submission of the relevant returns:

- an annual corporate income tax return (which must be accompanied by signed, audited accounts) must be filed within 150 days of the end of the accounting year;
- a half-year corporate income tax return must be filed within two months at the end of the first six months of the accounting year;
- all listed companies, banks, finance companies, securities companies, credit companies, and companies, whose auditors are approved by the Revenue Department, are required to pay half-year tax based on actual income. Other types of corporations are required to estimate net profits for the year and pay half of the tax thereon;
- the amount of tax paid against the half-year return, and tax withheld by income payers, are allowed as credits in the computation of the return at the end of the year.

The Revenue Department examines the accuracy and correctness of the tax returns and the accompanying audited accounts. The Revenue Department may then request further information to support claims for deductions or other matters it deems appropriate. The Revenue Department may select juristic corporations at random for an in-depth investigation or audit.

Foreign-owned companies incorporated under the laws of Thailand, and branches of foreign incorporated companies, are subject to the same filing requirements as Thai-owned companies.

Absent fraud or evasion, taxpayers' income tax returns will normally close after two years.

Every juristic corporation registered in Thailand must apply for a tax ID number, which must be quoted on all tax returns.

A non-resident juristic corporation that receives only Thai-source income that has been subjected to final withholding tax at source is not required to have a tax ID number.

A number of initiatives have been introduced by the Thai authorities to assist businesses in dealing with Asia's economic crisis. These include:

- tax exemptions to make the transfer and merger of businesses more attractive for new and existing investors; and
- tax exemptions on dividends or gains from transfer of shares received by venture capital companies investing in SMEs.

Audit and Accounting

Companies and businesses operating in Thailand are required by law to maintain thorough and up-to-date accounting records, and must prepare annual financial statements according to Thai Accounting Standards (TAS).

TAS essentially follows the International Financial Reporting Standards (IFRS) with some exceptions.

Corporate entities are able to choose a 12-month period for their accounting year that best suits their operations. Once decided, this cannot be altered without written approval from the Revenue Department.

A corporation's financial statements must be presented at least annually. Should the corporation's reporting period change and financial statements be prepared for a period other than a year, the entity must disclose the reason for this and make clear that the information is not exactly comparable to the previous reporting period.

A full range of accounting and other recordkeeping requirements must be observed by law: typically, a journal, general ledger and inventory records, all maintained in Thai, and must be kept. Thai translations must be provided where a foreign language is used.

These documents and records must be kept on the premises of the business, or the usual location where goods are produced or stored and retained for at least five years beyond the year to which they pertain unless otherwise agreed to the Accountants Inspector Office or the Chief Accounts Inspector.

A complete set of the required financial documents consists of a statement of financial position (balance sheet), a statement of comprehensive income, a statement of cash flows and a statement outlining any changes in equity, as well as any notes to the accounts.

All incorporated business entities—except partnerships registered under Thai law with a capital of THB 5 million or less as well as assets and income not exceeding THB 30 million—must submit financial statements (audited by a certified public accountant) to the Department of Business Development within five months of the end of its financial year. For limited companies or public limited companies established under Thai law, financial statements must be submitted within one month of the date of the general meeting at which they were approved.

Additionally, audited accounts must accompany the filing of the annual corporate income tax return with the Revenue Department. Audited financial statements (in THB and Thai) must be filed with the corporate income tax return and also the Ministry of Commerce.

Consistent with global accounting practice, auditors are required to declare whether in his or her opinion an entity's financial statements reflect honestly the financial position of the company, its financial performance, and its cash flow position for the designated period in accordance with Thai Financial Reporting Standards (TFRS).

Risk Assessment

The Second Governance and Anticorruption Action Plan of the Asian Development Bank constructed the basis for the country's governance risk and risk management plan.

Economic Risks

Despite recent political turmoil, Thailand's economy has been resilient due to developed infrastructure, an open economy, a diversified export industry and generally pro-business policies. However, levels of foreign direct investment have been negatively affected.

Traditionally, Thailand's economy had been based on agricultural exports; in recent decades, the economy has transformed. Current key economic drivers include the industrial and service sectors.

Low levels of inflation and weaker than expected growth have kept monetary policy accommodative.

Financial Risks

Thailand's insurance industry is regulated by the Office of the Insurance Commission under the Ministry of Commerce. To improve financial stability, the International Monetary Fund (IMF) recommended efforts to strengthen the supervision of financial institutions, foster coordination among regulators, update the macro-prudential policy framework and improve crisis prevention and resolution. Additionally, the IMF is concerned about high levels of household debt and interconnected financial conglomerates. In 2015, inflation moved into negative territory largely as a result of lower commodity prices and weak demand, undershooting the Bank of Thailand's inflation target band of 2.5% ± 1.5%. In 2020, inflation is expected to return to positive territory.

Political Risks

The military took control of the country in May of 2014 and remain in power through at least 2017. The country continues to be divided between the Red Shirts (supporters of former premier Shinawatra) and the Yellow Shirts (pro-royalist and supporters of the political and military elite). The delayed transition to civilian rule has the potential to increase the risk of violent protests. The monarchy in Thailand is highly regarded and is viewed as a unifying institution in the country.

VIETNAM

Official name
Socialist Republic of Vietnam
Capital
Hanoi
Area
331,210 sq. km
Population
95.5 mln
Languages
Vietnamese (official), English, French
Main ethnic groups
86% Vietnamese

Main religions
Buddhist 8%, Catholic 7%
Government type
Communist State
Urbanization
35.9%
Life expectancy ratio
77 years
Fertility rate
1.9 children born/woman
Currency
Dong VND

Vietnam

Country Introduction

Population, Location, Geography, Climate

There are about 95.5 million people in Vietnam. Eighty percent of them are ethnic Vietnamese while the remaining twenty percent are comprised of more than fifty separate ethnic groups. About seven million of these ethnic minorities are members of the hill tribes *ormontagnards* (French for mountain people). They make their homes and livelihoods in the spectacular mountains of the north and central highlands. In Vietnam people speak many languages, including Vietnamese, Chinese, English, French and Russian.

Shaped like an elongated *S*, Vietnam stretches the length of the Indochinese Peninsula and covers a surface area of 128,000 miles^2 making it roughly the size of Italy or in the US New Mexico. China lies to the north, Laos and Cambodia to the west and the South China Sea is situated in the east.

Topographically, Vietnam is a verdant tapestry of soaring mountains, fertile deltas, primeval forests inhabited by exotic fauna, sinuous rivers, mysterious caves, otherworldly rock formations, heavenly waterfalls and beaches. Beyond nature, the curious and open-minded visitor will find in Vietnam a feast of culture and history.

For convenience the country can be thought of as comprising three unique areas: north, central and south. The north is known for its alpine peaks, the Red River Delta, the plains of Cao Bang and Vinh Yen, enchanting Halong Bay, historic Hanoi as well as for the diversity of its ethnolinguistic minorities.

Central Vietnam, also home to many ethnic minorities, is characterized by high temperate plateaus rich in volcanic soil and by spectacular beaches, dunes and lagoons. It is also the location of the ancient imperial city of Hue. In the South, visitors encounter modern life in Ho Chi Minh City (formerly Saigon) and the fertile alluvial delta of the Mekong River. Vietnam's territory also encompasses a large continental shelf and thousands of archipelagic islands.

Vietnam's climate is as complex as its topography. Although the country lies entirely within the tropics its diverse range of latitude, altitude and weather patterns produce enormous climatic variation. North Vietnam, like China, has two basic seasons: a cold, humid winter from November to April and a warm, wet summer for the remainder of the year. Summer temperatures average around 70 °F (about 22 °C), with occasional typhoons to keep things exciting. The northern provinces of Central Vietnam share the climate of the North while the southern provinces share the tropical weather of the South. South Vietnam is generally warm, the hottest months being March through May, when temperatures rise into the mid-90's (low-30's °C). This is also the dry season in the south, which is followed by the April–October monsoon season.

Internal Policy

The President is the Head of State and he represents The Socialist Republic of Vietnam on internal and foreign affairs. The highest administrative state body is the Government. They are responsible for implementing and handling political, economic, cultural, social, national defence, security and foreign affairs of the state bodies. Ministries are responsible for the execution of state power in their industry or sector. People's Committee (province, district and commune) governs management affairs within its administrative location, manages, directs, operates daily activities of local state bodies and executes policies of the relevant People's Council and higher state bodies.

The Judiciary is comprised of the Supreme People's Court. It is headed by the Chief of Justice who is accountable to the National Assembly. Provincial and district People's Courts execute juridical power on criminal, civil, economic, labor and administrative issues.

People's Procuracy (province, district) checks all state authorities, organizations and individuals for law compliance. The power of prosecutor is executed by People's Procuracy in accordance with the law.

Vietnam's one-party political system, with the exclusive exercise of power by the Vietnam Communist Party (PCV), led by Ho Chi Minh's political heirs. However, the Vietnamese regime distinguishes itself from similar systems for its relatively dialectical character, partly the absence of a single leader. In fact, the country is ruled by a troika, consisting of the General Secretary of the Communist Party—the main constitutional position—the President of the Republic and the Prime Minister.

The reform process, launched in 1986, has not affected the monopoly of the party which contains a branched structure and a widespread presence at the local level and favored general acquiescence, despite its roots in the Confucian tradition. As of the end of the 80's the PCV has been confronted with the disaffection of the younger generation, foreign to the propaganda of war and independence and increasingly sensitive to cultural and alternative economic models.

The size of the new government (whose average age stood at 56.2 years) 'in addition to the PM—5 Deputy Prime Ministers, 19 Ministers, the Governor of the Central Bank and the Inspector General of Government, with the rank of Minister, 6 of them are part of the Politburo, 7 were re-elected at the helm of their respective Departments, 12 were deputies in the previous legislature and 7 come from other government departments. There was only one woman in government and she controlled department of Health.

As for the process of internal reforms, the X National Assembly plenary session (20.10–27.11.2015), has been a positive development in terms of due process, the protection of minors and the reduction of the death penalty. However, the rigid Criminal Code provisions are shady about the freedom 'of religion and people expressing their thoughts.

It is confirmed, however, the highest profile of AN gradually established itself as a chamber organ from the clearing. It has transformed and ratified the decisions of the Party in the debate about the countries reform. The Assembly is at the forefront in the process in the renewal of institutions and reform of the countries legal system. Their adaptations are necessary for Vietnam's integration into an international system and economy.

Vietnam is a one-party state which means the Communist Party's Politburo and Central Committee make policies for which the government are to implement. The National Assembly has the power to approve and revise Constitution and Law and make decisions on national matters (policies on internal and foreign affairs, socio-economic factors, political factors, security factors and operations of state bodies) and supervise all operations of state bodies. The government's policy to privatize State Owned Enterprises and form the Vietnam stock exchange in 2000 widened the door for foreign investors. The aim of the government is to control inflation, so CPI gradually goes down. After the Enterprise Law was passed in 2000, the number of private enterprises increased. More opportunities for foreign investors meant they were able to form partnerships with local firms in Vietnam due to changes to the Enterprise Law and Investment Law in 2005.

International Relations

Vietnam, part of the Soviet bloc during the Cold War, since the 90's has adopted a "political friendship with all countries." This approach has led to a growing integration and constructive international activism, with a renewed dynamism in the context of UN system (the country is currently a member of the UN Human Rights Council for the 2014–2016 term and participated in the international peacekeeping mission in South Sudan), with an increasingly influential role within ASEAN, established strengthen by the appointment, in 2013 the former Deputy Foreign Minister Le Luong Minh in Vietnam General Secretary and the recent establishment of ASEAN Economic Community (AEC) December 31, 2015.

Positive relations with former US foe accomplished long ago and Vietnam has become for the USA not only an important economic partner but also a strategic partner in the region.

Even relations with the European Union have experienced a continuous intensification, both bilaterally, with the conclusion of the Partnership and Cooperation (PCA, pending ratification), the EU-Vietnam Free Trade Agreement (when subjected to audits legal, before signing) and EU-ASEAN context. All of which gained an even higher profile and current agenda of the foreign policy.

Finally, increasingly profiled attention and participation of Vietnam to the issues of global climate change and environmental sustainability, as confirmed by the commitment during the COP21 and the setting up of a national pavilion to present and explain the actions taken and to be taken in the field of climate change.

Economy

Macroeconomic Overview

	Unit	2000A	2018	2020F
GDP, current prices	USD (billions)	31.18	241.27	282.372
GDP per capita, current prices	USD	401.57	2551.12	2928.96
GDP based on PPP per capita	Current International dollar	2058.15	7510.53	8682.95

Source IMF Outlook (2019)

Vietnam's Communist Party implemented an "economic renovation" (Doi Moi) policy in 1986, leading to a change from the planned economy model to a market economy. This and several other changes have created huge opportunities for foreign investors to expose their business to the Vietnam market, such as its accession into the WTO in 2007, establishment of securities market and equalization of state-owned sector. Other factors that will contribute to the upsurge of foreign capital and foreign enterprises are the dynamic, young and low-cost labor force, the positive prospect for economic growth and the increasing role of private sector.

In recent years, Vietnam has been one of the fastest growing economies in Asia and came second to China globally in the period 1991–2007. Despite on-going difficulties its prospects, currently, remain positive. Vietnam's real GDP average growth reached 7.34% in 2005–2009, before it dropped due to the 2008 global financial crisis to 5.3% but showed signs of recovery in 2009. Vietnam's long-term economic growth prospects remain positive. According to economists, the country's economic growth will be underpinned by rises in consumption, investment and exports.

Despite the more challenging global backdrop last year compared to the previous year, Vietnam's Trade Confidence Score rose markedly.

Exports are expected to grow from 2019–30 by 10% by annum. Three key drivers that will help activity grow strongly are the large and low-cost workforce, the increased openness to trade and FDI and more stable macroeconomic fundamentals. From 2021 to 2030 half of Vietnam's export growth will be made up of clothing, apparel, textiles, wood manufacturers sectors as well as the ICT equipment sector, which has seen rapid growth in recent years and will continue to expand. In the first eleven months of 2019, Vietnam's exports grew by 8.4% year-on-year showing resilience compared to China and other major Asian economies that saw a fall in exports for both oil and non-oil values and this resilience has been highlighted by more diverse export products and locations. In the long-term we will see exports growing very robustly.

Structure of output (% GDP)	2000	2005	2010	2015	2018
Agriculture	24.5	19.3	21.0	18.9	16.3
Industry	36.7	38.1	36.7	37.0	38.0
Services	38.7	42.6	42.2	44.2	45.7

Source Asian Development Bank (ADB, 2019)

Structure of expenditure (% GDP)	2000	2005	2010	2015	2018
Final consumption	72.9	71.0	72.6	74.3	74.0
Gross capital formation	29.6	33.8	35.7	27.7	26.5
Exports of goods and services	55.0	63.7	72.0	89.8	105.8
Imports of goods and services	57.5	67.0	80.2	89.0	102.5
Statistical discrepancy	0.0	−1.4	0.0	−2.8	−3.9

Source Asian Development Bank (ADB, 2019)

Economic Policy

Vietnam is gradually emerging from a centrally planned, socialist economy dominated by state-owned monopolies into an economy with a mix of public, private and foreign ownership. The Competition Law generally prohibits abuses of market power by companies but does not forbid monopolistic or market-dominant entities. Nevertheless, this law is expected to be applied more forcefully in the future. Any merger must undergo a regulatory examination. During 2014–2015, the government is attempting to reform hundreds of state-owned enterprises (SOEs), but the process may be slow and vulnerable to policy disagreements. In the period 2016–2018, more SOEs are undertaken reforms and be privatized or part-privatized while progress on ending market distortions are anticipated.

Vietnam's 2011–2020 Socio-Economic Development Strategy (SEDS) gives attention to structural reforms, environmental sustainability, social equity and emerging issues of macroeconomic stability. It defines three breakthrough areas which are promoting human resources/skills development (particularly skills for modern industry and innovation), improving market institutions and infrastructure development. In addition, to the elaboration of three SEDS breakthrough areas, the five-year Socio-Economic Development Plan (SEDP) for 2011–2015 focused on three critical restructuring areas the banking sector, state-owned enterprises and public investment that are needed to achieve these objectives. The SEDP for 2016–2020, approved in April 2016, acknowledges slow progress on certain SEDP reform priorities and emphasizes the need to accelerate these reforms over the next SEDP period, 2016–2020, to achieve the targets set out in the 10-year strategy.

Banking System

Direct Investment

Foreign invested enterprises and foreign parties to business cooperation contract must open a foreign currency account at an authorized credit institution to undertake transactions, such as:

- receipt of charter capital contributions, receipt of other capital and receipt of foreign loan;
- disbursement outside Vietnam of principle, interest and fees on a foreign medium or long-term loan.

All transfers of capital for a direct investment project in Vietnam and overseas must be conducted via a capital account in a foreign currency opened at an authorized credit institution. For their business transactions foreign invested enterprises may open current accounts/transaction accounts in foreign currency and Vietnamese Dong at authorized banks in Vietnam. In addition, foreign invested enterprises may be allowed to open offshore foreign currency bank accounts if approval is granted by the State Bank of Vietnam (SBV).

Indirect Investment

To conduct indirect investment in Vietnam, non-resident foreign investors must open a capital Vietnamese Dong account at an authorized credit institution. Before the indirect investment is carried out investment capital in a foreign currency must be converted to Vietnamese Dong.

An indirect investment capital Vietnamese Dong account shall be used to implement several transactions. For example:

- receipt from a sale of foreign currency to an authorized credit institution;
- receipt of salary, bonus and other lawful items of income by a non-resident being a foreign investor.

Overall, the inflow of foreign currencies into Vietnam is less constrained by the SBV compared to the outflow which has been restricted to certain transactions such as payment for imports of goods and services, repayment of loans contracted abroad and payment of interest accumulated thereafter. Banks, non-bank credit institutions and other authorized institutions are the only ones eligible to provide foreign exchange services.

The SBV announce the inert-bank average exchange rate against the US dollar (USD). Credit institutions authorized to take part in foreign exchange activity shall determine their own buying and selling rate within a 1% difference in the average exchange rate as stipulated by law. In the context of continued devaluation pressure of Vietnam Dong (VND) the inter-bank average exchange rate shall be adjusted by SBV more regularly to reflect market demand and supply hence improve the liquidity of currency market. The credit institutions authorized to engage in foreign exchange activity shall regulate their own buying and selling rate for all other foreign currencies.

The VND is the country's official currency and may be chosen as a means of payment and settlement. However, other currencies such as USD may also be chosen as a means of payment and remittance in certain situations (hereby called current transactions).

Generally, capital transaction means a transaction for transferring capital between a resident and a non-resident in the following sectors:

- foreign direct investment;
- investment in valuable papers;
- borrowing a foreign loan and repayment of a foreign loan;
- providing and recovery of a foreign loan.

Interest Rates (% per annum; period averages)	2000	2005	2010	2015	2018
On deposits					
Savings	0.20	3.00	3.00	0.7	0.5
Time: 6 months	4.80	7.80	11.14	5.6	6.5
12 months	6.24	8.40	11.50	6.3	7.1

Source Asian Development Bank (ADB, 2019)

Investment Area

As mentioned previously, the changes in Enterprise Law and Investment Law in 2005 created new opportunities for foreign investors in Vietnam via establishing partnerships with local private firms.

The establishment of Vietnam stock exchange in 2000 and the Government's policy of privatizing state-owned enterprises opened room for foreign investors to invest in Vietnam market.

The service industry accounts for approximately 77% of the GDP since 2001. However, we are witnessing a move in economic structure from agriculture to the service industry. Wealth and consumption are rising as a result creating opportunities for foreign investors in expanding business in Vietnam, especially in domestic retail market. Due to the ban of foreign investment in the retail distribution sector being lifted and the positive trends in the attraction of FDI into Vietnam, it is now directed not only at export processing industries but has also diversified and shifted fundamentally into highly value-added services, high technology and energy-saving industries sectors.

The integration into the world's largest economic organization, in general, has liberalized further the country's trade regime, renovated the regulatory environment to foster a safe and attractive investment environment simultaneously.

The Government of Vietnam is seeking to attract increased investment across a wide array of sectors. According to the Law on Investment the following sectors are encouraged:

- production of new materials and new energy, manufacture of products of high-technology, bio-technology, information technology and mechanical production;
- breeding, growing and processing agricultural, forestry and aquaculture products, salt production, creation of man-made varieties, new plant and animal varieties;
- use of high technology and advanced techniques, protection of the ecological environment, research, development and creation of high-technology;
- labor intensive industries;
- construction and development of infrastructure facilities and important industrial projects with a large scale.

Investment Incentives

Under the current laws of Vietnam, there are various investment preferences and incentives for investors who have investment projects in the preferential investment sectors and/or areas as follows:

- Corporate Income Tax (CIT) exemption and CIT reduction from the first profit making year;
- a preferential CIT rate of 10–20%;
- import duty exemption on the importation of equipment, materials, means of transportation and other goods for implementation of investment projects in Vietnam in accordance with the Law on Export and Import Duties;
- land rental exemption or reduction;
- accelerated depreciation of fixed assets;
- losses carry forward.

Domestic Markets

The agreement on good commitments (Goods Schedule) made when Vietnam joined the WTO required a 5–10% reduction in tariffs for imported goods for most cases including textiles, aquaculture products, automobile, automotive spare parts and consumer goods. The successful and rapid expansion of large retail groups such as: Espace Bourbon Group, Parkson and Metro Cash and Carry in Vietnam for the past years are among the most convincing examples of the more open Vietnam market to date thanks to Vietnam's WTO commitment.

The large growing low-cost workforce and the progress towards the TPP agreement and the ASEAN single market mean expectations of Vietnam continuing to attract low cost manufacturing firms and maintaining the strong foothold in the market for textiles and garments will continue to grow. Clothing and apparel will contribute 19% from 2021 to 30 while textiles and wood manufactures will account for 10%.

ICT equipment will account for around 10% of the increase from 2021 to 30 because of the strong foothold Vietnam has in the global telecoms sector and more broadly the gradual technical upgrading of the economy.

Textiles, wood manufactures and clothing account for close to 20% of the increase in imports. This reflects both intermediate demand from the domestic sector and final demand from the buoyant consumer market (household incomes in Vietnam are forecast to rise rapidly over the forecast period though they are expected to remain lower than China).

External trade (USD millions)	2000	2005	2010	2015	2018
Exports, fob	14,482.6	32,447.1	72,236.7	162,017	243,483
Imports, cif	15,636.5	36,761.1	84,838.6	165,776	236,688
Trade balance	−1153.9	−4314.0	−12,601.9	−3759	6795

Source Asian Development Bank (ADB, 2019)

Main commercial partners (USD millions)	2000	2005	2010	2015	2018
Exports					
1. United States	733	5924	14,238	33,475	46,974
2. China, People's Rep. of	1536	3228	7309	16,568	41,314
3. Japan	2575	4340	7728	14,100	18,885
4. Korea, Rep. of	353	664	3092	8915	18,042
5. Hong Kong, China	316	353	1464	6959	7974
6. Germany	730	1,085	2373	5707	6887
7. Netherlands	391	659	1688	4760	6986
8. United Arab Emirates	24	122	508	5691	5153
9. United Kingdom	479	1016	1682	4645	5943
10. Thailand	372	863	1183	3178	5510
Imports					
1. China, People's Rep. of	1401	5900	20,019	49,441	65,504
2. Korea, Rep. of	1753	3594	9761	27,579	47,784
3. Japan	2301	4074	9016	14,182	19,136
4. Taipei,China	1880	4304	6977	11,041	13,188
5. Thailand	811	2374	5602	8270	12,095
6. United States	364	863	3767	7793	12,707
7. Singapore	2694	4482	4101	6031	4478
8. Malaysia	389	1256	3413	4185	7470
9. Indonesia	345	700	1909	2738	4902
10. India	178	596	1762	2655	4117

Source Asian Development Bank (ADB, 2019)

Finance and Taxation

Tax

The main categories of tax imposed in Vietnam are Corporate Income Tax, Value Added Tax, Personal Income Tax, Foreign Contractor Tax, Special Sales Tax and Import and Export Duties. The Vietnamese taxation system has and will continue to undergo major transformations however the enforcement mechanism as well as the ruling process is often limited in capacity.

The Corporate Income Tax Law applies to all domestic and foreign entities that invest in Vietnam. The CIT Law expands the taxpayer pool to include all foreign enterprises having income from Vietnam regardless of whether they have a permanent establishment in Vietnam or not.

Taxable income is defined as income derived from production, operation and other sources from all business sectors and industries.

In general, deductible expenses for corporate income tax purposes are expenses incurred related to income-producing activities of the business with supporting legal documentation. The corporate tax rates are classified into three categories as follows:

- standard tax rate 25%;
- preferential tax rates 20% or 10%;
- other tax rates (e.g. oil and gas operations; natural resources industry) 32–50%.

Preferential tax treatments such as tax exemption, tax reduction and preferential rates (10 and 20%) are limited to:

- encouraged sectors such as: healthcare, education, high-tech, infrastructure development and software;
- encouraged special economic zones or areas with difficult socio-economic conditions.

The taxpayer must self-assess to check which incentives are applicable according to the current tax regulations.

Those paying corporate tax can choose to adopt a calendar or fiscal year ending on a quarter of a calendar year as the basis for the tax year.

The VAT system in Vietnam applies to goods and services used for production, business and consumption in Vietnam. Two methods can be used to calculate VAT payable/refund. Taxpayers meeting the requirements can apply the credit method. VAT payable/refund under the credit method are the difference between VAT Output (VAT collected for sales) and VAT Input (VAT paid for purchases). Taxpayer not qualified for the credit method can apply the direct method. Under the direct method, the taxpayer will pay VAT by applying a deemed rate on the added value of the transaction. Corporate taxpayer is required to file and pay VAT monthly. The standard VAT rate is 10% but the rates are classified into four groups: exempt, 0, 5 and 10%.

Special Sales Tax (SST) are imposed on a selected number of goods and services, either at the stage of production, provision of services or imports. Export products are exempted from SST. The tax is calculated based on the selling price at the place of production excluding this tax and VAT or CIF price plus import duty with respect to import products.

Both foreigners working in Vietnam and Vietnamese citizens are subject to PIT. For tax residents a progressive taxing system, where the marginal rate ranges from 5 to 35% is applied to the worldwide income. For non-tax residents a flat rate of 20% is applied on the income derived from Vietnam. In general, a tax resident is a person who is either:

- present in Vietnam for at least 183 days;
- having a regular resident location in Vietnam;
- cannot be a tax resident of another country (subject to applicable double tax agreement).

A tax resident is allowed VND 4 million as a personal deduction from his/her employment or business income and VND 1.6 million per dependent as qualified dependent deduction.

All goods entering Vietnam are generally subject to import duty. Import duty rates vary depending on the nature of goods involved and origin of the goods. There are three import duty rates, which are applicable (ordinary, preferential and especially preferential). They are based on the trading relationship between Vietnam and the exporting country.

A partial or full exemption from import duty may be granted on application. Raw materials and components imported into Vietnam for the manufacture of goods for export are usually exempt from import duty provided that the goods are exported within 275 days. Enterprises with foreign-invested capital and parties in BCC are especially encouraged projects, which are exempt from import duty in respect of certain imported goods which form part of their fixed assets.

Foreign organizations and individuals carrying on permitted businesses in Vietnam without a legal entity are subject to Foreign Contractors Tax (FCT) comprising VAT and CIT. Applicable taxation rates will vary depending on whether a foreign contractor registers to use the Vietnamese Accounting System (VAS). The standard FCT rate is 10%, but different rates can apply depending on the transactions and taxpayer's filing status.

As of June 2011, Vietnam has signed DTAs with more than 60 countries, out of which 50 DTAs are currently in force. Generally, these DTAs follow the basic principles contained in the OECD Model *Convention*.

For a country, which has a DTA with Vietnam, a foreign tax credit is also available to resident taxpayers in respect of foreign taxes paid. Generally, provisions of DTAs prevail over the domestic tax laws.

The amount of given credit is the lower of the tax suffered in the foreign country or Vietnamese CIT attributable to the foreign income. There is no provision in Vietnamese tax law allowing excess foreign tax credits to be carried forward.

The application of a DTA clause is not automatic. An official approval for tax relief must be obtained from the tax authorities.

Tax rate on salary	%
Corporate tax	20
Personal income tax	35
Sales tax	10

Source Trading Economics (2019)

Audit and Accounting

Enterprises with foreign-owned capital, foreign parties to business cooperation contracts and foreign contractors having resident base in Vietnam (collectively FIEs) are required to adopt the Vietnamese Accounting System (VAS), Vietnamese Accounting Standards and their interpretive guidance (also VAS).

The requirements of VAS include:

- the use of Vietnamese language or both Vietnamese language and another widely used language approved by the Ministry of Finance in the preparation of accounting records;
- Vietnam Dong as the currency unit in accounting. Only in limited cases can FIEs use a "foreign currency" as the currency unit in their accounting records;
- VAS chart of accounts must be complied with;
- all reports must be printed monthly;
- numerous reports must be produced as specified in the VAS regulations.

The fiscal year applicable to FIEs in Vietnam is normally 12 months commencing on 1 January and end on 31 December of each calendar year. FIEs may apply to the local tax authority for permission to adopt its own 12-month fiscal year, commencing from the first day of a quarter and ending on the last day of the previous quarter in the following year.

Where the first fiscal year is shorter than a 90-day duration it shall be permitted to add such a period to the following fiscal year. Also, the first fiscal year must be shorter than 15 consecutive months.

The enterprise is required to employ a Chief Accountant who must satisfy the criteria and conditions stipulated by the Law on Accounting. A foreigner may be appointed to act as the Chief Accountant of the enterprise and he/she must have a certificate of accounting expertise or an accounting/auditing certificate issued by a foreign organization, recognized by the MOF; or an accounting/auditing professional practicing certificate issued by the MOF; or a Chief Accountant certificate obtained after having passed the chief accountant's training course as prescribed in regulations of the MOF.

The annual financial statements of FIEs must be audited once a year in accordance with Vietnamese regulations. The audit must be carried out by an independent auditing company that is permitted to operate in Vietnam. The enterprise is legally responsible for providing timely and sufficient information as well as explanations to the auditor.

Risk Assessment

Economic growth accelerated in 2015 supported by both investment and private consumption. Net trade performance weakened due to high import growth compared to exports. Short-term economic prospects are positive and growth should pick up speed in future. A pro-growth policy mix (accommodative monetary policy and relaxed fiscal policy) coupled with increasing FDIs, rising incomes and firm private sector confidence will allow for a further improvement in domestic demand. Exports will likely rise but at a gradual pace reflecting modest external demand and low commodity prices. Going forward, GDP growth is projected to by 6% in 2016. Vietnam's ranking on the 'Ease of Doing Business' improved in 2016 as they moved to the 90th position (from 93rd). Progress was made on the tax environment and insolvency resolution. As a member of the TPP project further improvement is likely in the medium-term especially on investor protection, enforcing contract laws and insolvency resolution.

The most significant risks affecting this dynamic country are economic, supply chain disruption, recruitment challenges, natural catastrophes and the constantly changing regulations should also not be underestimated.

Challenging economic conditions, supply chain disruptions, regulatory changes and natural catastrophes are all major challenges to corporates operating in Vietnam. Further, since the placement of a Chinese oil rig in the disputed waters of the South China Sea in May (which sparked anti-Chinese riots on the Vietnamese mainland) Vietnam's risk landscape has become very interesting.

Roundtable contributors agreed Vietnam's top risks were primarily economic with inflation, interest rates and integration into regional and global economic development all of concern. An overheating economy, global economic failure and price volatility are viewed as threats to the country's economic well-being.

Vietnamese investment management and real estate development firm VinaCapital's head of risk and compliance Ly Xuan Thu said economic risk was indeed one of Vietnam's most pressing challenges. "The government is in the process of restructuring the banking sector because it has not performed well in the past and was affected by the economic crisis," she said. "The government is trying to restructure the sector to review the non-performing loans (NPLs) and control the inflation rate while still maintaining a reasonable economic growth rate. It established a company to buy NPLs back from companies to improve the liquidity of the local banking sector." Furthermore, it seems that although the published figure of NPLs is 4%, estimates of 10–20% are probably closer to the mark, much of this on the back of real estate lending.

Economic Risks

The complex interweaving of politics, economics and banking has created an environment that is making it difficult for Vietnam to reach its full potential. From an investment standpoint Vietnam is split between a great opportunity and a political concerns.

Chief executive officer at investment management company VietNam Holding Asset Management Pham Ngoc Bich says there is a pressing need to "encourage foreign investment, to build capacity for policy makers so, they can efficiently embrace the globalization of Vietnam's economy, to increase the participation of the private sector and to reduce the monopolistic role of many inefficient state-owned enterprises (SOEs)." Only through such means Vietnam will "efficiently use its main competitive advantages and vast potential in certain key sectors such as agriculture, tourism, original equipment manufacturing, outsourcing of technology and business processes and natural resources (mining, oil and gas), so as to bring the income level of the population and the abilities of the government to the next level".

Political Risks

The placement of a Chinese oil rig in the South China Sea in May led to collisions between ships from Vietnam and China as Vietnam tried to block what it views as Chinese encroachment into its waters. It is worth noting that Vietnam is not alone in questioning China's sovereignty in the South China Sea. Malaysia, Brunei and Taiwan also have claims to parts of the potentially energy rich waters, as does the Philippines, which submitted a case to an arbitration tribunal in The Hague earlier this year. This is also the first time Beijing has been subjected to international legal scrutiny over the waters. China has refused to participate and warned Manila that its submission could damage economic and political ties between the two countries.

This move of oil rig sparked anti-Chinese riots on the Vietnamese mainland. The violence first erupted at industrial parks in southern Vietnam where several foreign-owned factories were set on fire. At least two Chinese workers were killed and scores were injured. There were more than US$300 million in insured losses out of a market of US$ 1 billion in premium from this one 'event'. (The head of Gras Savoye Willis Vietnam Philippe Robineau reports many foreign investors are now looking at political cover in the light of the claims recorded).

Asia-Pacific director at specialist risk consultancy Control Risks Rupert Evill says that mainstream media coverage of anti-China sentiments in Vietnam "missed a lot". "The factories that had problems were the ones that had problems already," he says. "When China makes that kind of move because of the history between the countries the government must allow a valve to let off some nationalist steam and if some people have existing grievances, they should be provided with a window of opportunity to vent their grievances. That part of it has been massively overplayed and overblown."

Corruption Risks

Corruption is a significant issue in many emerging economies and Vietnam is no different. There is a more egregious tender space corruption in Vietnam. Evil says: "after some of the excesses of the state-owned companies, the prime minister is attracting serious criticism and there is now a will to deal with those issues. What we are hearing from clients partnering with the better-run state-owned enterprises (SOEs) is that this is not the issue. What you must be careful of is the downstream when you are further into the project and the SOE insists you use its subsidiary company for catering or logistics, quoting a jacked-up fee which is where the kickback is built in. It requires heavy investment of time, resources, creativity and choosing your project carefully to defend against predatory practices."

Interestingly, Japan is implementing new anti-fraud measures to ensure accountability within its foreign-aid operation after bribery allegations rocked three of its country programs earlier—Vietnam chief among them. A private contractor has been accused of paying local officials more than three-quarters of a million dollars to win development projects. The anti-bribery mechanism will be trialed in Vietnam first before potential adoption in Indonesia and Uzbekistan.

"Too much of the economy is still dependent on cash," she says. "An economy where large transactions are done in cash, where fees and fines to the government are collected in cash, is a recipe for corruption or delays and sometimes both. There are systems to implement legal fees structures, taxes and customs collection procedures—so that the amounts due and payments made are done in a transparent way and are uniformly assessed."

All in all, the public debt is high compared to regional peers with a GDP ratio above 60%. The fiscal deficit is large. Looking ahead, there are few if any signs that this trend will reverse significantly after 2016. First, weak commodities prices will remain a drag on government revenues growth despite some improvement in tax collection (broadened tax base e.g.) and higher duties on petroleum products. Second, the policy stances are likely to remain broadly accommodative with the reduction in corporate income tax in 2016 (20% from 22% in 2015) and still solid growth of public expenditures.

The external liquidity position is weak with FX reserves covering hardly 2–3 months of imports. Currency risk is elevated with 3 devaluations in 2015. External conditions are not fully supportive in the short run. The current account surplus is weakening as imports (led by high domestic demand) growth outpaced exports. FDI inflows are strong as the country is seen as a strong alternative to China, but strong short-term capital outflows (due to the Fed's tightening) are still a drag. Risks related to the banking system have receded with improved liquidity and lower NPL. However, a cause of concern still stems from weak profitability and low capital buffers.

In overall there are mainly two key risk factors in Vietnam:

Socialist-orientated Economy: Vietnam may have transitioned from a centrally planned economy, but the government still controls many key industries.
Early Stage Market Economy: Vietnam remains at an early and vulnerable stage of its economic development and is therefore, riskier than developed markets.

Country Profiles—Observers

PAPUA NEW GUINEA

Official name
Independent State of Papua New Guinea
Capital
Port Moresby
Area
462,840 sq. km
Population
8.25 mln
Languages
Tok Pisin (official), English (official), Hiri Motu
Main ethnic groups
Melanesian, Papuan, Negrito, Micronesian

Main religions
Protestant 70%, Roman Catholic 27%
Government type
Parliamentary Democracy
Urbanization
13.2%
Life expectancy ratio
66 years
Fertility rate
3.5 children born/woman
Currency
Kina PGK

L. Riccardi and G. Riccardi, *Invest in ASEAN*,
https://doi.org/10.1007/978-981-15-5378-3_2

Papua New Guinea

Country Introduction

Population, Location, Geography, and Climate

Papua New Guinea has a population of more than 8.25 million according to the 2018 census. The country has major 5 ethnic groups; they are categorized as Melanesian, Papuan, Negrito, Micronesian and Polynesian. Melanesian also referred as Papuans is the biggest ethnic group in Papua New Guinea and is divided into two ethnic groups; Papuans and Austronesians. Since Papuans and Austronesians have a different culture, geography, language, they are referred to as separate groups. Furthermore, Christianity is the dominant religion in Papua New Guinea. Around 96.4% of the country's population are Christians. In detail, 27% of the population refer to themselves as a Roman Catholic, and 69.4% are refer themselves as Protestant, according to the 2000s census. 0.3% of the remaining population belong to Baha'i religion, and the rest remaining percentage belong to indigenous beliefs.

Papua New Guinea has three official spoken languages. Those are Tok Pisin, English and Hiri Motu. Most of the population speaks Tok Pisin language; only 1–2% English, and less than 2% of the population speak Hiri Motu. Despite that, Papua New Guinea has 836 indigenous languages spoken which is about 12% of the world's total, and most languages have fewer than 1000 speakers.

Papua New Guinea consists of eastern New Guinea along with New Britain, New Ireland, Bougainville, and six hundred small islands and archipelagos. The land area is over 462,840 km^2, with the mainland accounting for 80%. The western half of the island is the Indonesian province of Irian Jaya. To the south is Australia, and to the east and southeast are the Solomon Islands and other Melanesian countries. To the north and northwest are the Philippines, South Korea, and Japan. The rest of the country is made up of about 600 small islands, the chief of which are the Bismarck Archipelago, the Trobriands, the Louisiade Archipelago, the D'Entrecasteaux Islands, and some of the islands in the Solomons group, including Bougainville. The country comprises 22 provinces including the National Capital District (greater Port Moresby) and the Autonomous Region of Bougainville.

The centre of the main island is a rugged mountainous ridge, with several wide valleys, and foothills north and south. The rivers Sepik and Ramu drain the foothills to the north, and the rivers Fly, Kikori and Purari those in the south. Though fast-flowing, many rivers are navigable. There are active volcanoes along the north coast, and some volcanoes and warm pools in the south-east islands. Furthermore, over 75% of the nation is covered in rain forest. Swamp forest is found in the poorly drained lowlands, and sago palm is a staple food of the people living there. Around Port Moresby and in drier areas to the west are grassy plains and savanna woodlands.

Papua New Guinea has a tropical monsoon climate and is generally hot and humid, although the climate varies from one area to another. Tropical monsoon type, hot and humid all year, though somewhat cooler in the highlands. Rainfall is chiefly from December to March. High mountains receive occasional frost, even snow.

Internal Policy

The eastern half of the island of New Guinea was divided between Germany (north) and the UK (south) in 1885. The latter area was transferred to Australia in 1902, which occupied the northern portion during World War I and continued to administer the combined areas until its independence and ratification of a constitution in 1975. A nine-year secessionist revolt on the island of Bougainville ended in 1997 after claiming 20,000 lives. Since 2001, Bougainville has experienced autonomy. Under the terms of a peace accord, 2015 is the year that a five-year window opens for a referendum on the question of independence.

Papua New Guinea is parliamentary democracy (National Parliament) under a constitutional monarchy; a Commonwealth realm. Similar to other Commonwealth Nations, Papua New Guinea's monarch stands as a ceremonial figurehead, while the governor-general represents the Monarch of the United Kingdom by acting upon the advice of the prime minister and the cabinet. The Governor-General is appointed by the monarch, and the governor-general appoints the prime minister.

Supreme Court hears appeals and reviews decisions made by the National Court. Chief justice appointed by the governor-general upon the advice of the National Executive Council after consultation with the National Justice Administration Minister. The Judicial and Legal Services Commission appoints the remaining judges. Citizen judges have 10-year terms while non-citizens have 3-year terms.

Constitution states that the legislative power of the people is vested in the National Parliament, and a member of the legislative powers are elected every 5 years through an alternative voting system.

International Relations

Papua New Guinea's foreign policy reflects its close ties with Australia and other allies. It is by far the largest Pacific Island nation and has traditionally viewed itself as part of the Pacific. In recent years, Papua New Guinea has also been cultivating relations with Asian nations. Its views on international political and economic issues are generally moderate. Papua New Guinea has diplomatic relations with 56 countries such as Australia, United Kingdom, China, United States of America, Australia, Cuba, Fiji, France, India, Indonesia, Japan, New Zealand, Philippines, and others. Papua New Guinea has good relationship with most of the Commonwealth Nations since the country itself is part of it.

Papua New Guinea belongs to a variety of regional organizations, including the Asia-Pacific Economic Cooperation (APEC) forum, the ASEAN Regional Forum, the South Pacific Commission, the Pacific Islands Forum, the Melanesian Spearhead Group, and the South Pacific Regional Environmental Program (SPREP).

Papua New Guinea is an observer member of the ASEAN and unlike Timor-Leste, Papua New Guinea has not applied to become a member of the association. Since the country has very good economy and joining the ASEAN will be beneficial for the country.

Economy

Macroeconomic Overview

	Unit	2000A	2018	2020F
GDP, current prices	USD (billions)	5.26	21.32	22.11
GDP per capita, current prices	USD	1025.04	2530.23	2518.48
GDP based on PPP per capita	Current International dollar	2015.10	3662.03	3907.99

Source IMF Outlook (2019)

Papua New Guinea's population of 8.25 million is young and growing. The country is rich with a vast endowment of natural resources and geographic proximity to rapidly growing Asian markets. Its population is strikingly diverse, speaking over 800 distinct languages.

Economically, PNG's economy remains dominated by two sectors which are agricultural, forestry, and fishing sector, which engages most of the labor force, and the minerals and energy extraction sector which accounts for the majority of export earnings and Gross Domestic Product.

Investment is needed to diversify Papua New Guinea's asset base and increase employment, and to strengthen capacity in institutions, human capital, and physical infrastructure. Electricity, telecommunications, roads, and other transport infrastructure remain critical to enabling private sector-led growth.

Obtaining more revenue from the mineral and petroleum sector by discontinuing the practice of providing significant tax concessions to companies operating in this sector will improve both the fiscal balance and the foreign exchange position in PNG. Further, translating revenues from strong, tangible improvements to living standards for all Papua New Guineans remains the key challenge for the Government of PNG, yet other challenges are also immense. It is inherent to improve public financial management and efficiency of public spending to convert resource revenues into inclusive growth and, consequently, a genuine improvement in the livelihoods.

Though the country is rich in mineral, agricultural, forestry and fisheries resources, development is still in the early stages, and has been hampered by volatile prices for agricultural and mineral exports. In addition, ocean or inhospitable terrain separates the main population centers. GDP grew by 1.9% p.a. 1980–90 and 3.8% p.a. 1990–2000.

Government policy has been to aim for steady, sustainable growth with an even sharing of the benefits throughout the country. To this end, it took minority shareholdings in most major industrial and mining developments (up to a maximum of 30% in mineral projects and 22.5% in petroleum projects).

GDP growth was uneven during the 1990s, registering 15% in 1993 as new mining investment came on stream, but falling to −3.6% in 1995, −3.9% in 1997 and −3.8% in 1998. By 1998 the country was in the most serious financial crisis since independence due to a prolonged drought, the continuing Bougainville crisis, the Asian economic downturn, and the falling value of the kina. With the support of the World Bank and IMF, the government embarked on economic reforms including a program of privatization.

The economy recovered strongly during 1999 but then stalled, with good growth returning from 2003, as new mining and hydrocarbon projects came on stream, recording 4.9% p.a. over 2005–09. There was strong growth in 2007–08, moderating slightly to 5.5% in 2009, in response to the global downturn and the collapse of world demand, before strengthening again to eight to nine% p.a. in 2010–12, slowing in 2013–14 before surging to a 12% in 2014, driven by exports of natural gas. Revenues from natural resource exploitation have resulted in high government spending and a construction boom. Yet, as the country suffers from endemic corruption and lacks a functioning legal system, inequality has been increasing. In 2018 the GDP growth rate was 0.5%.

Structure of output (% GDP)	2000	2005	2010	2015	2018
Agriculture	35.2	34.0	20.3	18.3	17.9
Industry	40.7	44.3	33.6	36.4	40.5
Services	24.1	21.7	46.0	45.3	41.6

Source Asian Development Bank (ADB, 2019)

Structure of expenditure (% GDP)	2000	2005	2010	2015	2018
Final consumption	61.2	64.1	N/A	N/A	N/A
Gross capital formation	21.9	17.5	N/A	N/A	N/A
Exports of goods and services	66.2	74.5	N/A	N/A	N/A
Imports of goods and services	49.2	56.1	N/A	N/A	N/A
Statistical discrepancy	0.0	0.0	N/A	N/A	N/A

Source Asian Development Bank (ADB, 2019)

Interest rates (% per annum; period averages)	2000	2005	2010	2015	2018
On deposits					
Savings	3.88	1.80	1.00	0.4	0.7
Time: 6 months	8.75	1.60	4.30	0.5	13
12 months	9.38	1.30	4.80	2.1	2.0

Source Asian Development Bank (ADB, 2019)

Investment Area

Papua New Guinea's enormous and largely untapped natural resources offer excellent investment opportunities. Coupled with the Government's positive attitude to foreign investment through the granting of incentives and concessions, and the recognition of the private sector's important contribution to the economic growth, it is clear why many international companies have invested in Papua New Guinea.

The Government places a high priority on the development of mining and petroleum projects even though this sector is relatively well-developed. There are huge opportunities for investors to establish businesses to provide support for the growing number of such large-scale projects.

Some of the priority economic sectors offering investment projects with good potential for investors include:

- Agriculture—production and processing.
- Fisheries.
- Forestry.
- Manufacturing.
- Tourism—large and small ventures.

Some of the specific projects offering good potential for investors (on a joint venture basis) include poultry farming and processing; processing of spices; coffee production and export; seafood processing and export; food production to replace imported goods; tanneries; timber management/production and export; building materials and furniture production; rubber production; garment and footwear production; the manufacture of a wide range of basic necessities such as processed food, paper and wood products, metal and glass products; printing services; and contractual cleaning services.

Currently, most of the market requirements in Papua New Guinea are satisfied by imports. As the economy expands in concert with the large resource projects, so does the number of opportunities.

Poor road conditions mean that for many people in Papua New Guinea, travel by road can be impossible, unsafe, or simply far too expensive. Without reliable access to roads, people cannot reach schools, hospitals or markets when they need to. Now more than 700 km of national roads have been already restored. Forty-six national and provincial bridges have been rehabilitated, maintained, and replaced and an estimated 1.3 million people have benefitted.

The Productive Partnership in Agriculture Project is Papua New Guinea's largest agriculture program. Launched in 2010, the project aims to improve the livelihoods of smallholder cocoa and coffee producers. More than 23,000 smallholder coffee and cocoa farmers have benefited from various activities supported under this project, with the number of farms adopting improved farming practices now estimated at more than 3600. And with additional funding of US$30 million, the project will be expanded into other areas of Papua New Guinea, increasing its support to women farmers.

In Port Moresby, the Urban Youth Employment Project is providing thousands of young Papua New Guineans with life skills and short-term employment opportunities. The project has been extended to 2018 with additional funding support of US$10.8 million from the Australian government. An estimated 15,000 young Papua New Guineans are set to benefit from the expansion of short-term employment and training program.

In the Autonomous Region of Bougainville, a World Bank project is supporting inclusive development and strengthening women's participation in development. Through the Inclusive Development in Post-Conflict Bougainville project, training has been delivered to 450 participants, and small grants have been awarded to 41 women's groups, including at least one project in each of Bougainville's 13 districts. It is estimated that over 48,000 people have benefitted from completed grant projects, representing nearly 25% of the Bougainville population.

All these projects have been funded by FDI meaning that foreign direct investment is required to improve the country's economy and overall living conditions.

The country is richly endowed with mineral and hydrocarbon resources. Since commercial gold-mining began in 1989, mining and oil and gas production has made a significant contribution to GDP. Oil production started in 1992. There are two oil refineries: one in the Gulf of Papua, and one at Port Moresby. A liquefied natural gas project linking fields in the Southern Highlands and Western Province with an LNG plant at Port Moresby began production and exports in 2014. Reserves of natural gas were estimated in January 2014 to be 200 billion cubic meters.

The principal copper mine at Ok Tedi in Western Province was developed and operated by an Australian company and then abandoned. Another important mine on the island of Bougainville closed in 1989 at the outbreak of political instability and after political resolution in Bougainville, rehabilitation needed huge investment. There are substantial reserves of nickel/cobalt at Ramu in Madang Province. Nickel and cobalt exports—from the new plant at Ramu—started in November 2012 and the plant was due to be producing at full capacity by 2016.

Domestic Market

Growth in Papua New Guinea continues to face headwinds from weaknesses in global prices for its export commodities and unfavorable weather caused by El Niño in 2015. Agriculture is expected to rebound to production levels achieved immediately before El Niño, but sustained growth in the sector is constrained by inadequate infrastructure and a weak business environment.

The top Trade partners of Papua New Guinea are Australia, Singapore, and Japan. The country's top exported goods are Precious Stones and Metals, Ores, and Fats and Oils.

Agriculture employs country's 85% of the population and contributes only 23% to the Papua New Guinea's GDP. The remaining 15% of Papua New Guinea's labor force employed in industry and services sector, however, industries contributed 37% to the country's GDP, and services contributed 40% to the Papua New Guinea's GDPs.

Papua New Guinea is richly endowed with natural resources, but exploitation has been hampered by rugged terrain, land tenure issues, and the high cost of developing infrastructure. The economy has a small formal sector, focused mainly on the export of those natural resources, and an informal sector, employing most of the population. Agriculture provides a subsistence livelihood for 85% of the people. The global financial crisis had little impact because of continued foreign demand for PNG's commodities.

Mineral deposits, including copper, gold, and oil, account for nearly two-thirds of export earnings. Natural gas reserves amount to an estimated 155 billion cubic meters. A consortium led by a major American oil company is constructing a liquefied natural gas (LNG) production facility that began exporting in April 2014. As the largest investment project in the country's history, it has the potential to double GDP in the near-term and triple Papua New Guinea's export revenue. An American-owned firm also opened PNG's first oil refinery in 2004 and is building a second LNG production facility. The government faces the challenge of ensuring transparency and accountability for revenues flowing from this and other large LNG projects. In 2011 and 2012, the National Parliament passed legislation that created an offshore Sovereign Wealth Fund to manage government surpluses from mineral, oil, and natural gas projects. In recent years, the government has opened up markets in telecommunications and air transport, making both more affordable to the people.

Numerous challenges still face the government of Papua New Guinea including, providing physical security for foreign investors, regaining investor confidence, restoring integrity to state institutions, promoting economic efficiency by privatizing moribund state institutions, and maintaining good relations with Australia; its former colonial ruler. Other socio-cultural challenges could upend the economy including chronic law and order and land tenure issues.

External trade (USD millions)	2000	2005	2010	2015	2018
Exports, fob	5813.0	10,271.1	15,601.8	23,323.0	32,986.0
Imports, cif	2779.0	4712.2	9576.2	8317.9	9353.5
Trade balance	3034.0	5558.9	6025.6	15,005.1	23,632.5

Source Asian Development Bank (ADB, 2019)

Main commercial partners (USD millions)	2000	2005	2010	2015	2018
Exports					
1. Australia	843	1507	2778	1178	2245
2. Singapore	226	214.0	226.4	1193	1318
3. Japan	317	450	906	1120	2465
4. China, People's Rep. of	182	281	709	853	1714
5. Taipei, China	9	14	10	609	587
6. India	1	65	137	352	187
7. Netherlands	7.8	36	99	74	313
8. Philippines	17	104	293	103	113
9. Germany	117	195	276	203	286
10. Korea, Rep. of	107	65	183	172	287
Imports					
1. Australia	608	1103	2068	1438	1828
2. China, People's Rep. of	27	73	388	1112	889
3. Singapore	244	271	645	700	596
4. Malaysia	42	84	243	400	472
5. Indonesia	37	54	169	227	240
6. Taipei, China	11	11	123	200	189
7. Japan	49	87	324	192	165
8. Thailand	21	39	154	155	189
9. New Zealand	47	79	151	160	131
10. United States	26	61	211	233	97

Source Asian Development Bank (ADB, 2019)

TIMOR LESTE

Official name
Democratic Republic of Timor Leste
Capital
Dili
Area
15,410 sq. km
Population
1.32 mln
Languages
Tetum (official), Portuguese (official)
Main ethnic groups
Austronesian, Papuan

Main religions
Roman Catholic 97%
Government type
Semi-presidential Republic
Urbanization
30.6%
Life expectancy ratio
70 years
Fertility rate
5.2 children born/woman
Currency
United States Dollar USD

Timor Leste

Country Introduction

Population, Location, Geography and Climate

Timor-Leste, officially the Democratic Republic of Timor-Leste, is a country in Southeast Asia, and has the population more than 1.32 million people according to the 2018 census. Commonly referred to the East Timor, the population is mostly concentrated around Dili, the largest city and capital, with a population of 234,000. The term Maubere was used by the Portuguese to refer to native East Timorese as a synonym for uneducated and illiterate however, now it is now used as a term of pride. Maubere is composed of several ethnic groups, mostly being Malayo-Polynesian and Melanesian/Papuan descent. The largest Malayo-Polynesian group are the Tetum (100,000), who live around Dili, followed by the Mambai (80,000) in the mountains, the Tukudede (63,000) around Liquica and Maubara, the Galoli (50,000), the Kemak (50,000) in north-central Timor island, and the Baikeno (20,000). The main groups of Papuan origin are the Bunak (50,000) in the central region of Timor island, the Fataluka (30,000) near Lospalos and the Makasae at the eastern end of the island. There is also a large population of people of mixed East Timorese and Portuguese origin called mesticos, and a small Chinese minority.

The national language of East Timor is Tetum, which is a Malayo-Polynesian language influenced by Portuguese, which also has status as an official language. Fataluku, is a Papuan language that is widely used in the eastern part of the country (often more than Tetum) and has official recognition under the constitution, as do other indigenous languages. Recognized languages include: Bekais, Bunak, Dawan, Fataluku, Galoli, Habun, Idalaka, Kawaimina, Kemak, Lovaia, Makalero, Makasai, Mambai, Tokodede and Wetarese. Furthermore, Indonesian is also widely spoken language due to Timor-Leste's history, although it does not have status as an official language. English and Indonesian are recognized as working languages and spoken a lot in business environment.

Timor is the Malay word for "East". The island of Timor is part of the Malay Archipelago and the largest and easternmost of the Lesser Sunda Islands. The country's total area is 14,874 km^2. To the north of the mountainous island are the Ombai Strait and Wetar Strait, in the south the Timor Sea separates the island from Australia and to the west lies the Indonesian Province of East Nusa Tenggara. The highest point of East Timor is Mount Tatamailau at 2963 m.

Christianity is the dominant religion in Timor-Leste. According to the 2010 census, more than 99% of the population stated their religion as Christian with almost 97% being Roman Catholic, and more than 2% Protestant. The remaining amount (less than 1%) are Muslim, Buddhist and others.

Timor-Leste has a tropical monsoon climate. It is very hot and dry from July to November with the western monsoon bringing the rains from December to March. It is cooler and more humid in the mountain region.

Internal Policy

In the sixteenth century, Timor-Leste was colonized by Portugal and known as Portuguese Timor. The Portuguese established outposts in the area. During World War II, it was occupied by the Japanese and struggled to defeat the Japanese with Allied forces and East Timorese volunteers. This led to the deaths of up to 70,000 East Timorese. Portugal effectively abandoned its colony in 1974, and Timor-Leste declared independence in 1975 but was invaded and occupied by Indonesia. The Indonesian occupation was marked by violence and brutality, which killed about

100,000 people. In 1999 Country had an independence referendum. On 20th May 2002 Timor-Leste finally declared its independence, and the country's constitution was adopted the same year after East Timor's independence declaration.

Timor-Leste is democratic republic and president is the head of the country. The president's powers are somewhat limited by the constitution, but he can veto legislation which, can be overridden by the parliament. President is elected every 5 years by absolute majority vote through a two-round system, and elected president appoints the prime minister.

Independent courts described as organs of sovereignty with competencies to administer justice in the name of the people. The judges are appointed by the president every 4 years.

Pass relevant, well drafted legislation in a timely manner, provide a counterbalance to the powers of the presidency, and establish and maintain proper, efficient, and effective communication between the various branches of government. National Parliament members are elected every 5 years through a closed-list proportional representation system.

International Relations

After declaring its independence Timor-Leste became part of the United Nations. Timor-Leste has diplomatic relationship with Russia, United States, Australia, Indonesia, Philippines, South Korea, Malaysia, Singapore, Portugal and Brazil. Furthermore, Timor-Leste has high interest in joining an ASEAN Association. Timor-Leste already has a good relationship with many of the ASEAN countries such as Indonesia, Malaysia, Singapore, and the Philippines. ASEAN is very beneficial to small countries and joining ASEAN will help Timor-Leste to achieve economic and financial progress.

Timor-Leste's foreign policy places high priority on its relationships with Indonesia, Australia, other neighbors, and friendly countries and donors, most notably the Community of Portuguese Language Countries (CPLP) and the member states of the Association of Southeast Asian Nations (ASEAN). Timor-Leste began its two-year presidency of the CPLP in 2014 by prioritizing economic integration between member states, as well as joint exploration and production of oil and gas. One of its top foreign policy objectives is to join ASEAN. Timor-Leste applied for ASEAN membership in 2011, but an ASEAN decision to admit the nation is still pending.

Timor-Leste and the United States belong to many of the same international organizations, including the United Nations, ASEAN Regional Forum, Asia/Pacific Group on Money Laundering, International Monetary Fund, and World Bank.

Asian Development Bank has close bilateral ties with Timor Leste, as such newly agreed Country Partnership Strategy which will include the provision of capital assistance during 2017–2019. It operationalizes the CPS objectives of human capital development, economic diversification, and sustainable and inclusive growth. Timor-Leste, a group B developing member country, is eligible for both regular ordinary capital resources (OCR) lending and concessional OCR lending

(COL). The indicative resources available for sovereign operations during 2017–2019 amount to $264.09 million, including $74.09 million for COL and $190.00 million for regular OCR lending.

Economy

IMacroeconomic Overview

	Unit	2000A	2018	2020F
GDP, current prices	USD (billions)	0.44	3.09	3.41
GDP per capita, current prices	USD	494.88	2435.05	2568.94
GDP based on PPP per capita	Current International dollar	1207.50	5241.80	5617.32

Source IMF Outlook (2019)

Over the past decade, Timor-Leste has created the conditions for successful development. It has credibly emerged from a crisis of internal violence and political instability in 2006–2007, and increased tangible services for the population, creating hard-won political stability, absence of conflict and a new confidence in the state. Largely peaceful democratic elections for the presidency and the parliament since 2012 reflect these achievements.

Timor-Leste has achieved tremendous progress since achieving its independence in 2002—drawing down money from the Petroleum Fund and channelling it through the budget to meet pressing needs. The effectiveness of this process is evident in the near-halving of infant and child mortality rates, significant gains in health and education, economic growth to rival regional neighbors, increasing citizen participation, and the gradual strengthening of state institutions.

According to World Bank 2018 data report, Economic activity saw a decline for a second consecutive year, owing to political and economic uncertainty. A new political cycle started in May 2018, but the cabinet was yet to be completed and two state budgets had to be prepared in a short period of time. Also, current account deficit narrowed to below 200 million USD, mainly due to higher primary income related to oil production.

Ensuring Timor-Leste's young people are educated, healthy, and productively employed are arguably the biggest development challenges facing Timor-Leste over the next decade. With 60% of the population under 25 years of age, Timor-Leste is one of the youngest countries in the world. Benefitting from high global oil prices, the country achieved lower middle-income status in 2011, but poverty remains high, particularly in rural areas, where most of the population lives.

Timor-Leste needs to diversify its economy and sources of revenue, elevate the quality of health and education services, and equip the population with viable skills to create job opportunities for youth, sustain inclusive growth, and prepare for a future of potentially declining natural resource returns. Capable institutions with a strong and consistent focus on quality of spending and policies that nurture private investment must underpin these efforts.

The World Development Report 2011 found that on average post-conflict countries take between 15 and 30 years to transition out of fragility and to build resilience. It is against this backdrop that Timor-Leste's social and economic development is noted as remarkable.

The government's Strategic Development Plan for 2011–2030 offers a vision, targets, and indicators for the next two decades. It is built around four pillars:

1. Social capital: health, education, and social protection.
2. Infrastructure: transport, telecommunication, power, and water supply and sanitation.
3. Economic foundations: targeting three sectors for development—agriculture, tourism, and petrochemicals—to bring about growth, jobs, and new sources of public revenues beyond oil.
4. Institutional framework: focusing on macroeconomic management and improving the capacity and effectiveness of government institutions.

Structure of output (% GDP)	2000	2005	2010	2015	2018
Agriculture	24.2	7.4	5.7	8.9	10.4
Industry	31.7	76.1	79.1	57.9	45.6
Services	44.1	16.5	15.2	33.2	44.0

Source Asian Development Bank (ADB, 2019)

Structure of expenditure (% GDP)	2000	2005	2010	2015	2018
Final consumption	182	36	37.9	58.9	75
Gross capital formation	28	4.0	12.0	19.2	22.5
Exports of goods and services	27.2	82.8	100.2	75.1	61.1
Imports of goods and services	139.5	23.7	50.7	54.7	59.9

Source Asian Development Bank (ADB, 2019)

Interest rates (% per annum; period averages)	2000	2005	2010	2015	2018
On deposits					
Savings	N/A	0.75	0.75	0.75	0.4
Time: 6 months	N/A	1.18	1.24	1.15	0.7
12 months	N/A	1.28	1.33	1.25	0.7

Source Asian Development Bank (ADB, 2019)

Investment Area

Petroleum and Minerals

The Government of Timor-Leste continues to support the training of Timorese in Geology, Chemical and Petroleum Engineering, Petroleum Finance and Project Management, though, among others, training of public servants, secondment of staff from international oil and gas companies, scholarship at reputable international higher education institution, and construction of a polytechnic training centre for oil and gas operation in Suai. Recent amendments to the Law on Petroleum Activities enabled the acquisition of a 56.6% stake in the Greater Sunrise Joint Venture through the Petroleum Fund.

Agriculture

Timor-Leste's Government focusing on Agriculture sector to promote economic growth and to provide jobs in the rural areas. The main agricultural products of Timor-Leste are coffee, sandalwood, cashew, cocoa, candlenut, nutmeg, coconut, vanilla, clove, cinnamon, cassava, corn, mangoes, horticulture (fruits and vegetables), fisheries, aquaculture, livestock and agro-forestry.

The main potential of agriculture sector in Timor-Leste are ensuring food security through the promotion of food production for the domestic market, as well as through diversification and improvement of production for export; improving agriculture practices in order to increase the production of rice, corn, coffee, vanilla, nutmeg and coconut oil, as well as strengthening the resilience of communities to climate change and population growth, through training and technical assistance to farmers; support to aquaculture activities, including fish crops, such as tilapia, as well as seaweed, shrimp and crab; and support for commercial fishing activities in the maritime area of the Exclusive Economic Zone. The weight of agriculture in overall output has once achieved to just 10%, while the main out-put is shared by industry and service sectors.

Tourism

The Pristine of Timor-Leste beauty, culture and history is a unique industry sector and an important avenue for the economic development of Timor-Leste.

The potential in this sector, lies within the development of Eco-Tourism, Agri-Tourism, Community Based-Tourism, Historical Tourism, Culture Tourism, rehabilitation and construction of infrastructure, including roads, pathways and resorts.

Industry and Manufacture

To strengthen the economic development and growth, the government of Timor-Leste has been trying to diversify its economic sector from petroleum sector.

Cement, mineral water, salt, marble, ceramic, apparel and mineral ores have high potential to contribute Timor-Leste economy and increase the country's GDP. However, the country needs FDI to develop these sectors.

In addition, Government of Timor-Leste continues support to its private sector by providing basic means to farmers, such as seed, fertilizers and spays. They also support the development of processing industries, particularly agriculture food product of the domestic market, construction material for the replacement of imported materials, and small-scale manufacturing industries of (currently imported) food products, such as salt and water.

Infrastructure

Timor-Leste expanded, improved, and maintained the national (urban and rural) road system and of about 450 bridges, in accordance with international standards, and implemented a traffic flow improvement and road safety program. Furthermore, country has established a regulatory body for the management of drinking water resources and of water and basic sanitation. In terms of electricity, Timor-Leste has already improved its revenue collection, operating costs reduction and service associated with electricity. In addition, country already implemented renewable energies, particularly solar and wind (e.g. solar power station in Hera, wind farms in Lariguto and Bobonaro for connection to the national grid).

Domestic Market

Public spending is the main source of economic demand, and the private sector is in the early stages of development. Revenues from off-shore petroleum production have fallen sharply since 2012, and are forecast to end in 2020. Timor-Leste's Petroleum Fund provides a large fiscal buffer, with a balance of $16.6 billion (10.5 times the non-oil gross domestic product) in September 2016, but declining oil revenues highlight the challenge of ensuring fiscal sustainability. GDP is forecast to grow by 3.9% under a scenario of greater political and economic stability. Increased government spending, coupled with stronger private consumption, will steer economic recovery. Inflation is expected stay under 4% in 2019.

Risks

Despite being fairly shielded from external shocks, the economy could be vulnerable to higher international prices, a falling US dollar, and worsening global financial conditions—the latter would impact on the Petroleum Fund balance. Domestic risks remain elevated, as political tensions have subsided but not dissipated.

With petroleum production declining and in the absence of greater fiscal prudence, large Petroleum Fund withdrawals will accelerate asset depletion and further threaten fiscal sustainability. A strong fiscal adjustment in response to tighter fiscal space would hurt living standards. Securing private investors for upstream and downstream development of the Greater Sunrise oil and gas fields would lessen exposure to commercial risks. Moreover, improving the quality of public spending can have multiplier effects on the economy—especially through greater efficiency and more strategic allocations. The key challenges facing Timor-Leste include accelerating economic growth and diversifying the economy, which will require stronger and better investments in human capital.

External trade (USD millions)	2000	2005	2010	2015	2018
Exports, fob	0.0	43.5	41.7	38.4	46.3
Imports, cif	0.0	109.1	298.1	491.2	565.2
Trade balance	0.0	−65.7	−256.4	−452.8	−518.9

Source Asian Development Bank (ADB, 2019)

Main commercial partners (USD millions)	2000	2005	2010	2015	2018
Exports					
1. Korea, Rep. of	N/A	0	0	0.2	0.2
2. United States	N/A	1.00	N/A	8.7	5.4
3. Indonesia	N/A	0.4	0.6	0.5	17
4. Germany	N/A	0.03	8	2.7	2
5. Japan	N/A	1	6	4.2	0.5
6. Portugal	N/A	0.2	0.1	3.2	1
7. China, People's Rep. of	N/A	N/A	0.2	0.9	4
8. Australia	N/A	17	16	0.8	1
9. Singapore	N/A	1	N/A	2.8	0.4
10. Hong Kong, China	N/A	0.1	0.1	0.6	1
Imports					
1. Indonesia	N/A	147	125	363.4	1
2. Singapore	N/A	1	N/A	283.0	71
3. China, People's Rep. of	N/A	1	30	70.7	89
4. Hong Kong, China	N/A	10	11	59.4	59
5. Viet Nam	N/A	29	63	66.9	41
6. Malaysia	N/A	28	32	40.0	9
7. Thailand	N/A	9	16	17.7	18
8. Australia	N/A	1	41	13.6	10
9. Belgium	N/A	0	0	19.8	0.1
10. Brazil	N/A	0	0.2	8.8	12

Source Asian Development Bank (ADB, 2019)

Relevant Treaties

Treaty of Amity and Cooperation in Southeast Asia

1976: Adopted by the Heads of State/Government at the 1st ASEAN Summit in Bali, Indonesia on 24 February 1976

The High Contracting Parties:

Conscious of the existing ties of history, geography and culture, which have bound their peoples together;
Anxious to promote regional peace and stability through abiding respect for justice and the rule or law and enhancing regional resilience in their relations;
Desiring to enhance peace, friendship and mutual cooperation on matters affecting Southeast Asia consistent with the spirit and principles of the Charter of the United Nations, the Ten Principles adopted by the Asian-African Conference in Bandung on 25 April 1955, the Declaration of the Association of Southeast Asian Nations signed in Bangkok on 8 August 1967, and the Declaration signed in Kuala Lumpur on 27 November 1971;
Convinced that the settlement of differences or disputes between their countries should be regulated by rational, effective and sufficiently flexible procedures, avoiding negative attitudes which might endanger or hinder cooperation;
Believing in the need for cooperation with all peace-loving nations, both within and outside Southeast Asia, in the furtherance of world peace, stability and harmony;
Solemnly Agree to enter into a Treaty of Amity and Cooperation as follows.

Chapter I. Purpose and Principles

Article 1

The purpose of this Treaty is to promote perpetual peace, everlasting amity and cooperation among their peoples which would contribute to their strength, solidarity and closer relationship.

L. Riccardi and G. Riccardi, *Invest in ASEAN*,
https://doi.org/10.1007/978-981-15-5378-3_3

Article 2

In their relations with one another, the High Contracting Parties shall be guided by the following fundamental principles:

a. Mutual respect for the independence, sovereignty, equality, territorial integrity and national identity of all nations;
b. The right of every State to lead its national existence free from external interference, subversion or coercion;
c. Non-interference in the internal affairs of one another;
d. Settlement of differences or disputes by peaceful means;
e. Renunciation of the threat or use of force;
f. Effective cooperation among themselves.

Chapter II. Amity

Article 3

In pursuance of the purpose of this Treaty the High Contracting Parties shall endeavour to develop and strengthen the traditional, cultural and historical ties of friendship, good neighbourliness and cooperation which bind them together and shall fulfill in good faith the obligations assumed under this Treaty. In order to promote closer understanding among them, the High Contracting Parties shall encourage and facilitate contact and intercourse among their peoples.

Chapter III. Cooperation

Article 4

The High Contracting Parties shall promote active cooperation in the economic, social, technical, scientific and administrative fields as well as in matters of common ideals and aspirations of international peace and stability in the region and all other matters of common interest.

Article 5

Pursuant to Article 4 the High Contracting Parties shall exert their maximum efforts multilaterally as well as bilaterally on the basis of equality, non-discrimination and mutual benefit.

Article 6

The High Contracting Parties shall collaborate for the acceleration of the economic growth in the region in order to strengthen the foundation for a prosperous and peaceful community of nations in Southeast Asia. To this end, they shall promote the greater utilization of their agriculture and industries, the expansion of their trade and the improvement of their economic infrastructure for the mutual benefit of their peoples. In this regard, they shall continue to explore all avenues for close and beneficial cooperation with other States as well as international and regional organisations outside the region.

Article 7

The High Contracting Parties, in order to achieve social justice and to raise the standards of living of the peoples of the region, shall intensify economic cooperation. For this purpose, they shall adopt appropriate regional strategies for economic development and mutual assistance.

Article 8

The High Contracting Parties shall strive to achieve the closest cooperation on the widest scale and shall seek to provide assistance to one another in the form of training and research facilities in the social, cultural, technical, scientific and administrative fields.

Article 9

The High Contracting Parties shall endeavour to foster cooperation in the furtherance of the cause of peace, harmony, and stability in the region. To this end, the High Contracting Parties shall maintain regular contacts and consultations with one another on international and regional matters with a view to coordinating their views actions and policies.

Article 10

Each High Contracting Party shall not in any manner or form participate in any activity which shall constitute a threat to the political and economic stability, sovereignty, or territorial integrity of another High Contracting Party.

Article 11

The High Contracting Parties shall endeavour to strengthen their respective national resilience in their political, economic, socio-cultural as well as security fields in conformity with their respective ideals and aspirations, free from external interference as well as internal subversive activities in order to preserve their respective national identities.

Article 12

The High Contracting Parties in their efforts to achieve regional prosperity and security, shall endeavour to cooperate in all fields for the promotion of regional resilience, based on the principles of self-confidence, self-reliance, mutual respect, cooperation and solidarity which will constitute the foundation for a strong and viable community of nations in Southeast Asia.

Chapter IV. Pacific Settlement of Disputes

Article 13

The High Contracting Parties shall have the determination and good faith to prevent disputes from arising. In case disputes on matters directly affecting them should arise, especially disputes likely to disturb regional peace and harmony, they shall refrain from the threat or use of force and shall at all times settle such disputes among themselves through friendly negotiations.

Article 14

To settle disputes through regional processes, the High Contracting Parties shall constitute, as a continuing body, a High Council comprising a Representative at ministerial level from each of the High Contracting Parties to take cognizance of the existence of disputes or situations likely to disturb regional peace and harmony.

Article 15

In the event no solution is reached through direct negotiations, the High Council shall take cognizance of the dispute or the situation and shall recommend to the parties in dispute appropriate means of settlement such as good offices, mediation, inquiry or conciliation. The High Council may however offer its good offices, or upon agreement of the parties in dispute, constitute itself into a committee of mediation, inquiry or conciliation. When deemed necessary, the High Council shall recommend appropriate measures for the prevention of a deterioration of the dispute or the situation.

Article 16

The foregoing provision of this Chapter shall not apply to a dispute unless all the parties to the dispute agree to their application to that dispute. However, this shall not preclude the other High Contracting Parties not party to the dispute from offering all possible assistance to settle the said dispute. Parties to the dispute should be well disposed towards such offers of assistance.

Article 17

Nothing in this Treaty shall preclude recourse to the modes of peaceful settlement contained in Article 33(l) of the Charter of the United Nations. The High Contracting Parties which are parties to a dispute should be encouraged to take initiatives to solve it by friendly negotiations before resorting to the other procedures provided for in the Charter of the United Nations.

Chapter V. General Provision

Article 18

This Treaty shall be signed by the Republic of Indonesia, Malaysia, the Republic of the Philippines, the Republic of Singapore and the Kingdom of Thailand. It shall be ratified in accordance with the constitutional procedures of each signatory State. It shall be open for accession by other States in Southeast Asia.

Article 19

This Treaty shall enter into force on the date of the deposit of the fifth instrument of ratification with the Governments of the signatory States which are designated Depositories of this Treaty and the instruments of ratification or accession.

Article 20

This Treaty is drawn up in the official languages of the High Contracting Parties, all of which are equally authoritative. There shall be an agreed common translation of the texts in the English language. Any divergent interpretation of the common text shall be settled by negotiation.

In Faith Thereof the High Contracting Parties have signed the Treaty and have hereto affixed their Seals.

Done at Denpasar, Bali, this twenty-fourth day of February in the year one thousand nine hundred and seventy-six.

For the Republic of Indonesia: **Soeharto**, President
For Malaysia: **DR. Husein Onn**, Prime Minister
For the Republic of the Philippines: **Ferdinand E. Marcos**, President
For the Republic of Singapore: **Lee Kuan Yew**, Prime Minister
For the Kingdom of Thailand: **Kukrit Pramoj**, Prime Minister.

Basic Agreement on ASEAN Industrial Projects

1980: Signed by the ASEAN Foreign Affairs Ministers at the 13th AMM in Kuala Lumpur, Malaysia on 6 March 1980

The Governments of the Republic of Indonesia, Malaysia, the Republic of the Philippines, the Republic of Singapore, and the Kingdom of Thailand.

Recalling the Declaration, of ASEAN Concord signed in Bali, Indonesia on 24 February 1976 which provides that member states shall take cooperative action in their national and regional development programs, utilizing as far as possible the resources available in the ASEAN region to broaden the complementarity of their respective economies;
Recalling the Agreement on ASEAN preferential Trading Arrangements which relates to the framework for ASEAN Economic Cooperation;
Desiring to intensify cooperation in the field of industry;
Considering that the establishment of ASEAN Industrial Projects, through joint endeavours in the spirit of equality and partnership, can contribute to the acceleration of economic growth in the region;
Have Agreed as follows.

Chapter I. Purposes and Principles

Article 1

The purposes of the present Agreement are:

1. To cooperate on establishing large-scale ASEAN Industrial Projects, particularly to meet regional requirements for essential products; and
2. To give priority to projects which utilize the available resources in the Member States and which contribute to the increase in food production and foreign exchange earnings or which save foreign exchange and create employment.

L. Riccardi and G. Riccardi, *Invest in ASEAN*,
https://doi.org/10.1007/978-981-15-5378-3_4

The provisions of this Agreement shall initially apply to the first five ASEAN Industrial Projects. They shall also apply to subsequent sets of projects, unless the ASEAN Economic Ministers decide otherwise. In the event modifications are found necessary in the subsequent sets in the light of experience gained under the first five ASEAN Industrial Projects, such modifications shall be effected in accordance with Chapter XVI of this Agreement.

Article 2

The Contracting States, in pursuance of the purposes stated in Article 1, shall act in accordance with the following principles:

1. Each Contracting State shall have at least one ASEAN Industrial Project in its country.
2. Upon the allocation of an ASEAN Industrial Project to an ASEAN member country, similar new national projects can only be established after consultation with member countries and also on condition that the basis for the ASEAN Industrial Project is not affected by the proposed new national projects. However, similar national projects which have already been firmly planned and are already in their early stage of implementation before the allocation of the ASEAN Industrial Projects shall be allowed to proceed as national projects. Such projects shall be specified with particulars in the relevant Supplementary Agreement attached hereto.
3. In the allocation of the subsequent sets of ASEAN Industrial Projects, the benefits derived from the preceding ASEAN Industrial Projects shall be taken into account with a view to equalizing benefits in the long term.

Chapter II. Equity

Article 3

1. Each of the first five ASEAN Industrial Projects shall have five (5) shareholder entities, except in the case of the ASEAN Industrial Project to be established in Thailand which shall have seven (7) shareholders.
2. Each shareholder entity shall be an agency or company which enjoys support and guidance from its respective Government of an ASEAN Member State and which is nominated by that Government to participate in the ASEAN Industrial Projects.
3. The shareholder entity of the host country shall have sixty per cent (60%) of the total equity of the respective ASEAN Industrial Project, with the balance to be shared by the shareholder entities of the other Contracting Parties.
4. The amount of equity participation in the shareholder entity by the Government itself, by the private sector in the country and by non-ASEAN interests shall be at the discretion of the respective Governments of the ASEAN Member States

concerned provided that each of the Governments of the ASEAN Member States shall have at least one third of the said equity.
5. Majority ownership interest should at all times be held by the ASEAN shareholders.

Chapter III. Board of Directors

Article 4

1. The Board of Directors of a company that is to undertake an ASEAN Industrial Project (hereinafter referred to in this Agreement as the Project company) shall consist of not more than eleven (11) members. As far as possible, the Board shall consist of nationals of ASEAN Member States only.
2. In the event it is necessary to appoint nationals of countries which are non-members of ASEAN to the Board of Directors, such appointment shall be approved by the members on the Board who are nationals of the ASEAN Member States.
3. In respect of membership in the Board of Directors of the Project company, membership in the Board of Directors by nationals of countries which are non-members of ASEAN representing portfolio investors who have sufficient capital participation directly or indirectly in the project to arrant participation in the Board of Directors may be considered. Proposed membership in the Board of Directors of the Project company by direct investors representing non-ASEAN interests with operational, marketing, engineering or similar involvement's in the project shall be approved by the members on the Board who are nationals of ASEAN Member States.

Chapter IV. Financing

Article 5

1. Wherever appropriate and after prior consultations, ASEAN shall approach prospective lenders as a group in securing loans for the AS Industrial Projects.
2. Notwithstanding paragraph 1 above, with regard to each ASEAN Industrial Project, the host country, after prior consultations with other ASEAN Member States, can act on behalf of the other ASEAN Member States in respect of securing loans, the result of which shall be reported to the other ASEAN Member States.

3. ASEAN Member States shall, in order to obtain the best possible terms in the securing of loans for the ASEAN Industrial Projects, adopt a coordinated approach to the raising of such loans whether simultaneous or staggered.
4. In the securing of loans for ASEAN Industrial Projects, it would be desirable to negotiate with the intention of attaining the three-fold objectives of:

   i. securing the maximum amount of concessional loans;
   ii. securing the greatest possible amount of untied financing; and
   iii. minimizing direct government guarantees.

   In the event that guarantees are necessary, the host country of the project shall be responsible for such guarantees.
5. Each member country shall endeavour to exempt ASEAN Industrial Projects from domestic borrowing ceilings or limits on foreign borrowings.
6. After the incorporation of the Project company, all additional financial requirements further to that initiated by ASEAN Member States, which have been negotiated or re being negotiated up to the time the company is incorporated, shall be the responsibility of the management of the Project company.
7. The Project company shall not be incorporated until all matters pertaining to the joint Venture Agreement have been resolved.

Chapter V. Preferential Trading Arrangements

Article 6

ASEAN trade preferences shall be accorded to the products of the ASEAN Industrial Projects, pursuant to Article 10 of the Agreement on ASEAN Preferential Trading Arrangements.

Chapter VI. Taxation

Article 7

1. An ASEAN Industrial Project shall be deemed to have its fiscal domicile in the State of the host country and shall be taxable in that State according to the taxation laws of that State.
2. Corporate taxes with holding taxes, dividend taxes and other forms of taxes applicable to each ASEAN Industrial Project shall be at the prevailing rate unless concessional rates have been granted by the host country of the ASEAN Industrial Project, taking into consideration the various incentives which may be granted under the provision of Article 8 and having regard to the nature and particular circumstances of the project.

3. An ASEAN Industrial Project shall not be subjected in the host country to any taxation or any requirement connected therewith which is more burdensome than the taxation and connected requirements to which similar enterprises in that country are or may be subjected.
4. In the negotiation and conclusion of bilateral tax treaties, special consideration shall be Oven to ASEAN industrial Projects.

Chapter VII. Incentives

Article 8

ASEAN countries shall offer ASEAN Industrial Projects the most favourable incentives under existing laws and policies and shall endeavour to make these incentives comparable to the treatment accorded to other ASEAN projects by the other host countries.

Chapter VIII. Repatriation of Foreign Exchange

Article 9

The host country shall guarantee the full repatriation of capital and the remittance of returns, including dividends and interest, without undue delay. Such repatriation and remittance shall be allowed to be made any freely usable currency as defined in the Articles of Agreement of the international Monetary Fund required by the recipient countries.

Chapter IX. Protection of Minority Shareholders

Article 10

The majority required for meetings of share- holders and the Board of Directors shall be two- thirds (2/3), whereas the majority required for liquidation, merger, increase and decrease of capital, issuance of debentures, and amendments to the Articles of Association or Articles of incorporation whichever is applicable, shall be three- fourths (3/4), unless a higher price is required by the respective law of the host country.

Chapter X. Pricing Principles

Article 11

1. The products of the ASEAN Industrial Projects shall be sold at world prices between floor and ceiling prices based on minimum and maximum project rates of return, which pricing arrangement shall be applicable to products purchased by or through ASEAN Member States from ASEAN Industrial Projects under long term contracts. However, the floor and ceiling prices may be reviewed in the event of unexpected and abnormal developments or in the event of either exigency in world market conditions.
2. There shall be one free-on-board (f.o.b) selling price based either on long term contracts, term supplies of any similar contracts for the host country and the ASEAN markets for each product of an ASEAN Industrial Project.
3. Where an identical product is produced by more than one ASEAN Industrial Project, the floor, ceiling and actual free-on-board (f.o.b) selling prices of such products once adopted for one project shall apply to the other project or projects.
4. The actual selling price shall be determined by the project company based on the prevailing world market prices generally applicable to the ASEAN region.
5. Not with standing paragraph 4 above, there shall be:

   a. A floor free-on-board (f.o.b) selling price for each product produced by the ASEAN Industrial Project to account for project commercial viability.
   b. A ceiling f.o.b. selling price for each product produced by the ASEAN Industrial Project to take into consideration the general protection of the host country and ASEAN consumers.

6. Floor and ceiling prices shall be calculated prior to commencement of commercial operation based on mini- mum and maximum rates of return on investment calculated by the discounted cash flow internal rate of return on investment (IRROI) method over the economic life of the project.
   Profit used in calculating the minimum and maximum IRROI percentages shall be profit before depreciation and interest on long term debt and after corporate income tax.
   Such floor and ceiling prices shall be adjusted periodically on account of:

   i. changes in cost of production
   ii. currency adjustment

7. Minimum and maximum IRROI percentages shall be assessed for each ASEAN Industrial Project taking into account the relevant factors of the project.
8. The floor and ceiling prices may be reviewed in the event of unexpected and abnormal developments in world conditions or in the event of either exigency. Such developments as aforesaid shall include the conditions when the prevailing

world market price exceeds the agreed ceiling price by more than ten per cent (10%) or when the prevailing market price goes below the agreed floor price by more than ten per cent (10%).

9. Selling prices throughout the project life shall be calculated in United States dollars.

Chapter XI. Project Scope

Article 12

1. Project cost shall include only the cost of infrastructure which can be shown to be directly a part of the project and only to the extent the infrastructure is required by the project itself and that such infrastructure costs are acceptable to the shareholders.
2. Such portions of infrastructure for the project that are larger than the minimum required by the project or are built to standards higher than needed by the project shall not be a part. of the project cost but shall be for the account of the host country.

Chapter XII. Institutional Arrangements

Article 13

1. For the purpose of implementing this Basic Agreement and the Supplementary Agreement hereinafter specified in Article 1 6, there shall be join, Venture Agreement among the participating shareholder entities from ASEAN Member States for each ASEAN Industrial Project. The joint Venture Agreement shall be in conformity with the provisions of the Basic Agreement and Supplementary Agreement.
2. The power to approve and review the joint Venture Agreement shall be vested in the ASEAN Economic Ministers based on recommendations of the Committee on industry, Minerals and Energy (COIME) in consultation with the Committee Finance and Banking and the Committee on Trade and Tourism.
3. COIME shall review, supervise and monitor the implementation of the Basic Agreement and the Supplementary Agreement hereinafter specified in Article 16 up to the time of incorporation of the project company. All decisions of COIME shall be taken by consensus.

Chapter XIII. Consultations

Article 14

1. Each Contracting State shall accord adequate opportunity for consultations regarding such representations as may be made by any Contracting State with respect to any matter affecting the implementation of this Agreement COIME may, at the request of any Contracting State, consult with any other Contracting State in respect of any matter for which it has not been posse to find a satisfactory solution during previous consultations.
2. If any Contracting State should consider that any other Contracting State has not carried out its obligations under this Agreement, the affected contracting State may make representations or proposals to the other Contracting State concerned which shall consider said representation or proposal within sixty (60) days from receipt thereof.
3. If no satisfactory solution is effected between the Contracting States, the matter may be referred to COIME which shall consult with the Contracting States concerned and arrive at a solution mutually acceptable to the States concerned. if no satisfactory solution is arrived at in COIME, the matter shall be referred to the ASEAN Economic Ministers for the final settlement.

Chapter XIV. Bankruptcy

Article 15

In order to maintain the required government equity in the shareholder entity, in the event that such entity becomes insolvent, the Contracting State responsible for the shareholder entity shall without undue delay, arrange the following:

1. Take all reasonable legal means to prevent the shares of the ASEAN Industrial Projects held by the said shareholder entity from being involved in any legal action taken by creditors.
2. If it is necessary for a new shareholder entity to take up all the shares owned by the insolvent shareholder entity, the new shareholder entity shall be accorded the same rights and shall undertake the same obligations as the insolvent entity.

Chapter XV. Supplementary Agreement

Article 16

Special provisions concerning each individual ASEAN Industrial Project shall be set out in a Supplementary Agreement which shall be deemed to be Part of this Basic Agreement.

Chapter XVI. Amendments

Article 17

All articles of this Agreement may be modified through amendments to this Agreement agreed upon by consensus. All amendments shall become effective upon acceptance by all Contracting States.

Chapter XVII. Entry into Force

Article 18

1. This Agreement shall enter into force on the thirtieth (30th) day after the deposit of the fifth Instrument of Ratification.
2. This Agreement may not be signed with reservation nor shall reservations be admitted at the time of ratification.
3. This Agreement shall be deposited with the Secretary-General of the ASEAN Secretariat who shall promptly furnish a certified copy thereof to each Contracting State.
4. Each Contracting State shall deposit its instrument of Ratification with the Secretary- General of the ASEAN Secretariat who shall promptly inform each, Contracting State of such deposit.

In Witness Whereof, the undersigned, being duly authorized thereto by their respective Governments, have signed the Basic Agreement on ASEAN Industrial Projects.

Done at Kuala Lumpur, in six originals in the English language this March 6, 1980.

For the Government of the Republic of Indonesia, **Dr. Mochtar Kusumaatmadja**, Minister for Foreign Affairs
For the Government of the Republic of Singapore, **S. Rajaratnam**, Minister for Foreign Affairs
For the Government of Malaysia, **Tengku Ahmad Rithadudeen**, Minister for Foreign Affairs
For the Government of the Kingdom of Thailand, **Upadit Pachariyangkun**, Minister for Foreign Affairs
For the Government of the Republic of Philippines, **Carlos P. Romulo**, Minister for Foreign Affairs.

ASEAN Agreement of Customs

1997: Done at Phuket, Thailand on the 1st March 1997

The Governments of Brunei Darussalam, the Republic of Indonesia, Malaysia, the Republic of the Philippines, the Republic of Singapore, the Kingdom of Thailand and the Socialist Republic of Vietnam of the Association of Southeast Asian Nations (hereinafter referred to as “ASEAN”):

Noting the Framework Agreement on Enhancing ASEAN Economic Cooperation of 28 January 1992 which provides that Member States shall explore further measures on border and non-border areas for cooperation to supplement and complement the liberalisation of trade;

Mindful that in 1992 the ASEAN Heads of Government declared that an ASEAN Free Trade Area (hereinafter referred to as “AFTA”) shall be established in the region and that in 1995 they agreed to accelerate its implementation to year 2003;

Recalling that in 1995, the ASEAN Heads of Governments adopted, in the Bangkok Summit Declaration, the Agenda for Greater Economic Integration which includes, among others, the harmonisation of tariff nomenclature, and the implementation of the GATT Valuation System by 1997;

Recognising that, further to the creation of the green lane system, the Seventh AFTA Council also agreed to the harmonisation of Customs procedures;

Mindful of the different levels of Customs and economic development, and diverse cultural backgrounds of ASEAN Member States;

Reiterating the commitment to the principles of the General Agreement on Tariffs and Trade 1994 (hereinafter known as “GATT”), the Agreement Establishing the World Trade Organisation (hereinafter known as “WTO”) and the World Customs Organisation (hereinafter known as “WCO”);

Recalling the former ASEAN Customs Code of Conduct signed in Jakarta on 18 March 1983 and the revised Code of Conduct signed on 18 July 1995;

L. Riccardi and G. Riccardi, *Invest in ASEAN*,
https://doi.org/10.1007/978-981-15-5378-3_5

Desiring to promote intra-ASEAN trade and investments by ensuring the smooth cross-border flow of goods and services within the region;
Mindful of the need to further strengthen enforcement and prevention among Customs Administration of ASEAN, particularly to combat, among others, the illicit trafficking of narcotics and psychotropic substances;
Recognising the need to provide a basis in Customs on general rules and procedures which will ensure the smooth implementation of ASEAN economic agreements and arrangements, in particular the ASEAN Free Trade Area;
Desiring to formulate a framework to deepen and broaden cooperation in Customs in ASEAN and to chart the future activities in this area.
Have Agreed as follows.

Article 1
Objectives

The objectives of this Agreement are:

1. to simplify and harmonise Customs valuation, tariff nomenclature and Customs procedures;
2. to ensure consistency, transparency and fair application of Customs laws and regulations, procedures and other administrative guidelines within each ASEAN Member State;
3. to ensure efficient administration and expeditious clearance of goods to facilitate intra-regional trade and investments;
4. to explore other appropriate intra-ASEAN cooperation arrangements in the field of Customs, particularly in the prevention and repression of all forms of smuggling and other Customs frauds.

Article 2
Principles

Member States will be guided by the following principles under this Agreement:

1. Consistency. Member States will ensure the continuous consistent application of Customs laws and regulations, procedures, administrative guidelines and other rulings within each ASEAN Member State;
2. Appeals. Member States will ensure the availability to traders of readily accessible means of review of Customs decisions in ASEAN;
3. Simplicity. Member States will endeavour to ensure the simplification of Customs procedures and requirements within ASEAN;
4. Transparency. Member States will make all laws, regulations, procedures and administrative notifications pertaining to Customs administration in their economies publicly available in a prompt, transparent and readily accessible manner;
5. Efficiency. Member States will ensure the efficient and effective administration and expeditious clearance of goods to facilitate intra-ASEAN trade and investment;

6. Mutual Assistance and Cooperation. Member States will endeavour their utmost cooperation and mutual assistance between Customs Authorities.

Article 3
General Provisions

1. The provisions of this Agreement shall apply to all Member States and all goods traded within ASEAN in accordance with their national laws, rules and regulations.
2. Goods eligible for preferential concessions whether tariff or non-tariff under any ASEAN economic arrangement shall be subject to the Rules of Origin for the CEPT for AFTA.

Article 4
Tariff Nomenclature

1. The ASEAN Harmonized Tariff Nomenclature shall be based on the 6-digit Harmonized Commodity Description and Coding System (HS) of the WCO and the amendments thereto.
2. Member States shall, for tariff purposes, use a common tariff nomenclature at the 8-digit level. The ASEAN Harmonized Tariff Nomenclature beyond the 8-digit level may be used for statistical and other purposes.
3. Member States may amend the ASEAN Harmonized Tariff Nomenclature in accordance with Article 10 of this Agreement.

Article 5
Customs Valuation

1. Member States shall not use Customs valuation for protective purposes or as a barrier to trade.
2. Member States shall implement the GATT Valuation Agreement, as per the Agreement on Implementation of Article VII of the General Agreement on Tariffs and Trade 1994, on an accelerated schedule.
3. Member States shall adopt a common interpretation of the GATT Valuation Agreement and standardize the systems used to operationalize the Agreement.

Article 6
Customs Procedures

1. Member States shall simplify and harmonize Customs procedures for the efficient and expeditious clearance of products traded in ASEAN.
2. Simplification and harmonization of Customs procedures in ASEAN shall conform with the standards and recommended practices in the Kyoto Convention, as amended, under the auspices of the Customs Cooperation Council (CCC) or WCO.
3. Nothing shall prevent two or more Member States, desiring to facilitate trade, from granting privileges more than those stipulated in this Agreement. Member States are however, encouraged to extend these privileges to all the other Member States.

4. Member States shall periodically review ASEAN Customs procedures to further simplify and harmonize ASEAN Customs procedures in accordance with Article 10 of this Agreement.

Article 7
Other Areas of Cooperation

1. Member States shall pursue other areas of Customs cooperation consistent with their respective national laws, rules and regulations and within the limits of the Customs Administration's competence and available resources.
2. Member States shall be encouraged to exchange vital information on the prevention and repression of smuggling, trafficking of narcotics and psychotropic substances, and other Customs frauds. Subject to Paragraph 1 of this Article, ASEAN Customs authorities shall cooperate among themselves in the conduct of investigation relating to smuggling and other Customs frauds.
3. Member States should accommodate any request by other Member States for studies and visits by Customs personnel.
4. Member States shall exchange information on international Customs issues and endeavour to coordinate ASEAN positions thereon in international Customs fora.
5. Member States should explore other activities to further enhance Customs cooperation in the region.

Article 8
Appeals

Subject to national laws and regulations in each ASEAN Member State, any affected person shall have the right to appeal decisions taken by the Customs authorities of Member States.

Article 9
Consultations and Settlement of Disputes

1. Member States shall, at the written request of a Member State, enter into consultations with a view to seeking a prompt, equitable and mutually satisfactory solution, if that Member State considers that:

   a. an obligation under this Agreement has not been fulfilled, is not being fulfilled, or may not be fulfilled; or,
   b. any objective of this Agreement is not being achieved or may be frustrated.

2. Any differences between Member States concerning the interpretation or application of this Agreement shall, as far as possible, be settled amicably between the parties. If a settlement between the parties cannot be reached, the dispute shall be submitted to the ASEAN Directors-General of Customs for settlement. If any such differences cannot be settled, it shall be subjected to the Dispute Settlement Mechanism of ASEAN.

Article 10
Institutional Arrangements

1. The ASEAN Directors-General of Customs, under the purview of the appropriate ASEAN Ministerial body, shall review, amend, supervise and monitor all aspects relating to the implementation of the Agreement.
2. The ASEAN Secretariat shall provide the support for supervising, coordinating and reviewing the implementation of the Agreement and assist the ASEAN Directors-General of Customs in all matters relating thereto.

Article 11
Private Sector Participation

1. Member States, pursuant to Article 6 of the Framework Agreement on Enhancing ASEAN Economic Cooperation (1992) recognise the importance of and encourage, among others, cooperation, consultations with the ASEAN private sector particularly on ways and means to further enhance intra-ASEAN trade facilitation.
2. The Meeting of the ASEAN Directors-General of Customs shall be the forum for such linkages with the private sector.

Article 12
Accession of New Members

New Members of ASEAN shall accede to this Agreement on terms and conditions agreed between them and existing Members of ASEAN. Accession shall be through the signing and depositing of the instrument of accession to this Agreement with the Secretary-General of ASEAN, who shall promptly furnish each Member State a certified copy thereof.

Article 13
Final Provisions

1. By Agreement of all Member States, the provisions of this Agreement may be reviewed or amended. Annexes may be introduced to this Agreement and shall form an integral part thereof.
2. Any reference to this Agreement is deemed to include also a reference to the Annexes.
3. Member States shall undertake appropriate measures to fulfill the agreed obligations arising from this Agreement.
4. Member States shall make no reservations with respect to any of the provisions of this Agreement.
5. This Agreement shall be deposited with the Secretary General of ASEAN, who shall promptly furnish each Member State a certified copy thereof.
6. This Agreement shall enter into force upon the signing and deposit of instrument of ratification or acceptance by all signatory governments with the Secretary-General of ASEAN.

In witness whereof the undersigned, being duly authorized to sign the Agreement, have signed this ASEAN Agreement on Customs.

Done at Phuket, Thailand, on the 1st day of March 1997, in a single copy in the English Language.

For Brunei Darussalam: **Pehin Dato Ahmad Wally Skinner**, Deputy Minister of Finance
For the Republic of Indonesia: **Ma'rie Muhammade**, Minister of Finance
For Malaysia: **Dato' Seri Anwar Bin Ibrahim**, Deputy Prime Minister and Minister of Finance
For the Republic of the Philippines: **Roberto F. De campo**, Secretary of Finance
For the Republic of Singapore: **Richard Hu Tsu Tau**, Minister of Finance
For the Kingdom of Thailand: **Amnuay Viravan**, Deputy Prime Minister and Minister of Finance
For the Socialist Republic of Viet Nam: **Nguyen Sinh Hung**, Minister of Finance.

ASEAN Agreement on Transboundary Haze Pollution

2002: Signed in Kuala Lumpur, Malaysia on the 10th June 2002

The Parties to this Agreement:

Reaffirming the commitment to the aims and purposes of the Association of Southeast Asian Nations (ASEAN) as set forth in the Bangkok Declaration of 8 August 1967, in particular to promote regional co-operation in Southeast Asia in the spirit of equality and partnership and thereby contribute towards peace, progress and prosperity in the region,

Recalling the Kuala Lumpur Accord on Environment and Development which was adopted by the ASEAN Ministers of Environment on 19 June 1990 which calls for, inter alia, efforts leading towards the harmonization of transboundary pollution prevention and abatement practices,

Recalling Also the adoption of the 1995 ASEAN Co-operation Plan on Transboundary Pollution, which specifically addressed transboundary atmospheric pollution and called for, inter alia, establishing procedures and mechanisms for co-operation among ASEAN Member States in the prevention and mitigation of land and/or forest fires and haze,

Determined to give effect to the 1997 Regional Haze Action Plan and to the Hanoi Plan of Action which call for fully implementing the 1995 ASEAN Cooperation Plan on Transboundary Pollution, with particular emphasis on the Regional Haze Action Plan by the year 2001,

Recognising the existence of possible adverse effects of transboundary haze pollution,

Concerned that a rise in the level of emissions of air pollutants within the region as forecast may increase such adverse effects,

Recognising the need to study the root causes and the implications of the transboundary haze pollution and the need to seek solutions for the problems identified,

L. Riccardi and G. Riccardi, *Invest in ASEAN*,
https://doi.org/10.1007/978-981-15-5378-3_6

Affirming their willingness to further strengthen international co-operation to develop national policies for preventing and monitoring transboundary haze pollution,
Affirming Also their willingness to co- ordinate national action for preventing and monitoring transboundary haze pollution through exchange of information, consultation, research and monitoring,
Desiring to undertake individual and joint action to assess the origin, causes, nature and extent of land and/or forest fires and the resulting haze, to prevent and control the sources of such land and/or forest fires and the resulting haze by applying environmentally sound policies, practices and technologies and to strengthen national and regional capabilities and co-operation in assessment, prevention, mitigation and management of land and/or forest fires and the resulting haze,
Convinced that an essential means to achieve such collective action is the conclusion and effective implementation of an Agreement,
Have Agreed as follows.

Part I. General Provisions

Article 1
Use of Terms

For the purposes of this Agreement:

1. "Assisting Party" means a State, international organization, any other entity or person that offer and/or render assistance to a Requesting Party or a Receiving Party in the event of land and/or forest fires or haze pollution.
2. "Competent authorities" means one or more entities designated and authorized by each Party to act on its behalf in the implementation of this Agreement.
3. "Controlled burning" means any fire, combustion or smouldering that occurs in the open air, which is controlled by national laws, rules, regulations or guidelines and does not cause fire outbreaks and transboundary haze pollution.
4. "Fire prone areas" means areas defined by the national authorities as areas where fires are most likely to occur or have a higher tendency to occur.
5. "Focal point" means an entity designated and authorized by each Party to receive and transmit communications and data pursuant to the provisions of this Agreement.
6. "Haze pollution" means smoke resulting from land and/or forest fire which causes deleterious effects of such a nature as to endanger human health, harm living resources and ecosystems and material property and impair or interfere with amenities and other legitimate uses of the environment.
7. "Land and/or forest fires" means fires such as coal seam fires, peat fires, and plantation fires.
8. "Member State" means a Member State of the Association of Southeast Asian Nations.

9. “Open burning” means any fire, combustion or smouldering that occurs in the open air.
10. “Party” means a Member State of ASEAN that has consented to be bound by this Agreement and for which the Agreement is in force.
11. “Receiving Party” means a Party that accepts assistance offered by an Assisting Party or Parties in the event of land and/or forest fires or haze pollution.
12. “Requesting Party” means a Party that requests from another Party or Parties assistance in the event of land and/or forest fires or haze pollution. “Transboundary haze pollution” means haze pollution whose physical origin is situated wholly or in part within the area under the national jurisdiction of one Member State and which is transported into the area under the jurisdiction of another Member State.
13. “Zero burning policy” means a policy that prohibits open burning but may allow some forms of controlled burning.

Article 2
Objective

The objective of this Agreement is to prevent and monitor transboundary haze pollution as a result of land and/or forest fires which should be mitigated, through concerted national efforts and intensified regional and international co-operation. This should be pursued in the overall context of sustainable development and in accordance with the provisions of this Agreement.

Article 3
Principles

The Parties shall be guided by the following principles in the implementation of this Agreement:

1. The Parties have, in accordance with the Charter of the United Nations and the principles of international law, the sovereign right to exploit their own resources pursuant to their own environmental and developmental policies, and the responsibility to ensure that activities within their jurisdiction or control do not cause damage to the environment and harm to human health of other States or of areas beyond the limits of national jurisdiction.
2. The Parties shall, in the spirit of solidarity and partnership and in accordance with their respective needs, capabilities and situations, strengthen co-operation and co-ordination to prevent and monitor transboundary haze pollution as a result of land and/or forest fires which should be mitigated.
3. The Parties should take precautionary measures to anticipate, prevent and monitor tranboundary haze pollution as a result of land and/or forest fires which should be mitigated, to minimize its adverse effects. Where there are threats of serious or irreversible damage from transboundary haze pollution, even without full scientific certainty, precautionary measures shall be taken by Parties concerned.

4. The Parties should manage and use their natural resources, including forest and land resources, in an ecologically sound and sustainable manner.
5. The Parties, in addressing transboundary haze pollution, should involve, as appropriate, all stakeholders, including local communities, non-governmental organizations, farmers and private enterprises.

Article 4
General Obligations

In pursuing the objective of this Agreement, the Parties shall:

1. Co-operate in developing and implementing measures to prevent and monitor transboundary haze pollution as a result of land and/or forest fires which should be mitigated, and to control sources of fires, including by the identification of fires, development of monitoring, assessment and early warning systems, exchange of information and technology, and the provision of mutual assistance.
2. When the transboundary haze pollution originates from within their territories, respond promptly to a request for relevant information or consultations sought by a State or States that are or may be affected by such transboundary haze pollution, with a view to minimizing the consequences of the transboundary haze pollution.
3. Take legislative, administrative and/or other measures to implement their obligations under this Agreement.

Part II. Monitoring, Assessment, Prevention and Response

Article 5
ASEAN Co-ordinating Centre for Transboundary Haze Pollution Control

1. The ASEAN Co-ordinating Centre for Transboundary Haze Pollution Control, hereinafter referred to as "the ASEAN Centre", is hereby established for the purposes of facilitating co-operation and co-ordination among the Parties in managing the impact of land and/or forest fires in particular haze pollution arising from such fires.
2. The ASEAN Centre shall work on the basis that the national authority will act first to put out the fires. When the national authority declares an emergency situation, it may make a request to the ASEAN Centre to provide assistance.
3. A Committee composed of representatives of the national authorities of the Parties shall oversee the operation of the ASEAN Centre.
4. The ASEAN Centre shall carry out the functions as set out in **Annex** and any other functions as directed by the Conference of the Parties.

Article 6
Competent Authorities and Focal Points

1. Each Party shall designate one or more Competent Authorities and a Focal Point that shall be authorized to act on its behalf in the performance of the administrative functions required by this Agreement.
2. Each Party shall inform other Parties and the ASEAN Centre, of its Competent Authorities and Focal Point, and of any subsequent changes in their designations.
3. The ASEAN Centre shall regularly and expeditiously provide to Parties and relevant international organizations the information referred to in paragraph 2 above.

Article 7
Monitoring

1. Each Party shall take appropriate measures to monitor:

   a. all fire prone areas,
   b. all land and/or forest fires,
   c. the environmental conditions conducive to such land and/or forest fires, and
   d. haze pollution arising from such land and/or forest fires.

2. Each Party shall designate one or more bodies to function as National Monitoring Centres, to undertake monitoring referred to in paragraph 1 above in accordance with their respective national procedures.
3. The Parties, in the event that there are fires, shall initiate immediate action to control or to put out the fires.

Article 8
Assessment

1. Each Party shall ensure that its National Monitoring Centre, at agreed regular intervals, communicates to the ASEAN Centre, directly or through its Focal Point, data obtained relating to fire prone areas, land and/or forest fires, the environmental conditions conducive to such land and/or forest fires, and haze pollution arising from such land and/or forest fires.
2. The ASEAN Centre shall receive, consolidate and analyze the data communicated by the respective National Monitoring Centres or Focal Points.
3. On the basis of analysis of the data received, the ASEAN Centre shall, where possible, provide to each Party, through its Focal Point, an assessment of risks to human health or the environment arising from land and/or forest fires and the resulting transboundary haze pollution.

Article 9
Prevention

Each Party shall undertake measures to prevent and control activities related to land and/or forest fires that may lead to transboundary haze pollution, which include:

1. Developing and implementing legislative and other regulatory measures, as well as programs and strategies to promote zero burning policy to deal with land and/or forest fires resulting in transboundary haze pollution;
2. Developing other appropriate policies to curb activities that may lead to land and/or forest fires;
3. Identifying and monitoring areas prone to occurrence of land and/or forest fires;
4. Strengthening local fire management and firefighting capability and co-ordination to prevent the occurrence of land and/or forest fires;
5. Promoting public education and awareness-building campaigns and strengthening community participation in fire management to prevent land and/or forest fires and haze pollution arising from such fires;
6. Promoting and utilizing indigenous knowledge and practices in fire prevention and management; and
7. Ensuring that legislative, administrative and/or other relevant measures are taken to control open burning and to prevent land clearing using fire.

Article 10
Preparedness

1. The Parties shall, jointly or individually, develop strategies and response plans to identify, manage and control risks to human health and the environment arising from land and/or forest fires and related haze pollution arising from such fires.
2. The Parties shall, as appropriate, prepare standard operating procedures for regional co-operation and national action required under this Agreement.

Article 11
National Emergency Response

1. Each Party shall ensure that appropriate legislative, administrative and financial measures are taken to mobilise equipment, materials, human and financial resources required to respond to and mitigate the impact of land and/or forest fires and haze pollution arising from such fires.
2. Each Party shall forthwith inform other Parties and the ASEAN Centre of such measures.

Article 12
Joint Emergency Response through the Provision of Assistance

1. If a Party needs assistance in the event of land and/or forest fires or haze pollution arising from such fires within its territory, it may request such assistance from any other Party, directly or through the ASEAN Centre, or, where appropriate, from other States or international organizations.
2. Assistance can only be employed at the request of and with the consent of the requesting Party, or, when offered by another Party or Parties, with the consent of the receiving Party.

3. Each Party to which a request for assistance is directed shall promptly decide and notify the requesting Party, directly or through the ASEAN Centre, whether it is in a position to render the assistance requested, and of the scope and terms of such assistance.
4. Each Party to which an offer of assistance is directed shall promptly decide and notify the assisting Party, directly or through the ASEAN Centre, whether it is in a position to accept the assistance offered, and of the scope and terms of such assistance.
5. The requesting Party shall specify the scope and type of assistance required and, where practicable, provide the assisting Party with such information as may be necessary for that Party to determine the extent to which it is able to meet the request. In the event that it is not practicable for the requesting Party to specify the scope and type of assistance required, the requesting Party and assisting Party shall, in consultation, jointly assess and decide upon the scope and type of assistance required.
6. The Parties shall, within the limits of their capabilities, identify and notify the ASEAN Centre of experts, equipment and materials which could be made available for the provision of assistance to other Parties in the event of land and/or forest fires or haze pollution resulting from such fires as well as the terms, especially financial, under which such assistance could be provided.

Article 13
Direction and Control of Assistance

Unless otherwise agreed:

1. The requesting or receiving Party shall exercise the overall direction, control, co-ordination and supervision of the assistance within its territory. The assisting Party should, where the assistance involves personnel, designate in consultation with the requesting or receiving Party, the person or entity who should be in charge of and retain immediate operational supervision over the personnel and the equipment provided by it. The designated person or entity should exercise such supervision in co-operation with the appropriate authorities of the requesting or receiving Party.
2. The requesting or receiving Party shall provide, to the extent possible, local facilities and services for the proper and effective administration of the assistance. It shall also ensure the protection of personnel, equipment and materials brought into its territory by or on behalf of the assisting Party for such purposes.
3. A Party providing or receiving assistance in response to a request referred to in paragraph (1) above shall co-ordinate that assistance within its territory.

Article 14
Exemptions and Facilities in Respect of the Provision of Assistance

1. The requesting or receiving Party shall accord to personnel of the assisting Party and personnel acting on its behalf, the necessary exemptions and facilities for the performance of their functions.

2. The requesting or receiving Party shall accord the assisting Party exemptions from taxation, duties or other charges on the equipment and materials brought into the territory of the requesting or receiving Party for the purpose of the assistance.
3. The requesting or receiving Party shall facilitate the entry into, stay in and departure from its territory of personnel and of equipment and materials involved or used in the assistance.

Article 15
Transit of Personnel, Equipment and Materials in Respect of the Provision of Assistance

Each Party shall, at the request of the Party concerned, seek to facilitate the transit through its territory of duly notified personnel, equipment and materials involved or used in the assistance to the requesting or receiving Party.

Part III. Technical Co-operation and Scientific Research

Article 16
Technical Co-operation

1. In order to increase the preparedness for and to mitigate the risks to human health and the environment arising from land and/or forest fires or haze pollution arising from such fires, the Parties shall undertake technical co-operation in this field, including the following:

   a. Facilitate mobilization of appropriate resources within and outside the Parties;
   b. Promote the standardization of the reporting format of data and information;
   c. Promote the exchange of relevant information, expertise, technology, techniques and know-how;
   d. Provide or make arrangements for relevant training, education and awareness-raising campaigns, in particular relating to the promotion of zero-burning practices and the impact of haze pollution on human health and the environment;
   e. Develop or establish techniques on controlled burning particularly for shifting cultivators and small farmers, and to exchange and share experiences on controlled-burning practices;
   f. Facilitate exchange of experience and relevant information among enforcement authorities of the Parties;
   g. Promote the development of markets for the utilization of biomass and appropriate methods for disposal of agricultural wastes;

h. Develop training programs for firefighters and trainers to be trained at local, national and regional levels; and
i. Strengthen and enhance the technical capacity of the Parties to implement this Agreement.

2. The ASEAN Centre shall facilitate activities for technical co-operation as identified in paragraph 1 above.

Article 17
Scientific Research

The Parties shall individually or jointly, including in co-operation with appropriate international organizations, promote and, whenever possible, support scientific and technical research programs related to the root causes and consequences of transboundary haze pollution and the means, methods, techniques and equipment for land and/or forest fire management, including fire fighting.

Part IV. Institutional Arrangements

Article 18
Conference of the Parties

1. A Conference of the Parties is hereby established. The first meeting of the Conference of the Parties shall be convened by the Secretariat not later than one year after the entry into force of this Agreement. Thereafter, ordinary meetings of the Conference of the Parties shall be held at least once every year, in as far as possible in conjunction with appropriate meetings of ASEAN.
2. Extraordinary meetings shall be held at any other time upon the request of one Party provided that such request is supported by at least one other Party.
3. The Conference of the Parties shall keep under continuous review and evaluation the implementation of this Agreement and to this end shall:

   a. Take such action as is necessary to ensure the effective implementation of this Agreement;
   b. Consider reports and other information which may be submitted by a Party directly or through the Secretariat;
   c. Consider and adopt protocols in accordance with the Article 21 of this Agreement;
   d. Consider and adopt any amendment to this Agreement;
   e. Adopt, review and amend as required any Annexes to this Agreement;
   f. Establish subsidiary bodies as may be required for the implementation of this Agreement; and
   g. Consider and undertake any additional action that may be required for the achievement of the objective of this Agreement.

Article 19
Secretariat

1. A Secretariat is hereby established.
2. The functions of the Secretariat shall include:
   a. Arrange for and service meetings of the Conference of the Parties and of other bodies established by this Agreement;
   b. Transmit to the Parties notifications, reports and other information received in accordance with this Agreement;
   c. Consider inquiries by, and information from, the Parties, and to consult with them on questions relating to this Agreement;
   d. Ensure the necessary co-ordination with other relevant international bodies and in particular to enter into administrative arrangements as may be required for the effective discharge of the Secretariat functions; and
   e. Perform such other functions as may be assigned to it by the Parties.
3. The ASEAN Secretariat shall serve as the Secretariat to this Agreement.

Article 20
Financial Arrangements

1. A Fund is hereby established for the implementation of this Agreement.
2. It shall be known as the ASEAN Transboundary Haze Pollution Control Fund.
3. The Fund shall be administered by the ASEAN Secretariat under the guidance of the Conference of the Parties.
4. The Parties shall, in accordance with the decisions of the Conference of the Parties, make voluntary contributions to the Fund.
5. The Fund shall be open to contributions from other sources subject to the agreement of or approval by the Parties.
6. The Parties may, where necessary, mobilize additional resources required for the implementation of this Agreement from relevant international organizations, in particular regional financial institutions and the international donor community.

Part V. Procedures

Article 21
Protocols

1. The Parties shall co-operate in the formulation and adoption of protocols to this Agreement, prescribing agreed measures, procedures and standards for the implementation of this Agreement.
2. The Conference of the Parties may, at ordinary meetings, adopt protocols to this Agreement by consensus of all Parties.

3. The text of any proposed protocol shall be communicated to the Parties by the Secretariat at least six months before such a session.
4. The requirements for the entry into force of any protocol shall be established by that instrument.

Article 22
Amendments to the Agreement

1. Any Party may propose amendments to the Agreement.
2. The text of any proposed amendment shall be communicated to the Parties by the Secretariat at least six months before the Conference of the Parties at which it is proposed for adoption. The Secretariat shall also communicate proposed amendments to the signatories to the Agreement.
3. Amendments shall be adopted by consensus at an ordinary meeting of the Conference of the Parties.
4. Amendments to this Agreement shall be subject to acceptance. The Depositary shall circulate the adopted amendment to all Parties for their acceptance. The amendment shall enter into force on the thirtieth day after the deposit with the Depositary of the instruments of acceptance of all Parties.
5. After the entry into force of an amendment to this Agreement any new Party to this Agreement shall become a Party to this Agreement as amended.

Article 23
Adoption and Amendment of Annexes

1. Annexes to this Agreement shall form an integral part of the Agreement and, unless otherwise expressly provided, a reference to the Agreement constitutes at the same time a reference to the annexes thereto.
2. Annexes shall be adopted by consensus at an ordinary meeting of the Conference of the Parties.
3. Any Party may propose amendments to an Annex.
4. Amendments to an Annex shall be adopted by consensus at an ordinary meeting of the Conference of the Parties.
5. Annexes to this Agreement and amendments to Annexes shall be subject to acceptance. The Depositary shall circulate the adopted Annex or the adopted amendment to an Annex to all Parties for their acceptance. The Annex or the amendment to an Annex shall enter into force on the thirtieth day after the deposit with the Depositary of the instruments of acceptance of all Parties.

Article 24
Rules of Procedure and Financial Rules

The first Conference of the Parties shall by consensus adopt rules of procedure for itself and financial rules for the ASEAN Transboundary Haze Pollution Control Fund to determine in particular the financial participation of the Parties to this Agreement.

Article 25
Reports

The Parties shall transmit to the Secretariat reports on the measures taken for the implementation of this Agreement in such form and at such intervals as determined by the Conference of the Parties.

Article 26
Relationship with Other Agreements

The provisions of this Agreement shall in no way affect the rights and obligations of any Party with regard to any existing treaty, convention or agreement to which they are Parties.

Article 27
Settlement of Disputes

Any dispute between Parties as to the interpretation or application of, or compliance with, this Agreement or any protocol thereto, shall be settled amicably by consultation or negotiation.

Part VI. Final Clauses

Article 28
Ratification, Acceptance, Approval and Accession

This Agreement shall be subject to ratification, acceptance, approval or accession by the Member States. It shall be opened for accession from the day after the date on which the Agreement is closed for signature. Instruments of ratification, acceptance, approval or accession shall be deposited with the Depositary.

Article 29
Entry into Force

1. This Agreement shall enter into force on the sixtieth day after the deposit of the sixth instrument of ratification, acceptance, approval or accession.
2. For each Member State ratifying, accepting, approving or acceding to the Agreement after the deposit of the sixth instrument of ratification, acceptance, approval or accession, the Agreement shall enter into force on the sixtieth day after the deposit by such Member State of its instrument of ratification, acceptance, approval or accession.

Article 30
Reservations

Unless otherwise expressly provided by this Agreement no reservations may be made to the Agreement.

Article 31
Depositary

This Agreement shall be deposited with the Secretary General of ASEAN, who shall promptly furnish each Member State a certified copy thereof.

Article 32
Authentic Text

This Agreement shall be drawn up in the English language, and shall be the authentic text.

In Witness Whereof the undersigned, being duly authorized by their respective Governments have signed this Agreement.

Done at **Kuala Lumpur, Malaysia** on the **tenth** day of **June** in the year **two thousand and two**.

For the Government of Brunei Darussalam: **H. E. Dr. Awang Haji Ahmad Bin Haji Juma**, Minister of Development
For the Government of the Kingdom of Cambodia: **H. E. Keo Puth Reamsey**, Ambassador
For the Republic of Indonesia: **MS. Liana Bratasida**, Deputy Minister for Environment Conservation
For the Government of Lao People's Democratic Republic: **H. E. Dr. Bountiem Phissamay**, Minister to the Prime Minister's Office
For the Government of Malaysia: **H. E. Dato Seri Law Hieng Ding**, Minister of Science, Technology and the Environment
For the Government of the Union of Myanmar: **U. Thane Myint**, Secretary of National Commission for Environmental Affairs
For the Government of the Republic of the Philippines: **H. E. Mr. Heherson T. Alvarez**, Secretary of Department of Environment and Natural Resources
For the Government of the Republic of Singapore: **H. E. Mr. Lim Swee Say**, Minister for the Environment
For the Government of the Kingdom of Thailand: **H. E. Mr. Chaisiri Anamarn**, Ambassador
For the Government of the Socialist Republic of Viet Nam: **H. E. Mr. Nguyen Van Dang**, Vice Minister of Agriculture and Rural Development.

Annex: Terms of Reference of the ASEAN Co-ordinating Centre for Transboundary Haze Pollution Control

The ASEAN Centre shall:

1. Establish and maintain regular contact with the respective National Monitoring Centers regarding the data, including those derived from satellite imagery and meteorological observation, relating to:

   a. Land and/or forest fire;
   b. Environmental conditions conducive to such fires; and
   c. Air quality and levels of pollution, in particular haze arising from such fires.

2. Receive from the respective National Monitoring Centers or Focal Points the data above, consolidate, analyze and process the data into.
3. Facilitate co-operation and co-ordination among the Parties to increase their preparedness for and to respond to land/or forest fires or haze pollution arising from such fires.
4. Facilitate co-ordination among the Parties, other States and relevant organizations in taking effective measures to mitigate the impact of land and/or forest fires or haze pollution arising from such fires.
5. Establish and maintain a list of experts from within and outside of the ASEAN region who may be utilized when taking measures to mitigate the impact of land and/or forest fires or haze pollution arising from such fires, and make the list available to the Parties.
6. Establish and maintain a list of equipment and technical facilities from within and outside of the ASEAN which may be made available when taking measures to mitigate the impact of land and/or forest fires or haze pollution arising from such fires, and make the list available to the Parties.
7. Establish and maintain a list of experts from within and outside of the ASEAN region for the purpose of relevant training, education and awareness-raising campaigns, and make the list available to the Parties.
8. Establish and maintain contact with prospective donor States and organizations for mobilizing financial and other resources required for the prevention and mitigation of land and/or forest fires or haze pollution arising from such fires and preparedness of the Parties, including fire-fighting capabilities.
9. Establish and maintain a list of such donors, and make the list available to the Parties.
10. Respond to a request for or offer of assistance in the event of land and/or forest fires or haze pollution resulting from such fires by:

    a. Transmitting promptly the request for assistance to other States and organizations; and
    b. Co-ordinating such assistance, if so requested by the requesting Party or offered by the assisting Party.

11. Establish and maintain an information referral system for the exchange of relevant information, expertise, technology, techniques and know-how, and make it available to the Parties in an easily accessible format.
12. Compile and disseminate to the Parties information concerning their experience and any other practical information related to the implementation of the Agreement.
13. Assist the Parties in the preparation of standard operating procedures (SOP).

Protocol Governing the Implementation of the ASEAN Harmonised Tariff Nomenclature

2003: Signed by Ministers of Finance in Makati, Philippines on 7 August 2003

The Governments of Brunei Darussalam, the Kingdom of Cambodia, the Republic of Indonesia, Lao People's Democratic Republic, Malaysia, Union of Myanmar, the Republic of Philippines, the Republic of Singapore, the Kingdom of Thailand and the Socialist Republic of Viet Nam of the Association of South East Asian Nations (hereinafter referred to as "ASEAN"):

Recalling the mandate of the Fifth ASEAN Summit to harmonize tariff nomenclature among all ASEAN Member States so as to enhance the flow of goods in the region;
Desiring to promote regional economic integration, and in particular, to support the establishment of the ASEAN Free Trade Area (AFTA) which envisages tariffs of 0–5% in the year 2002 for the original six ASEAN Member States, 2006 for Viet Nam, 2008 for Lao PDR and Myanmar, and 2010 for Cambodia, and further reduction to end tariffs of 0% by 2010/2015;
Recalling Article 4 of the ASEAN Agreement on Customs signed on 1 March 1997, which provides that Member States shall, for tariff purposes, use a common tariff nomenclature at the 8-digit level;
Recalling Further that Article 13(2) of the ASEAN Agreement on Customs provides that annexes may be introduced to the Agreement and shall form an integral part thereof;
Desiring to simplify intra-ASEAN trade transactions through a common tariff nomenclature, supported by clear and transparent implementation rules, explanatory notes and uniformity in its application;
Having Regard to the negotiations, which have been directed towards the formulation of an ASEAN Harmonized Tariff Nomenclature (hereinafter referred to as "AHTN"), its implementation rules and explanatory notes;
Desiring to establish a legal framework to govern the AHTN, its implementation rules and explanatory notes through this Protocol Governing the Implementation of the ASEAN Harmonized Tariff Nomenclature (hereinafter referred to as "the Protocol");

L. Riccardi and G. Riccardi, *Invest in ASEAN*,
https://doi.org/10.1007/978-981-15-5378-3_7

Have Agreed as follows:

Article 1
Objectives

The objectives of the Protocol are as follows:

1. to establish and implement the AHTN so as to facilitate trade in the region;
2. to establish clear rules which govern the implementation of the AHTN, its explanatory notes, and their amendments;
3. to establish uniformity of application in the classification of goods in ASEAN;
4. to enhance transparency in the classification process for goods in the region;
5. to simplify the AHTN; and
6. to create a nomenclature which conforms to international standards, which is a model of technical excellence and which reflects the changing patterns of international trade and technology.

Article 2
Principles

Member States will be guided by the following principles:

1. Transparency
2. Member States will publish all laws, regulations and administrative guidelines pertaining to the AHTN thus making them publicly available in a prompt, transparent and readily accessible manner;
3. Consistency
4. Member States will ensure the consistent application of the AHTN within each Member State;
5. Efficiency
6. Member States will ensure that the AHTN is used for the efficient administration and expeditious clearance of goods to facilitate trade;
7. Appeals;
8. Member States shall make available an appeal mechanism for importers and exporters on the classification decisions made on the AHTN.

Article 3
Structure of the ASEAN Harmonized Tariff Nomenclature

1. The AHTN shall be an 8-digit nomenclature, consisting of the latest version of the Harmonized Commodity Description and Coding System (hereinafter referred to as "HS Code") of the World Customs Organization and the amendments thereto, with the addition of the seventh and eighth digits and commodity descriptions for tariff purposes (the seventh and eighth digits and commodity descriptions hereinafter referred to as "ASEAN subheadings").
2. The AHTN and the Supplementary Explanatory Notes (SEN) relating to the ASEAN subheadings are annexed to the Protocol. The SEN shall form an integral part of the AHTN.

Article 4
Obligations of Member States

1. Member States shall abide by the HS Code, including its General Rules for the Interpretation of the Harmonized System, Section, Chapter and Subheading Notes, and its amendments thereto.
2. Member States shall apply the AHTN, up to the 8-digit level, for all trade transactions for tariff, the collection of statistical data and other purposes.
3. Member States may further sub-divide the AHTN, beyond the 8-digit level, for the collection of statistical data or other non-tariff purposes.
4. Amendments to the AHTN shall only be made in accordance with Articles 5 and 6 of the Protocol. Notwithstanding any provision to the contrary, no ASEAN subheading already incorporated in the AHTN can be removed without the consent of the affected Member State.

Article 5
Amendments to the ASEAN Harmonized Tariff Nomenclature

1. Procedures for amendments to the AHTN, as set out in Article 6 of the Protocol, may be effected if:

   a. amendments have been made to the HS Code and/or descriptions;
   b. amendments to the ASEAN subheadings in the AHTN for the purposes of simplification are being proposed;
   c. amendments are proposed which arise from the requirements of Member States, changes in technology or in patterns of international trade, or in other circumstances deemed desirable in accordance with the objectives of this Protocol as set out in Article 1.

2. The AHTN shall be continuously reviewed and amended with the view to simplifying the nomenclature, so as to facilitate trade. Member States shall regularly review their national tariff requirements and forward proposals for simplification of the AHTN.

Article 6
Amendment Procedures

1. Proposals for amendments shall be made by Member States to the ASEAN Directors-General of Customs, as referred to in Article 7 of the Protocol.
2. The ASEAN Directors-General of Customs shall study all proposals with the view to determining the acceptability of such amendments.
3. The ASEAN Directors-General of Customs shall be the body responsible for allowing amendments to the AHTN.

Article7
Institutional Arrangements

The ASEAN Directors-General of Customs, under the purview of the ASEAN Finance Ministers Meeting, shall be the body responsible for monitoring, reviewing and supervising all aspects relating to the implementation of the Protocol. The Experts Committee on Customs Matters (ECCM) shall assist the ASEAN Directors-General of Customs in all matters relating thereto.

Article 8
Responsibilities of the ASEAN Secretariat

1. The ASEAN Secretariat shall provide the necessary support for supervising, coordinating and reviewing the implementation of the Protocol, and shall assist the ASEAN Directors-General of Customs on matters relating thereto.
2. The ASEAN Secretariat shall have the responsibility of assisting the expert's panel, whenever it is convened, especially on procedural aspects of the matters dealt with, and of providing secretarial and technical support.
3. The ASEAN Secretariat shall have the responsibility of assisting Member States in monitoring and reviewing the AHTN with the view to simplification.

Article 9
Dispute Settlement

1. Member States shall, at the written request of a Member State, enter into consultations with a view to seeking a prompt, equitable and mutually satisfactory solution, if that Member State considers that:

   a. an obligation under the Protocol has not been fulfilled, is not being fulfilled or may not be fulfilled; or
   b. any objectives of the Protocol are not being achieved or may be frustrated.

2. Any differences between Member States concerning the interpretation or application of the Protocol shall, as far as possible, be settled amicably between the Member States. If a settlement cannot be reached, the dispute shall be submitted to the ASEAN Directors-General of Customs. If a settlement still cannot be reached by the ASEAN Directors-General of Customs, the dispute shall be referred to the ASEAN Finance Ministers Meeting.

Article 10
Final Provisions

1. The Protocol may be amended by mutual agreement of all Member States.
2. Annexes may be introduced to the Protocol and shall form an integral part thereof. Any reference to the Protocol is deemed to include also a reference to the Annexes.
3. Member States shall undertake appropriate measures to fulfill the obligations arising from the Protocol.
4. Member States shall make no reservations with respect to any of the provisions of the Protocol.
5. The Protocol shall enter into force on 7 August 2003. However, Member States may defer the obligation to apply the AHTN under paragraph 2 of Article 4 of the Protocol, to a date no later than 1 January 2004.

6. The Protocol shall be deposited with the Secretary-General of ASEAN, who shall promptly furnish a certified copy thereof to each Member State.

In Witness Whereof the undersigned, being duly authorized to sign the Protocol, have signed this Protocol Governing the Implementation of the ASEAN Harmonized Tariff Nomenclature.

Done at Makati, Philippines on the 7th day of August 2003, in a single copy in the English Language.

For the Government of Brunei Darussalam, **Pehin Dato Haji Abdul Aziz Umar**, Minister Representing the Ministry of Finance
For the Government of the Kingdom of Cambodia, **Keat Chhon**, Senior Minister, Minister of Economy and Finance
For the Government of the Republic of Indonesia, **Boediono**, Minister of Finance
For the Government of the Lao People's Democratic Republic, **Phouphet Khamphounyong**, Deputy Governor, Bank of Lao PDR
For the Government of Malaysia, **Dato Dr. Jamaludin Bin Mohd jarjis**, Finance Minister
For the Government of the Union of Myanmar, **Major General Hla Tun**, Minister of Finance and Revenue
For the Government of the Republic of the Philippines, **Jose Isidro Camacho**, Secretary of Finance
For the Government of the Republic of Singapore, **Lim Hng Kiang**, Second Minister for Finance
For the Government of the Kingdom of Thailand, **Suchart Jaovisidha**, Minister of Finance
For the Government of the Socialist Republic of Viet Nam, **Nguyen Sinh Hung**, Minister of Finance.

Interpretative Notes of the Protocol Governing the Implementation of the ASEAN Harmonised Tariff Nomenclature

Article 2

Importers and exporters shall not have recourse to the Dispute Settlement Mechanism as set out in Article 9 of the Protocol. Their recourse lies with their respective customs administrations.

Article 3 (1)

1. Within the AHTN, the HS Code must be adhered to. Where no further subdivisions of an HS 6-digit Code are made, the digits "00" shall appear in the seventh and eighth positions of the AHTN codes.

2. Where an HS Code and commodity description is sub-divided in the AHTN, the 6-digit HS Code shall be shown against the line which is sub-divided, and the text of the HS commodity description shall terminate with a colon. In the codes of the subdivisions, the seventh and eighth positions shall be filled with digits appropriate to the context.
3. The AHTN shall conform to the following dash system of integrated hierarchy:
   I. ASEAN subheadings, where the HS headings have no subheadings, will start at a one-dash level;
   II. ASEAN subheadings of a one-dash HS subheading will start at a two-dash level; and
   III. ASEAN subheadings of a two-dash HS subheading will start at a three-dash level.

Article 4 (3)

1. Additional subdivisions must adhere to the structure of the AHTN, as set out in Article 3 of the Protocol.
2. Member States must notify their national nomenclatures to the ASEAN Directors-General of Customs, through the ASEAN Secretariat, whenever amendments for the purposes of Article 4 (3) have been effected nationally.

Article 5 (1)

1. All amendments to the ASEAN subheadings must abide by the "Understanding on the Criteria for Classification in the ASEAN Harmonized Tariff Nomenclature", (hereinafter referred to as the "the Understanding"), signed by the ASEAN Directors-General of Customs. Additional ASEAN subheadings should be created only in exceptional circumstances.
2. Member States wishing to have additional subheadings shall forward details and reasons of the proposal to the ASEAN Directors-General of Customs, through the ASEAN Secretariat, wherein procedures for amendments under Article 6 of the Protocol shall be invoked.

Article 5 (2)

1. The process of review will be conducted in accordance with review guidelines to be formulated by the ASEAN Directors-General of Customs. A cycle of one-year duration will be established to institutionalize the review process.
2. Member States proposing simplification should also advise how the structure of a subheading could be simplified while meeting their respective national requirements.

Article 6 (1)

Proposals to the ASEAN Directors-General of Customs will be made through the ASEAN Secretariat, and shall include justifications.

Article 6 (2)

1. Assessment of the proposed amendments to the AHTN must take into account the Objectives of the Protocol as set out in Article 1, and the Understanding.
2. Where necessary, the ASEAN Directors-General of Customs shall convene an experts panel (as referred to in Article 7) to make an objective assessment of the acceptability of the proposal, including an examination of the facts of the proposal and the applicability of and conformity with the rules as referred to in 2 (a), and make such other findings as will assist the ASEAN Directors-General of Customs in making a decision. The meeting of the expert's panel must be unanimously agreed to by the ASEAN Directors-General of Customs. The expert's panel shall promptly submit their report to the ASEAN Directors-General of Customs to facilitate their decision making.
3. The expert's panel shall consist of representatives from all the Member States.
4. The expert's panel shall regulate its own procedures to perform its functions.
5. Measures should be undertaken to ensure that amendment procedures are efficient and effected expeditiously.
6. The ASEAN Secretariat shall provide the necessary secretariat support in the amendment procedures.

Article 6 (3)

1. Decisions by the ASEAN Directors-General of Customs shall be made by consensus.
2. Appropriate measures will be undertaken to bring any approved amendments to the AHTN into effect.

Article 9 (1)

1. Member States are encouraged to settle their differences through consultations. If a solution cannot be reached, Member States can submit the dispute to the ASEAN Directors-General of Customs for a decision without necessarily involving the dispute settlement procedures in Article 9.
2. In the interest of uniformity, settlements at the consultation level must be notified to the ASEAN Directors-General of Customs. Where applicable, such settlements shall be subject to agreement by the ASEAN Directors-General of Customs.

Article 9 (2)

1. Recourse can be made to the World Customs Organization for expert opinion on differences in the interpretation or application of the AHTN.
2. The ASEAN Finance Ministers Meeting shall be the final arbiter in any dispute relating to the implementation of the Protocol.

Agreement on the Establishment of the ASEAN Development Fund

2005: Signed by Foreign Ministers at the 38th ASEAN Ministerial Meeting in Vientiane, Lao PDR on 26 July 2005

The Governments of Brunei Darussalam, the Kingdom of Cambodia, the Republic of Indonesia, the Lao People's Democratic Republic, Malaysia, the Union of Myanmar, the Republic of the Philippines, the Republic of Singapore, the Kingdom of Thailand, and the Socialist Republic of Viet Nam:
Committing to realize the ASEAN Vision 2020 and build an ASEAN Community as articulated in the Declaration of ASEAN Concord II;
Desiring to implement expeditiously the Vientiane Action Program (VAP) and related ASEAN action plans towards the realization of an ASEAN Community that is open, dynamic and resilient;
Recognising the necessity of providing financial resources to support the implementation of the VAP and its successor Plans;
Do Hereby Agree as follows.

Article 1
Establishment of the ASEAN Development Fund

1. The ASEAN Development Fund (ADF) shall be established and implemented in accordance with the annexed Terms of Reference, which forms an integral part of this Agreement.
2. The initial contribution of each ASEAN Member Country to the ADF shall be one million US dollars (US$1,000,000). This initial contribution shall comprise the existing contributions of each ASEAN Member Country to the ASEAN Fund. These existing contributions of each ASEAN Member Country to the ASEAN Fund shall be transferred to the ADF upon the entry into force of this Agreement.
3. All other monies of the ASEAN Fund representing its accumulated unprogrammed earnings and its records shall also be transferred to the ADF.

L. Riccardi and G. Riccardi, *Invest in ASEAN*,
https://doi.org/10.1007/978-981-15-5378-3_8

Article 2
Entry into Force and Termination

1. This Agreement shall enter into force on the date of signature of all the ASEAN Member Countries and shall remain in force until it is terminated by the decision of the ASEAN Foreign Ministers.
2. The entry into force of this Agreement shall automatically constitute the termination of the Agreement for the Establishment of a Fund for ASEAN, signed by the ASEAN Foreign Ministers on 23 July 1994 in Bangkok, and the transfer of all monies and records of the ASEAN Fund to the ASEAN Development Fund.

Article 3
Final Provision

This Agreement shall be deposited with the Secretary-General of ASEAN who shall promptly furnish a certified copy thereof to each ASEAN Member Country.

In Witness Whereof, the undersigned, being duly authorized by their respective Governments, have signed this Agreement.

Done at **Vientiane, Lao PDR**, this Twenty-Sixth Day of July in the Year Two Thousand and Five, in a single original copy in the English language.

For Brunei Darussalam: **Mohamed Bolkiah**, Minister of Foreign Affairs
For the Kingdom of Cambodia: **Hor Namhong**, Deputy Prime Minister and Minister of Foreign Affairs and International Cooperation
For the Republic of Indonesia: **Dr. N. Hassan Wirajuda**, Minister for Foreign Affairs
For the Lao People's Democratic Republic: **Somsavat Lengsavad**, Deputy Prime Minister and Minister of Foreign Affairs
For Malaysia: **Dato' Seri Syed Hamid Albar**, Minister of Foreign Affairs
For the Union of Myanmar: **Nyan Win**, Minister for Foreign Affairs
For the Republic of the Philippines: **Alberto G. Romulo**, Secretary of Foreign Affairs
For the Republic of Singapore: **George Yong-Boon Yeo**, Minister for Foreign Affairs
For the Kingdom of Thailand: **Dr. Kantathi Suphamongkhon**, Minister of Foreign Affairs
For the Socialist Republic of Viet Nam: **Nguyen Dy Nien**, Minister for Foreign Affairs.

Terms of reference of the ASEAN Development Fund (ADF)

Objectives

1. The ASEAN Development Fund shall serve as ASEAN's common pool of financial resources to support the implementation of the Vientiane Action Programme (VAP) and its successor documents. In particular, the ADF shall be used for the following purposes:

i. To leverage funding of regional cooperation programmes and projects from Dialogue Partners and other external donors. When used for counterpart funding, the amount shall not exceed 20% of the total funding raised regardless of whether the co-funding source is an ASEAN Member Country or an external donor;
ii. To provide seed funding for initial activities of large-scale projects, requiring major financial support from a Dialogue Partner or donor institution; and
iii. To provide full funding support to small and short-term projects of a confidential or strategic nature.

Guiding Principles

2. The ADF shall be established and managed according to the following guiding principles:

   i. The basic element of the ADF shall be equal contributions by ASEAN Member Countries. The initial contribution of each ASEAN Member Country to the ADF shall be one million US dollars (US$1,000,000). This initial contribution shall comprise the existing contributions of each ASEAN Member Country to the ASEAN Fund. These existing contributions of each ASEAN Member Country to the ASEAN Fund shall be transferred to the ADF upon the Agreement's entry into force;
   ii. ASEAN Member Countries, at any time, are encouraged to make additional voluntary contribution(s) in any amount in addition to their initial contributions;
   iii. The ADF shall be open to contributions from other public and private sources. No restrictions or conditions shall be imposed by other public and private sources with regard to the use of their contributions; and
   iv. Contributions by the ASEAN Member Countries to the ADF shall be distinct and separate from their contributions to the operating budget of the ASEAN Secretariat, and to other ASEAN funds of a sectoral nature.

Arrangements for Managing and Utilizing the ADF

Custody and Management of the Fund

3. The ADF shall be held in trust at the ASEAN Secretariat, subject to the same rules and conditions that are applied to other existing trust funds in regard to investment, disbursement, accounting and auditing procedures.
4. The ADF will be increased by equal contributions of the ASEAN Member Countries in the amount US$100,000 by the end of the year 2007.

Programming and Appraisal of Proposed Projects

5. Use of the ADF shall be programmed on a regular basis every two years to realize each of the three pillars of the ASEAN Community and to narrow the development gap among ASEAN Member Countries. Selection of regional cooperation measures to be included in the ADF program shall take explicit

account of the need for: (a) priority measures in realizing each of the three pillars of the Community; (b) striking a parallel and balanced development and implementation of the three pillars of the Community; and (c) narrowing the development gap among ASEAN Member Countries so that they could move forward in a unified manner.

6. The two-yearly ADF program shall be approved by the ASEAN Standing Committee (ASC) as basis for preparation of specific project proposals for ADF funding support.
7. Projects seeking ADF support shall be appraised based on criteria including regionality, appropriateness and relevance in the context of the VAP and its successor documents, quality of design, cost effectiveness, and sustainability. Appraisal of projects shall be made by the ASEAN Secretariat Project Appraisal Committee (PAC) based on those criteria. The standard format for ASEAN project proposals shall be used.

Eligible Expenditures

8. Utilization of the fund is mainly for implementation of programs, projects and activities identified in the VAP and its successor Plans.
9. The ADF shall support projects and activities with clearly defined set of objectives and targets within a set timeframe for implementation.
10. The items of expenditure in a project budget shall be classified into three (3) general categories as follows:

    i. Administrative costs: rent, utilities, office space, salaries of locally engaged personnel, insurance and taxes;
    ii. Operational costs: project overhead costs, recruitment costs, compensation of professional staff engaged in the project, its related expenditure (e.g. travel, accommodation, per diem) equipment and supplies; and
    iii. Capital costs: land and building, and equipment costing more than US $10,000.

11. Only the operational costs of the project shall be eligible for support under the ADF.
12. The capital and administrative costs shall be borne by the Host Government of the project.
13. Travelling, accommodation and other expenses of delegations attending regular meetings of duly established ASEAN bodies are not eligible expenditures under the ADF.

Funding Approval

14. Approval authority for use of the fund by a project shall be obtained from the ASC taking into account the recommendations of the PAC of the ASEAN Secretariat submitted through the Secretary General of ASEAN, in consideration of the nature of activities eligible for support under the ADF.

Ownership of Property

15. The ownership of property acquired as a result of expenditures for financing capital costs as provided for in Paragraphs 10.iii and 12 shall be vested in the Host Government or the ASEAN Secretariat for projects which are hosted by the ASEAN Secretariat.
16. The ownership of office equipment such as computers, audio-video appliances; laboratory instruments; and the like, acquired as a result of expenditures for financing operational costs of projects shall be vested in the Host Government, or the ASEAN Secretariat for projects which are hosted by the ASEAN Secretariat to help ensure the sustainability of benefits after project completion. The Host Government or the ASEAN Secretariat, as applicable may redeploy property acquired under a project to other projects supported by the ADF under cost- effective arrangements, or it may sell such property when circumstances warrant. Any such redeployment or sale shall be reported by the Host Government or the ASEAN Secretariat, as applicable to the ASC. Any proceeds from the sale of property shall accrue to the ADF.
17. The Host Government or the ASEAN Secretariat, as applicable may not exercise their right to dispose of any property, the ownership of which has been vested to it under Paragraphs 15 and 16, until after the completion of the project.
18. The ownership of intellectual property acquired as a result of the project shall be vested in the ASEAN Member Countries. The disposition and use of intellectual property rights shall be governed by guidelines to be determined by the ASC

Reporting

19. All project implementing agencies receiving ADF support for projects of duration longer than six months are required to submit six-monthly financial reports to the ASEAN Secretariat, for consolidation into a regular six-monthly financial statement for review by the ASC.
20. At the end of a project, a project completion report including a full accounting of all funds received from the ADF shall be submitted by the project implementing agency within 60 days of project completion. Any excess funds unutilized by the project shall be returned by the project implementing agency to the ASEAN Secretariat within 90 days of project completion.
21. The ASEAN Secretariat shall provide a six-monthly financial statement to the ASC to update ASEAN Member Countries on the status of the ADF.

Amendments

22. ASEAN Member Countries or the ASEAN Secretariat may propose amendments at any time to these Guidelines and submit them for consideration by the ASC.

Utilization of Remaining Funds

23. At the end of the period of the implementation of the VAP, any funds remaining in the ADF shall be carried over for the implementation of the successor ASEAN action programs or for any other related purposes approved by the ASC.

Entry into Effect

24.

i. This TOR shall enter into effect upon the entry into force of the Agreement for the Establishment of an ASEAN Development Fund and shall remain in force until the Agreement is terminated.
ii. Upon the entry into effect of this TOR, the Agreement for the Establishment of a Fund for ASEAN signed in Bangkok on 23 July 1994 and the ASEAN Fund established by the said Agreement shall be terminated and all remaining monies and records of the ASEAN Fund shall form part of the ADF.

ASEAN Trade in Goods Agreement

2009: Adopted by the Economic Ministers at the 14th ASEAN Summit in Cha-am Thailand on 26th February 2009

The Governments of Brunei Darussalam, the Kingdom of Cambodia, the Republic of Indonesia, the Lao People's Democratic Republic (Lao PDR), Malaysia, the Union of Myanmar, the Republic of the Philippines, the Republic of Singapore, the Kingdom of Thailand and the Socialist Republic of Viet Nam, Member States of the Association of Southeast Asian Nations (hereinafter collectively referred to as "Member States" or singularly as "Member State"):

Recalling the Leaders' decision to establish the ASEAN Community, comprising three pillars, namely the ASEAN Political-Security Community (APSC), the ASEAN Economic Community (AEC) and the ASEAN Socio-Cultural Community (ASCC), made in the Declaration of ASEAN Concord II signed on 7 October 2003 in Bali, Indonesia, and in the ASEAN Charter signed on 20 November 2007 in Singapore;

Determined to realize the goals of establishing ASEAN as a single market and production base characterized by free flow of goods, services, investment, skilled labor and freer flow of capital envisaged in the ASEAN Charter and the Declaration on the ASEAN Economic Community Blueprint signed by the Leaders on 20 November 2007 in Singapore;

Recognising the significant achievements and contribution of the existing ASEAN economic agreements and instruments in various areas in facilitating free flow of goods in the region, including the Agreement on ASEAN Preferential Trading Arrangements (1977), the Agreement on the Common Effective Preferential Tariff Scheme for the ASEAN Free Trade Area (1992), the ASEAN Agreement on Customs (1997), the ASEAN Framework Agreement on Mutual Recognition Arrangements (1998), the e-ASEAN Framework Agreement (2000), the Protocol Governing the Implementation of the ASEAN Harmonized Tariff Nomenclature (2003), the ASEAN Framework Agreement for the Integration of Priority Sectors (2004), the Agreement to Establish and Implement the ASEAN Single Window (2005);

L. Riccardi and G. Riccardi, *Invest in ASEAN*,
https://doi.org/10.1007/978-981-15-5378-3_9

Desiring to move forward by developing a comprehensive ASEAN Trade in Goods Agreement which is built upon the commitments under the existing ASEAN economic agreements to provide a legal framework to realize free flow of goods in the region;
Confident that a comprehensive ASEAN Trade in Goods Agreement would minimize barriers and deepen economic linkages among Member States, lower business costs, increase trade, investment and economic efficiency, create a larger market with greater opportunities and larger economies of scale for the businesses of Member States and create and maintain a competitive investment area;
Recognising the different stages of economic development between and among Member States and the need to address the development gaps and facilitate increasing participation of the Member States, especially Cambodia, Lao PDR, Myanmar and Viet Nam, in the AEC through the provision of flexibility and technical and development co-operation;
Recognising Further the provisions of the ministerial declarations of the World Trade Organization on measures in favor of least-developed countries;
Acknowledging the important role and contribution of the business sector in enhancing trade and investment among Member States and the need to further promote and facilitate their participation through the various ASEAN business associations in the realization of the ASEAN Economic Community; and
Recognising the role of regional trade arrangements as a catalyst in accelerating regional and global trade liberalization and trade facilitation and as building blocks in the framework of the multilateral trading system;
Have Agreed as follows.

Chapter 1. General Provisions

Article 1
Objective

The objective of this Agreement is to achieve free flow of goods in ASEAN as one of the principal means to establish a single market and production base for the deeper economic integration of the region towards the realization of the AEC by 2015.

Article 2
General Definitions

1. For the purposes of this Agreement, unless the context otherwise requires:

    a. **ASEAN** means the Association of Southeast Asian Nations, which comprises Brunei Darussalam, the Kingdom of Cambodia, the Republic of Indonesia, Lao PDR, Malaysia, the Union of Myanmar, the Republic of the Philippines, the Republic of Singapore, the Kingdom of Thailand and the Socialist Republic of Viet Nam;

b. **customs authorities** mean the competent authorities that are responsible under the law of a Member State for the administration of customs laws;
c. **customs duties** mean any customs or import duty and a charge of any kind imposed in connection with the importation of a good, but does not include any:

    i. charge equivalent to an internal tax imposed consistently with the provisions of paragraph 2 of Article III of GATT 1994, in respect of the like domestic goods or in respect of goods from which the imported goods have been manufactured or produced in whole or in part;
    ii. anti-dumping or countervailing duty applied consistent with the provisions of Article VI of GATT 1994, the Agreement on Implementation of Article VI of GATT 1994, and the Agreement on Subsidies and Countervailing Measures in Annex 1A to the WTO Agreement; or
    iii. fee or any charge commensurate with the cost of services rendered.

d. **customs laws** means such laws and regulations administered and enforced by the customs authorities of each Member State concerning the importation, exportation, transit, transshipment, and storage of goods as they relate to customs duties, charges, and other taxes, or to prohibitions, restrictions, and other similar controls with respect to the movement of controlled items across the boundary of the customs territory of each Member State;
e. **customs value of goods** means the value of goods for the purposes of levying ad valorem customs duties on imported goods;
f. **days** means calendar days, including weekends and holidays;
g. **foreign exchange restrictions** mean measures taken by Member States in the form of restrictions and other administrative procedures in foreign exchange which have the effect of restricting trade;
h. **GATT 1994** means the General Agreement on Tariffs and Trade 1994, including its Notes and Supplementary Provisions, contained in Annex 1A to the WTO Agreement;
i. **Harmonized System or HS** means the Harmonized Commodity Description and Coding System set out in the Annex to the International Convention on the Harmonized Commodity Description and Coding System, including any amendments adopted and implemented by the Member States in their respective laws;
j. **MFN** means Most-Favored-Nation treatment in the WTO;
k. **non-tariff barriers** mean measures other than tariffs which effectively prohibit or restrict imports or exports of goods within Member States;
l. **originating goods** means goods that qualify as originating in a Member State in accordance with the provisions of chapter "Treaty of Amity and Cooperation in Southeast Asia";
m. **preferential tariff treatment** means tariff concessions granted to originating goods as reflected by the tariff rates applicable under this Agreement;

n. **quantitative restrictions** mean measures intended to prohibit or restrict quantity of trade with other Member States, whether made effective through quotas, licenses or other measures with equivalent effect, including administrative measures and requirements which restrict trade;
o. **this Agreement** or **ATIGA** means the ASEAN Trade in Goods Agreement;
p. **WTO** means the World Trade Organization; and
q. **WTO Agreement** means the Marrakesh Agreement Establishing the World Trade Organization, done on 15 April 1994 and the other agreements negotiated thereunder.

2. In this Agreement, all words in the singular shall include the plural and all words in the plural shall include the singular, unless otherwise indicated in the context.

Article 3
Classification of Goods

For the purposes of this Agreement, the classification of goods in trade between and among Member States shall be in accordance with the ASEAN Harmonized Tariff Nomenclature (AHTN) as set out in the Protocol Governing the Implementation of the ASEAN Harmonized Tariff Nomenclature signed on 7 August 2003 and any amendments thereto.

Article 4
Product Coverage

This Agreement shall apply to all products under the ASEAN Harmonized Tariff Nomenclature (AHTN).

Article 5
Most Favored Nation Treatment

With respect to import duties, after this Agreement enters into force, if a Member State enters into any agreement with a non-Member State where commitments are more favorable than that accorded under this Agreement, the other Member States have the right to request for negotiations with that Member State to request for the incorporation herein of treatment no less favorable than that provided under the aforesaid agreement. The decision to extend such tariff preference will be on a unilateral basis. The extension of such tariff preference shall be accorded to all Member States.

Article 6
National Treatment on Internal Taxation and Regulation

Each Member State shall accord national treatment to the goods of the other Member States in accordance with Article III of GATT 1994. To this end, Article III of GATT 1994 is incorporated into and shall form part of this Agreement, mutatis mutandis.

Article 7
Fees and Charges Connected with Importation and Exportation

1. Each Member State shall ensure, in accordance with Article VIII.1 of GATT 1994, that all fees and charges of whatever character (other than import or export duties, charges equivalent to an internal tax or other internal charge applied consistently with Article III.2 of GATT 1994, and anti-dumping and countervailing duties) imposed on or in connection with import or export are limited in amount to the approximate cost of services rendered and do not represent an indirect protection to domestic goods or a taxation on imports or exports for fiscal purposes.
2. Each Member State shall promptly publish details of the fees and charges that it imposes in connection with importation or exportation, and shall make such information available on the internet.

Article 8
General Exceptions

Subject to the requirement that such measures are not applied in a manner which would constitute a means of arbitrary or unjustifiable discrimination among Member States where the same conditions prevail, or a disguised restriction on international trade, nothing in this Agreement shall be construed to prevent the adoption or enforcement by a Member State of measures:

a. necessary to protect public morals;
b. necessary to protect human, animal or plant life or health;
c. relating to the importations or exportations of gold or silver;
d. necessary to secure compliance with laws or regulations which are not inconsistent with the provisions of this Agreement, including those relating to customs enforcement, the enforcement of monopolies operated under paragraph 4 of Article II and Article XVII of GATT 1994, the protection of patents, trademarks and copyrights, and the prevention of deceptive practices;
e. relating to the products of prison labor;
f. imposed for the protection of national treasures of artistic, historic or archaeological value;
g. relating to the conservation of exhaustible natural resources if such measures are made effective in conjunction with restrictions on domestic production or consumption;
h. undertaken in pursuance of the obligations under any intergovernmental commodity agreement which conforms to criteria submitted to the WTO and not disapproved by it or which is itself so submitted and not so disapproved;
i. involving restrictions on exports of domestic materials necessary to ensure essential quantities of such materials to a domestic processing industry during periods when the domestic price of such materials is held below the world price as part of a governmental stabilization plan, provided that such restrictions shall not operate to increase the exports of or the protection afforded to such domestic

industry, and shall not depart from the provisions of this Agreement relating to nondiscrimination; and

j. essential to the acquisition or distribution of products in general or local short supply, provided that any such measures shall be consistent with the principle that all Member States are entitled to an equitable share of the international supply of such products, and that any such measures, which are inconsistent with the other provisions of this Agreement shall be discontinued as soon as the conditions giving rise to them have ceased to exist.

Article 9
Security Exceptions

Nothing in this Agreement shall be construed:

1. to require any Member State to furnish any information, the disclosure of which it considers contrary to its essential security interests; or
2. to prevent any Member State from taking any action which it considers necessary for the protection of its essential security interests:

   a. relating to fissionable materials or the materials from which they are derived;
   b. relating to the traffic in arms, ammunition and implements of war and to such traffic in other goods and materials as is carried on directly or indirectly for the purpose of supplying a military establishment;
   c. taken so as to protect critical public infrastructure, including communications, power and water infrastructures, from deliberate attempts intended to disable or degrade such infrastructure;
   d. taken in time of domestic emergency, or war or other emergency in international relations; or to prevent any Member State from taking any action in pursuance of its obligations under the United Nations Charter for the maintenance of international peace and security.

Article 10
Measures to Safeguard the Balance-of-Payments

Nothing in this Agreement shall be construed to prevent a Member State from taking any measure for balance-of-payments purposes. A Member State taking such measure shall do so in accordance with the conditions established under Article XII of GATT 1994 and the Understanding on Balance-of-Payments Provisions of the General Agreement on Tariffs and Trade 1994 in Annex 1A to the WTO Agreement.

Article 11
Notification Procedures

1. Unless otherwise provided in this Agreement, Member States shall notify any action or measure that they intend to take:

   a. which may nullify or impair any benefit to other Member States, directly or indirectly under this Agreement; or

b. when the action or measure may impede the attainment of any objective of this Agreement.

2. Without affecting the generality of the obligations of Member States under paragraph 1 of this Article, the notification procedures shall apply, but need not be limited, to changes in the measures as listed in Annex 1 and amendments thereto.
3. A Member State shall make a notification to Senior Economic Officials Meeting (SEOM) and the ASEAN Secretariat before effecting such action or measure referred to in paragraph 1 of this Article. Unless otherwise provided in this Agreement, notification shall be made at least sixty (60) days before such an action or measure is to take effect. A Member State proposing to apply an action or measure shall provide adequate opportunity for prior discussion with those Member States having an interest in the action or measure concerned.
4. The notification of the intended action or measure submitted by a Member State shall include:

   a. a description of the action or measure to be taken;
   b. the reasons for undertaking the action or measure; and
   c. the intended date of implementation and the duration of the action or measure.

5. The contents of the notification and all information relating to it shall be treated with confidentiality.
6. The ASEAN Secretariat shall act as the central registry of notifications, including written comments and results of discussions. The Member State concerned shall furnish the ASEAN Secretariat with a copy of the comments received. The ASEAN Secretariat shall draw the attention of individual Member States to notification requirements, such as those stipulated in paragraph 4 of this Article, which remain incomplete. The ASEAN Secretariat shall make available information regarding individual notifications on request to any Member State.
7. The Member State concerned shall, without discrimination, allow adequate opportunities for other Member States to present their comments in writing and discuss these comments upon request. Discussions entered into by the Member State concerned with other Member States shall be for the purpose of seeking further clarification about the action or measure. The Member State may give due consideration to these written comments and the discussion in the implementation of the action or measure.
8. Other Member States shall present their comments within fifteen (15) days of the notification. Failure of a Member State to provide comments within the stipulated time shall not affect its right to seek recourse under Article 88.

Article 12
Publication and Administration of Trade Regulations

1. Article X of GATT 1994 shall be incorporated into and form an integral part of this Agreement, mutatis mutandis.

2. To the extent possible, each Member State shall make laws, regulations, decisions and rulings of the kind referred to in Article X of GATT 1994 available on the internet.

Article 13
ASEAN Trade Repository

1. An ASEAN Trade Repository containing trade and customs laws and procedures of all Member States shall be established and made accessible to the public through the internet.
2. The ASEAN Trade Repository shall contain trade related information such as (i) tariff nomenclature; (ii) MFN tariffs, preferential tariffs offered under this Agreement and other Agreements of ASEAN with its Dialogue Partners; (iii) Rules of Origin; (iv) non-tariff measures; (v) national trade and customs laws and rules; (vi) procedures and documentary requirements; (vii) administrative rulings; (viii) best practices in trade facilitation applied by each Member State; and (ix) list of authorized traders of Member States.
3. The ASEAN Secretariat shall maintain and update the ASEAN Trade Repository based on the notifications submitted by Member States as set out in Article 11.

Article 14
Confidentiality

1. Nothing in this Agreement shall require a Member State to provide confidential information, the disclosure of which would impede law enforcement of the Member State, or otherwise be contrary to the public interest, or which would prejudice legitimate commercial interests of any particular enterprise, public or private.
2. Nothing in this Agreement shall be construed to require a Member State to provide information relating to the affairs and accounts of customers of financial institutions.
3. Each Member State shall, in accordance with its laws and regulations, maintain the confidentiality of information provided as confidential by another Member State pursuant to this Agreement.
4. Notwithstanding the above, paragraphs 1, 2 and 3 of this Article shall not apply to chapter "ASEAN Agreement on Transboundary Haze Pollution".

Article 15
Communications

All official communications and documentation exchanged among the Member States relating to the implementation of this Agreement shall be in writing and in the English language.

Article 16
Participation Enhancement of Member States

Enhancing participation of Member States shall be facilitated through a negotiated pre-agreed flexibility on provisions under this Agreement. Such pre-agreed flexibility shall be captured in the respective provisions hereunder.

Article 17
Capacity Building

Capacity building shall be provided through effective implementation of programs to strengthen individual Member States' domestic capacity, efficiency and competitiveness, such as the Work Program under the Initiative for ASEAN Integration (IAI) and other capacity building initiatives.

Article 18
Regional and Local Government and Non-Governmental Bodies

1. Each Member State shall take such reasonable measures as may be available to it to ensure observance of provisions of this Agreement by the regional and local government and authorities within its territories.
2. In fulfilling its obligations and commitments under this Agreement, each Member State shall endeavor to ensure their observance by non-governmental bodies in the exercise of powers delegated by central, regional or local governments or authorities within its territory.

Chapter 2. Tariff Liberalisation

Article 19
Reduction or Elimination of Import Duties

1. Except as otherwise provided in this Agreement, Member States shall eliminate import duties on all products traded between the Member States by 2010 for ASEAN-6[1] and by 2015, with flexibility to 2018, for CLMV.[2]
2. Each Member State shall reduce and/or eliminate import duties on originating goods of the other Member States in accordance with the following modalities:
   a. Import duties on the products listed in Schedule A of each Member State's tariff liberalization schedule shall be eliminated by 2010 for ASEAN-6 and 2015 for CLMV, in accordance with the schedule set out therein. Schedule A of each Member State shall ensure the following conditions are met:

[1]"ASEAN-6" refers to Brunei Darussalam, Indonesia, Malaysia, the Philippines, Singapore and Thailand.
[2]"CLMV" refers to Cambodia, Lao PDR, Myanmar and Viet Nam.

i. For ASEAN-6, by 1 January 2009:

1. Import duties of at least eighty percent (80%) tariff lines are eliminated;
2. Import duties on all Information and Communications Technology (ICT) products, as defined in the e-ASEAN Framework Agreement, are eliminated;
3. Import duties on all Priority Integration Sectors (PIS) products are at zero percent (0%), except those listed in the accompanying negative lists to the Protocols of the ASEAN Framework Agreement for the Integration of Priority Sectors and any amendments thereto; and
4. Import duties on all products are equal to or less than five percent (5%);

b. For Lao PDR, Myanmar and Viet Nam, import duties on all products are equal to or less than five percent (5%) by 1 January 2009;

i. For Cambodia, import duties of at least eighty percent (80%) tariff lines are equal to or less than five percent (5%) by 1 January 2009; and
ii. Import duties on some products of CLMV, not exceeding seven percent (7%) of tariff lines, shall be eliminated by 2018. The list of the products and schedule of import duties reduction of these products shall be identified by CLMV no later than 1 January 2014;

c. Import duties on ICT products listed in Schedule B of each CLMV Member State shall be eliminated in three (3) tranches by 2008, 2009 and 2010 in accordance with the schedule set out therein;
d. Import duties on PIS products listed in Schedule C of each CLMV Member State shall be eliminated by 2012 in accordance with the schedule set out therein;
e. Import duties on unprocessed agricultural products listed in Schedule D of each Member State on its own accord shall be reduced or eliminated to zero to five percent (0-5%) by 2010 for ASEAN-6; 2013 for Viet Nam; 2015 for Lao PDR and Myanmar; and 2017 for Cambodia, in accordance with the schedule set out therein. Notwithstanding this, import duties on sugar products of Viet Nam shall be reduced to zero to five percent (0-5%) by 2010;
f. Unprocessed agricultural products placed in Schedule E of each Member State on its own accord shall have their respective applied MFN import duties reduced in accordance with the schedule set out therein;
g. The products listed in Schedule F of Thailand and Viet Nam, respectively, shall have their out-quota tariff rates reduced in accordance with the tariff reduction schedules corresponding to their respective product classification;

h. Import duties on petroleum products listed in Schedule G of Cambodia and Viet Nam, respectively, shall be reduced in accordance with the schedule as mutually agreed by all Member States and set out therein;
i. The products placed in Schedule H of each Member State shall not be subject to import duties reduction or elimination for the reasons as provided in Article 8;
j. Reduction and elimination of import duties shall be implemented on 1 January of each year; and
k. The base rates from which import duties are to be reduced or eliminated shall be the Common Effective Preferential Tariffs (CEPT) rates at the time of entry into force of this Agreement.

3. Except as otherwise provided in this Agreement, no Member State shall nullify or impair any tariff concessions applied in accordance with the tariff schedules in Annex 2 referred to in paragraph 5 of this Article.
4. Except as otherwise provided in this Agreement, no Member State may increase an existing duty specified in the schedules made pursuant to the provisions of paragraph 2 of this Article on imports of an originating good.
5. Except as provided in paragraph 2(a)(iv) of this Article, the detailed tariff schedules to implement the modalities of reduction and/or elimination of import duties set out in paragraph 2 of this Article shall be finalized before the entry into force of this Agreement for ASEAN-6 and six (6) months after the entry into force of this Agreement for CLMV, and form an integral part of this Agreement as Annex 2.

Article 20
Elimination of Tariff Rate Quotas

1. Unless otherwise provided in this Agreement, each Member State undertakes not to introduce Tariff Rate Quotas (TRQs) on the importation of any goods originating in other Member States or on the exportation of any goods destined for the territory of the other Member States.
2. Viet Nam and Thailand shall eliminate the existing TRQs as follows:

   a. Thailand shall eliminate in three (3) tranches by 1 January 2008, 2009 and 2010;
   b. Viet Nam shall eliminate in three (3) tranches by 1 January 2013, 2014 and 2015, with flexibility up to 2018.

Article 21
Issuance of Legal Enactments

1.

   a. Each Member State shall, no later than ninety (90) days for ASEAN-6 and six (6) months for CLMV after the entry into force of this Agreement, issue a legal enactment in accordance with its laws and regulations to give effect to the implementation of the tariff liberalization schedules committed under Article 19.

b. The legal enactments issued pursuant to paragraph 1(a) of this Article shall have retroactive implementation with effect from 1 January of the year of the entry into force of this Agreement.
c. In the case where a single legal enactment could not be issued, the legal enactments to give effect to the implementation of tariff reduction or elimination of each year shall be issued at least three (3) months before the date of its effective implementation.

2. Member States may decide to conduct reviews of the products in **Schedules D** and **E** with a view to improving the market access for these products. If a product subject to the review is agreed to be phased out of the said Schedules, it will be placed in **Schedule A** of the respective Member State(s) and be subjected to the import duty elimination of that Schedule.

Article 22
Enjoyment of Concessions

1. Products on which tariffs of the exporting Member State have reached or are at the rate of twenty percent (20%) or below, and satisfy the requirements on rules of origin as set out in chapter "Treaty of Amity and Cooperation in Southeast Asia" shall automatically enjoy the concessions offered by importing Member States as stated in accordance with the provisions of Article 19.
2. Products listed in **Schedule H** shall not be entitled for tariff concessions offered under this Agreement.

Article 23
Temporary Modification or Suspension of Concessions

1. In exceptional circumstances other than those covered under Article 10, Article 24 and Article 86 where a Member State faces unforeseen difficulties in implementing its tariff commitments, that Member State may temporarily modify or suspend a concession contained in its Schedules under Article 19.
2. A Member State which seeks to invoke the provision of paragraph 1 of this Article (hereinafter referred to as the "applicant Member State"), shall notify in writing of such temporary modification or suspension of concessions to the ASEAN Free Trade Area (AFTA) Council at least one hundred and eighty (180) days prior to the date when the temporary modification or suspension of concessions is to take effect.
3. Member States who are interested in engaging in consultations or negotiations with the applicant Member State, pursuant to paragraph 4 of this Article, shall notify all ASEAN Member States of this interest within ninety (90) days following the applicant Member State's notification of the temporary modification or suspension of concessions.

4. After making the notification pursuant to paragraph 2 of this Article, the applicant Member State shall engage in consultations or negotiations with the Member States who have made notification pursuant to paragraph 3 of this Article. In negotiations with Member States with substantial supplying interest,[3] the applicant Member State shall maintain a level of reciprocal and mutually advantageous concessions no less favorable to the trade of all other Member States of substantial supplying interest than that provided in this Agreement prior to such negotiations, which may include compensatory adjustments with respect to other goods. Compensatory adjustment measures in form of tariffs shall be extended to all Member States on a non-discriminatory basis.
5. The AFTA Council shall be notified of the outcome of the consultations or negotiations pursuant to paragraphs 3 and 4 of this Article at least forty-five (45) days before the applicant Member State intends to affect the temporary modification or suspension of concessions. The notification shall include the applicant Member State's justifications for needing to adopt such measures and shall provide the Member State's intended schedule pertaining to the modification or suspension of concessions and the time period for which the Member State intends to apply the measures.
6. In the event that no agreement is reached after the consultations or negotiations pursuant to paragraphs 3 and 4 of this Article, the notification to the AFTA Council shall also include the request for the AFTA Council's recommendation.
7. The AFTA Council shall issue its approval or recommendation within thirty (30) days upon receipt of the notification pursuant to paragraph 5 of this Article.
8. In the event that the circumstances giving rise to the request for the temporary modification or suspension of concessions cease to exist, the applicant Member State shall immediately restore the tariff concessions and notify the AFTA Council accordingly. Upon restoration of tariff concessions or termination of the suspension, the applicant Member State shall apply the rate which it would have applied according to the scheduled commitments as if the delay or suspension had not occurred.
9. In the event that there is no approval or recommendation by the AFTA Council pursuant to paragraph 7 of this Article, and the applicant Member State nevertheless proceeds with the temporary modification or suspension of the concession, Member States with substantial supplying interest shall be free to take action after thirty (30) days, but not later than ninety (90) days after the applicant Member State effects its modification or suspension of concessions, to

[3]A Member State shall be deemed to have "substantial supplying interest" if it has, or because of the tariff concessions, it is to be reasonably expected to have, a significant share of at least twenty percent (20%) of the total import from ASEAN of such products during the past three (3) years in average in the market of the applicant Member State.

modify or suspend substantially equivalent concessions from the applicant Member State. The concerned Member States shall immediately notify the AFTA Council of such actions.

Article 24
Special Treatment on Rice and Sugar

The Protocol to Provide Special Consideration for Rice and Sugar signed on 23rd August 2007 shall form an integral part of this Agreement.

Chapter 3. Rules of Origin

Article 25
Definitions

For the purposes of this chapter:

a. **aquaculture** means the farming of aquatic organisms including fish, mollusks, crustaceans, other aquatic invertebrates and aquatic plants, from feedstock such as eggs, fry, fingerlings and larvae, by intervention in the rearing or growth processes to enhance production such as regular stocking, feeding, or protection from predators;
b. **costs, insurance and freight (CIF)** means the value of the goods imported, and includes the costs of freight and insurance up to the port or place of entry into the country of importation. The valuation shall be made in accordance with Article VII of GATT 1994 and the Agreement on the Implementation of Article VII of GATT 1994 as contained in Annex 1A to the WTO Agreement;
c. **FOB** means the free-on-board value of the goods, inclusive of the costs of transport to the port or site of final shipment abroad. The valuation shall be made in accordance with Article VII of GATT 1994 and the Agreement on the Implementation of Article VII of GATT 1994 as contained in Annex 1A to the WTO Agreement;
d. **generally accepted accounting principles (GAAP)** means the recognized consensus or substantial authoritative support in the territory of a Member State, with respect to the recording of revenues, expenses, costs, assets and liabilities; the disclosure of information; and the preparation of financial statements. These standards may encompass broad guidelines of general application as well as detailed standards, practices and procedures;
e. **goods** shall include materials and/or products, which can be wholly obtained or produced, even if they are intended for later use as materials in another production process. For the purposes of this chapter, the terms "goods" and "products" can be used interchangeably;
f. **identical and interchangeable materials** mean materials being of the same kind and commercial quality, possessing the same technical and physical characteristics, and which after being incorporated into the finished product

cannot be distinguished from one another for origin purposes by virtue of any markings, etc.;

g. **materials** mean any matter or substance used or consumed in the production of goods or physically incorporated into another good or are subject to a process in the production of another good;
h. **originating goods** or **originating material** means goods or material that qualifies as originating in accordance with the provisions of this chapter;
i. **packing materials and containers for transportation** means the goods used to protect a good during its transportation, different from those containers or materials used for its retail sale;
j. **production** means methods of obtaining goods, including growing, mining, harvesting, raising, breeding, extracting, gathering, collecting, capturing, fishing, trapping, hunting, manufacturing, producing, processing or assembling goods; and
k. **product specific rules** mean rules that specify that the materials have undergone a change in tariff classification or a specific manufacturing or processing operation, or satisfy a Regional Value Content criterion or a combination of any of these criteria.

Article 26
Origin Criteria

For the purposes of this Agreement, a good imported into the territory of a Member State from another Member State shall be treated as an originating good if it conforms to the origin requirements under any one of the following conditions:

a. a good which is wholly obtained or produced in the exporting Member State as set out and defined in Article 27; or
b. a good not wholly obtained or produced in the exporting Member State, provided that the said goods are eligible under Article 28 or Article 30.

Article 27
Wholly Obtained or Produced Goods

Within the meaning of Article 26(a), the following shall be considered as wholly obtained or produced in the exporting Member State:

a. Plant and plant products, including fruit, flowers, vegetables, trees, seaweed, fungi and live plants, grown and harvested, picked or gathered in the exporting Member State;
b. Live animals, including mammals, birds, fish, crustaceans, mollusks, reptiles, bacteria and viruses, born and raised in the exporting Member State;
c. Goods obtained from live animals in the exporting Member State;

d. Goods obtained from hunting, trapping, fishing, farming, aquaculture, gathering or capturing conducted in the exporting Member State;
e. Minerals and other naturally occurring substances, not included in paragraphs (a) to (d) of this Article, extracted or taken from its soil, waters, seabed or beneath its seabed;
f. Products of sea-fishing taken by vessels registered with a Member State and entitled to fly its flag and other products[4] taken from the waters, seabed or beneath the seabed outside the territorial waters[5] of that Member State, provided that that Member State has the rights to exploit such waters, seabed and beneath the seabed in accordance with international law[6];
g. Products of sea-fishing and other marine products taken from the high seas by vessels registered with a Member State and entitled to fly the flag of that Member State;
h. Products processed and/or made on board factory ships registered with a Member State and entitled to fly the flag of that Member State, exclusively from products referred to in paragraph (g) of this Article;
i. Articles collected there which can no longer perform their original purpose nor are capable of being restored or repaired and are fit only for disposal or recovery of parts of raw materials, or for recycling purposes;
j. Waste and scrap derived from:
    i. production in the exporting Member State; or
    ii. used goods collected in the exporting Member State, provided that such goods are fit only for the recovery of raw materials; and
k. Goods obtained or produced in the exporting Member State from products referred to in paragraphs (a) to (j) of this Article.

Article 28
Not Wholly Obtained or Produced Goods

1.

    a. For the purposes of Article 26(b), goods shall be deemed to be originating in the Member State where working or processing of the goods has taken place:
        i. if the goods have a regional value content (hereinafter referred to as "ASEAN Value Content" or the "Regional Value Content (RVC)") of

[4]"Other products" refers to minerals and other naturally occurring substances extracted from the waters, seabed or beneath the seabed outside the territorial waters.

[5]For products of sea-fishing obtained from outside the territorial waters (e.g. Exclusive Economic Zone), originating status would be conferred to that Member State with whom the vessels used to obtain such products are registered with and whose flag is flown in the said vessel, and provided that that Member State has the rights to exploit it under international law.

[6]In accordance with international law, registration of vessels could only be made in one Member State.

not less than forty percent (40%) calculated using the formula set out in Article 29; or

ii. if all non-originating materials used in the production of the goods have undergone a change in tariff classification (hereinafter referred to as "CTC") at four-digit level (i.e. a change in tariff heading) of the Harmonized System.

b. Each Member State shall permit the exporter of the good to decide whether to use paragraph 1(a)(i) or 1(a)(ii) of this Article when determining whether the goods qualify as originating goods of the Member State.

2.

a. Notwithstanding paragraph 1 of this Article, goods listed in Annex 3 shall qualify as originating goods if the goods satisfy the product specific rules set out therein.
b. Where a product specific rule provides a choice of rules from a RVC-based rule of origin, a CTC-based rule of origin, a specific manufacturing or processing operation, or a combination of any of these, each Member State shall permit the exporter of the goods to decide which rule to use in determining whether the goods qualify as originating goods of the Member State.
c. Where product specific rules specify a certain RVC, it is required that the RVC of a good is calculated using the formula set out in Article 29.
d. Where product specific rules requiring that the materials used have undergone CTC or a specific manufacturing or processing operation, the rules shall apply only to non-originating materials.

3. Notwithstanding paragraphs 1 and 2 of this Article, a good which is covered by Attachment A or B of the *Ministerial Declaration on Trade in Information Technology Products* adopted in the Ministerial Conference of the WTO on 13 December 1996, set out as Annex 4, shall be deemed to be originating in a Member State if it is assembled from materials covered under the same Annex.

Article 29
Calculation of Regional Value Content

1. For the purposes of Article 28, the formula for calculating ASEAN Value Content or RVC is as follows:

a. Direct Method

$$RVC = \frac{ASEAN\ material\ cost + Direct\ labour\ cost + Direct\ overhead\ cost + other\ cost + profit}{FOB\ price} \times 100\%$$

Or

b. Indirect Method

$$RVC = \frac{FOB\,price - value\,of\,non\,originating\,materials, parts\,or\,goods}{FOB\,price} \times 100\%$$

2. For the purposes of calculating the RVC provided in paragraph 1 of this Article:
   a. **ASEAN Material Cost** is the CIF value of originating materials, parts or goods that are acquired or self-produced by the producer in the production of the good;
   b. Value of Non-Originating Materials, Parts or Goods shall be:
      i. The CIF value at the time of importation of the goods or importation can be proven; or
      ii. The earliest ascertained price paid for the goods of undetermined origin in the territory of the Member State where the working or processing takes place;
   c. **Direct labor cost** shall include wages, remuneration and other employee benefits associated with the manufacturing process;
   d. **The calculation of direct overhead cost** shall include, but is not limited to, real property items associated with the production process (insurance, factory rent and leasing, depreciation on buildings, repair and maintenance, taxes, interests on mortgage); leasing of and interest payments for plant and equipment; factory security; insurance (plant, equipment and materials used in the manufacture of the goods); utilities (energy, electricity, water and other utilities directly attributable to the production of the goods); research, development, design and engineering; dies, molds, tooling and the depreciation, maintenance and repair of plant and equipment; royalties or licenses (in connection with patented machines or processes used in the manufacture of the goods or the right to manufacture the goods); inspection and testing of materials and the goods; storage and handling in the factory; disposal of recyclable wastes; and cost elements in computing the value of raw materials, i.e. port and clearance charges and import duties paid for dutiable component; and
   e. **FOB price** means the free-on-board value of the goods as defined in Article 25. FOB price shall be determined by adding the value of materials, production cost, profit and other costs.
3. Member States shall determine and adhere to only one (1) method of calculating the RVC. Member States shall be given the flexibility to change their calculation method provided that such change is notified to the AFTA Council at least six (6) months prior to the adoption of the new method. Any verification to the ASEAN Value Content calculation by the importing Member State shall be done on the basis of the method used by the exporting Member State.
4. In determining the ASEAN Value Content, Member States shall closely adhere to the guidelines for costing methodologies set out in Annex 5.

5. Locally-procured materials produced by established licensed manufacturers, in compliance with domestic regulations, shall be deemed to have fulfilled the origin requirement of this Agreement; locally-procured materials from other sources shall be subjected to the origin verification pursuant to Article 57 for the purpose of origin determination.
6. The value of goods under this chapter shall be determined in accordance with the provisions of Article 57.

Article 30
Accumulation

1. Unless otherwise provided in this Agreement, goods originating in a Member State, which are used in another Member State as materials for finished goods eligible for preferential tariff treatment, shall be considered to be originating in the latter Member State where working or processing of the finished goods has taken place.
2. If the RVC of the material is less than forty percent (40%), the qualifying ASEAN Value Content to be cumulated using the RVC criterion shall be in direct proportion to the actual domestic content provided that it is equal to or more than twenty percent (20%). The Implementing Guidelines are set out in Annex 6.

Article 31
Minimal Operations and Processes

1. Operations or processes undertaken, by themselves or in combination with each other for the purposes listed below, are considered to be minimal and shall not be taken into account in determining whether a good has been originating in one Member State:

   a. ensuring preservation of goods in good condition for the purposes of transport or storage;
   b. facilitating shipment or transportation; and
   c. packaging or presenting goods for sale.

2. A good originating in the territory of a Member State shall retain its initial originating status, when exported from another Member State, where operations undertaken have not gone beyond those referred to in paragraph 1 of this Article.

Article 32
Direct Consignment

1. Preferential tariff treatment shall be applied to goods satisfying the requirements of this chapter and which are consigned directly between the territories of the exporting Member State and the importing Member State.
2. The following shall be considered as consigned directly from the exporting Member State to the importing Member State:

a. goods transported from an exporting Member State to the importing Member State; or
b. goods transported through one or more Member States, other than the exporting Member State and the importing Member State, or through a non-Member State, provided that:

   i. the transit entry is justified for geographical reason or by consideration related exclusively to transport requirements;
   ii. the goods have not entered into trade or consumption there; and
   iii. the goods have not undergone any operation there other than unloading and reloading or any other operation to preserve them in good condition.

Article 33
De Minimis

1. A good that does not undergo a change in tariff classification shall be considered as originating if the value of all non-originating materials used in its production that do not undergo the required change in tariff classification does not exceed ten percent (10%) of the FOB value of the good and the good meets all other applicable criteria set forth in this Agreement for qualifying as an originating good.
2. The value of non-originating materials referred to in paragraph 1 of this Article shall, however, be included in the value of non-originating materials for any applicable RVC requirement for the good.

Article 34
Treatment of Packages and Packing Materials

1. Packaging and Packing Materials for retail sale:

   a. If a good is subject to the RVC-based rule of origin, the value of the packaging and packing materials for retail sale shall be taken into account in its origin assessment, where the packaging and packing materials for retail sale are considered to be forming a whole with the good.
   b. Where paragraph 1 (a) of this Article is not applicable, the packaging and packing materials for retail sale, when classified together with the packaged good shall not be taken into account in considering whether all non-originating materials used in the manufacture of a product fulfils the criterion corresponding to a change of tariff classification of the said good.

2. The containers and packing materials exclusively used for the transport of a good shall not be taken into account for determining the origin of the said good.

Article 35
Accessories, Spare Parts and Tools

1. If a good is subject to the requirements of CTC or specific manufacturing or processing operation, the origin of accessories, spare parts, tools and instructional or other information materials presented with the good shall not be taken into account in determining whether the good qualifies as an originating good, provided that:

   a. the accessories, spare parts, tools and instructional or other information materials are not invoiced separately from the good; and
   b. the quantities and value of the accessories, spare parts, tools and instructional or other information materials are customary for the good.

2. If a good is subject to the RVC-based rule of origin, the value of the accessories, spare parts, tools and instructional or other information materials shall be taken into account as the value of the originating or non-originating materials, as the case may be, in calculating the RVC of the originating good.

Article 36
Neutral Elements

In order to determine whether a good originates, it shall not be necessary to determine the origin of the following which might be used in its production and not incorporated into the good:

a. fuel and energy;
b. tools, dies and molds;
c. spare parts and materials used in the maintenance of equipment and buildings;
d. lubricants, greases, compounding materials and other materials used in production or used to operate equipment and buildings;
e. gloves, glasses, footwear, clothing, safety equipment and supplies;
f. equipment, devices and supplies used for testing or inspecting the good;
g. catalyst and solvent; and
h. any other goods that are not incorporated into the good but of which use in the production of the good can reasonably be demonstrated to be a part of that production.

Article 37
Identical and Interchangeable Materials

1. The determination of whether identical and interchangeable materials are originating materials shall be made either by physical segregation of each of the materials or by the use of generally accepted accounting principles of stock control applicable, or inventory management practice, in the exporting Member States.
2. Once a decision has been taken on the inventory management method, that method shall be used throughout the fiscal year.

Article 38
Certificate of Origin

A claim that a good shall be accepted as eligible for preferential tariff treatment shall be supported by a Certificate of Origin (Form D), as set out in Annex 7 issued by a Government authority designated by the exporting Member State and notified to the other Member States in accordance with the Operational Certification Procedures, as set out in Annex 8.

Article 39
Sub-Committee on Rules of Origin

1. For the purposes of the effective and uniform implementation of this chapter, a Sub-Committee on Rules of Origin shall be established pursuant to Article 90.
2. The functions of the Sub-Committee on Rules of Origin shall include:

   a. monitoring of the implementation and operation of this chapter;
   b. reviewing, as and when necessary, this chapter to provide appropriate recommendations with the view to enhancing this chapter to make it responsive to the dynamic changes in the regional and global production processes so as to facilitate trade and investment among Member States, promote a regional production network, encourage the development of Small and Medium Enterprises (SMEs) and narrowing the development gaps;
   c. reviewing, as and when necessary, the operational procedures of this chapter with the view to simplifying the procedures and making them transparent, predictable and standardized, taking into account the best practices of other regional and international trade agreements;
   d. considering any other matter as Member States may agree related to this chapter; and
   e. carrying out other functions as may be delegated by the CCA, SEOM and the AFTA Council.

3. The Sub-Committee on Rules of Origin shall be composed of representatives of the Governments of Member States, and may invite representatives of relevant entities other than the Governments of the Member States with necessary expertise relevant to the issues to be discussed, upon agreement of all Member States.

Chapter 4. Non-tariff Measures

Article 40
Application of Non-tariff Measures

1. Each Member State shall not adopt or maintain any non-tariff measure on the importation of any good of any other Member State or on the exportation of any good destined for the territory of any other Member State, except in accordance with its WTO rights and obligations or in accordance with this Agreement.
2. Each Member State shall ensure the transparency of its non-tariff measures permitted in paragraph 1 of this Article in accordance with Article 12 and shall ensure that any such measures are not prepared, adopted or applied with the view to, or with the effect of, creating unnecessary obstacles in trade among the Member States.
3. Any new measure or modification to the existing measure shall be duly notified in accordance with Article 11.
4. The database on non-tariff measures applied in Member States shall be further developed and included in the ASEAN Trade Repository as referred in Article 13.

Article 41
General Elimination of Quantitative Restrictions

Each Member State undertakes not to adopt or maintain any prohibition or quantitative restriction on the importation of any goods of the other Member States or on the exportation of any goods destined for the territory of the other Member States, except in accordance with its WTO rights and obligations or other provisions in this Agreement. To this end, Article XI of GATT 1994, shall be incorporated into and form part of this Agreement, mutatis mutandis.

Article 42
Elimination of Other Non-Tariff Barriers

1. Member States shall review the non-tariff measures in the database referred to in paragraph 4 of Article 40 with a view to identifying non-tariff barriers (NTBs) other than quantitative restrictions for elimination. The elimination of the identified NTBs shall be dealt with by the Co-ordinating Committee for the Implementation of the ATIGA (CCA), the ASEAN Consultative Committee on Standards and Quality (ACCSQ), the ASEAN Committee on Sanitary and Phytosanitary (AC-SPS), the working bodies under ASEAN Directors-General of Customs and other relevant ASEAN bodies, as appropriate, in accordance with the provisions of this Agreement, which shall submit their recommendations on the identified non-tariff barriers to the AFTA Council through SEOM.
2. Unless otherwise agreed by the AFTA Council, the identified NTBs shall be eliminated in three (3) tranches as follows:

    a. Brunei, Indonesia, Malaysia, Singapore and Thailand shall eliminate in three (3) tranches by 1 January of 2008, 2009 and 2010;

b. The Philippines shall eliminate in three (3) tranches by 1 January of 2010, 2011 and 2012;
c. Cambodia, Lao PDR, Myanmar and Viet Nam shall eliminate in three (3) tranches by 1 January of 2013, 2014 and 2015 with flexibilities up to 2018.

3. The list of identified NTBs to be eliminated in each tranche shall be agreed upon by the AFTA Council meeting in the year before the effective elimination date of such NTBs.
4. Notwithstanding paragraphs 1 to 3 of this Article, the CCA, in consultation with the relevant ASEAN bodies, shall review any non-tariff measure notified or reported by any other Member State or by the private sector with a view to determining whether the measure constitutes as a NTB. If such review results in an identification of a NTB, the NTB shall be eliminated by the Member State applying such NTB in accordance with this Agreement.
5. The CCA shall serve as a focal point for the notification and review referred to in paragraph 4 of this Article.
6. Exceptions to this Article shall be allowed for the reasons provided in Article 8.
7. Nothing in this Agreement shall be construed to prevent a Member State, which is a party to the Basel Convention on the Control of Transboundary Movements of Hazardous Wastes and their Disposal or other relevant international agreements, from adopting or enforcing any measure in relation to hazardous wastes or substances based on its laws and regulations, in accordance with such international agreements.

Article 43
Foreign Exchange Restrictions

Member States shall make exceptions to their foreign exchange restrictions relating to payments for the products under this Agreement, as well as repatriation of such payments without prejudice to their rights under Article XVIII of GATT 1994 and relevant provisions of the Articles of Agreement of the International Monetary Fund (IMF).

Article 44
Import Licensing Procedures

1. Each Member State shall ensure that all automatic and nonautomatic import licensing procedures are implemented in a transparent and predictable manner, and applied in accordance with the Agreement on Import Licensing Procedures as contained in Annex 1A to the WTO Agreement.
2. Promptly after entry into force of this Agreement, each Member State shall notify the other Member States of any existing import licensing procedures. Thereafter, each Member State shall notify the other Member States of any new import licensing procedure and any modification to its existing import licensing procedures, to the extent possible sixty (60) days before it takes effect, but in any case, no later than the effective date of the licensing requirement.

A notification provided under this Article shall include the information specified in Article 5 of the Agreement on Import Licensing Procedures as contained in Annex 1A to the WTO Agreement.

3. Each Member State shall answer within sixty (60) days all reasonable enquiries from another Member State with regard to the criteria employed by its respective licensing authorities in granting or denying import licenses. The importing Member State shall also consider publication of such criteria.
4. Elements in non-automatic import licensing procedures that are found to be impeding trade shall be identified, with a view to remove such barriers, and to the extent possible work towards automatic import licensing procedures.

Chapter 5. Trade Facilitation

Article 45
Work Program on Trade Facilitation and its Objectives

1. Member States shall develop and implement a comprehensive ASEAN Trade Facilitation Work Program, which sets out all concrete actions and measures with clear targets and timelines of implementation necessary for creating a consistent, transparent, and predictable environment for international trade transactions that increases trading opportunities and help businesses, including small and medium sized enterprises (SMEs), to save time and reduce costs.
2. The ASEAN Trade Facilitation Work Program shall set out actions and measures to be implemented at both ASEAN and national levels.

Article 46
Scope of the ASEAN Trade Facilitation Work Program

The ASEAN Trade Facilitation Work Program referred to in Article 45 shall cover the areas of customs procedures, trade regulations and procedures, standards and conformance, sanitary and phytosanitary measures, ASEAN Single Window and other areas as identified by the AFTA Council.

Article 47
Principles on Trade Facilitation

Member States shall be guided by the following principles in relation to trade facilitation measures and initiatives at both ASEAN and national levels:

a. **Transparency**: Information on policies, laws, regulations, administrative rulings, licensing, certification, qualification and registration requirements, technical regulations, standards, guidelines, procedures and practices relating to trade in goods (hereinafter referred to as "rules and procedures relating to trade") to be made available to all interested parties, consistently and in a timely manner at no cost or a reasonable cost;

b. **Communications and Consultations**: The authorities shall endeavor to facilitate and promote effective mechanisms for exchanges with the business and trading community, including opportunities for consultation when formulating, implementing and reviewing rules and procedures relating to trade;
c. **Simplification, practicability and efficiency**: Rules and procedures relating to trade to be simplified to ensure that they are no more burdensome or restrictive than necessary to achieve their legitimate objectives;
d. **Non-discrimination**: Rules and procedures relating to trade to be applied in a non-discriminatory manner and be based on market principles;
e. **Consistency and predictability**: Rules and procedures relating to trade to be applied in a consistent, predictable and uniform manner so as to minimize uncertainty to the trade and trade related parties. Rules and procedures relating to trade to provide clear and precise procedural guidance to the appropriate authorities with standard policies and operating procedures and be applied in a non-discretionary manner;
f. **Harmonization, standardization and recognition**: While accepting the need of each Member State to regulate or set rules for legitimate objectives such as protection of health, safety or public morals and conservation of exhaustible natural resources, regulations, rules and procedures affecting the acceptance of goods between Member States to be harmonized as far as possible on the basis of international standards where appropriate. The development of mutual recognition arrangements for standards and conformity assessment results, and continuing co-operation on technical infrastructure development, are encouraged;
g. **Modernization and use of new technology**: Rules and procedures relating to trade to be reviewed and updated if necessary, taking into account changed circumstances, including new information and new business practices, and based on the adoption, where appropriate, of modern techniques and new technology. Where new technology is used, relevant authorities shall make best efforts to spread the accompanying benefits to all parties through ensuring the openness of the information on the adopted technologies and extending co-operation to authorities of other economies and the private sector in establishing inter-operability and/or inter-connectivity of the technologies;
h. **Due process**: Access to adequate legal appeal procedures, adding greater certainty to trade transactions, in accordance with the applicable laws of Member States; and
i. **Co-operation**: Member States shall strive to work closely with private sector in the introduction of measures conducive to trade facilitation, including by open channels of communication and co-operation between both governments and business. Member States shall continue to work in partnership to focus on

opportunities for increased co-operation including integrated technical assistance and capacity-building; exchanges of best practices critical to implementing trade facilitation initiatives and the co-ordination of positions concerning topics of common interest discussed in the framework of regional and international organizations.

Article 48
Progress Monitoring of Trade Facilitation

1. Member States, individually and collectively, shall undertake assessments once in every two (2) years, on implementation of the trade facilitation measures set out in this Agreement and in the ASEAN Trade Facilitation Work Program to ensure effective implementation of trade facilitation measures. For this purpose, an ASEAN Trade Facilitation Framework shall be agreed by Member States within six (6) months after entry into force of this Agreement, to serve as a guideline to further enhance trade facilitation in ASEAN.
2. The ASEAN Work Program on Trade Facilitation shall be reviewed based on the results of the regular assessment pursuant to paragraph 1 of this Article. The ASEAN Trade Facilitation Work Program and the ASEAN Trade Facilitation Framework and any revisions thereto shall be administratively annexed to this Agreement and serve as an integral part of this Agreement.

Article 49
Establishment of the ASEAN Single Window

Member States shall undertake necessary measures to establish and operate their respective National Single Windows and the ASEAN Single Window in accordance with the provisions of the Agreement to Establish and Implement the ASEAN Single Window and the Protocol to Establish and Implement the ASEAN Single Window.

Article 50
Implementation Arrangement

1. The progress in the implementation of the ASEAN Work Program on Trade Facilitation and the outcomes of its assessment shall be reported to the AFTA Council. The SEOM, assisted by the CCA, shall be the main coordinator in monitoring the progress of the implementation of the ASEAN Work Program on Trade Facilitation, in close co-ordination with the various ASEAN Committees in charge of the implementation of the measures under the Work Program.
2. Each Member State shall establish a Trade Facilitation Coordinating Committee or relevant focal point at the national level.

Chapter 6. Customs

Article 51
Objectives

The objectives of this chapter are to:

a. ensure predictability, consistency and transparency in the application of customs laws of Member States;
b. promote efficient and economical administration of customs procedures, and expeditious clearance of goods;
c. simplify and harmonize customs procedures and practices to the extent possible; and
d. promote cooperation among the customs authorities.

Article 52
Definitions

For the purposes of this chapter:

a. **Authorized Economic Operator** means a party involved in the international movement of goods in any function that has been approved by the customs authorities as complying with statutory and/or regulatory requirements of Member States, taking into account international supply chain security standards;
b. **customs control** means measures applied by the customs authorities to ensure compliance with customs laws of Member States;
c. **customs procedures** means the treatment applied by the customs authorities of each Member State to goods, which are subject to customs laws;
d. **Customs Valuation Agreement** means the Agreement on Implementation of Article VII of the General Agreement on Tariffs and Trade 1994, contained in Annex 1A to the WTO Agreement;
e. **drawback** means the amount of import duties and taxes repaid under the drawback procedure;
f. **drawback procedure** means customs procedures which, when goods are exported, provide for a repayment (total or partial) to be made in respect of the import duties and taxes charged on the goods, or on materials contained in them or consumed in their production;
g. **goods declaration** means a statement made in the manner prescribed by the customs authorities, by which the persons concerned indicate the customs procedure to be applied to the goods and furnish the particulars which the customs authorities require for its application;
h. **repayment** means the refund, in whole or in part, of duties and taxes paid on goods and the remission, in whole or in part, of duties and taxes where payment has not been made;

i. **security** means that which ensures to the satisfaction of the customs authorities that an obligation to the customs authorities will be fulfilled; and
j. **temporary admission** means customs procedures under which certain goods can be brought into a customs territory conditionally relieved totally or partially from payment of import duties and taxes; such goods must be imported for a specific purpose and must be intended for re-exportation within a specified period and without having undergone any change except normal depreciation due to the use made of them.

Article 53
Scope

This chapter applies, in accordance with the Member States' respective laws, regulations and policies, to customs procedures applied to goods traded among Member States.

Article 54
Customs Procedures and Control

1. Each Member State shall ensure that its customs procedures and practices are predictable, consistent, transparent and trade facilitating, including through the expeditious clearance of goods.
2. Customs procedures of Member States shall, where possible and to the extent permitted by their respective customs law, conform to standards and recommended practices of the World Customs Organization and other international organizations as relevant to customs.
3. The customs authorities of each Member State shall review its customs procedures with a view to their simplification to facilitate trade.
4. Customs control shall be limited to that which is necessary to ensure compliance with customs laws of Member States.

Article 55
Pre-arrival Documentation

Member States shall endeavor to make provision for the lodging and registering or checking of the goods declaration and its supporting documents prior to the arrival of the goods.

Article 56
Risk Management

Member States shall use risk management to determine control measures with the view to facilitate customs clearance and release of goods.

Article 57
Customs Valuation

1. For the purposes of determining the customs value of goods traded between and among the Member States, provisions of Part I of Customs Valuation Agreement, shall apply mutatis mutandis.[7]
2. Member States shall harmonize, to the extent possible, administrative procedures and practices in the assessment of value of goods for customs purposes.

Article 58
Application of Information Technology

Member States, where applicable, shall apply information technology in customs operations based on internationally accepted standards for expeditious customs clearance and release of goods.

Article 59
Authorized Economic Operators

1. Member States shall endeavor to establish the program of Authorized Economic Operators (AEO) to promote informed compliance and efficiency of customs control.
2. Member States shall endeavor to work towards mutual recognition of AEO.

Article 60
Repayment, Drawback and Security

1. Decisions on claims for repayment shall be reached, and notified in writing to the persons concerned, without undue delay, and repayment of amounts overcharged shall be made as soon as possible after the verification of claims.
2. Drawback shall be paid as soon as possible after the verification of claims.
3. Where security has been furnished, it shall be discharged as soon as possible after the customs authorities are satisfied that the obligations under which the security was required have been duly fulfilled.

Article 61
Post Clearance Audit

Member States shall establish and operate Post Clearance Audit (PCA) for expeditious customs clearance and enhanced customs control.

Article 62
Advance Rulings

1. Each Member State, through its customs authorities and/or other relevant authorities, shall, to the extent permitted by its respective laws, regulations and

[7]In the case of Cambodia, the Agreement on Customs Valuation, as implemented in accordance with the provision of the protocol on the Accession of the Kingdom of Cambodia to the WTO, shall apply mutatis mutandis.

administrative determinations, provide in writing advance rulings on the application of a person described in paragraph 2(a) of this Article, in respect of the tariff classification, questions arising from the application of the principles of Customs Valuation Agreement and/or origin of goods.

2. Where available, each Member State shall adopt or maintain procedures for advance rulings, which shall:

   a. provide that an importer in its territory or an exporter or producer in the territory of another Member State may apply for an advance ruling before the importation of goods in question;
   b. require that an applicant for an advance ruling provide a detailed description of the goods and all relevant information needed to process an application for an advance ruling;
   c. provide that its customs authorities may, at any time during the course of evaluation of an application for an advance ruling, request that the applicant provide additional information within a specified period;
   d. provide that any advance ruling be based on the facts and circumstances presented by the applicant, and any other relevant information in the possession of the decision-maker; and
   e. provide that an advance ruling be issued to the applicant expeditiously, within the period specified in each Member State's respective laws, regulations or administrative determinations.

3. A Member State may reject requests for an advance ruling where the additional information requested in accordance with paragraph 2(c) of this Article is not provided within a specified time.
4. Subject to paragraphs 1 and 5 of this Article and where available, each Member State shall apply an advance ruling to all importations of goods described in that ruling imported into its territory for three (3) years from the date of that ruling, or such other period as specified in that Member State's respective laws, regulations or administrative determinations.
5. A Member State may modify or revoke an advance ruling upon a determination that the ruling was based on an error of fact or law (including human error), the information provided is false or inaccurate, there is a change in its law consistent with this Agreement, or there is a change in a material fact, or circumstances on which the ruling was based.
6. Where an importer claims that the treatment accorded to an imported good should be governed by an advance ruling, the customs authorities may evaluate whether the facts and circumstances of the importation are consistent with the facts and circumstances upon which an advance ruling was based.

Article 63
Temporary Admission

Member States shall facilitate movement of goods under temporary admission to the greatest extent possible.

Article 64
Customs Co-operation

To the extent permitted by their laws, Member States may, as deemed appropriate, assist each other on customs matters.

Article 65
Transparency

1. Member States will facilitate the timely publication, dissemination of statutory and regulatory information, decisions and rulings on customs matters.
2. Each Member State shall publish on the internet and/or in print form all statutory and regulatory provisions and any customs administrative procedures applicable or enforceable by its customs administration, except law enforcement procedures and internal operational guidelines.

Article 66
Enquiry Points

Each Member State shall designate one (1) or more enquiry points to address enquiries from interested persons concerning customs matters, and shall make available on the internet and/or in print form information concerning procedures for making such enquiries.

Article 67
Consultation

The customs authorities of Member States will encourage consultation with each other regarding customs issues that affect goods traded between and among Member States.

Article 68
Confidentiality

1. Nothing in this chapter shall be construed to require any Member State to furnish or allow access to confidential information pursuant to this chapter the disclosure of which it considers would:

    a. be contrary to the public interest as determined by its laws;
    b. be contrary to any of its laws, including but not limited, to those protecting personal privacy or the financial affairs and accounts of individual customers of financial institutions;
    c. impede law enforcement; or
    d. prejudice legitimate commercial interests, which may include competitive position of particular enterprises, public or private.

2. Where a Member State provides information to another Member State in accordance with this chapter and designates the information as confidential, the Member State receiving the information shall maintain the confidentiality of the information, use it only for the purposes specified by the Member State

providing the information, and not disclose it without the specific written permission of the Member State providing the information.

Article 69
Review and Appeal

1. Each Member State shall ensure that any person, in its territory, being aggrieved by any customs decision pertinent to this Agreement have access to administrative review within the customs authorities that issued the decision subject to review or, where applicable, by the higher authority supervising the administration and/or judicial review of the determination taken at the final level of administrative review, in accordance with the Member State's law.
2. The decision on appeal shall be given to the appellant and the reasons for such decision shall be provided in writing.

Article 70
Implementation and Institutional Arrangements

The ASEAN Directors-General of Customs, supported by customs working bodies, shall be responsible to implement the provisions of this chapter and any other provisions relevant to customs in this Agreement.

Chapter 7. Standards, Technical Regulations and Conformity Assessment Procedures

Article 71
Objective

The objective of this chapter is to establish provisions on standards, technical regulations and conformity assessment procedures to ensure that these do not create unnecessary obstacles to trade in establishing ASEAN as a single market and production base, and at the same time ensure that the legitimate objectives of Member States are met.

Article 72
Terms and Definitions

General terms concerning standardization and conformity assessment used in this chapter have the meaning given to them in the definitions contained in the appropriate editions of ISO/IEC Guide 2 and ISO/IEC 17000 of the International Organization for Standardization (ISO) and the International Electrotechnical Commission (IEC) as cited in the ASEAN Framework Agreement on Mutual Recognition Arrangements and the relevant ASEAN Sectoral Mutual Recognition Arrangements.

Article 73
General Provisions

1. Member States reaffirm and are committed to abide by the rights and obligations under the Agreement on Technical Barriers to Trade contained in Annex 1A to the WTO Agreement.
2. Member States shall take any of the following possible measures or their combinations to mitigate, if not totally eliminate, unnecessary technical barriers to trade:

    a. harmonize national standards with relevant international standards and practices;
    b. promote mutual recognition of conformity assessment results among Member States;
    c. develop and implement ASEAN Sectoral Mutual Recognition Arrangements and develop ASEAN Harmonized Regulatory Regimes in the regulated areas where applicable; and
    d. encourage the co-operation among National Accreditation Bodies and National Metrology Institutes (NMIs) including relevant legal metrology authorities in ASEAN to facilitate the implementation of Mutual Recognition Arrangements (MRAs) in regulated and non-regulated sectors.

3. To facilitate the free movement of goods within ASEAN, Member States shall develop and implement a Marking Scheme, where appropriate, for products covered under the ASEAN Harmonized Regulatory Regimes or Directives.

Article 74
Standards

1. Each Member State undertakes that its national standards authorities accept and follow the Code of Good Practice for the Preparation, Adoption and Application of Standards as provided for in Annex 3 of the Agreement on Technical Barriers to Trade as contained in Annex 1A to the WTO Agreement.
2. In harmonizing national standards, Member States shall, as the first and preferred option, adopt the relevant international standards when preparing new national standards or revising existing standards. Where international standards are not available, national standards shall be aligned among Member States.
3. Member States are encouraged to actively participate in the development of international standards, particularly in those sectors that have trade potential for ASEAN.
4. Harmonization of the existing national standards and adoption of international standards into new national standards should be based on "Adoption of International Standards as Regional or National Standards", as contained in the ISO/IEC Guide 21 or its latest edition.
5. Whenever modifications of contents and structure of the relevant international standards are necessary, Member States shall ensure an easy comparison of the contents and structure of their national standards with the referenced

international standards and provide information to explain the reason(s) for such modifications.

6. Member States shall ensure that:

   a. the modifications of contents of international standards are not prepared and adopted with a view to, or with the effect of, creating unnecessary technical barriers to trade; and
   b. the modifications of contents shall not be more restrictive than necessary.

Article 75
Technical Regulations

1. In adopting technical regulations, Member States shall ensure that:

   a. these are not adopted with a view, to or with the effect of, creating technical barriers to trade;
   b. these are based on international or national standards that are harmonized to international standards, except where legitimate reasons for deviations exist;
   c. alternative means that are least trade restrictive to achieve the desired objectives are considered before a decision is taken on the adoption of technical regulations;
   d. the adoption of prescriptive standards is avoided to ensure that unnecessary obstacles to trade are not introduced, to enhance fair competition in the market or that it does not lead to a reduction of business flexibility; and
   e. treatment accorded to products imported from Member States is no less favorable than that accorded to like products of national origin and to like products originating from any other Member State.

2. Member States shall ensure that only those parts of a standard that represent minimum requirements to fulfill the desired objectives are referred to in the technical regulations.
3. Member States shall also ensure that, wherever applicable, the preparation, adoption and application of technical regulations are to facilitate the implementation of the respective ASEAN Sectoral Mutual Recognition Arrangements.
4. Whenever the need for technical regulations is urgent for overcoming problems that arise or threaten to arise within the territory of a Member State and the available time does not allow such Member State to harmonize the relevant national standards, that Member State shall consider using the appropriate international standards or the relevant parts of them as the first alternative.
5. Member States shall comply with the notification procedures as stipulated in Article 11. However, in the case of technical regulations under this Article, other Member States shall present their comments, if any, within sixty (60) days of the notification. Member States shall, upon request, provide to other Member States the draft of the technical regulation and other information regarding the deviations from the relevant international standards and the applicable pre-market conformity assessment procedure.

6. Except in urgent circumstances, Member States shall allow at least six (6) months between the publication of technical regulations and their entry into force in order to provide sufficient time for producers in exporting Member States to adapt their products or methods of production to the requirements of importing Member States.

Article 76
Conformity Assessment Procedures

1. Member States shall ensure that conformity assessment procedures are not prepared, adopted or applied with a view to, or with the effect of, creating unnecessary technical barriers to trade and that conformity assessment procedures that have to be complied with by suppliers of products originating in the territories of other Member States are not more stringent than those accorded to suppliers of like products of national origin.
2. Member States shall adopt conformity assessment procedures that are consistent with international standards and practices and wherever such procedures cannot be achieved because of differences in legitimate objectives, the differences of conformity assessment procedures shall be minimized as far as possible.
3. Member States shall develop and implement ASEAN Sectoral Mutual Recognition Arrangement in the regulated areas, where appropriate, in accordance with the provisions of the ASEAN Framework Agreement on Mutual Recognition Arrangements.
4. Member States shall accept the results of conformity assessment produced by conformity assessment bodies designated by other Member States in accordance with the provisions of the ASEAN Framework Agreement on Mutual Recognition Arrangements and the provisions of the respective ASEAN Sectoral Mutual Recognition Arrangements in all regulated areas.
5. Member States shall establish co-operation among National Accreditation Bodies and National Metrology Institutes (NMIs), including legal metrology in ASEAN to facilitate the implementation of MRAs in regulated and non-regulated sectors.

Article 77
Post Market Surveillance

1. Member States shall establish post market surveillance systems to complement the implementation of the ASEAN Sectoral Mutual Recognition Arrangements and ASEAN Harmonized Regulatory Regimes and/or Directives.
2. The relevant authority that undertakes the post market surveillance system of the Member States shall take the necessary actions to ensure compliance of products placed in the market with the applicable ASEAN Sectoral Mutual Recognition Arrangements and ASEAN Harmonized Regulatory Regimes and/or Directives.
3. Member States should ensure that the necessary laws and technical infrastructure are in place to support post market surveillance systems.

4. The effectiveness of the post market surveillance systems shall be further enhanced through the establishment of Alert Systems among Member States.

Article 78
Implementation

1. Member States shall take all necessary measures to ensure implementation of all the ASEAN Sectoral Mutual Recognition Arrangements, ASEAN Harmonized Regulatory Regimes and the relevant provisions of this Agreement within the time frame stipulated in the aforesaid agreements and to ensure compliance with aforesaid harmonized requirements.
2. The following instruments, and any future instruments agreed by Member States to implement the provisions of this Agreement, shall form an integral part of this Agreement:

   a. ASEAN Framework Agreement on Mutual Recognition Arrangements;
   b. ASEAN Sectoral Mutual Recognition Arrangement for Electrical and Electronic Equipment;
   c. Agreement on the ASEAN Harmonized Electrical and Electronic Equipment (EEE) Regulatory Regime; and
   d. Agreement on the ASEAN Harmonized Cosmetic Regulatory Scheme.

3. The ASEAN Consultative Committee for Standards and Quality (ACCSQ) shall be responsible for:

   a. identifying and initiating sectoral MRAs;
   b. monitoring the effective implementation of the relevant provisions of this Agreement in respect of standards, technical regulations and conformity assessment procedures;
   c. providing support to the respective Joint Sectoral Committees when required; and
   d. collaborating with the ASEAN Secretariat to provide regular feedback on the implementation of this Agreement.

4. The ACCSQ shall provide support and co-operation under the relevant ASEAN Free Trade Agreements (FTAs) with Dialogue Partners, including capacity building and institutional strengthening programs for Standards, Technical Regulations and Conformity Assessment Procedures Chapters in such ASEAN FTAs.
5. The ACCSQ shall take the necessary actions to ensure effective implementation of the ASEAN Sectoral Mutual Recognition Arrangements and ASEAN Harmonized Regulatory Regimes.

Chapter 8. Sanitary and Phytosanitary Measures

Article 79
Objectives

The objectives of this chapter are to:

a. facilitate trade between and among Member States while protecting human, animal or plant life or health in each Member State;
b. provide a framework and guidelines on requirements in the application of sanitary and phytosanitary measures among Member States, particularly to achieve commitments set forth in the ASEAN Economic Community Blueprint;
c. strengthen co-operation among Member States in protecting human, animal or plant life or health; and
d. facilitate and strengthen implementation of this chapter in accordance with the principles and disciplines in the Agreement on the Application of Sanitary and Phytosanitary Measures contained in Annex 1A to the WTO Agreement and this Agreement.

Article 80
Definitions

For the purposes of this chapter:

a. **international standards, guidelines and recommendations** shall have the same meaning as in Annex A of paragraph 3 to the SPS Agreement;
b. **sanitary or phytosanitary measures** shall have the same meaning as in Annex A of paragraph 1 to the SPS Agreement; and
c. **SPS Agreement** means the Agreement on the Application of Sanitary and Phytosanitary Measures contained in Annex 1A to the WTO Agreement.

Article 81
General Provisions and Obligations

1. The provisions of this chapter apply to all sanitary and phytosanitary measures of a Member State that may, directly or indirectly, affect trade between and among Member States.
2. Member States affirm their rights and obligations with respect to each other under the SPS Agreement.
3. Each Member State commits to apply the principles of the SPS Agreement in the development, application or recognition of any sanitary or phytosanitary measures with the intent to facilitate trade between and among Member States while protecting human, animal or plant life or health in each Member State.
4. In the implementation of their sanitary or phytosanitary measures, Member States agree to be guided, where applicable, by relevant international standards, guidelines and recommendations developed by international organizations such as, the Codex Alimentarius Commission (Codex), the World Organization for

Animal Health (OIE), the International Plant Protection Convention (IPPC) and ASEAN.

5. Member States hereby agree that the laws, regulations, and procedures for application of SPS measures in their respective territories shall be listed in Annex 9, which form an integral part of this Agreement. Member States hereby agree to ensure that their respective national sanitary and phytosanitary laws, regulations and procedures as listed in Annex 9 are readily available and accessible to any interested Member States.
6. Any change to national sanitary and phytosanitary laws, regulations and procedures shall be subject to Article 11.

Article 82
Implementation and Institutional Arrangements

1. For effective implementation of this chapter, an ASEAN Committee on Sanitary and Phytosanitary Measures (AC-SPS) shall be established to conduct committee meetings at least once a year among Member States.
2. The functions of the AC-SPS shall be to:

   a. facilitate exchange of information on such matters as occurrences of sanitary or phytosanitary incidents in the Member States and non-Member States, and change or introduction of sanitary and phytosanitary-related regulations and standards of the Member States, which may, directly or indirectly, affect trade between and among Member States;
   b. facilitate co-operation in the area of sanitary or phytosanitary measures including capacity building, technical assistance and exchange of experts, subject to the availability of appropriated funds and the applicable laws and regulations of each Member State;
   c. endeavor to resolve sanitary and phytosanitary matters with a view to facilitate trade between and among Member States. The AC-SPS may establish ad hoc task force to undertake science-based consultations to identify and address specific issues that may arise from the application of sanitary or phytosanitary measures; and
   d. submit regular reports of developments and recommendations in the implementation of this Chapter to the AFTA Council, through SEOM for further action.

3. Each Member State shall establish a contact point for effective communication and co-operation. The list of respective designated contact points appears in Annex 10.
4. Each Member State shall ensure the information in Annex 10 is updated.

Article 83
Notification under Emergency Situation

1. Each Member State acknowledges the value of exchanging information, particularly in an emergency situation on food safety crisis, interception, control of pests and/or disease outbreaks and its sanitary or phytosanitary measures.

2. Member States shall immediately notify all contact points and the ASEAN Secretariat should the following situations occur:

   a. in case of food safety crisis, pest or disease outbreaks; and
   b. provisional sanitary or phytosanitary measures against or affecting the exports of the other Member States are considered necessary to protect the human, animal or plant life or health of the importing Member State.

3. The exporting Member State should, to the extent possible, endeavor to provide information to the importing Member State if the exporting Member State identifies that an export consignment which may be associated with a significant sanitary or phytosanitary risk has been exported.

Article 84
Equivalence

1. Each Member State shall initiate and further strengthen cooperation on equivalence in accordance with the SPS Agreement and relevant international standards, guidelines and recommendations, in order to facilitate trade between and among the Member States.
2. To facilitate trade, Member States may develop equivalence arrangements and recommend equivalence decisions, in particular in accordance with Article 4 of the SPS Agreement and with the guidance provided by the relevant international and regional standard setting bodies namely Codex, OIE, IPPC and ASEAN and by the Committee on Sanitary and Phytosanitary Measures established in accordance with Article 12 of the SPS Agreement.
3. Each Member State shall, upon request, enter into consultations with the aim of achieving bilateral and/or regional recognition arrangements of the equivalence of specified sanitary or phytosanitary measures.

Article 85
Co-operation

1. Each Member State shall explore opportunities for further cooperation, technical assistance, collaboration and information exchange with other Member States on sanitary and phytosanitary matters of mutual interest consistent with the objectives of this Chapter and the commitments set forth in the ASEAN Economic Community Blueprint.
2. Member States shall further strengthen co-operation for the control and eradication of pests and disease outbreaks, and other emergency cases related to sanitary or phytosanitary measures as well as to assist other Member States to comply with SPS requirements.
3. In implementing the provisions of paragraph 1 of this Article, Member States shall co-ordinate their undertakings with the activities conducted in the regional and multilateral context, with the objectives of avoiding unnecessary duplication and maximizing efficiency of efforts of the Member States in this field.

4. Any two (2) Member States may, by mutual agreement, cooperate on adaptation to regional conditions including the concept of pests and disease-free areas and areas of low pests or disease prevalence, in accordance with the SPS Agreement and relevant international standards, guidelines and recommendations, in order to facilitate trade between the Member States.

Chapter 9. Trade Remedy Measures

Article 86
Safeguard Measures

Each Member State which is a WTO member retains its rights and obligations under Article XIX of GATT 1994, and the Agreement on Safeguards or Article 5 of the Agreement on Agriculture.

Article 87
Anti-dumping and Countervailing Duties

1. Member States affirm their rights and obligations with respect to each other relating to the application of anti-dumping under Article VI of GATT 1994 and the Agreement on Implementation of Article VI of General Agreement on Tariffs and Trade 1994 as contained in Annex 1A to the WTO Agreement.
2. Member States affirm their rights and obligations with respect to each other relating to subsidies and countervailing measures under Article XVI of GATT 1994 and the Agreement on Subsidies and Countervailing Measures as contained in Annex 1A to the WTO Agreement.

Chapter 10. Institutional Provisions

Article 88
Advisory and Consultative Mechanism

The ASEAN Consultations to Solve Trade and Investment Issues (ACT) and the ASEAN Compliance Monitoring Body (ACB) as contained in the Declaration on ASEAN Concord II (Bali Concord II) may be invoked to settle disputes that may arise from this Agreement. Any Member State who does not wish to avail of the ACT/ACB may resort to the mechanism provided in the ASEAN Protocol on Enhanced Dispute Settlement Mechanism.

Article 89
Dispute Settlement

The ASEAN Protocol on Enhanced Dispute Settlement Mechanism, signed on 29 November 2004 in Vientiane, Lao PDR and amendments thereto, shall apply in relation to any dispute arising from, or any difference between Member States concerning the interpretation or application of this Agreement.

Article 90
Institutional Arrangements

1. The ASEAN Economic Ministers (AEM) shall, for the purposes of this Agreement, establish an ASEAN Free Trade Area (AFTA) Council comprising one (1) ministerial-level nominee from each Member State and the Secretary-General of ASEAN. In the performance of its functions, the AFTA Council shall also be supported by the Senior Economic Officials' Meeting (SEOM). In the fulfilment of its functions, the SEOM may establish bodies, as appropriate, to assist them such as the Coordinating Committee on the implementation of ATIGA (CCA). The SEOM, assisted by the CCA, shall ensure the effective implementation of this Agreement and, shall coordinate and be supported by technical bodies and committees under this Agreement.
2. Each Member State shall establish a National AFTA Unit, which shall serve a national focal point for the coordination of the implementation of this Agreement.
3. The ASEAN Secretariat shall:
    a. provide support to the AEM and AFTA Council in supervising, coordinating and reviewing the implementation of this Agreement as well as assistance in all related matters; and
    b. monitor and regularly report to the AFTA Council on the progress in the implementation of this Agreement.

Chapter 11. Final Provisions

Article 91
Relation to Other Agreements

1. Subject to paragraph 2 of this Article, all ASEAN economic agreements that exist before the entry into force of ATIGA shall continue to be valid.
2. Member States shall agree on the list of agreements to be superseded within six (6) months from the date of entry into force and such list shall be administratively annexed to this Agreement and serve as an integral part of this Agreement.

3. In case of inconsistency between this Agreement and any ASEAN economic agreements that are not superseded under paragraph 2 of this Article, this Agreement shall prevail.

Article 92
Amended or Successor International Agreements

If any international agreement or a provision therein referred to, or incorporated into, this Agreement, and such agreement or provision is amended, the Member States shall consult on whether it is necessary to amend this Agreement, unless this Agreement provides otherwise.

Article 93
Annexes, Attachments and Future Instruments

1. The Annexes and Attachments to this Agreement shall form an integral part of this Agreement.
2. Member States may adopt legal instruments in the future pursuant to the provisions of this Agreement. Upon their respective entry into force, such instruments shall form part of this Agreement.

Article 94
Amendments

1. The provisions of this Agreement may be modified through amendments mutually agreed upon in writing by the Member States.
2. Notwithstanding paragraph 1 of this Article, the Annexes and Attachments to this Agreement may be modified through amendments endorsed by the AFTA Council. The said amendments shall be administratively annexed to this Agreement and serve as an integral part of this Agreement.

Article 95
Review

The AFTA Council or their designated representatives shall meet within one (1) year of the date of entry into force of this Agreement and then every two (2) years or otherwise as appropriate to review this Agreement for the purpose of fulfilling the objective of this Agreement.

Article 96
Entry into Force

1. This Agreement shall be signed by the ASEAN Economic Ministers.
2. This Agreement shall enter into force, after all Member States have notified or, where necessary, deposited instruments of ratifications with the Secretary-General of ASEAN upon completion of their internal procedures, which shall not take more than one hundred and eighty (180) days after the signing of this Agreement.

3. The Secretary-General of ASEAN shall promptly notify all Member States of the notifications or deposit of each instrument of ratification referred to in paragraph 2 of this Article.

Article 97
Reservations

No reservations shall be made with respect to any of the provisions of this Agreement.

Article 98
Depositary

This Agreement shall be deposited with the Secretary-General of ASEAN who shall promptly furnish a certified copy thereof to each Member State.

In Witness Whereof, the undersigned, being duly authorized thereto by their respective Governments, have signed the ASEAN Trade in Goods Agreement.

Done at Cha-am, Thailand, this Twenty Sixth Day of February in the Year Two Thousand and Nine, in a single original copy in the English language.

For the Government of Brunei Darussalam, **Lim Jock Seng**, Second Minister of Foreign Affairs and Trade
For the Royal Government of Cambodia, **Cham Pradish**, Senior Minister and Minister of Commerce
For the Government of the Republic of Indonesia, **Mari Elka Pangestu**, Minister of Trade
For the Government of the Lao People's Democratic Republic, **Nam Viyaketh**, Minister of Industry and Commerce
For the Government of Malaysia, **Muhyiddin Bin Mohammad Yassin**, Minister of International Trade and Industry
For the Government of the Union of Myanmar, **U. Soe Tha**, Minister for National Planning and Economic Development
For the Government of the Republic of Philippines, **Peter B. Favila**, Secretary of Trade and Industry
For the Government of the Republic of Singapore, **Lim Hng Kiang**, Minister for Trade and Industry
For the Government of the Kingdom of Thailand
For the Goverment of the Socialist Republic of Vietnam, **Vu Huy Hoang**, Minister of Industry and Trade.

ASEAN Petroleum Security Agreement

2009: Signed by the Foreign Ministers at the 14th ASEAN Summit in Cha-am, Thailand on 1st March 2009

The Governments of Brunei Darussalam, the Kingdom of Cambodia, the Republic of Indonesia, Lao People's Democratic Republic (Lao PDR), Malaysia, the Union of Myanmar, the Republic of the Philippines, the Republic of Singapore, the Kingdom of Thailand and the Socialist Republic of Viet Nam being members of the Association of Southeast Asian Nations, hereinafter refer to collectively as "ASEAN" or "ASEAN Member States", or individually, as "ASEAN Member State":

Recalling the Agreement on ASEAN Energy Cooperation signed in Manila, Philippines, on 24th June 1986, which emphasized co-operation among the ASEAN Member States in developing energy resources to strengthen the economic resilience of the individual ASEAN Member States as well as solidarity and integrity of ASEAN;

Noting the ASEAN Petroleum Security Agreement (APSA) 1986 signed in Manila, Philippines, on 24th June 1986, which established the ASEAN Emergency Petroleum Sharing Scheme for crude oil and/or petroleum products in times or circumstances of both shortages and oversupply;

Recalling further the Protocol Amending the Agreement on ASEAN Energy Cooperation signed in Bangkok, Thailand on 15th December 1995, which provided for focused energy co-operation in ASEAN to pursue cooperative activities in various areas of energy;

Realising that energy security and self-sufficiency can be achieved through national and multinational efforts geared towards indigenous energy resource exploration, development, exploitation, distribution and transportation, and undertaken in a manner that both conserve the resources and preserve the environment and human habitat;

Noting further that the importance of ASEAN energy co-operation was further underscored in the Bangkok Summit Declaration of 1995, which states that ASEAN

L. Riccardi and G. Riccardi, *Invest in ASEAN*,
https://doi.org/10.1007/978-981-15-5378-3_10

shall ensure greater security and sustainability of energy through diversification, development and conservation of resources, the efficient use of energy, and the wider application of environmentally-sound technologies; and as reinforced in the ASEAN Second Informal Summit on 15th December 1997 in Kuala Lumpur, Malaysia, calling for cooperative activities aimed at establishing interconnecting arrangements for power and natural gas, among others, within ASEAN Power Grid (APG) and Trans-ASEAN Gas Pipeline (TAGP) Project;
Aware that the development of the APG and the TAGP Project are two important Energy Programs in the Hanoi Plan of Action endorsed by the ASEAN Heads of Government on 16th December 1988, the ASEAN Plan of Action for Energy Cooperation (APAEC) 1999–2004 adopted by the 17th ASEAN Ministers on Energy Meeting (AMEM) in Bangkok, Thailand on 3rd July 1999, and the APAEC 2004–2009 further adopted by the 22nd AMEM in Manila, Philippines on 9th June 2004, which had entrusted the responsibility of implementing the ASEAN Power Grid to the ASEAN Heads of Power Utilities and Authorities (HAPUA) and TAGP to the ASEAN Council on Petroleum (ASCOPE) through the auspices of the ASEAN Energy Ministers;
Mindful that ASEAN is increasingly becoming more dependent on petroleum resources outside the region, there is a need to recognize, coordinate and rationalize these efforts, plans and programs to enhance security of petroleum supply for ASEAN Member States;
Aware of the future threats and risks to the ASEAN security of petroleum supply coupled with the fact that some ASEAN Member States, which are now net oil exporters will in the near future become net oil importers with high dependence on petroleum resources outside the region, particularly the Middle East;
Also Aware that the ability to respond to an energy emergency situation in the ASEAN Member States can be greatly enhanced by ensuring the physical availability of oil and oil products through the establishment of stockpiles on voluntary and commercial basis;
Further Aware of the changes in global energy market landscape, including but not limited to deregulation and liberalization, and the increasing global concerns on environmental issues;
Noting that ASEAN energy security is the key to economic resilience and that the ASEAN Vision 2020 and the ASEAN Energy Co-operation were conceived in view of such consideration;
Realising that a review of the APSA among ASEAN Member States is necessary to further strengthen the economic resilience of the individual ASEAN Member State as well as the solidarity and integrity of ASEAN;
Have Agreed on the following.

Article 1
Objective

The objective of this Agreement is to enhance petroleum security, either individually or collectively, and minimize exposure to an emergency situation, through the implementation of short, medium and long term measures as hereinafter provided.

Article 2
Definition

For the purposes of this Agreement, the following definitions shall apply unless the context otherwise requires:

1.1 "ASEAN Member State in Distress" refers to an ASEAN Member State that had given appropriate notice to the ASCOPE Secretariat of the occurrence of a critical shortage due to an emergency situation that undermines energy security;
1.2 "Coordinated Emergency Response Measures" means the Coordinated Emergency Response Measures annexed as a Schedule to this Agreement and hereinafter referred to as "CERM";
1.3 "Critical Shortage" refers to the situation when an ASEAN Member State in Distress is experiencing a shortfall of at least ten percent (10%) of the Normal Domestic Requirement for a continuous period of at least 30 days;
1.4 "Crude Oil" means oil extracted from bituminous shales and other rock formations before any such oil has been refined or otherwise treated and includes all natural Gas Liquids and Condensates from Natural Gas;
1.5 "Emergency Situation" refers to a situation when an ASEAN Member State is faced with Critical Shortage in petroleum supply due to natural calamity (such as earthquake and tsunami), explosion of facilities or war only;
1.6 "Natural Gas" means a mixture of hydrocarbons and varying quantities of non-hydrocarbons that exist either in the gaseous phase or in association with Crude Oil in natural underground reservoirs and is classified as either Associated Gas or Non-Associated Gas;
1.7 "Normal Domestic Requirement" refers to the daily average domestic petroleum consumption over the twelve (12) months period immediately preceding the occurrence of the emergency situation;
1.8 "Oil Stockpile" refers to strategic crude oil and petroleum products stored in ground level storage tanks or underground storage tanks to be used for both operational and strategic reasons, and
1.9 "Petroleum" refers to crude oils, products and natural gas in its natural condition.

Article 3
Strategic Options to Enhance Petroleum Security

1.1 The ASEAN Member States shall endeavor to implement short, medium and long-term measures to minimize the exposure to emergency situation.
1.2 Short term measures

   a. The ASEAN Member States shall endeavor to establish the following short-term measures:

      i. ASEAN Member State in Distress Emergency Response to Petroleum Supply Disruption

1. During the critical shortage period, the ASEAN Member State in Distress will implement short-term measures to reduce the demand of its Normal Domestic Requirement before requesting assistance under the CERM.
2. Such emergency response may include, amongst others, Demand Restraint (recognizing the diversity and sovereignty of each ASEAN Member State), Fuel Switching, Surge Protection and Information Sharing/e-trading;

b. Coordinated Emergency Response Measures (CERM)

i. All ASEAN Member States shall endeavor to supply petroleum to the ASEAN Member State in Distress at the aggregate amount equal to ten percent (10%) of the Normal Domestic Requirement of the ASEAN Member State in Distress based on the terms and conditions to be negotiated among the appropriate parties in the spirit of assistance and no undue advantage shall be taken by the ASEAN Member States concerned;
ii. The assistance rendered under CERM shall be on a voluntary and commercial basis, and
iii. The details of the mechanism for the operationalization of the CERM are set out in the Annex to this Agreement.

1.3 Medium- and long-term measures

1.3.1 The ASEAN Member States shall endeavor to adopt the following as medium and long-term measures taking into account the ASEAN Member States' own supply situation, commitments and reliance on petroleum:

a. ASEAN Energy Co-operation, which includes APG, TAGP, Regional Energy Policy and Planning (REPP), Coal, Renewable Energy, Energy Efficiency and Conservation;
b. Exploring for new petroleum resources, whereby interested or relevant parties of the ASEAN Member States may endeavor to participate on a commercial and voluntary basis in joint ventures to explore and develop petroleum resources particularly in deep water and new frontier areas, both globally and regionally;
c. Energy Diversification and Improvement of Energy Efficiency include leveraging on the APG and TAGP, Fuel Switching to other alternative energy, joint Research Development & Demonstration (RD & D) in Renewable Energy, Energy Efficiency and New Energy Technologies;
d. Diversification of energy supply sources, whereby ASEAN Member States are to reduce the dependence on import from a single petroleum source;

e. Oil and Gas markets liberalization, whereby ASEAN Member States recognize that the deregulation and liberalization of petroleum industry would enhance the petroleum security by allowing more players into the playing field; and
f. Oil Stockpiling, whether individually or jointly by ASEAN Member States, shall be on a voluntary and commercial basis. The joint stockpiling may be commenced by ASEAN Member States who are ready and willing to make the commitments and cooperation.

Article 4
International Cooperation

ASEAN Member States shall endeavor to participate in international dialogues to enhance ASEAN's energy and/or petroleum security with ASEAN Dialogue Partners and relevant international organizations.

During periods of petroleum shortages and emergencies affecting the whole ASEAN region, the ASCOPE Secretary In Charge shall support any mechanism formalized pursuant to the 22nd AMEM in Manila, Philippines on 9 June 2004, on regional consultation and coordination.

Article 5
Institutional Framework for the CERM

1.1 The ASEAN Member States shall establish:

- 1.1.1 a Governing Board as the main policy making body for the CERM, which shall comprise one or more Ministers or their designated representatives from each ASEAN Member State.
- 1.1.2 a Management Committee which shall carry out the functions in accordance with the CERM assigned to it by the Governing Board; examine and make proposals to the Governing Board on matters related to the CERM and shall be composed of one or more senior representatives of the Government of each ASEAN Member State.
- 1.1.3 a Coordinating Agency to liaise with ASCOPE Secretariat and the Executing Agencies of ASEAN Member States for immediate assistance to activate the CERM to assist the ASEAN Member State in Distress.

1.2 The ASCOPE Secretariat shall be the designated institution to coordinate the implementation of the CERM.
1.3 The meetings of the Governing Board and Management Committee shall be called by the ASCOPE Secretariat.
1.4 The Governing Board shall appoint the Industry Advisory Group as and when necessary which shall compose of Senior Members of the Oil Companies of each ASEAN Member State.

Article 6
Settlement for Disputes

1.1 Any differences between the ASEAN Member States concerning the interpretation or application of this Agreement or any arrangements arising therefrom shall, as far as possible, be settled amicably between those ASEAN Member States.
1.2 In case the consultation referred to in Article 6.1 fails to settle the dispute within a period of 30 days or a period agreed between those ASEAN Member States, the matter shall be settled in accordance with the ASEAN Protocol on Enhanced Dispute Settlement Mechanism signed in Vientiane Lao PDR on 29th November 2004.

Article 7
Final Provisions

1.1 This Agreement shall be deposited with the Secretary-General of ASEAN who shall promptly furnish a certified true copy to each ASEAN Member State.
1.2 This Agreement is subject to ratification or acceptance by all the ASEAN Member States. The Instrument of Ratification or Acceptance shall be deposited with the Secretary-General of ASEAN who shall promptly inform each ASEAN Member State of such deposit.
1.3 This Agreement shall enter into force on the thirtieth (30th) day after the deposit of the tenth (10th) Instrument of Ratification or Acceptance.
1.4 No reservations may be made to this Agreement either at the time of signature or ratification or acceptance.
1.5 The Annex on CERM shall constitute an integral part of this Agreement.
1.6 Any amendment to the provisions of this Agreement and its Schedule on the Mechanism for the Operationalization of the CERM shall be effected by consent of all the ASEAN Member States and shall become effective on a mutually agreed date.
1.7 This Agreement shall supersede the ASEAN Petroleum Security Agreement signed on 24th June 1986 in Manila, Philippines.
1.8 This Agreement shall remain in force for a period of ten (10) years, unless terminated earlier by agreement of all the ASEAN Member States. The expiry or termination of this Agreement shall be without prejudice to the rights and obligations of the ASEAN Member States arising from this Agreement prior to the effective date of expiry or termination of this Agreement.
1.9 An ASEAN Member State may at any time give notice of its intention to withdraw from this Agreement, by giving written notice to the Secretary-General of ASEAN, who shall immediately notify all other ASEAN Member States. Such withdrawal shall take effect six (6) months from the date of the said notice.

1.10 This Agreement may be extended beyond its period of validity, as stipulated in paragraph 7.8 of this Article, with the agreement of all ASEAN Member States.

1.11 Any ASEAN Member State may propose any amendment to the provisions of this Agreement. Such amendment shall be effected by written consent of all the ASEAN Member States. Any amendment to this Agreement shall be without prejudice to the rights and obligations of the ASEAN Member States, prior to the effective date of such amendment.

In Witness Whereof, the undersigned, being duly authorized thereto by their respective Governments, have signed this ASEAN Petroleum Security Agreement.

Done at Cha-am, Thailand, this First Day of March in the Year Two Thousand and Nine, in a single original copy in the English Language.

For Brunei Darussalam, **Mohamed Bolkiah**, Minister of Foreign Affairs and Trade
For the Kingdom of Cambodia, **Hor Namhong**, Deputy Prime Minister and Minister of Foreign Affairs and International Cooperation
For the Republic of Indonesia, **Dr. N. Hassan Wirajuda**, Minister for Foreign Affairs
For the Lao People's Democratic Republic, **Dr. Thongloun Sisoulith**, Deputy Prime Minister and Minister of Foreign Affairs
For Malaysia, **Dr. Rais Yatim**, Minister of Foreign Affairs
For the Union of Myanmar, **Nyan Win**, Minister for Foreign Affairs
For the Republic of the Philippines, **Alberto G. Romulo**, Secretary of Foreign Affairs
For the Republic of Singapore, **George Yong-Boon Yeo**, Minister for Foreign Affairs
For the Kingdom of Thailand, **Wannarat Channukul**, Minister of Energy
For the Socialist Republic of Vietnam, **Vu Huy Hoang**, Minister of Industry and Trade.

ASEAN Multilateral Agreement on Air Services

2009: Adopted by the Transport Ministers of ASEAN Member States at the 14th ASEAN Transport Ministers Meeting in Manila, Philippines on 20th May 2009

Governments of Brunei Darussalam, the Kingdom of Cambodia, the Republic of Indonesia, the Lao People's Democratic Republic (hereinafter referred as "Lao PDR"), Malaysia, the Union of Myanmar, the Republic of the Philippines, the Republic of Singapore, the Kingdom of Thailand and the Socialist Republic of Viet Nam, Member States of the Association of Southeast Asian Nations (ASEAN) (hereinafter collectively referred to as "Contracting Parties" or individually as "Contracting Party"):

Recalling the Declaration of ASEAN Concord II (Bali Concord II) issued in Bali, Indonesia on 7 October 2003, pursuant to which ASEAN is committed to deepen and broaden its internal economic integration and linkages with the world economy to realize an ASEAN Economic Community;

Affirming the policy agenda for progressive implementation of full liberalization and integration of air services in ASEAN as laid down in the Action Plan for ASEAN Air Transport Integration and Liberalization adopted at the Tenth (10th) ASEAN Transport Ministers' (ATM) Meeting on 23 November 2004 in Phnom Penh, Cambodia;

Recalling the Vientiane Action Program adopted at the Tenth (10th) ASEAN Summit on 29 November 2004 in Vientiane, Lao PDR, which calls for accelerating open sky arrangements and advancing liberalization in air transport services;

Recalling also the decision of the Tenth (10th) ATM Meeting in Phnom Penh, Cambodia, on 23 November 2004 to adopt the Roadmap for Integration of Air Travel Sector and the Action Plan for ASEAN Air Transport Integration and Liberalization 2005-2015, which provides strategic actions to further liberalize air services in ASEAN and promotes an enabling environment for a single and unified aviation market in ASEAN;

Being committed to maintain, further develop and strengthen friendly relations and cooperation between and among their countries;

L. Riccardi and G. Riccardi, *Invest in ASEAN*,
https://doi.org/10.1007/978-981-15-5378-3_11

Recognising that efficient and competitive international air services are important to develop trade, benefit consumers, and promote economic growth;
Desiring to ensure the highest degree of safety and security in international air transport and reaffirm their grave concern about acts or threats against the security of aircraft, which jeopardize the safety of persons or property, adversely affect the operation of air transportation, and undermine public confidence in the safety of civil aviation;
Desiring to facilitate and enhance air services and their related activities, to complement the other transport facilitation and liberalization efforts in ASEAN;
Desiring to remove restrictions, on a gradual basis, so as to achieve greater flexibility and capacity in the operation of air services in ASEAN with a view to build a single unified aviation market of ASEAN by 2015;
Being Parties to the Convention on International Civil Aviation, opened for signature at Chicago on 7 December 1944, and desiring to adhere to the principles and provisions of the aforesaid Convention; and
Desiring to conclude a Multilateral Agreement on Air Services.
Have Agreed as follows.

Article 1
Definitions

For the purpose of this Agreement only, unless the context otherwise requires:

1. The term "the Convention" means the Convention on International Civil Aviation opened for signature at Chicago on 7 December 1944, and includes: (i) any amendment that has entered into force under Article 94(a) of the Convention and has been ratified by all the Contracting Parties to this Agreement, and (ii) any Annex or any amendment thereto adopted under Article 90 of the Convention, insofar as such Annexes or amendments are, at any given time, effective for all the Contracting Parties to this Agreement;
2. The term "aeronautical authority" means the Minister responsible for Civil Aviation, or any person or body authorized to perform any functions at present exercisable by him or similar functions;
3. The term "designated airline" means an airline which has been designated and authorized in accordance with Article 3 (Designation and Authorization of Airlines) of this Agreement;
4. The term "territory" means the land territory, internal waters, territorial sea, archipelagic waters, the seabed and the sub-soil thereof and the airspace above them;
5. The terms "air service", "international air service", and "airline" have the meanings respectively assigned to them in Article 96 of the Convention;
6. The term "tariff" means the prices to be paid for the carriage of passengers and cargo and the conditions under which those prices apply, including prices and conditions for agency and other auxiliary services but excluding remuneration and conditions for the carriage of mail;

7. The term "specified routes" means the routes specified in the route schedule annexed to this Agreement;
8. The term "agreed services" means scheduled air services performed for the carriage of passengers, cargo and/or mail, separately or in combination, for remuneration or hire on the specified routes;
9. The term "stop for non-traffic purposes" means a landing for any purpose other than taking on or discharging passengers, cargo and/or mail in international air services;
10. The term "user charges" means a charge imposed on airlines by the competent authorities, or permitted by them to be imposed, for the provision of airport property or facilities or of air navigation facilities, including related services and facilities for aircraft, their crew, passengers and cargo;
11. The term "Agreement" means this Agreement, its Annexes and its Implementing Protocols and any amendments thereto;
12. The term "Depository" means the Secretary-General of ASEAN; and
13. All references to the singular shall include the plural, and all references to the plural shall include the singular.

Article 2
Grant of Right

1. Each Contracting Party grants to the other Contracting Parties the following rights for the conduct of international air services by the designated airlines of the other Contracting Parties:

   a. the right to fly across its territory without landing;
   b. the right to make stops in its territory for non-traffic purposes; and
   c. the rights otherwise specified in this Agreement, including those rights stated in the Annex I (Scheduled Air Transportation) and, where applicable, Annex II (the Implementing Protocols 1–6 listed) of this Agreement.

2. The airline(s) of each Contracting Party, other than those designated under Article 3 (Designation and Authorization of Airlines) of this Agreement, shall also enjoy the rights specified in paragraphs 1(a) and (b) of this Article. That airline shall be required to meet other conditions prescribed under the laws, regulations and rules normally applied to the operation of the international air services by the Contracting Party considering the application.
3. Nothing in this Agreement shall be deemed to confer on the airline or airlines of one Contracting Party the right to take on board, in the territory of another Contracting Party, passengers, baggage, cargo, or mail carried for remuneration and destined for another point in the territory of that other Contracting Party.

Article 3
Designation and Authorization of Airline

1. Each Contracting Party shall have the right to designate as many airlines as it wishes for the purpose of conducting international air services in accordance with this Agreement and to withdraw or alter such designation. Such designation

shall be transmitted in writing through diplomatic channels to the Depository who shall subsequently inform all the Contracting Parties.

2. On receipt of such a designation, and of application from the designated airline, in the form and manner prescribed for operating authorization and technical permission, each Contracting Party shall grant the appropriate authorization and technical permission with minimum procedural delay, provided that:

   i. substantial ownership and effective control of that airline are vested in the Contracting Party designating the airline, nationals of that Contracting Party, or both; or
   ii. subject to acceptance by a Contracting Party receiving such application, the designated airline which is incorporated and has its principal place of business in the territory of the Contracting Party that designates the airline, is and remains substantially owned and effectively controlled by one or more ASEAN Member States and/or its nationals, and the Contracting Party designating the airline has and maintains effective regulatory control; or
   iii. subject to acceptance by a Contracting Party receiving such application, the designated airline is incorporated in and has its principal place of business in the territory of the Contracting Party that designates the airline in which the Contracting Party designating the airline, has and maintains effective regulatory control of that airline, provided that such arrangements will not be equivalent to allowing airline(s) or its subsidiaries access to traffic rights not otherwise available to that airline(s); and

   b. the designated airline is qualified to meet other conditions prescribed under the laws, regulations and rules normally applied to the operation of international air services by the Contracting Party considering the application or applications; and
   c. the Contracting Party designating the airline is in compliance with the provisions set forth in Article 5 (Safety) and Article 6 (Aviation Security) of this Agreement.

3. The Contracting Parties granting operating authorizations in accordance with paragraph 2 of this Article shall notify such action to the Depository who will subsequently inform all the Contracting Parties.

Article 4

Withholding, Revocation, Suspension and Limitation of Authorization

1. Each Contracting Party shall have the right to withhold, revoke, suspend, impose conditions on or limit the operating authorizations or technical permission referred to in Article 3 (Designation and Authorization of Airlines) of this Agreement with respect to an airline designated by another Contracting Party, temporarily or permanently where:

   a. the airline has failed to prove that it is qualified under Article 3 paragraphs 2 (a) (i) or (ii) or (iii) as applicable; or

b. the airline has failed to comply with laws, regulations, and rules referred to in Article 14 (Application of Laws and Regulations) of this Agreement; or
c. the other Contracting Party is not maintaining and administering the standards as set forth in Article 5 (Safety) of this Agreement.

2. Unless immediate action is essential to prevent further non-compliance with paragraphs 1(b) or 1(c) of this Article, the rights established by this Article shall be exercised only after consultations with the Contracting Party designating the airline, in accordance with the provisions set forth in Article 16 (Consultations and Amendment).
3. A Contracting Party that has exercised its right to withhold, revoke, suspend, impose conditions on or limit the operating authorizations or technical permission of an airline or airlines in accordance with paragraph 1 of this Article shall notify its action to the Depository and the Depository shall subsequently inform all the Contracting Parties.
4. This Article does not limit the rights of any Contracting Party to withhold, revoke, suspend, impose conditions on or limit the operating authorizations or technical permission of an airline or airlines of the other Contracting Parties in accordance with the provisions of Article 6 (Aviation Security).

Article 5
Safety

1. Each Contracting Party shall recognize as valid, for the purpose of operating the air services provided for in this Agreement, certificates of airworthiness, certificates of competency, and licenses issued, or validated by the Contracting Party that designates that said airline and still in force, provided that the requirements for such certificates or licenses are at least equal to the minimum standards which may be established pursuant to the Convention. Each Contracting Party reserves the right, however, to refuse to recognize as valid for the purpose of flight above its own territory, certificates of competency and licenses granted to or validated for its own nationals by another Contracting Party.
2. Each Contracting Party may request consultations concerning the safety and security standards maintained by another Contracting Party relating to aeronautical facilities, air crew, aircraft, and operation of that other Contracting Party's designated airline(s). If, following such consultations, the first Contracting Party finds that the other Contracting Party does not effectively maintain and administer safety and security standards and requirements in these areas that are at least equal to the minimum standards which may be established pursuant to the Convention, the other Contracting Party shall be notified of such findings and the steps considered necessary to conform with these minimum standards; and the other Contracting Party shall take appropriate corrective action. Each Contracting Party reserves the right to withhold, revoke, suspend, impose conditions on or limit the operating authorization or technical permission of an airline or airlines designated by the other Contracting Party in the

event the other Contracting Party does not take such appropriate corrective action within a reasonable time.

Article 6
Aviation Security

1. In accordance with their rights and obligations under international law, the Contracting Parties reaffirm that their obligation to one another to protect the security of civil aviation against acts of unlawful interference forms an integral part of this Agreement. Without limiting the generality of their rights and obligations under international law, the Contracting Parties shall in particular act in conformity with the provisions of the Convention on Offences and Certain Other Acts Committed on Board Aircraft, signed at Tokyo on 14 September 1963, the Convention for the Suppression of Unlawful Seizure of Aircraft, signed at The Hague on 16 December 1970, the Convention for the Suppression of Unlawful Acts against the Safety of Civil Aviation, signed at Montreal on 23 September 1971, as well as any other convention or protocol relating to the security of civil aviation which all the Contracting Parties adhere to.
2. The Contracting Parties shall provide upon request all necessary assistance to one another to prevent acts of unlawful seizure of civil aircraft and other unlawful acts against the safety of such aircraft, their passengers and crew, and airports and air navigation facilities, and to address any other threat to the security of civil aviation.
3. The Contracting Parties shall, in their mutual relations, act in conformity with the aviation security provisions established by the International Civil Aviation Organization and designated as Annexes to the Convention; they shall require that operators of aircraft of their registry, operators of aircraft who have their principal place of business or permanent residence in their territory, and the operators of airports in their territory act in conformity with such aviation security provisions.
4. Each Contracting Party shall observe the security provisions required by the other Contracting Parties for entry into, departure from, and while within their respective territories and to take adequate measures to protect aircraft and to inspect passengers, crew, and their carry-on items, as well as cargo and aircraft stores, prior to and during loading or unloading. Each Contracting Party shall also give positive consideration to any request from another Contracting Party for special security measures to meet a particular threat.
5. When an incident or threat of an incident of unlawful seizure of civil aircraft or other unlawful acts against the safety of aircraft, passengers and crew, airports or air navigation facilities occurs, the Contracting Parties shall assist one another by facilitating communications and other appropriate measures intended to terminate rapidly and safely such incident or threat.
6. When a Contracting Party has reasonable grounds to believe that another Contracting Party has departed from the aviation security provisions of this Article, the aeronautical authorities of that Contracting Party may request immediate consultations with the aeronautical authorities of the other

Contracting Party. Failure to reach a satisfactory agreement within fifteen (15) days from the date of receipt of such request shall constitute grounds to withhold, revoke, suspend, impose conditions on or limit the operating authorization and technical permission of an airline or airlines of that Contracting Party. When required by an emergency, a Contracting Party may take interim action prior to the expiry of fifteen (15) days.

7. Each Contracting Party shall require the airline(s) of another Contracting Party providing service to that Contracting Party to submit a written operator security program which has been approved by the aeronautical authority of the Contracting Party of that airline for acceptance.

Article 7
Tariffs

1. The tariffs to be applied by the designated airline or airlines of a Contracting Party for air services covered by this Agreement shall be established at reasonable levels, due regard being paid to all relevant factors, including interests of users, cost of operation, characteristics of service, reasonable profit, tariffs of other airlines, and other commercial considerations in the market-place.
2. Tariffs charged by airlines shall not be required to be filed with, or approved, by either Contracting Party. However, in the event the national law of a Contracting Party requires prior approval of a tariff, the tariff application shall be dealt with accordingly. In such cases, the principle of reciprocity may be applied by the Contracting Parties concerned at their discretion.
3. The Contracting Parties agree to give particular attention to tariffs that may be objectionable because they appear unreasonably discriminatory, unduly high or restrictive because of the abuse of a dominant position, or artificially low because of direct or indirect governmental subsidy or support or other anti-competitive practices.
4. The Contracting Parties shall ensure that the designated airlines provide the general public with full and comprehensive information on their air fares and rates and the conditions attached in advertisements to the public concerning their fares.

Article 8
Operation of Leased Aircraft

1. When a designated airline proposes to use an aircraft other than one owned by it on the air services provided hereunder, this would only be done subject to the following conditions:

   a. that such arrangements will not be equivalent to allowing a lessor airline access to traffic rights not otherwise available to that airline;
   b. that the financial benefit to be obtained by the lessor airline will not be dependent on the profit or loss of the operation of the designated airline concerned; and

   c. that the responsibility for the continued airworthiness and the adequacy of operating and maintenance standards of any leased aircraft operated by an airline designated by one Contracting Party will be established in conformity with the Convention.

2. A designated airline is not otherwise prohibited from providing services using leased aircraft provided that any lease arrangement entered into satisfies the conditions listed in paragraph 1 of this Article.

Article 9
Commercial Activities

1. In accordance with the laws and regulations of the other Contracting Parties, the designated airline of a Contracting Party shall have the right:

   a. in relation to entry, residence and employment, to bring in and maintain in the territory of the other Contracting Parties managerial and other specialist staff, office equipment and other related equipment and promotional materials required for the operation of international air services;
   b. to establish offices in the territory of the other Contracting Party for the purposes of provision, promotion and sale of air services;
   c. to engage in the sale of air services in the territory of the other Contracting Party directly and, at its discretion, through its agents; to sell such air services, and any person shall be free to purchase such services in local currency of that territory or, subject to the national laws and regulations, in freely convertible currencies of other countries;
   d. to convert and remit to the territory of its incorporation, on demand, local revenues in excess of sums locally disbursed. Conversion and remittance shall be permitted promptly without restrictions or taxation in respect thereof at the rate of exchange applicable to current transactions and remittance on the date the airline makes the initial application for remittance. Such conversion and remittance shall be made in accordance with the foreign exchange regulations of the Contracting Party concerned; and
   e. to pay for local expenses, including purchases of fuel, in the territories of the other Contracting Parties in local currency. At their discretion, the airlines of each Contracting Party may pay for such expenses in the territory of the other Contracting Parties in freely convertible currencies according to local currency regulation.

2. In operating or holding out the authorized services on the agreed routes, the designated airline(s) may, subject to national laws and regulations and policies, enter into cooperative marketing arrangements which may include but are not limited to code-sharing or block-space with:

   a. an airline or airlines of the same Contracting Party; and
   b. an airline or airlines of the other Contracting Parties. provided that all participants in such arrangements hold the underlying traffic rights and appropriate authorization and meet the requirements applied to such arrangements.

3. The marketing airline may be required to file for approval to the aeronautical authority of each Contracting Party of any cooperative marketing arrangements entered into with an operating airline, in accordance with paragraph 2 of this Article, before its proposed introduction.
4. When holding out air services for sale, the marketing airline will make it clear to the purchaser of tickets for such services, at the point of sale, which airline will be the operating airline on each sector of the services and with which airline or airlines the purchaser is entering into a contractual relationship.

Article 10
User Charges

1. No Contracting Party shall impose or permit to be imposed on the designated airlines of another Contracting Party user charges higher than those imposed on its own airlines operating similar international air services.
2. Each Contracting Party shall encourage consultations on user charges between its competent charging authorities and airlines using the services and facilities provided by those charging authorities, where practicable through those airlines' representative organizations. Reasonable notice of any proposals for changes in user charges should be given to such users to enable them to express their views before changes are made. Each Contracting Party shall further encourage its competent charging authorities and such users to exchange appropriate information concerning user charges.

Article 11
Customs Duties

1. Each Contracting Party shall on the basis of reciprocity exempt a designated airline of another Contracting Party to the fullest extent possible under its national law from customs duties, excise taxes, inspection fees and other national duties and charges on aircraft, fuel, ground equipment, lubricating oils, consumable technical supplies, spare parts including engines, regular aircraft equipment, aircraft stores and other items, such as printed air waybills, any printed material which bears the insignia of the company printed thereon and usual publicity material distributed free of charge by that designated airline, intended for use or used solely in connection with the operation or servicing of aircraft of the designated airline of such other Contracting Party operating the agreed services.
2. The exemptions granted by this Article shall apply to the items referred to in paragraph 1:

   a. introduced into the territory of the Contracting Party by or on behalf of the designated airline of another Contracting Party;
   b. retained on board aircraft of the designated airline of one Contracting Party upon arrival in or leaving the territory of another Contracting Party; or
   c. taken on board aircraft of the designated airline of one Contracting Party in the territory of another Contracting Party and intended for use in operating

the agreed services whether or not such items are used or consumed wholly within the territory of the Contracting Party granting the exemption, provided the ownership of such items is not transferred in the territory of the said Contracting Party.

3. The regular airborne equipment, as well as the materials and supplies normally retained on board the aircraft of a designated airline of any Contracting Party, may be unloaded in the territory of another Contracting Party only with the approval of the customs authorities of that territory. In such case, they may be placed under the supervision of the said authorities up to such time as they are re-exported or otherwise disposed of in accordance with customs regulations.
4. The exemptions provided by this Article shall also be available where the designated airline(s) of one Contracting Party has contracted with another designated airline, which similarly enjoys such exemptions from another Contracting Party or Contracting Parties, for the loan or transfer in the territory of the other Contracting Party or Contracting Parties of the items specified in paragraph 1 of this Article.

Article 12
Fair Competition

Each Contracting Party agrees:

1. that each designated airline shall have a fair and equal opportunity to compete in providing the international air services governed by this Agreement; and
2. to take action to eliminate all forms of discrimination and/or anti-competitive practices by that Contracting Party and/or its designated airline(s) that it deems to adversely affect the competitive position of a designated airline of any other Contracting Party.

Article 13
Safeguards

1. The Contracting Parties agree that the following airline practices may be regarded as possible anti-competitive practices that may merit closer examination:

   a. charging fares and rates on routes at levels which are, in the aggregate, insufficient to cover the costs of providing the air services to which they relate;
   b. the addition of excessive capacity or frequency of air services;
   c. the practices in question are sustained rather than temporary;
   d. the practices in question have a serious negative economic effect on, or cause significant damage to another airline;
   e. the practices in question reflect an apparent intent or have the probable effect, of crippling, excluding or driving another airline from the market; and
   f. behavior indicating an abuse of dominant position on the route.

2. The grant of state aid and/or subsidy shall be transparent among the Contracting Parties, and shall not distort competition among the designated airlines of the Contracting Parties. The Contracting Parties concerned shall furnish other interested Contracting Parties, upon their requests, with complete information on such grant and any revision to or extension of such grant. Such information shall be treated with the utmost sensitivity and confidentiality.
3. If the aeronautical authorities of one Contracting Party consider that an operation or operations intended or conducted by the designated airline of another Contracting Party may constitute unfair competitive behavior in accordance with the indicators listed in paragraph 1, or any discrimination by means of undue state aid and/or subsidy by that other Contracting Party, they may request consultations in accordance with Article 16 (Consultations and Amendment) with a view to resolving the problem. Any such request shall be accompanied by notice of the reasons for the request, and the consultations shall begin within fifteen (15) days of the receipt of such request.
4. If the Contracting Parties fail to reach a resolution of the problem through consultations, any Contracting Party may invoke the dispute resolution mechanism under Article 17 (Settlement of Disputes) to resolve the dispute.
5. Each Contracting Party shall have the right to withhold, revoke, suspend, impose conditions on or limit the operating authorizations with respect to an airline designated by another Contracting Party temporarily, should there be reasonable ground to believe that unfair or anti-competitive practices related to paragraphs 1 and 2 of this Article committed by a Contracting Party or its designated airline seriously affect the operation of its designated airline.

Article 14
Application of Laws and Regulations

1. While entering, within, or leaving the territory of one Contracting Party, its laws, regulations and rules relating to the operation and navigation of aircraft shall be complied with by the airlines designated by any other Contracting Party. While entering, within, or leaving the territory of one Contracting Party, its laws, regulations and rules relating to the admission to or departure from its territory of passengers, crew or cargo on aircraft (including regulations relating to entry, clearance, aviation security, immigration, passports, customs and quarantine or, in the case of mail, postal regulations).
2. Shall be complied with by, or on behalf of, such passengers, crew or cargo of the airlines of any other Contracting Party.
3. Passengers, baggage and cargo in transit through the territory of any Contracting Party and not leaving the area of the airport reserved for such purpose shall not undergo any examination except for reasons of aviation security, narcotics control, prevention of illegal entry or in special circumstances.

Article 15
Statistic

The aeronautical authority of each Contracting Party shall provide the aeronautical authorities of the other Contracting Parties, upon request, with periodic statistics or other similar information relating to the traffic carried on the agreed services.

Article 16
Consultation and Amendment

1. The aeronautical authorities of the Contracting Parties shall consult with one another from time to time with a view to ensuring the implementation of, and satisfactory compliance with, the provisions of this Agreement. Unless otherwise agreed, such consultations shall begin at the earliest possible date, but not later than sixty (60) days from the date the other Contracting Party or Parties receive, through diplomatic or other appropriate channels, a written request, including an explanation of the issues to be raised. When the date for consultations has been agreed, the requesting Contracting Party shall also notify all the other Contracting Parties of the consultations and the issues to be raised. Any Contracting Party may attend. Once the consultations have been concluded, all the Contracting Parties as well as the Depository shall be notified of the results.
2. If one third of the Contracting Parties consider it desirable to amend any provision of this Agreement they shall be entitled, by request addressed to the Secretary-General of ASEAN, given not earlier than twelve (12) months after the entry into force of this Agreement, to call a meeting of all the Contracting Parties in order to consider any amendments which they may propose to this Agreement. Such amendment, if agreed among all the Contracting Parties and if necessary after consultations in accordance with paragraph 1 of this Article, shall come into effect when more than half of the Contracting Parties have deposited their Instruments of Ratification or Acceptance of such amendment.
3. In the event of the conclusion of any general multilateral convention concerning international air services by which all the Contracting Parties become bound, this Agreement shall be so modified as to conform with the provisions of such convention.

Article 17
Settlement of Disputes

The provisions of the ASEAN Protocol on Enhanced Dispute Settlement Mechanism, done at Vientiane, Lao PDR, on 29 November 2004 and any amendment thereto, shall apply to disputes arising under this Agreement.

Article 18
Relationship to Other Agreement

1. This Agreement or any actions taken thereto shall not affect the rights and obligations of the Contracting Parties under any existing agreements or

international conventions to which they are also Contracting Parties, except as provided in paragraph 3 of this Article.

2. Nothing in this Agreement shall prejudice the rights or the exercise of these rights by any Contracting Party under the provisions of the United Nations Convention on the Law of the Sea of 1982, in particular with regard to freedom of the high seas, rights of innocent passage, archipelagic sea lanes passage or transit passage of ships and aircraft, and consistent with the Charter of the United Nations.
3. In the event of any inconsistency between a provision of this Agreement and a provision of any existing bilateral or multilateral air services agreement(s) (including any amendments thereto), by which two or more of the ASEAN Member States are bound or which is not covered by this Agreement, the provision which is less restrictive or more liberal or which is not covered by this Agreement, shall prevail. If the inconsistency concerns provisions relating to safety or aviation security, the provisions prescribing a higher or more stringent standard of safety or aviation security shall prevail to the extent of the inconsistency.

Article 19
Final Provision

1. This Agreement shall be deposited with the Depository who shall promptly furnish a certified true copy thereof to each Contracting Party.
2. This Agreement is subject to ratification or acceptance by the Contracting Parties. The Instruments of Ratification or Acceptance shall be deposited with the Depository and the Depository shall promptly inform each Contracting Party of such deposit.
3. This Agreement shall enter into force on the date of the deposit of the third (3rd) Instrument of Ratification or Acceptance with the Secretary-General of ASEAN and shall become effective only among the Contracting Parties that have ratified, or accepted it.
4. Subject to paragraph 3 of this Article, the Implementing Protocols as listed in Annex II of this Agreement shall enter into force upon ratification or acceptance as set out in the "Final Provisions" of each of the respective Implementing Protocol(s). The provisions of this Agreement shall only apply in respect of the Implementing Protocol that has entered into force among the Contracting Parties that have ratified or accepted it.
5. The Depository shall maintain a centralized register of airline designations and operating authorization in accordance with Article 3 (Designation and Authorization of Airlines) of this Agreement.
6. The Depository shall register this Agreement with the International Civil Aviation Organization as soon as it enters into force.

In Witness Whereof, the undersigned, being duly authorized by their respective Governments, have signed this ASEAN Multilateral Agreement on Air Services.

Done at Manila, Philippines, this 20th day of May in the Year Two Thousand and Nine, in a single original copy in the English language.

For Brunei Darussalam, **Pehin Dato Abu Bakar Apong**, Minister of Communications
For the Kingdom of Cambodia, **Mao Havannall**, Secretary of State of Civil Aviation
For the Republic of Indonesia, **Jusman Syafii Djamal**, Minister for Transportation
For the Lao People's Democratic Republic, **Sommad Pholsena**, Minister of Public Works and Transport
For Malaysia, **Dato's Sri Ong Tee Keat**, Minister of Transport
For the Union of Myanmar, **Major General Thein Swe**, Minister for Transport
For the Republic of the Philippines, **Leandro R. Mendoza**, Secretary of Transportation and Communications
For the Republic of Singapore, **Raymond Lim**, Minister for Transport
For the Socialist Republic of Vietnam, **Ho Nghia Dzung**, Minister of Transport.

Annex I: Scheduled Air Services

Section 1 Routing

1. The designated airline(s) of each Contracting Party shall, in accordance with the terms of their designation, be allowed to operate from any points in the territory of the Contracting Party designating the airline via any intermediate points to any points in the territory of any other Contracting Party and to any points beyond in any combination or order, provided that all the points are international airports.
2. Notwithstanding the above provisions, the right to take on board or put down, in the territory of any other Contracting Party, passengers, baggage, cargo, or mail carried for remuneration and destined for or coming from points in the territory of any non-Contracting Party, shall be subject to the agreement between the aeronautical authorities of the Contracting Parties concerned.

Section 2 Operational Flexibility

1. Each designated airline may, on any or all flights and at its option:
   a) operate flights in either or both directions;
   b) combine different flight numbers within one aircraft operation;
   c) serve behind, intermediate, and beyond points and points in the territories of the Contracting Parties on the routes in any combination and in any order;
   d) omit stops at any point or points;
   e) transfer traffic from any of its aircraft to any of its other aircraft at any point on the routes; and
   f) serve points behind any point in its territory with or without change of aircraft or flight number and may hold out and advertise such services to the public as through services without directional or geographic limitation and without loss of any right to carry traffic otherwise permissible under this

Agreement; provided that the service serves a point in the territory of the Contracting Party designating the airline.

2. On any segment or segments of the routes above, any designated airline may perform international air services without any limitation as to change, at any point on the route, on an one-on-one basis (with the exception of code-sharing) provided that, in the outbound direction, the air services beyond such point is a continuation of the air services from the territory of the Contracting Party that has designated the airline and, in the inbound direction, the air services to the territory of the Contracting Party that has designated the airline is a continuation of the air services from beyond such point.
3. The designated airline(s) of each Contracting Party may be required to submit its envisaged flight schedules for approval to the aeronautical authorities of the other Contracting Party at least thirty (30) days prior to the operation of the agreed services. Any modification thereof shall be submitted for consideration at least fifteen (15) days prior to the operation.
4. For supplementary flights which the designated airline(s) of one Contracting Party wishes to operate on the agreed services outside the approved timetable, that airline must request prior permission from the aeronautical authorities of the other Contracting Party. Such requests shall usually be submitted at least four (4) working days prior to the operation of such flights.

Annex II: Implementing Protocols

The Contracting Parties shall conclude the following Implementing Protocols which shall form integral parts of this Agreement:

a) Protocol 1 Unlimited Third and Fourth Freedom Traffic Rights Within ASEAN Sub-Region;
b) Protocol 2 Unlimited Fifth Freedom Traffic Rights Within ASEAN Sub-Region;
c) Protocol 3 Unlimited Third and Fourth Freedom Traffic Rights Between ASEAN Sub-Regions;
d) Protocol 4 Unlimited Fifth Freedom Traffic Rights Between ASEAN Sub-Regions;
e) Protocol 5 Unlimited Third and Fourth Freedom Traffic Rights Between ASEAN Capital Cities; and
f) Protocol 6 Unlimited Fifth Freedom Traffic Rights Between ASEAN Capital Cities.

Framework Agreement on the Facilitation of Inter-State Transport

2009: Signed by Ministers of Transport in Manila, Philippines on 10th December 2009

Preamble

The Members of the Association of Southeast Asian Nations (hereinafter referred to as **Contracting Parties**):

Recognising the importance of facilitating inter-state transport of goods to support greater trade and bring about closer economic integration;

Noting that nations in the region have taken steps bilaterally and multilaterally to facilitate inter-state transport;

Recalling ASEAN Transport Action Plan 2005–2010 with a policy direction to operationalize the ASEAN Framework Agreements on the Facilitation of Goods in Transit, Inter-State Transport and Multimodal Transport in order to create an integrated and efficient logistics and multimodal transportation system for cargo movement between logistics bases and trade centers within and beyond ASEAN.

Recalling also the ASEAN Framework Agreement on the Facilitation of Goods in Transit signed in Ha Noi on 16 December 1998 which, inter alia, provides for inter-state transport to be agreed upon by all Contracting Parties;

Recalling further paragraph 3 of Article I of the Framework Agreement on Enhancing ASEAN Economic Cooperation signed on 28 January 1992 in Singapore, that in the implementation of economic arrangements, two or more Member Countries may proceed first if other Member Countries are not ready to implement these arrangements;

Desiring to establish an effective, efficient, integrated and harmonized regional transport system that addresses all aspects of inter-state transport;

Undertaking to encourage and facilitate inter-state traffic among the Contracting Parties;

Have Agreed as follows.

L. Riccardi and G. Riccardi, *Invest in ASEAN*,
https://doi.org/10.1007/978-981-15-5378-3_12

Article 1
Objectives

The objectives of this Agreement are:

a. to facilitate inter-state transport of goods between and among the Contracting Parties, to support the implementation of the ASEAN Free Trade Area, and to further integrate the region's economies;
b. to simplify and harmonize transport, trade and customs regulations and requirements for the purpose of facilitation of inter-state transport of goods; and
c. to work in concert towards establishing an effective, efficient, integrated and harmonized regional transport system that addresses all aspects of inter-state transport.

Article 2
Principles

The Contracting Parties shall be guided by the following principles under this Agreement:

1. Most Favored Nation Treatment: Contracting Parties shall accord to inter-state transport between the territories of any other Contracting Parties treatment no less favorable than the treatment accorded to inter-state transport between any other country;
2. Consistency: Contracting Parties shall ensure the consistent application of the relevant laws and regulations, procedures, and administration guidelines and other rulings within each Contracting Party;
3. Simplicity: Contracting Parties shall endeavor to ensure the simplification of all inter-state transport procedures and requirements in ASEAN;
4. Transparency: Contracting Parties shall make all laws, regulations, procedures and administrative notifications pertaining to the relevant authorities publicly available in a prompt, transparent and readily accessible manner;
5. Efficiency: Contracting Parties shall ensure the efficient and effective administration of inter-state transport to facilitate the movement of goods into and/or from the Contracting Parties;
6. Appeals: Contracting Parties shall ensure that an effective mechanism for the review of the decisions by the relevant authorities of Contracting Parties is made available and accessible to users and providers of inter-state transport within ASEAN; and
7. Mutual Assistance: Contracting Parties shall endeavor their utmost cooperation and mutual assistance between the concerned agencies involved in the facilitation of inter-state transport in ASEAN.

Part I. General Provision

Article 3
Definitions

For the purposes of this Agreement:

1. "Cabotage" means the carriage of goods loaded in the territory of a Contracting Party for unloading at a place within the territory of the same Contracting Party;
2. "Competent National Body" means the body designated by each Member Country for the registration of inter-state transport operators;
3. "Dangerous goods" means those substances and article which may affect the interest of environment, health, safety and national security;
4. "Host Contracting Party" means the Contracting Party where transport is performed;
5. "Inter-state transport" means transport of goods and the movement of means of transport into and/or from Contracting Parties;
6. "Means of transport" means road vehicles, including those on-board roll-on/roll-off vessels;
7. "Perishable goods" means goods that are easily damaged under the influence of time, temperature or transport movement if they are not carried in good condition. These may include fresh, chilled or frozen fish, crustacean, mollusks, fruits, vegetables, chilled or frozen meat or poultry, dairy and dairy products, eggs and egg products, and swine and pork products;
8. "Secretary-General" means Secretary-General of the Association of Southeast Asian Nations, and

   a. "Transport Operator" means owners, drivers, and/or agents of road transport vehicles who i) have the appropriate national permit or license to operate inter-state transport services and who have a proven compliance record to the rules and procedures under said permit or license; and
   b. are duly registered as inter-state transport operators by the respective Competent National Body or the National Transit Transport Coordinating Committee (NTTCC) among the Contracting Parties.

Article 4
Scope of Application

The provisions of this Agreement shall apply to inter-state transport. Cabotage is not covered by this Agreement.

Article 5
Grant of Rights

1. Subject to the provisions of this Agreement, each Contracting Party shall grant to other Contracting Parties the right to inter-state transport by:

a. allowing transport operators duly established in one Contracting Party to undertake transport of goods into and/or from the territories of other Contracting Parties; and
b. granting the right to load and discharge goods destined for or coming from Contracting Parties.

2. The Contracting Parties shall endeavor to provide facilities for inter-state transport in accordance with the provisions of this Agreement.
3. Inter-state transport, provided that it complies with the relevant laws and rules of the host Contracting Party, shall not be subject to any unnecessary delays or restrictions.

Part II. Designation of Inter-State Transport Routes and Frontier Posts

Article 6
Inter-State Transport Routes and Facilities

1. The Contracting Parties agree that the list of transit transport routes as specified in the Annex of Protocol 1: Designation of Transit Transport Routes and Facilities, under the ASEAN Framework Agreement on Facilitation of Goods in Transit, signed at Bangkok on 8 February 2007, shall be the designated inter-state transport routes and facilities for the purpose of this Agreement.
2. The Contracting Parties may initiate proposals for the modifications and/or expansion of the designated inter-state transport routes from time to time. Any proposed modifications/changes by one Contracting Party shall be with the mutual agreement of the immediate neighboring Contracting Party or Parties. Subsequent amendments shall be deposited with the Secretary-General of ASEAN.
3. For the benefit of safety, the Contracting Parties shall endeavor to provide in their territories vehicle rest areas on these designated routes at appropriate intervals.

Article 7
Frontier Posts and Facilities

1. The Contracting Parties agree that the frontier posts as specified in Protocol 2: Designation of Frontier Posts, under the ASEAN Framework Agreement on Facilitation of Goods in Transit, shall be the designated frontier posts for the purpose of inter-state transport under this Agreement.
2. The Contracting Parties may initiate proposals for the modifications and/or expansion of the designated frontier posts from time to time. Any proposed modifications/changes by one Contracting Party shall be with the mutual agreement of the immediate neighboring Contracting Party or Parties.

Subsequent amendments shall be deposited with the Secretary-General of ASEAN.

3. The Contracting Parties shall provide adequate facilities and related installations at frontier posts over the inter-state transport routes.
4. The Contracting Parties shall endeavor to:

   a. Provide, whenever possible, and within their national jurisdiction, frontier posts which are physically adjacent to those of other Contracting Parties concerned with control areas with checking requirements in order to facilitate the clearance and examination of the means of transport and goods under this Agreement, so that repeated unloading and reloading of these foods may be avoided. Nothing shall prevent two or more Contracting Parties from conducting joint examination at the same place by officials of these Contracting Parties;
   b. Ensure that adequate manpower resources are made available for the speedy completion and clearance of frontier formalities, such as immigration, customs, health and foreign exchange controls;
   c. Coordinate working hours of adjacent posts; and
   d. Provide, wherever possible, adequate parking space for containers and for vehicles awaiting goods clearance.

5. The Contracting Parties agree to be guided, wherever possible, by the provisions of the International Convention on Harmonization of Frontier Control of Goods, signed at Geneva on 21 October 1982, in their efforts to harmonize frontier facilities for goods transported under this Agreement.

Part III. General Conditions for Road Transport

Article 8
Traffic Regulations

The Contracting Parties shall endeavor to take appropriate measures to ensure the harmonization of road traffic regulations in force in their territories conform in substance to the provisions of the Convention on Road Traffic, signed at Vienna on 8 November 1968, and the Convention on Road Sign and Signals, signed at Vienna on 8 November 1968.

Article 9
Inter-State Transport Services

1. Each Contracting Party shall allow the use of means of transport registered in other Contracting Parties to provide inter-state transport services on its territory in accordance with Article 5 of this Agreement.

2. The Contracting Parties agree that the number of inter-state transport vehicles allowed to be used for inter-state transport shall be no more than five hundred (500) vehicles per Contracting Party. Thereafter, the number of inter-state transport vehicles shall be discussed from time to time between the Contracting Parties.
3. Except for the provisions relating to the number of road transit transport vehicles as provided for in Article 4 of Protocol 3: Types and Quantity of Road Vehicles, under the ASEAN Framework Agreement on Facilitation of Goods in Transit, signed at Ha Noi on 15 September 1999, the principles as specified in the said Protocol shall apply to this Agreement.

Article 10
Road Transport Permits

The Contracting Parties undertake to harmonize road transport permit requirements in order to facilitate inter-state transport.

Article 11
Technical Requirements of Road Vehicles

Means of transport used in inter-state transport shall conform to the technical requirements regarding vehicle dimensions, maximum weights and loads, emissions standards and related matters as specified in Protocol 4: Technical Requirements of Vehicles, under the ASEAN Framework Agreement on the Facilitation of Goods in Transit, signed at Ha Noi on 15 September 1999.

Article 12
Mutual Recognition of Inspection Certificates

1. The Contracting Parties undertake to institute periodic inspection of road vehicles registered in their respective territories and used for inter-state transport.
2. The Contracting Parties shall recognize periodic inspection certificates of road vehicles used for inter-state transport issued by the other Contracting Parties, in accordance with the Agreement on the Recognition of Commercial Vehicle Inspection Certificates for Goods Vehicles and Public Services Vehicles Issued by ASEAN Member Countries signed at Singapore on 10 September 1998.

Article 13
Mutual Recognition of Driving Licenses

The Contracting Parties shall recognize domestic driving licenses issued by all other Contracting Parties for the purpose of inter-state transport in accordance with the Agreement on the Recognition of Domestic Driving Licenses Issued by ASEAN Countries signed at Kuala Lumpur on 9 July 1985.

Article 14
ASEAN Scheme of Compulsory Motor Vehicle Insurance

1. Motor vehicles travelling to the territory of other Contracting Parties shall comply with the compulsory motor vehicle insurance required in the host Contracting Party.
2. The Contracting Parties agree to conform to the scheme of compulsory motor vehicle insurance as specified in Protocol 5: ASEAN Scheme of Compulsory Motor Vehicle Insurance, under the ASEAN Framework Agreement on the Facilitation of Goods in Transit, signed at Kuala Lumpur on 8 April 2001.

Article 15
Charges and Other Financial Obligations

The Contracting Parties shall endeavor to simplify, consolidate and harmonize charges and other financial obligations which are levied on the means of transport.

Article 16
Temporary Admission of Road Vehicles

For the purpose of this Agreement, the Contracting Parties shall grant temporary admission to road vehicles (and the fuel contained in its supply tanks, its lubricants, maintenance supplies, and spare parts in reasonable quantities) registered in the territory of another Contracting Party, without payment of import duties and import taxes, without depositing a Customs' guarantee bond and free of import prohibitions and restrictions, subject to re-exportation and other related conditions.

Part IV. Customs Control, Sanitary and Phytoanitary Measures

Article 17
Harmonization and Simplification Of Customs Procedures

1. The Contracting Parties shall simplify and whenever possible harmonize the customs control procedures of inter-state transport to ensure compliance with the laws and regulations which the Customs are responsible for enforcing.
2. The Contracting Parties shall facilitate joint customs inspection, wherever possible, of inter-state transport at their designated frontier points.

Article 18
Establishment of Sanitary and Phytosanitary Measures

The Contracting Parties agree to establish sanitary and phytosanitary measures as specified in Protocol 8: Sanitary and Phytosanitary Measures, under the ASEAN Framework Agreement on the Facilitation of Goods in Transit, signed at Phnom

Penh on 27 October 2000, to facilitate inter-state transport of goods into and/or from their territories and ensure compliance with the laws and regulations which the relevant authorities are responsible for enforcing.

Part V. Miscellaneous Provisions

Article 19
Special Provisions on Inter-State Transport of Dangerous Goods

The Inter-State Transport of Dangerous Goods shall not be permitted under this Agreement, unless there is a special permit of the Contracting Party in whose territory the transport is undertaken, as specified in Protocol 9: Dangerous Goods, under the ASEAN Framework Agreement on the Facilitation of Goods in Transit, signed at Jakarta on 20 September 2002.

Article 20
Special Provisions on Transport of Prohibited and/or Restricted Goods

The Inter-State Transport of prohibited and/or restricted goods shall not be permitted under this Agreement.

Article 21
Special Provisions on Inter-State Transport of Perishable Goods

Subject to the provisions of this Agreement, the Contracting Parties shall endeavor to facilitate inter-state transport of perishable goods.

Article 22
Provision of Greater Facilities

This Agreement does not entail in any way the withdrawal of facilities which are greater than those provided for in this Agreement as long as the terms and conditions are consistent with the principles embodied in this Agreement. This Agreement also does not preclude the granting of greater facilities which may be agreed between Contracting Parties in the future.

Article 23
Domestic Legislation

1. Unless otherwise provided for by this Agreement, the domestic laws and regulations of the Contracting Parties relating to transport of goods, shall apply equally and without discrimination to inter-state transport.
2. The Contracting Parties shall endeavor to harmonize and simplify their rules, regulations and administrative procedures relating to inter-state transport in accordance with the provisions of this Agreement.

Article 24
Compliance with National Laws

Except where otherwise provided in Agreements between the Contracting Parties, including this Agreement:

1. means of transport of one Contracting Party including persons and goods shall, when in the territory of the other Contracting Party, comply with national laws and regulations in force in that territory;
2. neither of the Parties shall impose on persons or goods of the other Contracting Party requirements which are more restrictive than those applied by its national laws and regulations on its own means transport; and
3. the host Contracting Party may temporarily or permanently deny access to its territory to a person, driver, transport operator, means of transport that has infringed national laws and regulations or this Agreement.

Article 25
Transparency

1. The Contracting Parties shall ensure transparency of their respective laws, regulations and administrative procedures which affect the facilitation of inter-state transport of goods under this Agreement and its Protocols.
2. For this purpose, all Contracting Parties shall deposit with the ASEAN Secretariat, not later than six months after this Agreement has entered into force, their aforementioned laws, regulations and administrative procedures.
3. If the aforementioned documents are not in the English language, their English translation shall also be deposited within one year after this Agreement has entered into force.

Article 26
Assistance for Traffic Accidents

Should the means of transport of one Contracting Party including persons and goods be involved in traffic accidents in the territory of another Contracting Party, the latter shall provide all possible assistance to the means of transport, including persons and goods, and notify the appropriate authorities of the Contracting Party concerned as soon as possible.

Part VI. Institutional Arrangements

Article 27
Institutional Arrangements

1. The National Transit Transport Coordinating Committee, established under Article 29 of the ASEAN Framework Agreement on the Facilitation of Goods in

Transit signed in Ha Noi on 16 December 1998, of each Contracting Party shall also be responsible for the coordination and implementation of this Agreement.

2. The Transit Transport Coordinating Board, established under Article 29 of the ASEAN Framework Agreement on the Facilitation of Goods in Transit signed in Ha Noi on 16 December 1998, shall also oversee the overall coordination and implementation of this Agreement. The Board is further authorized to invite and seek the assistance of other relevant ASEAN coordinating bodies, for all matters related to the implementation of this Agreement.
3. The Transit Transport Coordinating Board shall make periodic reports on the implementation of this Agreement, and seek appropriate guidance on significant issues as necessary, from the relevant ASEAN Ministerial bodies.
4. The ASEAN Secretariat shall assist the Transit Transport Coordinating Board in its functions and responsibilities under this Agreement, and in particular, in the monitoring and reporting of the progress of the implementation of this Agreement. The ASEAN Secretariat shall submit evaluation reports to the Transit Transport Coordinating Board, for further action.

Part VII. Final Clauses

Article 28
Dispute Settlement

The provisions of the ASEAN Protocol on Enhanced Dispute Settlement Mechanism, done at Vientiane, Lao PDR on the 29th day of November 2004 and any amendment thereto, shall apply to disputes arising under this Agreement.

Article 29
Other Agreements in Force

This Agreement or any actions taken thereto shall not affect the rights and obligations of the Contracting Parties under any existing agreements or International Conventions to which they are also Contracting Parties

Article 30
Implementation Arrangements

1. In the implementation of this Agreement, or more Contracting Parties who are ready can negotiate, conclude and sign implementing agreements/arrangements in line with the ASEAN-X Formula, on a plurilateral, multilateral or sub-regional basis. The other Contracting Parties can join in the implementation when they are ready.
2. The Protocols under the ASEAN Framework Agreement on Facilitation of Goods in Transit which are referred to under this Agreement, and any

amendments to such Protocols, shall apply mutatis mutandis to inter-state transport under this Agreement. Such Protocols, and any amendments thereto, shall be regarded as an integral part of this Agreement.

3. With respect to each Contracting Party, the effect of those Protocols for this Agreement shall be from the date of depositing the Instrument of Ratification or Acceptance of those Protocols or the date of depositing the Instrument of Ratification or Acceptance of this Agreement with the Secretary-General of ASEAN, whichever is later.

Article 31
Final Provisions

1. This Agreement is subject to ratification or acceptance by the Contracting Parties.
2. The Instrument of Ratification or Acceptance shall be deposited with the Secretary-General of ASEAN, who shall promptly inform each Contracting Party of such deposit.
3. This Agreement shall enter into force upon the thirtieth day after the deposit of the second Instrument of Ratification or Acceptance, and shall be effective only among the Contracting Parties who have ratified or accepted it. For each Contracting Party ratifying or accepting this Agreement after the deposit of the second Instrument of Ratification or Acceptance, this Agreement shall enter into force on the thirtieth day after the deposit of such Contracting Party of its Instrument of Ratification or Acceptance.
4. No reservation may be made to this Agreement either at the time of signature, ratification or acceptance.
5. Any amendment to the provisions of this Agreement shall be affected by consent of all Contracting Parties.

In Witness Whereof, the undersigned, being duly authorized to sign by their respective Governments, have signed this ASEAN Framework Agreement on the Facilitation of Inter-State Transport.

Done at **Manila, Philippines**, this **10th** Day of **December** in the Year **Two Thousand and Nine** in a single original copy in the English Language

For Brunei Darussalam, **Pehin Dato Abu Bakar Apong**, Minister of Communications
For the Kingdom of Cambodia, **Tauch Chankosal**, Secretary of State Ministry of Public Works and Transport
For the Republic of Indonesia, **Jusman Syafii Djamal**, Minister of Transportation
For the Lao People's Democratic Republic, **Sommad Pholsena**, Minister of Public Works and Transport
For Malaysia, **Dato' Sri Ong Tee Keat**, Minister of Transport
For the Union of Myanmar, **Major General Thein Swe**, Minister of Transport

For the Republic of the Philippines, **Leandro R. Mendoza**, Secretary of Transportation and Communications
For the Republic of Singapore, **Raymond Lim**, Minister for Transport
For the Kingdom of Thailand, **Sophon Zaram**, Minister of Transport
For the Socialist Republic of Vietnam, **Ho Nghia Dzung**, Minister of Transport.

ASEAN Agreement on the Movement of Natural Persons

2012: Signed in Phnom Penh, Cambodia on 19th November 2012

The Governments of Brunei Darussalam, the Kingdom of Cambodia, the Republic of Indonesia, Lao People's Democratic Republic, Malaysia, the Republic of the Union of Myanmar, the Republic of the Philippines, the Republic of Singapore, the Kingdom of Thailand, and the Socialist Republic of Viet Nam, Member States of the Association of South East Asian Nations ("ASEAN"), hereinafter collectively referred to as "Member States" or singularly as "Member State":

Noting the mandate of the ASEAN Economic Community Blueprint adopted at the 13th ASEAN Summit held on 20 November 2007 in Singapore that free flow of skilled labors one of the core elements of an ASEAN single market and production base; which allows for managed mobility or facilitated entry for the movement of natural persons engaged in trade in goods, trade in services and investment, according to the prevailing regulations of the receiving country;

Recalling the ASEAN Framework Agreement on Services ("AFAS") signed by ASEAN Economic Ministers ("AEM") on 15 December 1995 in Bangkok, Thailand and its subsequent Implementing Protocols, which lays the foundation for elimination of restrictions to trade in services amongst Member States in all modes of supply, including mode 4 (Movement of Natural Persons);

Desiring for an effective mechanism to further liberalize and facilitate movement of natural persons towards free flow of skilled laboring ASEAN through close cooperation among related ASEAN bodies in the areas, including and not limited to trade in goods, trade in services, investment, immigration, and labor;

Also Desiring to eliminate substantially all restrictions in the temporary cross-border movement of natural persons involved in the provision of trade in goods, trade in services and investment within the provisions of this Agreement;

L. Riccardi and G. Riccardi, *Invest in ASEAN*,
https://doi.org/10.1007/978-981-15-5378-3_13

Have Agreed as follows:

Article 1
Objectives

The objectives of this Agreement are to:

a. provide within the scope of this Agreement the rights and obligations additional to those set out in the ASEAN Framework Agreement on Services and its Implementing Protocols in relation to the movement of natural persons between Member States;
b. facilitate the movement of natural persons engaged in the conduct of trade: in goods, trade in services and investment between Member States;
c. establish streamlined and transparent procedures for applications for immigration formalities for the temporary entry or temporary stay of natural persons to whom this Agreement applies; and
d. protect the integrity of Member States' borders and protect the domestic labor force and permanent employment in the territories of Member States.

Article 2
Scope

1. This Agreement shall apply to measures affecting the temporary entry or temporary stay of natural persons of a Member State into the territory of another Member State. Such natural persons may include:

    i. business visitors;
    ii. intra-corporate transferees;
    iii. contractual service suppliers;
    iv. other categories as may be specified in the Schedules of Commitments for the temporary entry and temporary stay of natural persons of the Member State.

2. This Agreement shall not apply to measures affecting natural persons seeking access to the employment market of another Member State, nor shall it apply to measures regarding citizenship, residence or employment on a permanent basis.
3. Nothing contained in this Agreement shall prevent a Member State from applying measures to regulate the entry into, or temporary stay, of natural persons of the other Member State in its territory, including those measures necessary to protect the integrity of its territory and to ensure the orderly movement of natural persons across its borders, provided that such measures are not applied in a manner so as to nullify or impair the benefits accruing to the other Member State under the terms of a specific commitment.
4. The sole fact of requiring natural persons to meet visa requirements prior to entry into the territory of a Member State shall not be regarded as nullifying or impairing benefits under this Agreement.

Article 3
Definitions

For the purposes of this Agreement, the following definitions shall apply:

1. Business Visitor means a natural person seeking to enter or stay in the territory of another Member State temporarily, whose remuneration and financial support for the duration of the visit is derived from outside of that other Member State;
    a. as a representative of a goods seller/service supplier, for the purpose of negotiating the sale of goods or supply of services or entering into agreements to sell goods or supply services for that goods seller/service supplier, where such negotiations do not involve direct sale of goods or supply of services to the general public;
    b. as an employee of a juridical person as defined in subparagraphs e(i), e(ii) and e(iii) of this Article only for the purpose of establishing an investment or setting up a commercial presence, for the juridical person in the territory of another Member State;
    c. for the purpose of participating in business negotiations or meetings; or
    d. for the purpose of establishing an investment or setting up a commercial presence in the territory of another Member State;
2. Contractual Service Supplier means a natural person who is an employee of a juridical person established in the territory of a Member State which has no commercial presence in the territory of the other Member State where the services will be provided, who
    a. enters the territory of that other Member State temporarily in order to supply a service pursuant to a contract(s) between his/her employer and service consumer(s) in the territory of the other Member State;
    b. is either an executive, manager, or specialist as defined in subparagraph e(i), e(ii) and e(iii) of this Article, who receives remuneration from his/her employer;
    c. must possess the appropriate educational and professional qualifications relevant to the service to be provided; and
    d. as may be applicable, has been an employee of the juridical person for a period as may be specified in the Schedule of Commitments;
3. Granting Member State means a Member State who receives an application for temporary entry or temporary stay from a natural person of another Member State who is covered by Article 2 (Scope);
4. Immigration Formality means a visa, permit, pass or other documents or electronic authority granting a natural person of one Member State the right to temporarily enter, stay, work, or to establish commercial presence in the territory of the granting Member State;
5. Intra–Corporate Transferee (ICT) means a natural person who is an employee of a juridical person established in the territory of a Member State, who is transferred temporarily for the supply of a service through commercial presence

(either through a representative office, branch, subsidiary or affiliate) in the territory of another Member State, and who has been an employee of the juridical person for a period as may be specified in the Schedule of Commitments, and who is:

a. an Executive: a natural person within the organization who primarily directs the management of the organization and exercises wide latitude in decision making and receives only general supervision or direction from higher level executives, the board of directors, or stockholders of the business; an executive would not directly perform tasks related to the actual provision of the service or services of the organization;
b. a Manager: a natural person within the organisation who primarily directs the organisation/department/subdivision and exercises supervisory and control functions over other supervisory, managerial or professional staff; does not include first line supervisors unless employees supervised are professionals; does not include employees who primarily perform tasks necessary for the provision of the service; or
c. a Specialist: a natural person within the organisation who possesses knowledge at an advanced level of expertise essential to the establishment/ provision of the service and/or possesses proprietary knowledge of the organisation's service, research equipment, techniques or management; may include, but is not limited to, members of a licensed profession;

6. Natural Person means a natural person who is a national of a Member State, in accordance with its laws, regulations and national policies; and
7. Temporary Entry or Temporary Stay means entry into or stay by a natural person covered by this Agreement, without the intent to establish permanent residence.

Article 4
Grant of Temporary Entry or Temporary Stay

1. Each Member State shall, in accordance with that Member State's Schedule of Commitments in ANNEX 1, grant temporary entry or temporary stay in accordance with this Agreement to natural persons of another Member State provided those natural persons:

   a. follow prescribed application procedures for the immigration formality sought; and
   b. meet all relevant eligibility requirements for temporary entry or temporary stay of the granting Member State.

2. Any fees imposed in respect of the processing of an immigration formality shall be reasonable and in accordance with domestic law.
3. A Member State may deny temporary entry or temporary stay to natural persons of another Member State who do not comply with paragraphs 1(a) and 1(b) of this Article.

Article 5
Processing of Applications

1. Where an application for an immigration formality is required by a Member State, that Member State shall promptly process complete applications for immigration formalities or extensions received from natural persons of another Member State covered by Article 2 (Scope).
2. Each Member State shall, upon request and within a reasonable period after receiving a complete application for an immigration formality from a natural person of another Member State covered by Article 2 (Scope), notify the applicant of:

    a. the receipt of the application;
    b. the status of the application; and
    c. the decision concerning the application including, if approved, the period of stay and other conditions.

2. In the case of an incomplete application, at the request of the applicant, the Member State shall notify the applicant of all the additional information that is required to complete the application and provide the applicant with the opportunity to remedy deficiencies in his/her application.

Article 6
Schedules of Commitments for the Temporary Entry and Temporary Stay of Natural Persons

1. Each Member State shall set out in ANNEX 1 a schedule containing its commitments for the temporary entry or temporary stay in its territory of natural persons of other Member States covered in Article 2 (Scope). These Schedules shall specify the: general conditions and limitations governing those commitments, including the length of stay, for each category of natural persons included in each Member State's Schedule of Commitments.
2. Upon entry into force of this Agreement, the Schedules of Commitments as referred to in paragraph 1 of this Article shall supersede commitments made under the AFAS in relation to mode 4 (Movement of Natural Persons).

Article 7
Further Liberalisation

1. Member States shall enter into discussion to review the Schedules of Commitments under this Agreement with a view to achieving further liberalisation on the movement of natural persons. The initial discussion to review the Schedules of Commitments shall take place one year from entry into force of the Agreement. Subsequent discussions shall take place at intervals to be agreed by Member States.
2. The revisions of the Schedules of Commitments as a result of the discussions referred to in paragraph 1 of this Article shall be incorporated into this

Agreement, subject to paragraphs 2, 3, 4 and 5 of Article 15 (Revisions, Modifications and Amendments).

Article 8
Transparency

Each Member State shall:

a. publish or otherwise make publicly available explanatory material on all relevant immigration formalities which pertain to or affect the operation of this Agreement;
b. maintain or establish contact points or other mechanisms to respond to inquiries from interested persons regarding regulations affecting the temporary entry or temporary stay of natural persons;
c. to the extent possible, allow reasonable time between publication of new regulations affecting the temporary entry or temporary stay of natural persons and their effective date. Such publication may be made electronically available;
d. no later than six month after entry into force of this Agreement publish, such as on its immigration website, or otherwise make publicly available in its own territory and to persons in the territory of the other Member States, the general requirements for temporary entry or temporary stay under this Agreement, including explanatory material and relevant forms and documents that will enable natural persons of other Member States to become acquainted with those requirements; and
e. upon modifying or amending any immigration measure that affects the temporary entry or temporary stay of natural persons, ensure that the information published or otherwise made available pursuant to subparagraph (d) of this Article is updated as soon as possible within 90 days.

Article 9
General Exceptions

Subject to the requirement that such measures are not applied in a manner which would constitute a means of arbitrary or unjustifiable discrimination between countries where like conditions prevail, or a disguised restriction on the movement of natural persons, nothing in this Agreement shall be construed to prevent the adoption or enforcement by any Member State of measures:

1. necessary to protect public morals or to maintain public order;
2. necessary to protect human, animal or plant life or health;
3. necessary to secure compliance with laws or regulations which are not inconsistent with the provisions of this Agreement including those relating to:

    a. the prevention of deceptive and fraudulent practices or to deal with the effects of a default on services contracts;

b. the protection of the privacy of individuals in relation to the processing and dissemination of personal data and the protection of confidentiality of individual records and accounts;
c. safety.

Article 10
Security Exceptions

1. Nothing in this Agreement shall be construed:

   a. to require any Member State to furnish any information, the disclosure of which it considers contrary to its essential security interests; or
   b. to prevent any Member State from taking any action which it considers necessary for the protection of its essential security interests:

      i. relating to the supply of services as carried out directly or indirectly for the purpose of provisioning a military establishment;
      ii. relating to fissionable and fusionable materials or the materials from which they are derived;
      iii. taken in time of war or other emergency in international relations; or

   c. to prevent any Member State from taking any action in pursuance of its obligations under the United Nations Charter for the maintenance of international peace and security.

2. The AEM shall be informed to the fullest extent possible of measures taken under paragraphs 1(b) and 1(c) of this Article and of their termination.

Article 11
Dispute Settlement

1. Member States shall endeavor to settle any differences arising out of the implementation of this Agreement through consultations.
2. A Member State shall not recourse to the ASEAN Protocol on Enhanced Dispute Settlement Mechanism, signed on 29 November 2004 in Vientiane, Lao PDR and amendments thereto, regarding a refusal to grant temporary entry or temporary stay under this Agreement unless:

   a. the matter involves a pattern of practice on the part of the granting Member State; and
   b. the natural persons affected have exhausted all available domestic remedies regarding this particular matter.

Article 12
Relation with ASEAN Comprehensive Investment Agreement

1. This Agreement does not apply to measures adopted or maintained by each Member State to the extent that they are covered by the ASEAN Comprehensive Investment Agreement ("ACIA").

2. Notwithstanding paragraph 1 of this Article, this Agreement shall apply, mutatis mutandis, to measures adopted or maintained under Article 22 of the ACIA (Entry, Temporary Stay and Work of Investors and Key Personnel) affecting the movement of natural persons of a Member State in the territory of any one of the other Member States.
3. For greater certainty, Section B (Investment Dispute Between an Investor and a Member State) of the ACIA shall not apply to this Agreement.

Article 13
Recognition

1. A Member State, by agreement or arrangement with another Member State, may recognize the education or experience obtained, requirements met, licenses or certifications granted in the other Member State for the purposes of the fulfilment, in whole or in part, of its standards or criteria for authorization, licensing and certification of service suppliers of the other Member State and subject to the requirements of paragraph 3 of this Article.
2. Where a Member State recognizes, by agreement or arrangement with a non-Member State or unilaterally whether in favor of another Member State or a non-Member State, the education or experience obtained, requirements met, licenses or certifications granted in the other Member State or non-Member State, the Member State shall afford adequate opportunity for any other Member State to demonstrate that education, experience, licenses, or certifications obtained or requirements met in the territory of that Member State should be recognized.
3. A Member State shall not accord recognition in a manner which would constitute a means of discrimination against another Member State in the application of its standards or criteria for the authorization, licensing or certification of service suppliers, or a disguised restriction on trade in services. Where appropriate, recognition should be based on multilaterally agreed criteria.
4. Each Member State shall encourage competent bodies in its territory to enter into cooperation, agreement or arrangement, multilaterally or bilaterally, on recognition of professional:

   a. qualification requirements;
   b. qualification procedures; and
   c. licensing, certification or registration requirements and procedures.

Article 14
Institutional Mechanism

1. The AEM shall be responsible for the implementation of this Agreement.
2. The AEM shall coordinate and oversee the implementation of this Agreement across Member States and across related ASEAN bodies.
3. The ASEAN Coordinating Committee on Services ("CCS") and, for the purposes of this Agreement, other relevant government officials shall assist the AEM in implementing this Agreement.

4. In the fulfilment of its functions, the AEM may establish subsidiary bodies and assign them to perform/undertake/accomplish certain tasks or delegate its responsibilities to any subsidiary bodies.

Article 15
Revisions, Modifications and Amendments

1. Any Member State may request in writing a revision, modification, or amendment of all or any part of this Agreement.
2. The provisions of this Agreement may only be revised, modified or amended when mutually agreed upon in writing by the Governments of all Member States.
3. Any revision, modification, or amendment agreed to and in writing shall form an integral part of this Agreement.
4. Such revision, modification, or amendment shall come into force on such date as may be determined by all Member States.
5. Any revision, modification, or amendment shall not prejudice the rights and obligations arising from or based on this Agreement prior or up to the date of such revision, modification, or amendment.

Article 16
Entry into Force

1. This Agreement shall enter into force after all Member States have notified or, where necessary, deposited instruments of ratification with the Secretary-General of ASEAN, which shall not take more than 180 days after the signing of this Agreement.
2. The Secretary-General of ASEAN shall promptly notify all Member States of the notifications or deposit of each instrument of ratification referred to in paragraph 1 of this Article.

Article 17
Depositary

This Agreement shall be deposited with the ASEAN Secretary-General, who shall promptly furnish a certified copy thereof to each Member State.

In Witness Whereof, the undersigned, being duly authorized by their respective Governments, have signed the ASEAN Agreement on Movement of Natural Persons.

Done at Phnom Penh, Cambodia, this Nineteenth day of November in the Year Two Thousand and Twelve, in a single copy in the English Language.

For the Government of Brunei Darussalam, **Lim Jock Seng**, Second Minister of Foreign Affairs and Trade
For the Royal Government of Cambodia, **Cham Pradish**, Senior Minister and Minister of Commerce
For the Government of the Republic of Indonesia, **Gita Irawan Wirjawan**, Minister of Trade

For the Government of the Lao People's Democratic Republic, **Nam Viyaketh**, Minister of Industry and Commerce
For the Government of Malaysia, **Mustapa Mohamed**, Minister of International Trade and Industry
For the Government of the Union of Myanmar, **Kan Zaw**, Minister for National Planning and Economic Development
For the Government of the Republic of Philippines, **Gregory l. Domingo**, Secretary of Trade and Industry
For the Government of the Republic of Singapore, **Lim Hng Kiang**, Minister for Trade and Industry
For the Government of the Kingdom of Thailand, **Boonsong Teriyapirom**, Minister of Commerce
For the Government of the Socialist Republic of Vietnam, **Vu Huy Hoang**, Minister of Industry and Trade.

The manufacturer's authorised representative in the EU is Springer Nature Customer Service Centre GmbH, Europaplatz 3, 69115 Heidelberg, Germany. If you have any concerns regarding our products, please contact ProductSafety@springernature.com

Printed and bound by CPI Group (UK) Ltd, Croydon, CR0 4YY
05/10/2026
02228124-0015